Data Structures
(Theory and Practicals)

AUTHOR

Dr. NB Venkateswarlu
GVPCEW, Visakhapatnam

REVIEWER

Dr. Ravi Shankar Singh
IIT(BHU), Varanasi

KHANNA BOOK PUBLISHING CO. (P) Ltd.
4C/4344, Ansari Road, Darya Ganj,
New Delhi, India

All India Council for Technical Education
Nelson Mandela Marg, Vasant Kunj,
New Delhi, India

Dear Readers,

To prevent the piracy, this book is secured with HIGH SECURITY HOLOGRAM on the front title cover. In case you don't find the hologram on the front cover title, please write us to at contact@khannabooks.com or whatsapp us at +91-99109 09320 and avail special gift voucher for yourself.

Specimen of Hologram on front Cover title:

Moreover, there is a SPECIAL DISCOUNT COUPON for you with EVERY HOLOGRAM.

How to avail this SPECIAL DISCOUNT:

Step 1: Scratch the hologram

Step 2: Under the scratch area, your "coupon code" is available

Step 3: Logon to www.khannabooks.com

Step 4: Use your "coupon code" in the shopping cart and get your copy at a special discount

Step 5: Enjoy your reading!

ISBN: 978-93-5538-768-4
Book Code: DIP438EN

Data Structures (Theory & Practicals)

by Dr. NB Venkateswarlu

First Edition: 2025

Originally Published by:
All India Council for Technical Education, Ministry of Education, GOI

Exclusively Published & Distributed by: **Khanna Book Publishing Co. (P) Ltd.**
4C/4344, Ansari Road, Daryaganj,
New Delhi (INDIA)

Visit us at: **www.khannabooks.com**
Write us at: **contact@khannabooks.com**

To view complete list of books, Please scan the QR Code:
KPH

Printed in Bharat.

प्रो. म. जगदीश कुमार
अध्यक्ष
Prof. M. Jagadesh Kumar
Chairman

सत्यमेव जयते

आज़ादी का अमृत महोत्सव

अखिल भारतीय तकनीकी शिक्षा परिषद्
(भारत सरकार का एक सांविधिक निकाय)
(शिक्षा मंत्रालय, भारत सरकार)
नेल्सन मंडेला मार्ग, वसंत कुंज, नई दिल्ली–110070
दूरभाष : 011–26131498
ई–मेल : chairman@aicte-india.org

ALL INDIA COUNCIL FOR TECHNICAL EDUCATION
(A STATUTORY BODY OF THE GOVT. OF INDIA)
(Ministry of Education, Govt. of India)
Nelson Mandela Marg, Vasant Kunj, New Delhi-110070
Phone : 011-26131498
E-mail : chairman@aicte-india.org

FOREWORD

Engineers are the backbone of the modern society. It is through them that engineering marvels have happened and improved quality of life across the world. They have driven humanity towards greater heights in a more evolved and unprecedented manner.

The All India Council for Technical Education (AICTE), led from the front and assisted students, faculty & institutions in every possible manner towards the strengthening of the technical education in the country. AICTE is always working towards promoting quality Technical Education to make India a modern developed nation with the integration of modern knowledge & traditional knowledge for the welfare of mankind.

An array of initiatives have been taken by AICTE in last decade which have been accelerate now by the National Education Policy (NEP)2020. The implementation of NEP under the visionary leadership of Hon'ble Prime Minister of India envisages the provision for education in regional languages to all, thereby ensuring that every graduate becomes competent enough and is in a position to contribute towards the national growth and development through innovation & entrepreneurship.

One of the spheres where AICTE had been relentlessly working since 2021-22 is providing high quality books prepared and translated by eminent educators in various Indian languages to its engineering students at Under Graduate & Diploma level. For the second year students, AICTE has identified 87 books at Under Graduate and Diploma Level courses, for translation in 12 Indian languages - Hindi, Tamil, Gujarati, Odia, Bengali, Kannada, Urdu, Punjabi, Telugu, Marathi, Assamese & Malayalam. In addition to the English medium, the 1044 books in different Indian Languages are going to support to engineering students to learn in their mother tongue. Currently, there are 39 institutions in 11 states offering courses in Indian languages in 7 disciplines like Biomedical Engineering, Civil Engineering, Computer Science & Engineering, Electrical Engineering, Electronics & Communication Engineering, Information Technology Engineering & Mechanical Engineering, Architecture, and Interior Designing. This will become possible due to active involvement and support of universities/institutions in different states.

On behalf of AICTE, I express sincere gratitude to all distinguished authors, reviewers and translators from different IITs, NITs and other institutions for their admirable contribution in a very short span of time.

AICTE is confident that these out comes based books with their rich content will help technical students master the subjects with factor comprehension and greater ease.

(Prof. M. Jagadesh Kumar)

ACKNOWLEDGEMENT

The authors are grateful to the authorities of AICTE, particularly Prof. M. Jagadesh Kumar, Chairman; Prof. M. P. Poonia, Vice-Chairman; Prof. Rajive Kumar, Member-Secretary and Dr Amit Kumar Srivastava, Director, Faculty Development Cell for their planning to publish the books on (Data Strctures: Theory & Practicals). We sincerely acknowledge the valuable contributions of the reviewer of the book Dr. Ravi Shankar Singh, Assoc. Prof., IIT(BHU), Varanasi.

The authors are thankful to Prof MN Murthy, IISC, Bangalore, Prof Roger D Boyle, University of Leeds, UK for providing "Foreword" for the book. Also, authors appreciate Sri Vishnu Raju garu, Dr Nagendra, Dr Suryanarayana of Vishnu Institute of Technology, Bhimavaram for allowing the authors to use their plagiarism checking SW account.

The authors appreciate the support of Dr JVR Murthy, Dr MHM Prasad of JNTUK, Kakinada, Prof PVGD Prasada Reddy, VC, Andhra University, management members of GVP, Principal, Vice Principal of GVPCEW.

This book is an outcome of various suggestions of AICTE members, experts and authors who shared their opinion and thought to further develop the engineering education in our country. Acknowledgements are due to the contributors and different workers in this field whose published books, review articles, papers, photographs, footnotes, references and other valuable information enriched us at the time of writing the book.

Dr. NB Venkateswarlu

PREFACE

Undoubtedly there are hundreds of books on data structures. However this book is written with the following salient flavors:

1. All India Council for Technical Education (AICTE) was aptly identified to offer the data structures course as a skill oriented course. Thus, while writing this book we have included hundreds of solved and unsolved questions so that students can implement them in C (or some other programming language) and enrich their coding skills. An addendum having discussions on the unsolved questions is available for teachers.
2. During the last 4 to 5 years, placement examinations in India are demanding aspiring students to solve some number of programming puzzles online. It is very open that many of the programming puzzles are around data structures and algorithms courses. Thus, in this book we have attempted to motivate students/faculty to introduce programming puzzles around linked lists, stacks, trees, graphs such that their chances of getting an aspiring job gets hyped. In order to achieve this, we have also created a competition site/group for the perusal of the readers of this book.
3. We did include some number of questions that appeared in various competitive examinations such as Bebras, IOI so as to motivate students to inculcate more interest in data structures concepts in a determined manner.
4. Many authors have employed program tracing to elucidate most intricate concepts. In this book, we have included program visualizations for the majority of programs which readers can pass through step by step fashion and understand the intricate concepts in a better way. Here, we have used pythontutor.com services to visualize our programs.

First Unit introduces the reader to the need of data structures with many practical examples such as long integers in programming languages such as Python. Also, this unit introduces empirical and theoretical algorithmic analysis along with the need for data abstraction, abstract data types, etc., allied themes in the easiest possible manner.

Unit on stacks and queues contains many illustrious discussions on their use in practical SW systems such as operating systems, compilers. This unit discusses how to implement various operations on stacks and queues using arrays. Also, how stacks can be used for evaluating arithmetic expressions by employing postfix or reverse polish notation is explained in a lucid manner with many illustrious examples.

Unit on linked lists begins with many interesting example usages of the "link" concept in our real day to day life. Also, how the "link" concept is used in practical SW systems such as free data block management, garbage collection, etc. Operations on the single linked lists, doubly linked lists, circular lists are explained along with their practical implementations in C language. Also, this unit contains the implementation of stacks and queues using linked lists.

Unit on non-linear data strctures introduces fundamental aspects of trees and graphs. Binary search trees, their traversals are with the recursive implementations. Also, sequential representation of binary search trees is explained along with its implementation. In addition graph theory, graph representations, graph traversals (breadth first traversal, depth first traversal), path matrix, Marshalls algorithm, minimum spanning tree, Kruskal algorithm, Prim's algorithm, Dijkstra's algorithm, topological sorting, etc., are explained in a lucid manner.

Every unit is designed to have a set of objective questions and laboratory problems to test and enrich the students.

Dr. NB Venkateswarlu

OUTCOME BASED EDUCATION

For the implementation of an outcome based education the first requirement is to develop an outcome based curriculum and incorporate an outcome based assessment in the education system. By going through outcome based assessments evaluators will be able to evaluate whether the students have achieved the outlined standard, specific and measurable outcomes. With the proper incorporation of outcome based education there will be a definite commitment to achieve a minimum standard for all learners without giving up at any level. At the end of the programme running with the aid of outcome based education, a student will be able to arrive at the following outcomes:

PO1: **Engineering knowledge:** Apply the knowledge of mathematics, science, engineering fundamentals, and an engineering specialization to the solution of complex engineering problems.

PO2: **Problem analysis:** Identify, formulate, review research literature, and analyze complex engineering problems reaching substantiated conclusions using first principles of mathematics, natural sciences, and engineering sciences.

PO3: **Design / development of solutions:** Design solutions for complex engineering problems and design system components or processes that meet the specified needs with appropriate consideration for the public health and safety, and the cultural, societal, and environmental considerations.

PO4: **Conduct investigations of complex problems:** Use research-based knowledge and research methods including design of experiments, analysis and interpretation of data, and synthesis of the information to provide valid conclusions.

PO5: **Modern tool usage:** Create, select, and apply appropriate techniques, resources, and modern engineering and IT tools including prediction and modeling to complex engineering activities with an understanding of the limitations.

PO6: **The engineer and society:** Apply reasoning informed by the contextual knowledge to assess societal, health, safety, legal and cultural issues and the consequent responsibilities relevant to the professional engineering practice.

PO7: **Environment and sustainability:** Understand the impact of the professional engineering solutions in societal and environmental contexts, and demonstrate the knowledge of, and need for sustainable development.

COURSE OUTCOMES

By the end of the course the students are expected to learn:

CO-1: Identify types of rocks and sub soil strata of earth.

CO-2: Interpret the physical properties of soil related to given construction activities.

CO-3: Use the results of permeability and shear strength test for foundation analysis.

CO-4: Interpret the soil bearing capacity results.

CO-5: Compute optimum moisture content values for maximum dry density of soil through various tests.

Mapping of Course Outcomes with Programme Outcomes to be done according to the matrix given below:

Course Outcomes	EXPECTED MAPPING WITH PROGRAMME OUTCOMES (1- Weak Correlation; 2- Medium correlation; 3- Strong Correlation)						
	PO-1	PO-2	PO-3	PO-4	PO-5	PO-6	PO-7
CO-1	3	2	2	2	1	–	–
CO-2	3	2	2	1	1	–	–
CO-3	3	3	2	1	1	–	–
CO-4	3	3	3	2	1	–	–
CO-5	3	3	2	1	1	1	–

GUIDELINES FOR TEACHERS

To implement Outcome Based Education (OBE) the knowledge level and skill set of the students should be enhanced. Teachers should take a major responsibility for the proper implementation of OBE. Some of the responsibilities (not limited to) for the teachers in OBE system may be as follows:

- Within reasonable constraints, they should maneuver time to the best advantage of all students.
- They should assess the students only upon certain defined criterion without considering any other potential ineligibility to discriminate them.
- They should try to grow the learning abilities of the students to a certain level before they leave the institute.
- They should try to ensure that all the students are equipped with quality knowledge as well as competence after they finish their education.
- They should always encourage the students to develop their ultimate performance capabilities.
- They should facilitate and encourage group work and team work to consolidate newer approaches.
- They should follow Bloom's taxonomy in every part of the assessment.

Bloom's Taxonomy

Level	Teacher should Check	Student should be able to	Possible Mode of Assessment
Creating	Students ability to create	Design or Create	Mini project
Evaluating	Students ability to Justify	Argue or Defend	Assignment
Analysing	Students ability to distinguish	Differentiate or Distinguish	Project/Lab Methodology
Applying	Students ability to use information	Operate or Demonstrate	Technical Presentation/ Demonstration
Understanding	Students ability to explain the ideas	Explain or Classify	Presentation/Seminar
Remembering	Students ability to recall (or remember)	Define or Recall	Quiz

GUIDELINES FOR STUDENTS

Students should take equal responsibility for implementing the OBE. Some of the responsibilities (not limited to) for the students in OBE system are as follows:

- Students should be well aware of each UO before the start of a unit in each and every course.
- Students should be well aware of each CO before the start of the course.
- Students should be well aware of each PO before the start of the programme.
- Students should think critically and reasonably with proper reflection and action.
- Learning of the students should be connected and integrated with practical and real life consequences.
- Students should be well aware of their competency at every level of OBE.

LIST OF FIGURES

LIST OF TABLES

CONTENTS

1 Introduction to Data Structures

UNIT COVERAGE

Introduction to Data Structures: Basic Terminology, Classification of Data Structures, operations on Data Structures.

OBJECTIVES OF THE UNIT

By the end of this unit, student will be able to:

- describe and use the following notions; **data type, abstract data type and data structure.**
- outline the **classification of data type**.
- give **typical examples** of data type.
- explain the **relevance of data structures** in programming.
- describe and use: **time complexity** of the algorithm, best case, worst case complexities.
- explain the relevance of data structures in **programming language design**.
- give typical examples of **overflow, underflow** conditions.
- give typical examples of **stack growth, stack rewinding, call tree**, in recursive solutions.

LEARNING OUTCOMES OF THE UNIT

After completing the Unit 1, the student

- is able to apply the basic techniques covered in the course in **designing algorithms** and implementing them in C **(U1-01)**.
- is able to analyse the **time and space complexity** of an algorithm using big-O notation and justify the correctness of an algorithm using, for example, a loop invariant and/or fundamental step **(U1-02)**.
- has detailed knowledge of **abstract data type (U1-03)**.
- is able to implement the most important **tree algorithms** and knows their time complexities **(U1-04)**.
- is familiar with the basic concepts **overflow, underflow (U1-05)**.
- has detailed knowledge of how d**ata structures are instrumental** in programming language design **(U1-06)**.

- applies the basic concepts covered in the unit such as **iterative** solutions, **recursive** solutions, **divide and conquer** solutions **(U1-07).**
- is able to **pick a suitable algorithm** for an application based on, e.g., time complexity **(U1-08).**

Unit-1 Outcome	EXPECTED MAPPING WITH COURSE OUTCOMES (1 - Weak Correlation; 2 - Medium Correlation; 3 - Strong Correlation)				
	CO-1	CO-2	CO-3	CO-4	CO-5
U1-O1	1	-	-	-	-
U1-O2	2	-	-	-	-
U1-O3	3	-	-	-	-
U1-O4	1	-	-	-	-
U1-O5	1	-	-	-	-
U1-O6	2	-	-	-	-
U1-O7	1	-	-	-	-
U1-O8	2	-	-	-	-

Note: We will be using a program visualization tool in our book extensively in order to let students understand a piece of logic in a better manner and in a visual manner. The application contains the following buttons:

<< First | < Prev | Next > | Last >>

The button "First" takes you to the beginning of our code, "Prev" takes you to the previous instruction, "Next" takes you to the next instruction, and the "Last" takes you to the last instruction of our program. While we move in our program, all the variables values, stack content, heap content will be displayed in a marvelous manner so as to understand the logic of the code which we are trying to visualize. If we encounter any problem with the server, try again. Also, this visualization tool cannot support interactive input(scanf) in C language. Thus, we may be using some random numbers that are generated from the rand() function as input. However, if we want another set of input values, you may call srand() function with some integer value as argument.

1.1 INTRODUCTION TO DATA STRUCTURES

According to Wikipedia[1]

In computer science, a data structure is a data organization, management, and storage format that is usually chosen for efficient access to data. More precisely, a data structure is a collection of data values, the relationships among them, and the functions or operations that can be applied to the data, ie, it is an algebraic structure about data.

According to Britannica[2]

data structure, way in which data is stored for efficient search and retrieval.

1. https://en.wikipedia.org/wiki/Data_structure
2 https://www.britannica.com/technology/data-structure

Some authoritative authors of Computer Science consider **Algorithms + Data Structures = Program.** In fact, Niklaus Wirth wrote a book with the title "Algorithms + Data Structures = Program" that was published by Prentice-Hall in 1975.

Question 1: How many comparisons are needed to find the maximum out of three integers (of any type)?. Before answering, please do explore the following links which contain various solutions from our side. In fact, there are many more possible solutions for this problem.

https://tinyurl.com/AICTEDSBOOK2c

https://tinyurl.com/AICTEDSBOOK2d

https://tinyurl.com/AICTEDSBOOK2e

Out of the above code samples, which one takes less number of comparisons? Can you plan another approach that uses a lesser number of comparisons?

We think the readers are exposed or convergent with one high level programming language such as C. Thus, we love to construct their data structures foundations on that C knowledge.

Question 2: How many comparisons are needed to find both the maximum and minimum of out of the given four integers (of any type)3. Before answering, please do explore the following link which contains one possible solution from our side.

https://tinyurl.com/NBVMAXABCD

In our solution given at the above link uses divide and conquer approach. It finds the maximum and minimum of the first two numbers then maximum and minimum of next two numbers. Then, maximum of the maximums and minimum of minimums are computed as the final solution. Have a look at the above link. Thus, we will be spending four comparisons.

Can you plan another approach that uses a lesser number of comparisons?

Can you plan another approach that uses exactly six comparisons (three comparisons for finding maximum and three more comparisons for finding minimum of the given four numbers) to find the required things?

Question 3: This question was asked in Kansas State University High School Programming contest HSPC 2004. Assume that given three integers a, b, and c to be ordered such that a will be having smallest value, c to be having largest value while b to be having intermediate value. Assume that we have some working code made it available for your experimentation at

https://tinyurl.com/AICTEDSBOOK5

When do we need the worst number of comparisons? When will you need the smallest number of comparisons? Can you think of any other efficient method for doing the same?

If all the given three are in natural order, how many comparisons it needs?

If all the given three are in descending order, how many comparisons is demands?

When this approach used in the above link takes exactly one comparison?

Data structures are the backbones of High-Level Languages[4]

We are sure most of you are aware about low level, medium level, high level programming languages. Also, you know that programming languages have evolved from machine languages to high level languages

3 Can you think of implementing our solution on given four strings and find the strings which comes first and last in the alphabetical order out of the given four strings?

4 http://orion.lcg.ufrj.br/Dr.Dobbs/books/book2/chap01.htm

via assembly languages. However, many assembly languages along with BCPL (Basic Combined Programming Language) like low level languages rarely contain rich data structures. Whereas most of the high-level programming(HLL) languages are popular because of their rich data structures such as arrays/records. Of course, some higher-level assembly languages such as MASM(Microsoft Assembler), NASM(GNU Assembler) have some built-in support for certain data structures. For example C,[5] supports user defined types known as structures, unions, enumerators, and derived types called as arrays (one-dimensional arrays, two dimensional arrays and multidimensional arrays) while Pascal languages support records and vectors.

Question 4: Assume that C language or some other assembly language does not have a modulus operator(%). How to realize the same. You know in C language, if a and b are two integer type variables then a%b is defined as reminder of |a|/|b| with the sign as that of the first operand(a). That is, 10%3=1, 10%-3=1, -10%3=-1, -10%-3=-1, 3%19=3, 10%2=0, 11%2=1, and vice versa. Also, do remember that the language uses integer mode arithmetics if all of the operands of any operator are integers. Thus, 10/3=1, 5/9=0, 34/3=11, and vice versa. See the following link where a sample program is proposed by us. Identify the logic we have used in implementing modulus operators using integer division, multiplication and subtraction.

https://tinyurl.com/AICTEDSBOOK4

Did you understand the logic behind this solution? What happens if the division operation does not follow integer arithmetic?

For the ease of humans' specification to machine what they want, high level languages are developed. However, the machine/CPU very much takes instructions in its machine language. Thus, we need translators that convert high level language programs to machine language. For example, if we write an arithmetic expression in C language, how with the help of a data structure stack it will be verified for its validity and then evaluated is introduced in the chapter on stacks and queues?. Also, related themes known as expression trees are explained in chapter on "trees and graphs". Let us take a funny example. Assume you are hungry and ordered an Item from a restaurant. Then what happens? We don't know. What we know is that the parcel is going to arrive within 10 minutes. What SW system, what delivery boy's organization it uses is masked from us. In the same sense, when we write a program in high level language without the knowledge of ourselves, the compiler uses many data structures (some may be already available in the HLL and some or specially designed) to convert the same into machine language for possible execution.

Just, try to open your Windows task manager app that shows details about processes running on your computer, memory and CPU performance etc. For example, you can find my task manager window as shown below. You find that I am running more than one Google Chrome process. What does that convey further? Windows support multi tasking and also the Chrome app SW is designed to have multiple or concurrent versions. In the same lines, sometimes some applications demands their data

5 a direct descendant of BCPL

structures to be concurrently (or parallel) in multiple computing **threads**[6].

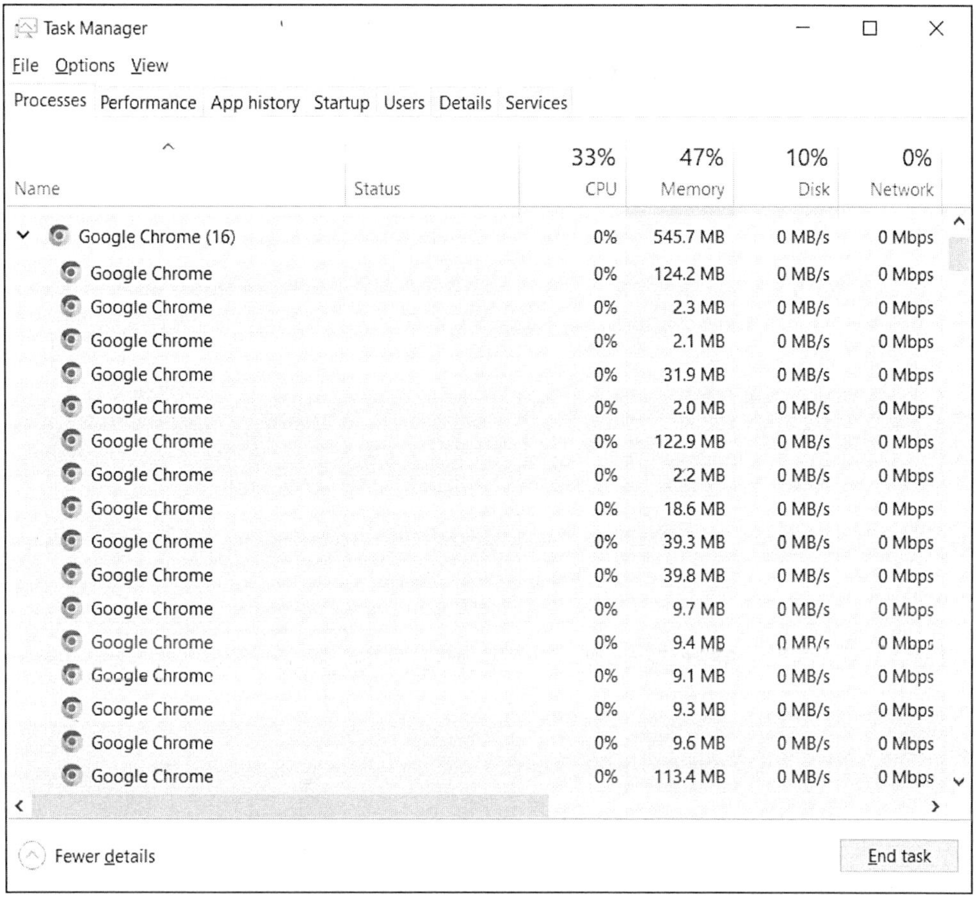

Let us try to construct the foundations of data structures based on your current C language knowledge. You know that **Computers are finite devices**; i.e., they will have finite memory like 16GB RAM, and finite clock rate, etc. Also, you know that programming languages are also **finite** languages. The built-in variables such as int, float, char, long, double of C language will be taking **finite memory**. For example, int type variable takes 4 bytes (32 bits in C), and vice versa. In the following picture (Fig. 1.1), you will find a C program and its output. It tries to add two int types of variables, two long types of variables with large possible values. Readers may refer to https://en.wikibooks.org/wiki/C_Programming/limits.h for possible limits for various data types in C language.

6 The high level language program explicitly typed by us is called the **source program** which is available as files in our secondary memory systems such as Hard disk, etc.,. After successful compilation, the compiler generates a machine language file (in the case of Windows it is **EXE**; whereas in the case of Unix/Linux it is **ELF** binary or **a.out** binary). When we really start this program file, it will be loaded into RAM then it is called as process. Thus, the **process** is an executable entity that is in RAM. Process creation takes lots of computational resources and thus it is called as heavy weight while thread is also an executable entity but demands less computational resources. Detailed discussion on this theme is beyond the scope of this book

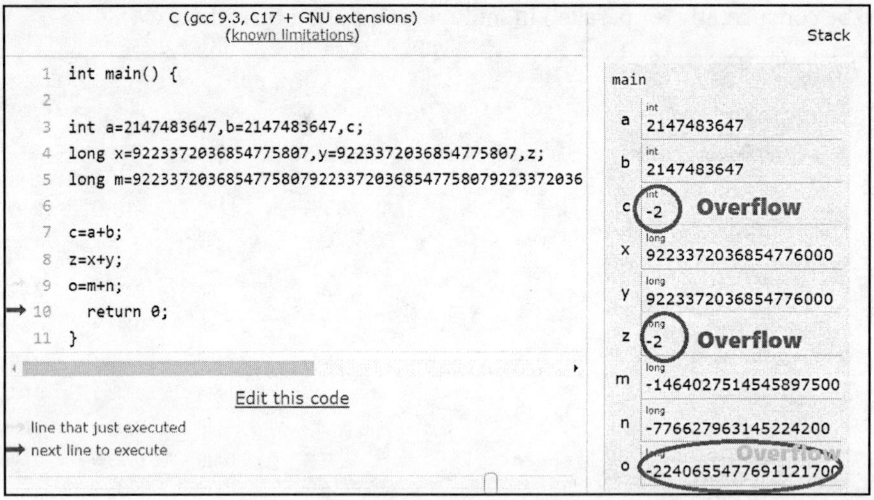

Fig. 1.1: Demonstration of overflow in C language addition.

The addition(+) instructions (among two integers(a&b)), two long (x & y, m & n) of the above program leads to overflow (see the above picture) because of finiteness of the memory that is allocated for the variables. That is, in an int type variable in C language, we can store a maximum value of 2147483647. When we try to add two such variables a and b and store their results in the third variable c, we bump into **overflow** (we cannot store more than 2147483647 in variable c as it is also int type) and thus c variable value is not the actual value we expect; instead we are getting -2 into the c variable. This is happening because of the finiteness of language.

Note: Of course, after seeing the above picture, you may be having a doubt "in the above C program why 9223372036854775807 becoming 9223372036854776000 in long type in C language?". Though, we love to clarify it here, because of the book size limitations we are not explaining here.

The following C program also shows similar behavior.

```
#include <stdio.h>
int main(void) {
int a=2147483647,b=2147483647,c;
c=a+b;
printf("%d\n",c);
a=9223372036854775807;
b=9223372036854775807;
c=a+b;
printf("%d\n",c);
a=922337203685477580792233720368547758079223372036854775807;
b=92233720368547758079223372036854775807;
c=a+b;
printf("%d\n",c);
  return 0;
}
```

Output of the above program is given below. You find overflow at every c=a+b statement.

-2

-2

-332398594

The following link contains the above code for readers for their experimentation.

https://tinyurl.com/AICTEDSBOOK0b

The following C program also shows similar behavior.

```
int main() {
int a=2147483647,b=2147483647,c;
c=a+b;
a=9223372036854775807;
b=9223372036854775807;
c=a+b;

a=922337203685477580792233720368547758079223372036854775807;
b=92233720368547758079223372036854775807;
c=a+b;
return 0;
}
```

The following link contains the above code for readers experimentation.

https://tinyurl.com/AICTEDSBOOK0a

The following link contains the Python variant of the above programs for readers experimentation.

https://tinyurl.com/AICTEDSBOOK1 .

We welcome readers to experiment the same. Do remember **you need not be required to be knowing Python language to understand the following Python code.** Here, also we are adding two variables and trying to print the results. While experimenting with the following code, you may remove # from the statement #print(c).

```
import sys
a=2147483647
b=2147483647
c=a+b
print(type(a),type(b), type(c))
print(sys.getsizeof(a),sys.getsizeof(b),sys.getsizeof(c))
#print(c)

a=9223372036854775807
b=9223372036854775807
c=a+b
print(type(a),type(b),type(c))
print(sys.getsizeof(a),sys.getsizeof(b),sys.getsizeof(c))

a=922337203685477580792233720368547758079223372036854775807
b=922337203685477580792233720368547758072233720368547758079 2
c=a+b
print(type(a),type(b),type(c))
print(sys.getsizeof(a),sys.getsizeof(b),sys.getsizeof(c))
#print(c)
```

```
a=99223372036854775807922337203685477580792233720368547758079223
37203685477580792233720368547758079223372036854775807922337203 6
85477580792233720368547758079223372036854775807922337203685477 58
07922337203685477580792233720368547758072233720368547758079223 37
2036854775807922337203685477 5807
```

```
c=a+b
print(type(a),type(b),type(c))
print(sys.getsizeof(a),sys.getsizeof(b),sys.getsizeof(c))
#print(c)
```

```
a=9922337203685477580792233720368547758079223372036854775807922337203685477580792233720368547758
0792233720368547758079223372036854775807922337203685477580792233720368547758079223372036854775807
9223372036854775807922337203685477589922337203685477580792233720368547758079223372036854775807922
3372036854775807922337203685477580792233720368547758079223372036854775807922337203685477580792233
7203685477580792233720368547758079223372036854775807922337203685477580722337203685477580792233720
3685477580792233720368547758079922337203685477580792233720368547758079223372036854775807922337203
6854775807922337203685477580792233720368547758079223372036854775807922337203685477580792233720368
5477580792233720368547758079223372036854775807922337203685477580722337203685477580792233720368547
7580792233720368547758079922337203685477580792233720368547758079223372036854775807922337203685477
5807922337203685477580792233720368547758079223372036854775807922337203685477580792233720368547758
0792233720368547758079223372036854775807922337203685477580722337203685477580792233720368547758079
2233720368547758079922337203685477580792233720368547758079223372036854775807922337203685477580792
2337203685477580792233720368547758079223372036854775807922337203685477580792233720368547758079223
3720368547758079223372036854775807922337203685477580722337203685477580792233720368547758079223372
0368547758079922337203685477580792233720368547758079223372036854775807922337203685477580792233720
3685477580792233720368547758079223372036854775807922337203685477580792233720368547758079223372036
8547758079223372036854775807922337203685477580722337203685477580792233720368547758079223372036854
7758079922337203685477580792233720368547758079223372036854775807922337203685477580792233720368547
7580792233720368547758079223372036854775807922337203685477580792233720368547758079223372036854775
8079223372036854775807922337203685477580722337203685477580792233720368547758079223372036854775807
9922337203685477580792233720368547758079223372036854775807922337203685477580792233720368547758079
2233720368547758079223372036854775807922337203685477580792233720368547758079223372036854775807922
3372036854775807922337203685477580722337203685477580792233720368547758079223372036854775807992233
7203685477580792233720368547758079223372036854775807922337203685477580792233720368547758079223372
0368547758079223372036854775807922337203685477580792233720368547758079223372036854775807922337203
6854775807922337203685477580722337203685477580792233720368547758079223372036854775807072233720368
5477580792233720368547758079223372036854775807
```

```
b=9922337203685477580792233720368547758079223372036854775807922337203685477580792233720368547758
0792233720368547758079223372036854775807922337203685477580792233720368547758079223372036854775807
9223372036854775807922337203685477580722337203685477580792233720368547758079223372036854775807992
2337203685477580792233720368547758079223372036854775807922337203685477580792233720368547758079223
3720368547758079223372036854775807922337203685477580792233720368547758079223372036854775807922337
2036854775992233720368547758079223372036854775807922337203685477580792233720368547758079992233720
3685477580792233720368547758079223372036854775807922337203685477580792233720368547758079223372036
8547758079223372036854775807922337203685477580792233720368547758079223372036854775807922337203685
4775807922337203685477580722337203685477580792233720368547758079223372036854775807992233720368547
7580792233720368547758079223372036854775807922337203685477580792233720368547758079223372036854775
8079223372036854775807922337203685477580792233720368547758079223372036854775807922337203685477580
7922337203685477580722337203685477580792233720368547758079223372036854775807992233720368547758079
```

```
22337203685477580792233720368547758079223372036854775807922337203685477580792233720368547758079 22
33720368547758079223372036854775807922337203685477580792233720368547758079223372036854775807922 33
72036854775807223372036854775807922337203685477580792233720368547758079922337203685477580792233 72
036854775807922337203685477580792233720368547758079223372036854775807922337203685477580792233 7203
68547758079223372036854775807922337203685477580792233720368547758079223372036854775807922337 20368
5477580722337203685477580792233720368547758079223372036854775807223372036854775807922337203 685477
580792233720368547758079223372036854775807922337203685477580792233720368547758079223372036 8547759
92233720368547758079223372036854775807922337203685477580792233720368547758079223372036854 77580792
233720368547758079223372036854775807922337203685477580792233720368547758079223372036854 758079223
37203685477580792233720368547758072233720368547758079223372036854775807922337203685477 58079922337
2036854775807922337203685477580792233720368547758079223372036854775807922337203685477 580792233720
368547758079223372036854775807922337203685477580792233720368547758079223372036854775 8079223372036
85477580792233720368547758072233720368547758079223372036854775807922337203685477580 79922337203685
4775807922337203685477580792233720368547758079223372036854775807922337203685477580 792233720368547
758079223372036854775807922337203685477580792233720368547758079223372036854775807 9223372036854775
80792233720368547758072233720368547758079223372036854775807922337203685477580799 22337203685477580
7922337203685477580792233720368547758079223372036854775807922337203685477580792 233720368547758079
22337203685477580792233720368547758079223372036854775807922337203685477580792 2337203685477 5807922
33720368547758072233720368547758079223372036854775807922337203685477580780792 2337203685477 5807223
37203685477580792233720368547758079223372036854775807
c=a+b
print(type(a),type(b),type(c))
print(sys.getsizeof(a),sys.getsizeof(b),sys.getsizeof(c))
#print(c)
```

The above program gives the following results.

```
<class 'int'> <class 'int'> <class 'int'>
32 32 32
<class 'int'> <class 'int'> <class 'int'>
36 36 36
<class 'int'> <class 'int'> <class 'int'>
52 52 52
<class 'int'> <class 'int'> <class 'int'>
152 128 152
<class 'int'> <class 'int'> <class 'int'>
1164 1380 1380
```

Interestingly, you find from the above Python program that in the Python language, we are able to add huge integers also without any overflow (One can verify with this program that it cannot give any underflow also by taking huge negative values). This became possible as Python uses **BigInteger/ Bignum** data structure (refer https://peps.python.org/pep-0237/, https://levelup.gitconnected.com/how-python-represents-integers-using-bignum-f8f0574d0d6b for more details) to achieve this in run time as a dynamic language unlike C.

From the above examples, we find Python language uses Bignum data structure because of which it rarely gives overflow!. This is an example that shows how data structures are used in high level language design/development.

Why do we need arrays?

Do remember that I am not asking "What is an array?". An array occupies consecutive memory locations in the RAM and is used to store similar data. That is, all the elements of an array are of the same type. However, I am asking "Why do we need arrays?".

Some people give the answer as "to refer to a group of values with a single name". Of course, I am not convinced with this answer fully. To answer my question, pose yourself a question: what if our language does not support arrays at all? We already understood that some low level programming languages do not have arrays or vectors.

For example, let us assume that we want a program to calculate average marks of those students whose marks are more than the class average. Of course, class average also has to be calculated by your program itself.

See the following solution. 1. We go on reading the students' marks one after another and calculate their total marks. 2. Now, we calculate class average (avg) using the computed class total marks. 3. Now, we again read students' marks one after another and compare with class average (avg) and calculate the number of students whose marks are more than class average (n1) and their total marks (avg1). 4. Now, we compute the average marks of the students whose marks are more than the class average as avg1/n1.

```
#include <stdio.h>
/*Average of students whose marks are more than class average*/
int main(void) {
   int i,n,avg=0,n1,avg1,m;
   scanf("%d",&n);
   for(i=0;i<n;i++){
         scanf("%d",&m);
         avg+=m;
   }
   avg=avg/n;
   for(i=0,n1=0,avg1=0;i<n;i++){
         scanf("%d",&m);
   if(m>avg){
         avg1+=m;
         n1++;
   }
   }
   printf("%d\n", avg1/n1);
   return 0;
}
```

The above code is available at https://ideone.com/WHmq6H for readers experimentation.

In the above solution, we are reading all the student's marks **two times.** By chance if we make a mistake in entering the last value during the second time, we are forced to run the program again and enter all the students marks another two more times. That is, the above solution is demanding more program I/O bandwidth.

Now, see the following solution where all the student's marks are read only once into an array and use them a second time without reading again interactively. In fact, once the data is available in the array (in the memory, RAM), we can use the same as many times as we want without spending any more program I/O bandwidth. **Thus, use of arrays reduces program I/O bandwidth.** So, do you think the program becomes fast? Of course, you are a very very very fast data entry operator then things may be different. Do you know that we need a few milliseconds to press and release a key while to read one word from RAM we need a few nanoseconds?

```
#include <stdio.h>
/*Average of students whose marks are more than class average using
array*/
```

```
int main(void) {
   int a[10],i,n,avg=0,n1,avg1;
   scanf("%d",&n);
   for(i=0;i<n;i++){
         scanf("%d",&a[i]);
         avg+=a[i];
   }
   avg=avg/n;
   for(i=0,n1=0,avg1=0;i<n;i++){

   if(a[i]>avg){
         avg1+=a[i];
         n1++;
   }
   }
   printf("%d\n", avg1/n1);
   return 0;
}
```

The above code is available at https://ideone.com/CrbIhN for your experimentation.

Thus, an array is a good example for a data structure. From the above two coding examples, we found that the use of arrays reduces program's I/O bandwidth. Also, to know the importance of arrays, one program we have written without arrays while the other with arrays. **In practice also, in order to know the importance of one thing, we need to study what happens if we don't have it in our system. This is one of the famous engineering requirements known as risk analysis or failure analysis!.** Also, if a is an array, while accessing ith of it element through a[i], compiler spends one (implicit) multiplication in computing the address of a[i] with the formula a+i*sizeof(type of a), where we know that here 'a' is the base address of the array 'a'. In the same lines, if a is a two dimensional array with four rows and 7 columns then while accessing a[i][j], compiler will be employing a+(i*7+j)*sizeof(type of a). This is true with multidimensional arrays also. Thus, array data structure of high level language is masking many technical aspects from its programmers!.

We recommend readers to refer to the following video to understand more about this (addressing) concept which is also called as storage order of the arrays. We have two prominent storage orders known as row major and column major order. C, C++, Java etc., uses row major order while FORTRAN uses column major order.

https://www.youtube.com/watch?v=aPQM-SQfe2A&list=PLXX7XiUxnzzWoLDfgad4s4dwleb4NMtVN&index=61

Question 5: In the above discussion, we have compared two programs. The second one that employs arrays is declared to be taking less time. But, what about memory requirements[7] of both the methods? If you observe the first program, it is taking a scalar variable, m, only to read students' marks. **Is it also the most important difference?**

Let us debate things further around your knowledge set on C language. We are sure your teacher might have taught you how to compute the product of two matrices and the same you might have carried out in the laboratory also.

7 Space complexity section we shall discuss some more examples on this theme

If A is an m1xn1 matrix, B is an n1xm2 matrix then the product of AB matrices(C) becomes a m1xn2 matrix. We are sure the same thing is your Mathematics course is represented as:

$$C_{ij} = \sum_{k=1}^{n1} A_{ik} B_{kj} \quad ,1 <= i <= m1, 1 <= j <= n2$$

The same in the C language is implemented as follows with A, B, C as two dimensional arrays. We are skipping instructions to read the data into arrays A, B for the reasons of brevity or conciseness of the book.

```
for(i=0;i<m1;i++)
for(j=0;j<n2;j++){
C[i][j]=0;
for(k=0;k<n1;k++) C[i][j]+=A[i][k]*B[k][j];
}
```

The following link contains our sample code to compute the matrix product. You are welcome to experiment with its working.

https://tinyurl.com/AICTEDSBOOK3

The following picture (Fig. 1.2) contains the snapshot of our matrix multiplication code.

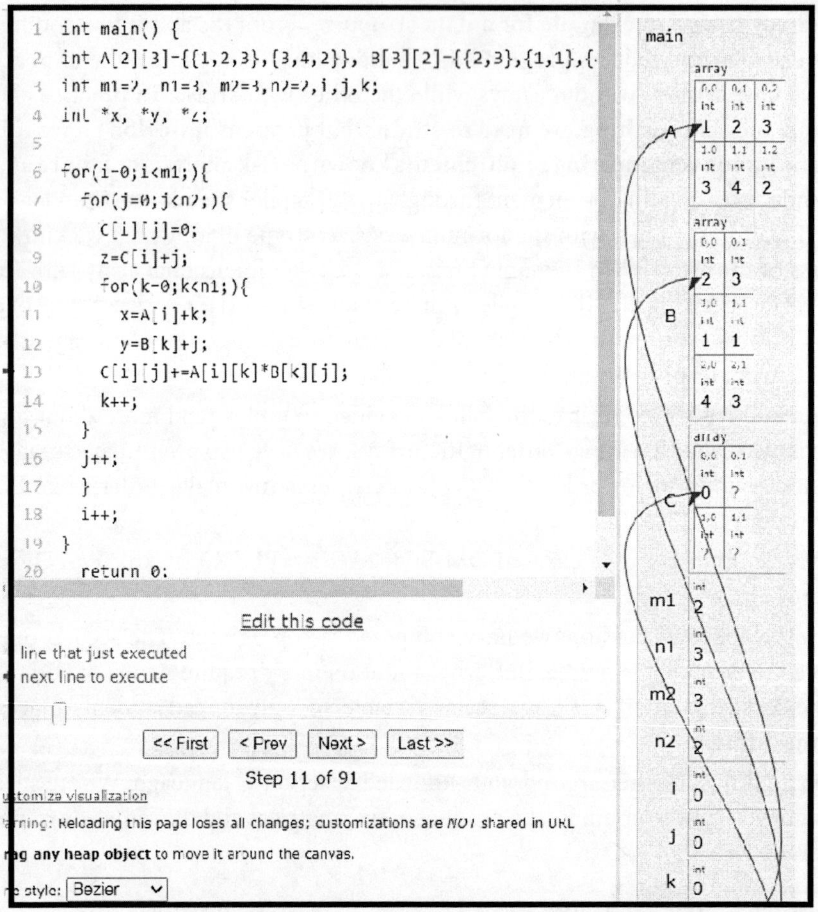

Fig. 1.2: A snapshot of matrix multiplication program

Assume that our C language does not support the two dimensional array concept and we want a flexible matrix multiplication program. Is it possible to write in C? Do remember that we need a flexible program. That is, to multiply any sized matrix with any sized matrix and of course meet the essential requirement of 1st matrix columns to be the same as the second matrix's number of rows. Did you catch the point? **Thus, the two dimensional array data structure of the C language is the one that is allowing us to write a flexible matrix multiplication program.** In this manner, data structures of a language helps us to implement the solutions in an easy manner[8].

Thus, the main objective of the data structures is to manipulate/store the data efficiently in the primary memory by possibly designing data structures. Of course, it is wiser to relate this to other areas of Computer Science also. In Computer Science, we do have another area known as Database Management Systems (DBMS). It also deals with efficient storage and manipulation of the data. However, there we assume that the data is in secondary memory devices such as hard disks, optical disks, etc.,. Many algorithms which are used in data structures are equally applicable in DBMS also. Because of the same reason, sorting methods which are when applied to the data items in the primary memory (RAM), are referred to as internal **sorting** techniques; the same, when applied to the data items available in the secondary memory devices (either as a databases or as a file), are referred to as external **sorting** techniques. **Of course, a data structure method that is found to be good on the data in RAM is not guaranteed to be good if the data is in secondary memory devices as both the devices (RAM and hard disks) work on different accessing approaches in their physical forms.**

Moreover, the Computer Science curriculum of most of the Universities contains courses such as 1. Design And Analysis of Algorithms 2. Graph Theory 1 and 2[9] 3. Computational Geometry, 4. Distributed and Parallel Algorithms, etc.. There exists some overlap between these courses.

More or less, some of the prime objectives of these courses including data structures are:

1. To study algorithms in detail so as to find means of making it efficient in terms of its CPU time and memory requirements.
2. To study algorithm to find out suitable storage (organization) and manipulation procedures for a problem,
3. To compare the algorithms which are available for a problem such that one of them can be recommended in a practical system,
4. To study an algorithm and its computational requirements such as CPU time, memory(RAM) in terms of its problem size; a.k.a. scalability studies/analysis. What happens if the program is run on a large data set; does the running time become an issue?. Is the program computationally inefficient or does it need lots of memory?.
5. Just writing a syntax-error-free program is acceptable when you are in your 1st level computing course. In reality in practice, we need to know whether the algorithm is correct or not, i.e. whether it can give correct answers for the inputs (or called instances)?.
6. We can compare algorithms without implementation. This is called the analysis of algorithms, theoretically. If we implement in a language and carry experimentations, then it is called experimental study.

---

8 Some authors refer this as tractability

9 This reminds me of my BITS, Pilani stay during the 1990's. I did not get a chance to see BITS, Pilani syllabus in the recent years.

It is observed with most of the practical algorithms that if we try to reduce its CPU time requirements it is bound to consume more memory; if we try to reduce its memory requirements, it is going to consume more CPU time. This behavior is called the memory **space-time tradeoff**. Analysis of an algorithm's CPU time and memory space requirements helps us in selecting suitable versions of the algorithm for our practical SW systems[10]. For example, if we happened to have a system with fast processor and less RAM, then we may select an algorithm which consumes more CPU time and less RAM. If we happen to have a machine with a less powerful processor with a lot of RAM, then we can select the algorithm which takes more RAM and less CPU time.

Let us try to explain the first reason with one strong example.

Example 1: Polynomial Evaluation

Let us assume that we have been given a polynomial with its coefficients to evaluate its value at a given point x as:

$$a_0 + a_1x + a_2x^2 + \ldots\ldots\ldots a_nx^n$$

Now, if we employ a naïve approach, we may need 1+2+...+n multiplications = n(n+1)/2 multiplications. See the function FD in the following pages. Here, we assume to calculate x^2 with one multiplication, x^3 with two multiplications etc., One more multiplication for multiplying them with coefficients.

A second version is shown in function FD1. Here, with only one multiplication (without using pow function), we propose to calculate x^2, x^3, x^4 ...etc.,. Thus, to calculate any term, we may need in total, two multiplications. Thus, this version needs 2n multiplications.

The third version, FD2, is called Horner's method. It needs only n multiplications. This became possible by reordering the equation as: (we are taking 6th order equation for clarity reasons):

$$a_0 + x^*(a_1 + x^*(a_2 + x^*(a_3 + x^*(a_4 + x^*(a_5 + a_6{}^*x)))))$$

If we observe the above equation, we may find that with 6 multiplications, we can evaluate the polynomial value at x. The same thing can be generalized to nth order polynomials also. Thus, we may need n multiplications to calculate polynomial value using this method.

Program for evaluating a Polynomial using Horner's method in relation to other methods.

```
#include<stdio.h>
#include<math.h>
float FD(float c[], int ord, float x){
    float s=c[0];
    int i;
    for(i=1;i<=ord;i++) s += c[i]*pow(x,i);
    return s;
}
float FD1(float c[], int ord, float x){
    float s=c[0],T=1;
    int i;
    for(i=1;i<=ord;i++) {T=T*x;
                         s += c[i]*T;
                        }
    return s;
}
```

10 SW localization. Users will be asked which type of algorithm while configuring a SW system.

```
float FD2(float c[], int ord, float x){
    float s=c[ord];
    int i;
    for(i=ord;i;i--) s = s*x+c[i-1];
     return s;
}
int main(){
        int i;
        float coeff[10], P,Q,R,x;
        int n;
        printf("Enter the order of the polynomial\n");
        scanf("%d", &n);
        printf("Enter the coefficients of the polynomial\n");
        for(i=0;i<=n;i++) scanf("%f", &coeff[i]);
        printf("Enter x value\n");
        scanf("%d", &x);
        P=FD(coeff,n,x);
        Q=FD1(coeff,n,x);
        R=FD2(coeff,n,x);
        printf("Polynomial Values using three approaches=%f %f %f\n",
P,Q,R);
        return 0;
}
```

Output:

```
Enter the order of the polynomial
4
Enter the coefficients of the polynomial
1 2 -3 4 1
Enter x value
3
Polynomial Values using three approaches=169.000000 169.000000 169.000000
```

The above program is made available on a visualization server for the perusal of readers.

https://tinyurl.com/AICTEDSBOOK6

Example 2: In the following pages, an efficient means of evaluating xn, for some positive value of n is proposed[11]. Normal iterative12 procedure if we follow, we need **n-1** multiplications.

Solution: We propose to write n as the binary polynomial.

$n = a_k 2^k + a_{k-1} 2^{k-1} + \cdots\cdots + a_1 2^1 + a_0 2^0$, Where, **k** is the largest integer such that **2k<=n, ak** values can be either 0 or 1.

Thus,

11 This method is known as repeated squaring or exponentiation by squaring

12 for(prod=1,i=1;i<n;i++)prod=prod*x; //this for loop runs for n times and thus takes (n-1) multiplications while computing x^n.

$$x^n = x^{a_k 2^k + a_{k-1} 2^{k-1} + \dots\dots + a_1 2^1 + a_0}$$

$$= x^{(a_k 2^k)} . x^{(a_{(k-1)} 2^{(k-1)})} \dots\dots . x^{(a_1 2^1)} . x^{(a_0)}$$

$$= (x^{(2^k)})^{(a_k)} (x^{(2^{(k-1)})})^{(a_{(k-1)})} \dots . (x^2)^{(a_1)} (x^1)^{(a_0)}$$

$$= y_k^{a_k} y_{k-1}^{a_{k-1}} \dots . y_1^{a_1} y_0^{a_0}$$

To calculate $\mathbf{y_i}$ value, we can multiply $\mathbf{y_{i-1}}$ with $\mathbf{y_{i-1}}$. Moreover, if **ai** value is zero we don't consider the respective $\mathbf{y_i}$ value into a product otherwise we will consider. Thus, we may need **2k** multiplications to calculate $\mathbf{x_n}$.

That is, initially we verify **LSB** (least significant bit) of the **binary code**[13] of n, if it is 0 then the product is taken as 1; else it will be taken as x. The number n, will be right shifted by 1 bit. We take y value as x. We execute a loop till n value becomes zero. Each time y value is updates as y*y. If LSB of the n is 1, product is multiplied with y else not.

```
#include<stdio.h>
#include<stdlib.h>
long pow2(long int x, long int n){
        long int t,s;
        s=(n&1)?x:1;
        t=x;
        n=n>>1;
        while(n)
        {
        t=t*t;
        if(n&1)s*=t;
        n=n>>1;
        }
        return s;
}
int main(){
        printf("%ld\n", pow2(2,24) );
        return (0);
}
```

Output:

16777216

Snapshot of the above program.

n (24)	t	s	We assume n value as 24.
0001100**0**		1	As the least significant bit of n is 0, we consider s value as 1.
	x		Initially, t value is taken as x.
0000110**0**			Right shift the n value by 1 bit.
0000110**0**			
	x^2		
0000110**0**			As the least significant bit of n is 0, we don't multiply s with t.

13 Why don't you try to visualize how binary code of a number is computed using recursive implementation. https://tinyurl.com/NBVbinarycode

00000110			Right shift the n value by 1 bit.
00000110	x^4		
00000110			As the least significant bit of n is 0, we don't multiply s with t.
00000011			Right shift the n value by 1 bit.
	x^8		
00000011		x^8	As the least significant bit of n is 0, we multiply s with t.
00000001			Right shift the n value by 1 bit.
00000001	x^{16}		
00000001		x^{24}	As the least significant bit of n is 0, we multiply s with t.
00000000			Right shift the n value by 1 bit.

The above program is made available on a visualization server for the perusal of readers.

https://tinyurl.com/AICTEDSBOOK7

You are also welcome to view a video on this theme.

https://www.youtube.com/watch?v=JFH0C4wCKEg&list=PLXX7XiUxnzzWoLDfgad4s4dwleb4NMtVN&index=19

By the way, how many times does the loop run in the above program? If you observe the table, you find that we are executing the loop body once per one bit of the binary code of the required power, n. Then the question arises is how many bits will be there in the binary code of the required power n?. It is log2(n). Thus, the above loop can be said to be running for log2(n) times. We strongly recommend the readers to read our primer on logarithms that is given in the Appendix of this book.

1.2 CLASSIFICATIONS OF DATA STRUCTURES

There are three main data structure classifications, each consisting of a pair of characteristics.

Linear and Nonlinear

Linear structures: We know that the elements of an array are organized in memory in sequential manner. To support our statement or to educate yourself, we have written the following program that displays the addresses of the elements of static and dynamic arrays from a C program.

```
int main() {
int a[10],i, *p;
char *q;
p=(int*)malloc(10*sizeof(int));
q=(char*)malloc(10);
```

```
printf("Elements addresses of static integer array:\n");
for(i=0;i<10;i++)printf("%X ", &a[i]);

printf("\n\nElements addresses of dynamic integer array:\n");
for(i=0;i<10;i++)printf("%X ", p+i);

printf("\n\nElements addresses of dynamic character array:\n");
for(i=0;i<10;i++)printf("%X ", q+i);
 return 0;
}
```

The above program gives the following output. You will find that from their displayed addresses, all the elements of an array (both static and dynamic) are consecutive in RAM. That is, they are linear or sequential in RAM(memory). As an integer takes 4 bytes on my machine, the element address difference is 4. Of course, you will also find in the following output that the character array elements address difference is 1 as in C language a character takes one byte of memory.

```
Elements addresses of static integer array:
FF000BB0  FF000BB4  FF000BB8  FF000BBC  FF000BC0  FF000BC4  FF000BC8  FF000BCC  FF000BD0  FF000BD4
          Difference=4
Elements addresses of dynamic integer array:
5402040  5402044  5402048  540204C  5402050  5402054  5402058  540205C  5402060  5402064
         Difference=4
Elements addresses of dynamic character array:
54020B0  54020B1  54020B2  54020B3  54020B4  54020B5  54020B6  54020B7  54020B8  54020B9
         Difference=1
```

Arrays are thus linear in RAM; rather they are physically linear (one after another). What about door numbers of two consecutive individual houses in a city? They are consecutive with a difference value of 1 in them. BTW, what about roll numbers of an attendance register? They are too consecutive or linear. Sometimes some objects may be logically linear. That is, they may not be physically linear in memory, but in one sense they are consecutive or linear. We will be knowing more about such things like linked lists, queues and stacks in the coming chapters.

Let me take one example. You are in an Ice cream shop and found your favorite ice cream is 5 rupees. If you buy two, the cost will be 10, if you buy four, the cost will be 20; if you buy k number of ice creams, the cost will be 5k. What is the power for k? One. Isn't it? Thus, your cost is linear in k. Consider the total cost of your car fuel. Does it exactly depend on the number of kilometers traveled? Not at all. It depends on your car age, fuel quality, road type(plain or hilly), weather conditions(sunny or rainy), your mood(whether you are with your girlfriend or not), etc. That is, the car fuel charge is said to be nonlinear and depends on the above parameters.

If the data doesn't form a sequence (physically or logically), they are said to be nonlinear data structures. Consider an example of a family tree where we find grand grand parent, grand parent, parent, children, grand children etc., in the tree. Here, persons may be having a hierarchical relationship. We shall introduce in this book two most popular nonlinear data structures, trees (binary trees) and graphs in forthcoming chapters.

Static and Dynamic

This classification is based on the memory that is allocated for a data structure. Consider an example of a C array which is declared with the instruction like **int a[10]**. You may already know that the memory that is allocated for the array, a, will stay till the end of the program. It will not change, I mean it is static. How much memory needed for this array can be found at compile time itself; of course the compiler knows this. Dynamic data structures are uniquely identified by their non-fixed memory sizes and which can grow or shrink while the program is executing. Also, the location of their associated memory can change during the execution of the program. Marvelous examples of dynamic data structures are C++ language's standard template libraries(STL)[14].

We welcome readers to visit the following link and visualize the code available there. We find that the memory for the array x will be allocated when we enter into the function and the same memory gets deallocated when we return from the function. This is because the array x is a static array. However, the other two arrays a and b whose memory is allocated through malloc() will be available even if the program control exits from the function. This is because they are dynamic arrays.

https://tinyurl.com/NBVstaticvsdynamicarrays

Mutable/Immutable[15]

Mutable ones are the ones whose state(data) can be changed once it is created like adding, updating or deleting elements.

Ex: Lists, Dictionary, Set, bytearray are mutable object types in python, queues, linked lists, stacks, trees.

Immutable ones are the ones whose state (data or content) cannot be modified after creation; we cannot add, remove or update their elements (data or content).

Ex: String, Integer, Tuples, Frozenset are some of the immutable object types in Python.

For instance, C++ language supports "const" with which we can declare a variable as constant type such that its value cannot be changed and any attempt to change its value gives error during the compilation time itself.

If we try to compile the following single line program at https://ideone.com/NiduLs

```
#include <iostream>
using namespace std;
int main(void) {
   // your code goes here
   const int N=10;
   N=100;
   return 0;
}
```

We get the following error:

Compilation error #stdin compilation error #stdout 0s 0KB

```
prog.cpp: In function 'int main()':
prog.cpp:6:4: error: assignment of read-only variable 'N'
 N=100;
```

However, "const" and "immutable" are different. Readers are welcome to read this discussion. https://softwareengineering.stackexchange.com/questions/149555/difference-between-immutable-and-const

14 Many people advises people to use these STLs in solving programming competitions.

15 https://www.cronj.com/blog/immutable-mutable-data-structures-functional-javascript/

Homogenous and Non-Homogenous

A data structure is said to be homogenous data structure if it consists of the same data elements, like elements of a C array; otherwise non-homogeneous data structure. That is, in non-homogenous data structures, the data or members/elements don't have to be the same type[16]. For example, see the following two images that are borrowed from alamy.com. The left side image is the inside of a passenger aircraft whereas the right side image is of a balla kattu that is used in many parts of India. The left side one carries humans (not animals or vehicles) whereas the right side carries humans, cattle, goods, vehicles. By the way, which is homogeneous and which is non-homogeneous?

Persistent and non-persistent data structures

According to Wikipedia[17]: In computing, a persistent data structure preserves the previous version when it gets changed. These data structures also can be said as not ephemeral data structures. When some changes take place on these data structures, a new version of it will be available. They can be also referred to as immutable as the operations on them do not (visibly) update their structure in-place.

Text and File Editing

Do you remember *Undo and Redo* operations that exist in many applications. These two are the most common operations that are available in most of the Text or File editing tools and allow us to have (or recall or go back) persisted (all historical) versions through a persistent data structure. Are you able to catch our point? Let us take one more example. We are sure that you have created some Google Doc files, Presentations using Google Doc. In fact, I am writing or creating this manuscript using Google Doc only. See the following picture. It shows when the file is edited. This filename is Unit1.doc. At any time I can go back to the file status or content of any date and any time.

That is, the Google Doc document is persistent. Did you come across Github? It is a widely used SW repository and we can access the contents of our source files that are committed in it of any data and any time.

16 Python lists are good examples for this category of data structures.

17 https://en.wikipedia.org/wiki/Persistent_data_structure#:~:text=The%20data%20structure%20is%20fully,not%20persistent%20are%20called%20ephemeral.

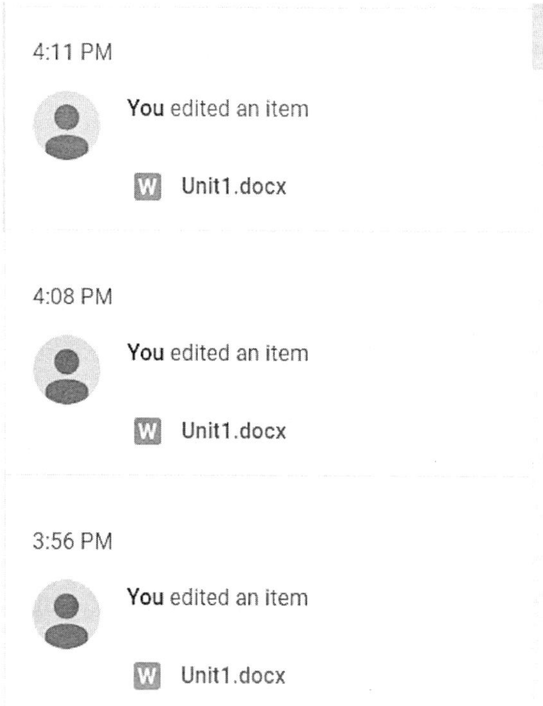

An operation on an ordinary data structure leaves a new version, destroying their old version. However, a persistent structure allows access to any version, old or new[18]. Multiple versions of a data structure is a must while working with the allocations such as computational geometry, 3D graphics, CAD, etc.. **A data structure is persistent if it supports access to its multiple versions.**

A partially persistent data structure is the one which extends freedom to access all of its versions with the constraint of being unable to modify all versions except the most recent one. A fully persistent extends freedom for accessing and modifying all its versions.

Array data structures which are available in C, Java, Python can be said to be non-persistent; if you change it, you have changed it eternally.

Consider the following two C language statements.

```
int c=10;
c++;
```

We know that after the execution of the second statement, variable c value is 11. Is it having c's previous value also? No. If we can store the operation that we have applied on c to get this current value 11, then we can get back c's previous value. That is, we can achieve persistence for the variable c. However, as the C language is not storing anything with respect to variable c except its current value, we say that variable c value is non-persistent.

Non-persistent data structures are efficient, but hard to reason about in complex systems. Persistent systems are a bit slower and need some semantics about what a reference is. For example, many databases

18 https://www.cs.cmu.edu/~sleator/papers/another-persistence.pdf

provide persistence at least within a transaction. Some more advanced systems give even greater persistence promises: given a timestamp T, the server/system can always return the exact state of the data at time T.

For example consider a Linked List.

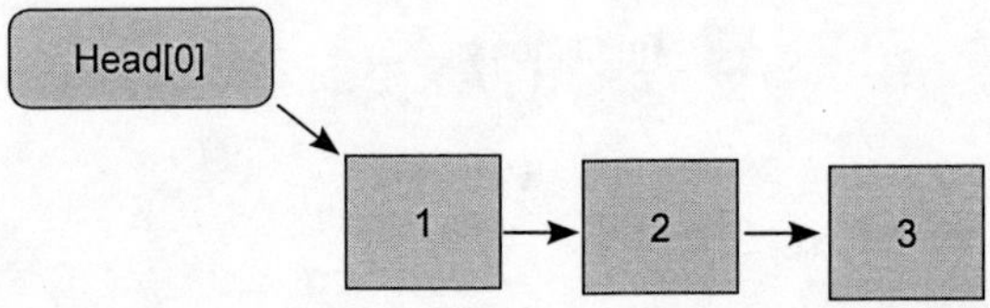

(Courtesy: https://www.hackerrank.com/topics/persistent-data-structures Last accessed: 10th Aug 2022)

Assume that we want to insert two new nodes just before the head of an existing linked list. To achieve this, we will create a new node and point (link) it to the current head of the linked list. See the following picture where Head[0] is made pointing to the first linked list, Head[1] is pointing to the linked list after adding 4, while Head[2] is the that points to the linked list after adding number 5. That is, we can access the old linked list through Head[0], modified linked list after adding 4 through Head[1], and further modified linked list through Head[2]. If we do like this then we can say we have the persistent linked list. At any time, we can access any version of the linked list. This became possible with the overhead of two extra pointers, Head[1] and Head[2].

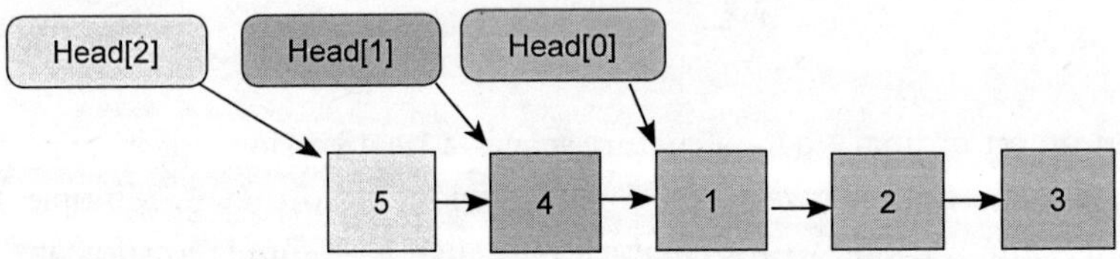

(Courtesy: https://www.hackerrank.com/topics/persistent-data-structures Last accessed: 10th Aug 2022)

We welcome readers to play with this to experience the above explanation. Anyway, we shall be dwelling linked lists in detail in the third chapter.

https://tinyurl.com/AICTEDSBOOK117

By chance, if we add a new node in between an existing linked list, we cannot have original linked list and modified linked list; we have the modified one only. That is, it is a non-persistent operation.

Consider a binary tree T:

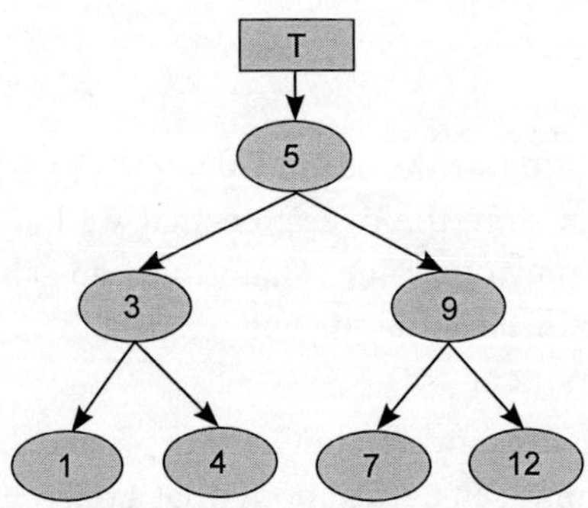

(Courtesy: https://www.hackerrank.com/topics/persistent-data-structures Last accessed: 10th Aug 2022)

To insert a new value into a persistent binary tree, first we create a new tree with the nodes which are along the path from the root to the node to which the new node to be added then new node will be added to it. The remaining nodes of the original persistent tree that are not along the path are shared between the original and the updated versions of the tree.

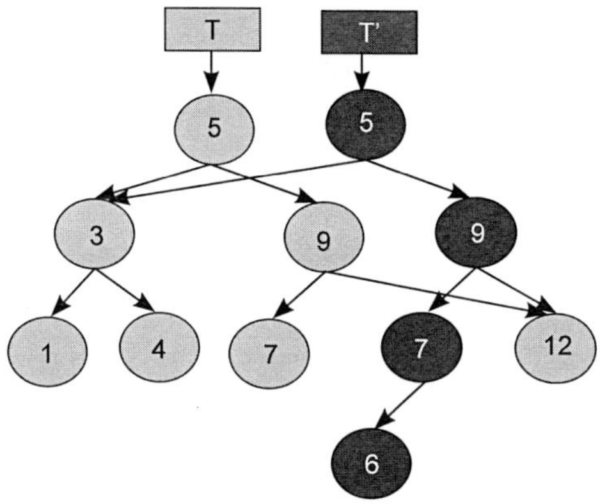

(Courtesy: https://www.hackerrank.com/topics/persistent-data-structures Last accessed: 10th Aug 2022)

Partially Persistent

We already understood that in partially persistent data structures we can access all versions but modify the most recent version only. This means historical versions of the data structure are immutable (read-only). Consider the previous example of the linked list. If we try to add a new node to an existing linked list at the end, the remaining or original list will not change.

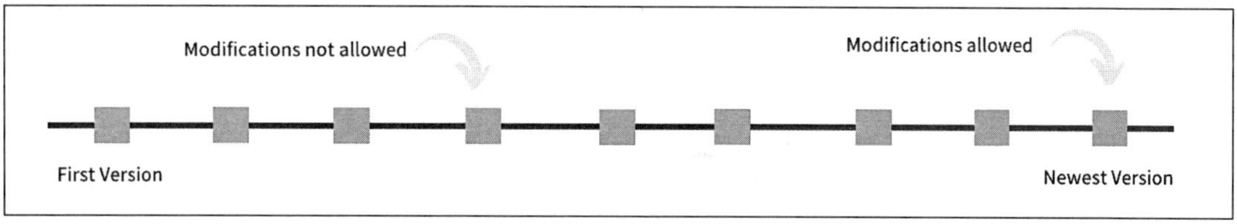

(Courtesy: https://arpitbhayani.me/blogs/persistent-data-structures-introduction Last accessed: 10th Aug 2022)

Fully Persistent

Fully Persistent Data Structures does not restrict any modifications on any version of the data structure whatsoever it may be at any time. This means we can typically revisit any historical version and modify it.

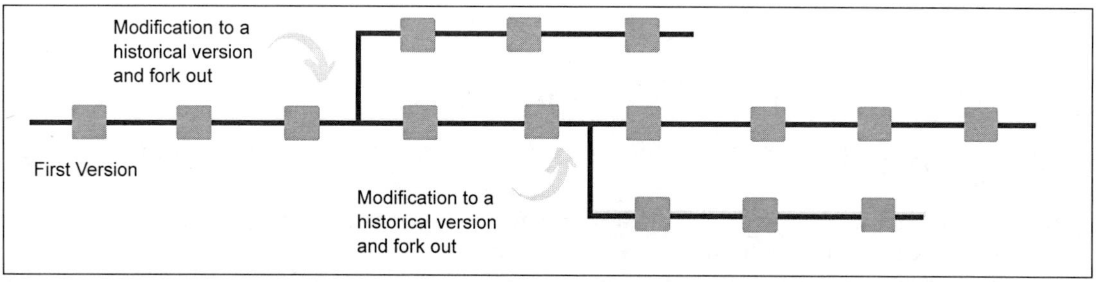

(Courtesy: https://arpitbhayani.me/blogs/persistent-data-structures-introduction Last accessed: 10th Aug 2022)

Confluently Persistent

Confluently Persistent Data Structures not only allows modifications to historical versions (past or previous versions) but also allows to merge with the existing ones so as to create a new version.

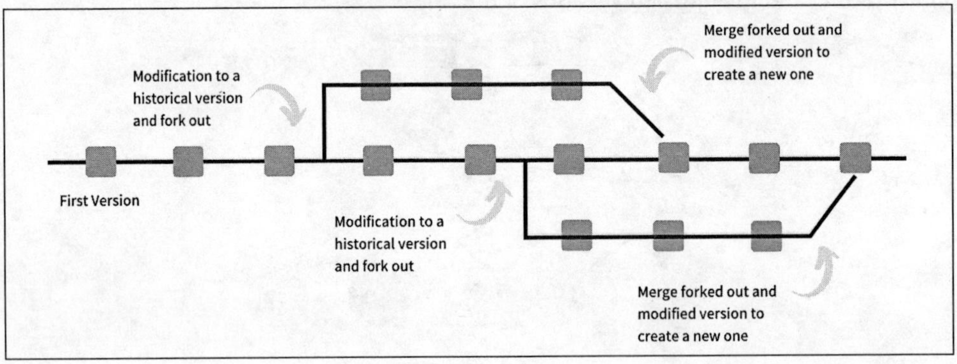

(Courtesy: https://arpitbhayani.me/blogs/persistent-data-structures-introduction Last accessed: 10th Aug 2022)

Note: Certainly one is expected to relate persistence with mutability also. However, as this book is aimed at first level readers, it is beyond the scope of the book.

Primitive vs non-primitive(aka derived)

Primitive data types are predefined by the particular programming language. This includes int, float, decimal, number, char, string and so on, depending on the language.

Non-primitive data types are defined by the programmer. The language will provide keywords like struct, class, and interface for defining these.

1.2.1 Advantages of Data structures

1. Effective data storage (RAM or secondary memory) is possible by the use of data structures.
2. The use of data structures makes it easier to retrieve data from a storage device in addition to RAM. However, the data structure that is used to access RAM may not be suitable for other devices such as hard disks.
3. An aptly designed data structure can extend similar benefits when used with both little and huge amounts of data. That is, they are scalable.
4. The use of a good data structure may assist a programmer to save a lot of time or processing time while performing tasks such as data storage, retrieval, or processing.
5. Anybody can use data structures such as arrays, trees, linked lists, stacks, graphs, and so on as they are thoroughly verified and proved. This may reduce their SW development time.

1.3 OPERATIONS ON DATA STRUCTURES

Usually, we will be doing a variety of operations on data structures which may change from data structure to data structure.

For instance, on an array which we already understood as a data structure, we can **access** a specific element, we can **change** a specific element, we can **traverse** all the elements of an array, and vice versa. Also, we need to **search(find)** whether a given element in the array or not; we may need to **sort** all the elements of the array, we may need to **partition** the array based on some criterion.

Also, we may be using **inserting (adding)** an element, **removing (deleting)** an element, **removing all** elements (cleaning), etc.,.

As such, we did not touch the real subject of data structures, so it is not wise from our side to talk in the air. Thus, we postpone our discussion on operations on data structures to next chapters.

1.3.1 Algorithms: a briefing

An **algorithm** may be defined in simple terms as a finite sequence of instructions that solves a problem. A computer program is simply an implementation of an algorithm on a computer. The word Algorithm comes from the name of Abu Ja'afar Mohamed ibn Musa Al Khowarizmi (c. 825 A.D.). An Algorithm is a procedure to do a certain task. An Algorithm is supposed to solve a general, well-specified problem.

How to make your breakfast?

See the following figure (Fig. 1.3) having steps in making breakfast.

Fig. 1.3: Algorithm for breakfast

In Yoga, surya namaskar is one form (see Fig. 1.4). The sequence of poses that we carry can be also considered as an algorithm, of course to do this prakriya.

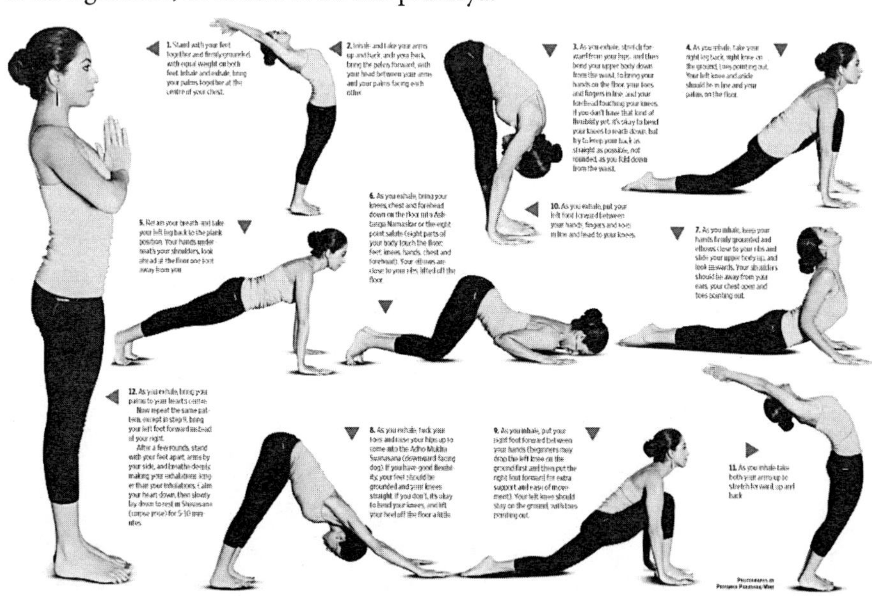

Fig. 1.4: Algorithm for surya namaskar

Picture courtesy of: https://www.timeslifestyle.net/wp-content/uploads/2018/03/Surya-Namaskara-benefits-and-how-to-do.jpg

Algorithms are written for a human, rather than for a computer to understand. In this way algorithms differ from programs.

Thus, an Algorithm is a set of rules or steps used to solve a problem. An algorithm is a sequence of instructions or a set of rules to get something done.

An algorithm can be also thought off as a solution to a problem with three properties:

- having list of step-by-step of instructions
- It is a finite process. This means it is guaranteed to finish at some point.
- All the possible instances(situations or cases) of the problem have to be solved.

In computer science, a problem is solved in the following fashion. 1. Analyzing the problem and preparing the algorithm, 2. Implement the algorithm probably in some language, 3. Test the algorithm (program) 4. Use the algorithm (program or Software). This sequence of steps also can be called an algorithm. Ha. Ha. **Algorithm for algorithm**(see Fig. 1.5).

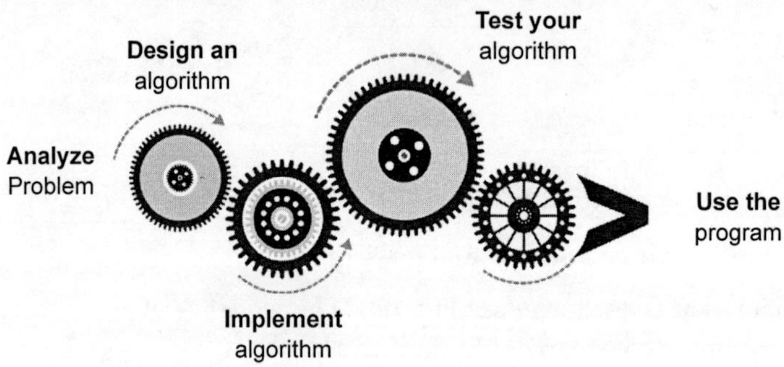

Fig. 1.5: Algorithm for realizing algorithm

I am happy to know that a board of directors are being appointed by algorithms!. https://www.bbc.com/news/technology-27426942?ocid=wsnews.chat-apps.in-app-msg.whatsapp.trial.link1_.auin&fbclid=IwAR2yalns1tNDHPS-Q8Rbuwc075vAtq9kDI_3J8KxJe9iqNbM4YEugQmPj2w

Example 3: Let us enjoy a real life example and its algorithm

A simple real life example to illustrate what an algorithm is. Assume that there is a mother with two children. Both the children are having their favourite cups, probably their names on them. They will have their drinks only when they are served in their respective cups. One loves coffee and the other loves Horlicks. One fine morning, mother wanted to serve them drinks, but made a mistake in selecting the cups; rather cups got exchanged. Now, how she can solve the situation. Assume both the cups are of same size(volume) and she is also having an empty cup also at her disposal.

She transfers coffee to the empty cup.

Then, she transfers Horlicks to the cup labelled coffee.

Now, she transfers coffee to the cup labeled as Milk.

The steps that the mother followed can be said as an algorithm to solve her problem.

Now, let us visualize the above operation in a programming language point of view. That is, we want to exchange the values of two variables(or objects). We have the following six solutions for our discussion.

Let us analyze swap

A	B
temp=a	a=a^b
a=b	b=a^b
b=temp	a=a^b

a=a+b	a=a-b	a=a*b	a=a/b
b=a-b	b=a+b	b=a/b	b=a*b
a=a-b	a=b-a	a=a/b	a=b/a
C	D	E	F

Solution A is akin to the cups example which we have explained above. That is, we are using a temporary variable. That is, assign the value of the variable, a, to temp variable, value of variable b to variable a, then value of temp variable to variable a. Three steps like the above example.

The following link contains a C language implementation of solution A which is hosted on a visualization server. We welcome readers to experiment and understand the working of this.

https://tinyurl.com/y84zkj8n

Solution B uses bitwise exclusive-OR operator. The following workout will clarify the steps of solution B. Observe the original and final bit patterns of a and b.

a=	11000101	(197)
b=	01111010	(122)
a=a^b=	10111111	
b=a^b=	11000101	(197)
a=a^b=	01111010	(122)

The following link contains a C language implementation of solution A which is hosted on a visualization server. We welcome readers to experiment and understand the working of this.

https://tinyurl.com/yab53z3z

Let us explore whether the above solutionB works for float type variables or not.

```
#include <stdio.h>
int main(void) {
        float a=12.2,b=12.343;
        a=a^b;
        b=a^b;
        a=a^b;
        printf("%f %f\n",a,b);
        return 0;
}
```

Try to run the above. Refer any book on C language to find whether bitwise operators are meaningful between float type arguments or not.

Maybe the following corrections will make this work with floats also.

```
#include <stdio.h>
int main(void) {
        float a=12.2,b=12.343;
        int x=*((int *)&a);
        int y=*((int *)&b);
                x=x^y;
                y=x^y;
                x=x^y;
                a=*((float*)&x);
                b=*((float*)&y);
        printf("%f %f\n",a,b);
        return 0;
}
```

The above is available at https://ideone.com/1WPtp1 for experimentation.

Now let us debate on Solution C. The following link contains the above Solution Cs code on a visualization server.

https://tinyurl.com/y9vq86os

Example 4: Experiment the above Solution C with

a. Very large values (in the order of $2^{64} - 1$) for a and b.
b. Very large negative values in the order of $-(2^{64} - 1)$ for a and b.
c. Variable a is very huge positive and while b is very large negative.
d. Both a and b are zeros.
e. Either of a and b are zeroes.
f. Both are positives.
g. Both are negatives.
h. One positive and one negative.
i. Repeat the above for float type values of a and b.

Approach D is available at https://tinyurl.com/y75kabfw and you are most welcome to trace the same on the visualization server.

Approach E code is available at https://tinyurl.com/y7puvwof and you are most welcome to trace the same on the visualization server.

Approach F code is available at https://tinyurl.com/y9c3n687 and you are most welcome to trace the same on the visualization server. **Find a flaw in this code given above link.**

Question 8: Observe with all the above examples when you get overflow/underflow or floating point exception or NaN(not a number) etc?.

1.3.2 Empirical vs theoretical algorithm time complexity analysis

Most of the Computer Science professionals may encounter one or other day the following type of doubt. What happens to their SW system if input size is doubled or tripled? If we feed it with a different input, how will it behave? To answer this, we may employ time complexity analysis which is a tool to explain how our algorithms behave with the input size.

When we speak of the time complexity, we are **not** at all interested in **absolute** times, i.e. how many CPU seconds it is taking to solve a particular problem for a given input size. The actual absolute CPU time consumed depends on a number of factors: how fast the computer is, the quality of code generated by the compiler, the number of users using the computer at that time etc. If you change any of these, then the absolute time changes.

Thus, absolute time is not useful as a measure of an algorithm's performance.

Also, do remember we want algorithm performance; not the code performance!

Reasons to analyze the efficiency of an algorithm:

- Analysis helps choose which solution to use to solve a particular problem.
- Experimentation tells us about one test case, while analysis can tell us about all test cases(performance guarantees).
- Performance can be predicted before programming. If you wait until you've coded a large project and then discover that it runs slowly, much time has been wasted.
- If you can tell which parts of your solution execute quickly and which parts execute slowly, then you know which to work on to improve the overall solution.

In addition to the above reasons for analyzing the algorithms, we wanted to bring another important reason. All of us know that there can be a multitude of algorithms to solve a given problem. Consider the situation where you have a horrible day in the office because of a picky boss and his brain eating five clock interaction session. You are relieved at 8.00 pm and eager to reach home and relax. Also, assume that you don't have your own vehicle. There are many options available for you to reach home. 1. Pooled bus service provided by the office, 2. Public service such as bus/train/metro, 3. Calling Uber/Ola, 4. Calling your elder son to come from home by vehicle and pick you up, 5. Ask your better half who is still in her office to pick you up. Which one do you select to reach your home? Of course, we know that you know the correct answer. You pick a better one. Better in the sense of time if you are too rich; better in the sense of cost if you are an average salaried employ.In the same lines, if an algorithm has a multitude of solutions, an immediate question that arises is "which is better?". This necessitates the relative **analysis of algorithms.** In the example above, if he selects option 3 (Uber/Ola cab), he will reach the house quickly. In the same lines, to compare algorithms we need to arrive at their computational performance. Also, we may need to compare algorithms in terms of the amount of space (memory) they consume.

We know that each algorithm consists of a finite sequence of instructions/steps. If the algorithm contains more instructions, the longer it will take to execute. Thus one way to compare algorithms would be to count the instructions that the algorithm requires to solve a problem. Rather, we compute the **number of instructions as a function of the input size (or problem size which we explain in the coming pages).**

In general algorithms can be analyzed either empirically or theoretically as discussed above.

Empirical analysis involves:

- Implementing an algorithm in some programming language like C, Pascal
- Compiling and generating executable/binary file

- Running the executable/binary file on a specific computer platform and gathering runtime data for various possible input sizes
- Analyzing the runtime versus size of the input

However, empirical analysis suffers from

1. Empirical analyses conclusions are biased on how it is implemented. How nicely one has coded, which apt programming language is used in developing the code, etc., influence a lot.

Theoretical analysis which is also called as the **time complexity analysis**:

- uses a high-level description of the algorithm instead of an implementation of some programming language
- explore running time versus input size, n.
- considers all possible inputs, often analyzing the worst case and best case
- Algorithm speed is evaluated independent of the hardware/software environment

As per this book, it is assumed that instructions of an algorithm are executed one after another, serially or sequentially (We are not going to discuss parallel algorithms here). We consider serial algorithms only. Also, the computer uses RAM (Random Access Model), in which each operation (e.g. +, -, x, /,=) and each memory access take one run-time unit. Loops and functions can take multiple time units.

The time complexity of an algorithm, T(n), is represented as a function of its problem size, say n. The time required is counted in terms of the **primitive operations** involved in the algorithm. Primitive operations include

1. Assigning a value to a variable (independent of the size of the value; but the variable must be a scalar).
2. calling a function such as printf, scanf, pow, sqrt.
3. Performing a (simple) arithmetic operation .
4. Indexing into an array .
5. accessing an object from its reference i.e., pointer.
6. Returning from a function.

As the time complexity of an algorithm, T(n) is represented in terms of number of operations involved, it becomes "device-independent" measure[19]. That is, rather than expressing the time consumed in seconds in empirical analysis, we attempt here to represent how many "elementary operations" the algorithm executes when presented with instances of different input sizes. This measure is more useful for answering questions like:

- If I want to run on a problem on input of double size, how long will it take?
- If we can buy a machine twice as fast as the existing one, what is the size of the input which we can solve in the same time?

Let us take a simple example, to illustrate what is meant by complexity analysis.

Alice and Bob proposed sorting algorithms with time complexities 256n lg n and n^2 comparisons respectively. Assume that their algorithms are implemented and benchmarked on a machine that takes 10^{-3} seconds for one comparison operation and input size of 1024. The following shows the observed

19 Analysis is done before coding. Profiling (a.k.a. benchmarking) is done after the code is written.

times. From the table, clearly Bob's algorithm is better.

Size	Alice	Bob
1024	2621	1049

However, they are asked to observe their algorithms' behaviors for various possible input sizes also. The following table illustrates their observations.

Size	Alice	Bob
1024	2621	1049
2048	5767	4194
4096	12583	16777
8192	27363	67109

The table conveys Alice's algorithm is much better placed for expansion.

Let us try to compute how many items each of these two algorithms sorts in one hour. As one comparison on the selected machine takes 10^{-3} seconds, within an hour it can make $3600/10^{-3} = 3600000$ comparisons. Assume nA, nB as the number of items that can be sorted by Alice and Bob's algorithms in one hour time. Thus,

$$3600000 = 256nA \lg nA = n^2B$$

We can find nA = 1352, nB = 1897.

That is, Bob's algorithm seems to be too workaholic!.

Let us analyze what happens if we replace the current machine with another machine that is four times faster in carrying comparison operations. That is, on the new machine, comparison takes $1/4 \times 10^{-3}$ seconds. Thus, we can make $3600/(1/4 \times 10^{-3})$=14400000 comparisons in the same one hour. Let us try to compute nA , nB for this situation also. That is,

$$14400000 = 256nA \lg nA = n^2B, \text{ yields}$$

$$nA = 4620, nB = 3794.$$

Faster the machine, faster are both the algorithms. However, nA value rose by 3.41 (4620/1352), whereas nB value doubled (3794/1987) only when we replaced the CPU with a four times faster machine. So, we can say Alice's algorithm is gaining much more rate from the faster machines compared to Bob's algorithm.

Note: We do have some other complexities related to computer science. They are 1. Circuit Complexity 2. Language complexity. However, the discussion on them is beyond the scope of this book.

1.3.2.1 Problem Size

Usually algorithm's computational complexities are represented in terms of problem size. For example, in the case of sorting a set of elements, the number of elements can be considered as problem size. Similarly, while estimating the complexity of the matrix multiplication problem, matrix size is taken. For number-theoretic algorithms, the input parameter or problem size is the measure of how big the number is. So it is the number of bits occupied by the number. Thus, this is very much associated with the problem.

The time complexity of an algorithm, T(n), is represented as a function of its problem size, say n. The following table 1.1 summarizes some common problems and their problem sizes.

Table 1.1: Problem size with examples

Problem	Problem Size
Searching for an element in an array	Number of elements in the array.
Sorting elements of an array.	Number of elements in the array.
Testing uniqueness of a 1-D, 2-D, 3-D or n-Dimensional array.	Number of elements in the array or size of the array.
Checking whether a string is palindrome or not.	Number of characters in the given string.
Searching for a node with a given value in a binary tree.	Number of node of the tree.
Graph traversal	Number of node and edge in the graph.
Matrix multiplication	Size of the matrix which we want to multiply.
Finding LCM of two positive integers	The number of bits needed to represent both the numbers.
Factorial calculation	The input number.
Finding average of a 1-D array.	The number of elements in the array.

For instance, take a physical real life example where a store manager will be giving gifts to customers. Assume there are n customer's in the queue. That is, here the problem size is this, the number of customers(n) in the queue. Assume that the Manager brings one gift at a time. Handover it to one customer. Returns to collect the next gift. What is the time complexity of handling a gift to a customer?

Answer:

Time complexity = 1 step as manager will take exactly the same time irrespective of the line length.

What is the time complexity of the whole gift distribution activity?

Answer: n steps.

Let us explore another physical example. Shifting n items from one room to another room in our house.

Answer: n pick-ups, n forward moves to the other room, n drops and n reverse moves to the first room. Total, we have 4 n operations. That is, T(n)=4n steps.

What about exploring another real life example?. Shifting n items from one room to another room in our house.

At the beginning you are the only one to start the task of items shifting. After you transferred an item and returned to the first room, one more friend of yours joined. When you have transferred the second item, two more friends of yours have joined. If we assume your friends are joining you, how many transfer operations are needed to transfer n items? Assume all the people are equally energetic. Also, once anyone starts transferring an item, he will not terminate or stop the same in between. Also, when a friend has joined, he will stay till the end of the room shifting. Transferring an item involves picking an item, taking it to the other room, placing it, then returning to the first room. All the people start at the same time and complete at the same time.

Answer: $\log_2 n$ transfers. Let us analyze the situation of shifting chronologically.

The 1st item is moved by you and returned.

New friend of yours did join you.

Both of you carry one item and return to the room.

Two more friends of yours have joined you.

Four of you carry one item and return to the room.

Four more friends of yours join you.

Like this, the items are transferred: 1, 2, 4,8 and vice versa. If we have n items then we need $\log_2(n)$ transfers. If we have 15, we need ceil($\log_2(15)$)=4 transfers.

Example 5: What made us use computational complexity analysis of algorithms in an abstract manner instead of empirically?

Answer: Empirical analysis conclusions are very influenced by processor architecture, memory architecture, compiler implementation, and also many platform(both HW/SW) dependent run-time factors like the current load(number of processes) of the CPU, the current memory usage, availability of cache memory and swap memory. Thus, in time complexity analysis, we try to understand the algorithm's behavior independent of the above so as to answer some questions.

1.3.2.2 The Big-Oh Notation

"Big-O notation is a relative representation of the complexity of an algorithm"[20]. Let us explore the words of this statement.

Relative: Let us try to recall an old saying "you can only compare apples to apples, you cannot compare an apple with a pineapple". In the same lines in practice, you can compare the performance of a Prime Minister with another country's Prime Minister; but not with a lady doctor!!. Consider an algorithm two compute the inner product of two n dimensional vectors and another algorithm to find(search) whether a given element x is available in a n element 1-D array or not. In the first one, multiplications are needed whereas in the second one comparisons are needed. You can't compare these two algorithms. However, you can compare two separate searching algorithms on a 1-D array.

Representation: Big-O (in its simplest form) reduces the comparison between algorithms to a single variable. That variable is chosen based on observations or assumptions, out of them are already mentioned while discussion T(n). For example, sorting algorithms are typically compared based on comparison operations. This assumes that comparison is expensive. We know the majority of sorting algorithms do spend element exchanges. But what if the comparison is cheap but swapping (exchanging) is expensive? It changes the comparison exchanges.

Complexity: if it takes my program one second to sort 100,000 elements, how long will it take to sort one billion elements? Complexity in this instance is a relative measure to something else.

The big O does not give an idea of the time duration of the computation. It just gives how the duration's scales with input size or problem size[21].

20 Refer http://ssp.impulsetrain.com/big-o.html for some misconceptions on time complexity orders.

21 Big O domain calculator https://www.wolframalpha.com/widgets/view.jsp?id=57ad04c0f04cc92e742205985c18023e

Definition: Let f(n) and g(n) be real-valued functions of a single non-negative integer argument. We write f(n) is O(g(n)) if there is a positive real number c and a positive integer n_0 such that $f(n) \leq cg(n)$ for all $n \geq n_0$ (see Fig. 1.6).

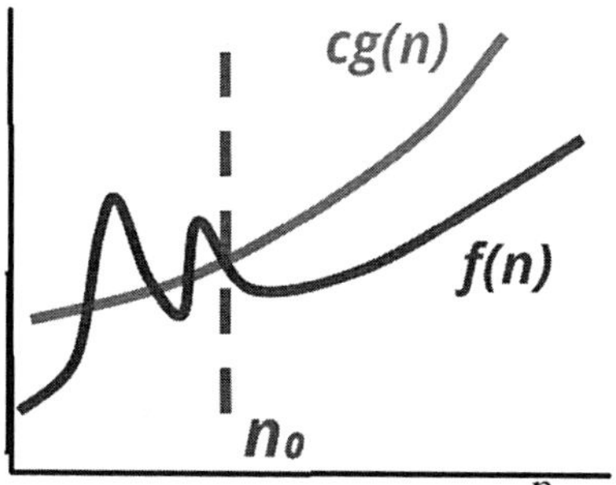

Fig. 1.6: Big-Oh definition

What is the meaning of this?

For large inputs ($n \leq n_0$), f is not much bigger than g ($f(n) \leq cg(n)$). Consider a symbolic example to elucidate this concept.

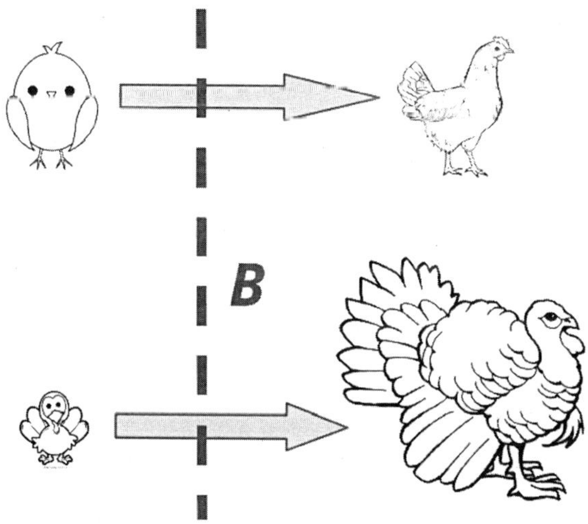

Fig. 1.7: Growth of chicken and turkey

We know in general a chicken grows slower than turkey(Fig. 1.7), rather we can say that chicken size is in O(turkey size). What does it really mean?. We know the following facts of real life.

- Baby chickens might be larger than baby turkeys when they are born.
- After some days(breakpoint), the turkey size will start become more than chicken size.
- Rather, from that breakpoint day onwards, the chicken size will always be smaller than the turkey size.

In the same fashion, the given function f(n) is guaranteedly smaller than cg(n) for values of n >= n0.

To practically explain about this, consider a live problem. Suppose a company tracks its autos that are shipped around the world on rail, truck, and water vessel. At the end of each day, this company uses an algorithm to summarize all auto movement in some meaningful way. Let us consider that the algorithm does its job in three steps.

- The algorithm takes 50,000 msecs to read the data from the database. Do remember that this time is independent of the number of autos in the company.
- The algorithm takes 1 msec to process each auto movement into summarized data.
- The algorithm takes 5,000 msecs to write the summarized data back to the database. Do remember that this time is independent of the number of autos in the company.

So, processing *n* auto movements takes

- (50,000 + 1*n + 5,000) msecs
- The *n* term will become more important as *n* becomes very large
- **As it turns out, in the real world, *n* may be in the order of 100,000,000 !!**

Thus, *n* be the input size (number of autos) or problem size here and T(*n*) becomes the time complexity of the processing. That is, T(n)= 50,000 + 1*n + 5,000. Obviously, you find that T(n) is a function of problem size, here it is the number of autos, n.

Let f(*n*) be another function, preferably without constant factors… n, n^2, $\log_2 n$, etc., We can say that T(*n*) is Big-Oh of f(*n*), or, T(*n*) is on the order of f(*n*), or, T(*n*) = *O*(f(*n*)) if:

T(*n*) ≤ *c**f(*n*) for some positive constant *c*, starting at the point where *n* is ≥ some other positive constant *n0*.

What we are saying is *c**f(*n*) is a bounding function T(*n*) asymptotically.

Think of *c**f(*n*) is like a ceiling for T(*n*); in other words, we can guarantee that our algorithm will never run in worse time than on the order of f(*n*).

From the above, the time complexity equation becomes:

$$T(n) = (50{,}000 + 1*n + 5{,}000) \text{ msecs}$$

$$T(n) = n + 55{,}000$$

Choose f(*n*) = *n* to see if T(*n*) = O(*n*)

Definition of Big-Oh: $T(n) \le c*f(n)$

$$n + 55{,}000 \le c*n \qquad \text{solve for } \boldsymbol{c}$$

$$1 + 55{,}000/n \le c$$

As *n* gets bigger and bigger (and approaches infinity), 55,000/*n* will approach zero.

$$1 + 55{,}000/1 \le c \;\; \text{->} \;\; c \ge 55{,}001 \quad \text{if } n = 1$$

$$1 + 55{,}000/2 \le c \;\; \text{->} \;\; c \ge 27{,}500 \quad \text{if } n = 2$$

$$1 + 55{,}000/\infty \le c \;\; \text{->} \;\; c \ge 1 \qquad \text{if n approaches infinity.}$$

We need to show this holds for positive constants *c* and n_0 where $n \ge n_0$

Pick $n_0 = 1$

$$1 + 55{,}000/1 \le c, \;\; \text{so } c = 55{,}001$$

Does this *c* = 55,001 still work for *n* = 2 (because *n* keeps growing)?

$$1 + 55{,}000/2 \le 55{,}001$$

$$27{,}501 \le 55{,}001 \qquad \text{TRUE!}$$

So, $T(n) = O(f(n))$ because we can find c and n_0 that hold as n grows to infinity!. Thus, this algorithm's asymptotic complexity is said to be O(n).

Consider another example:

Suppose we have an algorithm that takes $3n2$ steps given n inputs(that is, problem size is n).

Does $3n2 = O(n2)$?

The definition of Big-Oh says...

$T(n) \leq c^*f(n)$ for c and $n0$ where $n \geq n0$

Given: $3n2 \leq c\ n2$

Choose $n0 = 1$ and $c = 3$. That is, LHS and RHS are the same, Which means that the given $3n2$ is $O(n2)$.

Does it still work as n grows? Now, let us try for $n = 2$. It will work. It will work for values of n more than 2 also. Thus, we can say that $3n2 = O(n2)$.

Let us consider another example. The following figure shows the possible operations in a C++ function that is written to find the maximum of a vector(a container).

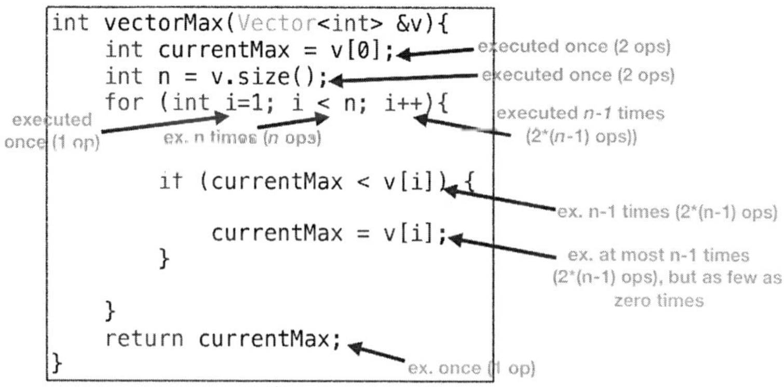

The possible number of operations are:

at best: $2 - 2 + 1 + n + 4(n - 1) - 1 = 5n - 2$

at worst: $2 - 2 + 1 + n + 6(n - 1) + 1 = 7n$

If there are n items in the vector, the number of operations needed will be between 5n+2 operations and 7n operations. If the vector contains elements in descending order then the if condition will never become true as all the elements will be smaller than the first element. Thus, we need 5n+2 operations. Instead if the vector contains elements in ascending order, each time the if condition becomes true and maximum changes. Thus, it needs 7n operations. We can prove that it is of O(n) by taking c=7 and n_0=1.

Example 6: Let us explore the algorithm for computing the inner product of two vectors A, B of size n elements each. the inner product of the two arrays A and B is A[0]*B[0] + A[1]*B[1] +....A[n-1]*B[n-1], which is the sum of pairwise products. See the following algorithm for this purpose.

```
1 prod ← 0
2 for i ← 0 to n-1 do
3     prod ← prod + A[i]*B[i]
4 return prod
```

- Line 1 can be taken as one operation (assigning a value).
- Initializing the loop also can be taken as one more operation (assigning a value).
- Third statement involves five operations per iteration of the loop (mult, add, two array references for A[i], B[i], assignment).
- Also, the third statement is executed n times.
- Also, loop control variable, i, incrementation is two operations (an addition and an assignment)
- Also, loop incrementation is done for n times.
- Also, loop condition testing for termination or continuation is one operation (a comparison i<n) each time.
- Do remember that loop termination takes place (n+1)th time (n successes, one failure).
- We need to consider that 'return' is also one operation when implemented really in any language..

The total is thus 1+1+5n+2n+(n+1)+1 = 8n+4.

That is, time complexity T(n)=8n+4. You may prove with c=9 and n0=1, this can be proved as O(n) using the big O definition.

Example 7: Let us explore the following algorithm for computing the inner product of two vectors A, B of size n elements each. the inner product of the two arrays A and B is A[0]*B[0] + A[1]*B[1] +....A[n-1]*B[n-1], which is the sum of pairwise products. See the following algorithm for this purpose. Is there any advantage of this over the previous one?

```
1 prod ← A[0]*B[0]
2 for i ← 1 to n-1 do
3     prod ← prod + A[i]*B[i]
4 return prod
```

- Line 1 is four operations (accessing A[0], B[0], calculating their product, and assigning the result to the variable prod).
- Initializing the loop also can be taken as one more operation (assigning a value).
- Third statement involves five operations per iteration of the loop (mult, add, two array references for A[i], B[i], assignment).
- Also, the third statement is executed n-1 times.
- Also, loop control variable, i, incrementation is two operations (an addition and an assignment)
- Also, loop incrementation is done for n-1 times.
- Also, loop condition testing for termination or continuation is one operation (a comparison i<n) each time.

- Do remember that loop termination takes place nth time (n-1 successes, one failure).
- We need to consider that 'return' is also one operation when implemented really in any language.

The total cost of the above code fragment, T(n) = 4+1+5(n-1)+2(n-1)+n+1 = 8n−1. We may take c=8 and n_0=1 so as to claim its order is O(n) in accordance with the big O definition.

We find both the above two solution's complexity orders are the same, O(n).

1.3.2.2.1 Fundamental step

Example 8: What do you know about fundamental step while carrying out algorithm analysis?

Answer: Fundamental step is "a single line or short group of lines of code that will be executed the most times". It will be typically of order O(1) for the following code fragment.

```
def sum(lis):
    total = 0
    for i in range(0,len(lis)):
        total += lis[i]
    return total
```

N = length of lis.

How many times is the fundamental step executed? N times

So this algorithm is O(N).

In the following code, the fundamental step is marked with a red square.

```
def seqSearch(lis, target):
    for i in range(0,len(lis)):
        if target == lis[i]:
            return i
    return None
```

Also, the fundamental step is marked with a red square in the following code.

```
// problem size is n
x = 2 * n
y = n - 4
total = 0
while x > 0:
    if x is even:
        total = total + y
    else:
        total = total - y
    x = x - 1
```

Similarly consider another example of a function call along with the operations involved. We find that the time complexity T(n) is 6n+4. According to the big O definition, we find that for c=7 and n_0=5 values, its complexity order is O(n).

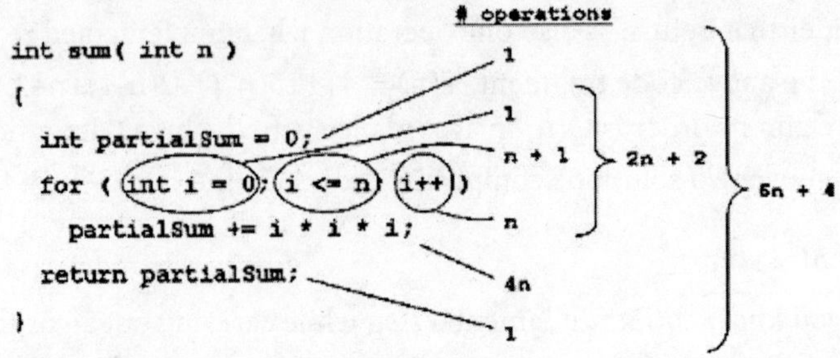

So, T(n) for this algorithm is 6n+4 and T(n)=O(n).

Example 9: Compare the following two algorithms?

Algorithm1	**Algorithm2**
arr[0] = 0; **arr[1] = 0;** **arr[2] = 0;** **...** **arr[N-1] = 0;**	**for(i=0; i<N; i++)** **arr[i] = 0;**

Answer: There is a high chance people will conclude that Algorithm1 as O(1) while Algorithm 2 as O(N). However, both are O(N). See the following analysis with some simple assumptions. Assume c1 is the cost of accessing a memory location, c2 is the cost of incrementing variable i value, comparing i with N etc. As the loop runs N+1 times and in (N+1)th time the condition becomes false. Thus, we have taken (N+1)*c2. Of course, we did not take into account the i=0 statement's cost. Because, i++ statement is in principle executed for N times while i<N is executed for N+1 times. We thought it would balance!. See the following workout for time complexity computation for both the algorithms.

Algorithm 1	Cost	*Algorithm 2*	Cost
arr[0] = 0;	c1	for(i=0; i<N; i++)	c2
arr[1] = 0;	c1	arr[i] = 0;	c1
arr[2] = 0;	c1		
...			
arr[N-1] = 0;	c1		
	-----------		------------
c1+c1+...+c1 = c1 x N		(N+1) x c2 + N x c1 = (c2 + c1) x N + c2	

O(n)

According to the big O definition, for Algorithm 1, c=c1 and n_0=1 while for Algorithm 2, c=c1+c2+1 and n_0=c2+1 to prove their complexity orders are O(n).

Consider another example involving nested loops. Here, each loop runs for n+1 times. Thus, the innermost k++ statement executes (n+1)*(n+1) times.

```
for ( int i = 0; i <= n; i++ )          <---- 1 + (n + 1) + n
  for ( int j = 0; j <= n; j++ )        <---- (n+1)*(1+ (n + 1) + n)
    k++;                                <---- (n+1) * (n+1)
                                              ____________________
                                              2n + 2
                                               + 2n² + 3n +1
                                               + n²  + 2n  + 1
                                              ____________________
                                              3n² + 7n + 4
```

T(n) = 3n² + 7n + 4

So O(n) = n²

Let us take c=8 and try to prove:

$3n^2+7n+4 <= 8n^2$.

$-5n^2+7n+4 <= 0$

If we solve the above quadratic equation[22], we find roots as -0.43578167 and 1.83578167. We take the ceiling of positive root as n_0. That is, $n_0=2$. According to the big O definition, we can say that the above algorithm's order is $O(n^2)$. To cross check, for n=1, $3n^2+7n+4=14$ while $8n^2$ value is 8. For n=2, $3n^2+7n+4=30$ while $8n^2$ value is 32. We find that for all values of n=2, $3n^2+7n+4 <8n^2$.

Example 10: In the following, we have two functions prefixAverages1() and prefixAverages2(). Which one is better in terms of their computational complexity order?

Answer: Operations needed for both the methods are also shown below. First one needs 4n+1+n(n+1) operations while second one needs 4n+2 operations. As, the first one is having n^2 term while the second one is not; thus, the second one is most preferred as it is computationally cheaper.

```
Algorithm prefixAverages1(X,n)
Input: an array X with n integer elements
Output: An array having prefix averages of A          #Operations
A<- new array of n integers                           n
for i=0 to n-1 do                                     n
        s=X[0]                                        n
        for j=1 to i do                               1+2+3+...+(n-1)
                s=s+X[j]                              1+2+3+...+(n-1)
        A[i]=s/(i+1)                                  n
return A                                              1

Algorithm prefixAverages2(X,n)
Input: an array X with n integer elements
Output: An array having prefix averages of A          #Operations
A<- new array of n integers                           n
s=0                                                   1
for i=0 to n-1 do                                     n
        s=s+X[j]                                      n
        A[i]=s/(i+1)                                  n
return A                                              1
```

22 https://quadraticsolver.com/

Example 11: What c and n_0 values are needed to prove $7 \in O(1)$?

Answer: We need to find c, n_0 such that for all $n \geq n_0$ we have

$$7 \leq c \cdot 1$$

Take c = 7, n_0 = 1.

Example 12: What c and n_0 values are needed to prove 2n+1 big-Oh order is O(n)?

Answer: We need to find c, n_0 such that for all $n \geq n_0$ we have

$$2n + 1 \leq c \cdot n$$

We choose c = 3, n_0 = 1. Then $3 \cdot n = 2n + n \geq 2n + 1$. Thus, we can say that 2n + 11 is of order O(n).

Example 13: What c and n_0 values are needed to prove 7n – 2 big-Oh order is O(n)?

Answer: We need to find c, n_0 such that for all $n \geq n_0$. We have

$$7n - 2 \leq c \cdot n$$

We choose c = 7, n_0 = 1.

Example 14: $3x^4 + 5x^2 - 19 = O(x^4)$. Does it convey that there's a function $O(x^4)$ and which is equal to $3x^4 + 5x^2 - 19$?

Answer: No. Rather the example is read as: "$3x^4 + 5x^2 - 19$ is big-Oh of x^4". Which actually means:" $3x^4 + 5x^2 - 19$ is asymptotically dominated by x^4"

Example 15: What c and n_0 values are needed to prove $(3n^3 + 5n^2 + 2 \in O(n^3))$?

Answer: We need to find c, n_0 such that for all n ≥ n0 we have $3n^3 + 5n^2 + 2 \leq c \cdot n^3$.

Here, the highest ordered term is n^3 and its coefficient is 3. For this coefficient, we need to add something such that $5n^2 + 2$ contribution is also taken into account. For which value of n, $n^3 > 5n^2 + 2$?.

n	1	2	3	4	5	6	7	8
n^3	1	8	27	64	125	256	343	512
$5n^2 + 2$	7	22	47	82	127	182	247	322

Thus, we add 1 to the coefficient of n^3 term, that is 3 and thus 3 + 1 is taken as c. Also, n_0 value can be taken as 6 from the above table. Thus, c = 4 and n_0 = 6.

Example 16: Consider an example in which data has to be read from a file. This inturn involves reading a filename interactively and opening the file with a function like fopen() or through system call like open(). Assume for this initial activity it needs 500 operations. Assume to read one item from disk, it needs 10 operations. Thus, T(n)=500+10n. Assume that we want to compare this with two other algorithms whose complexities n, 20n respectively. The following picture (Fig. 1.8) shows the function 500 + 10n plotted against n, the problem size.

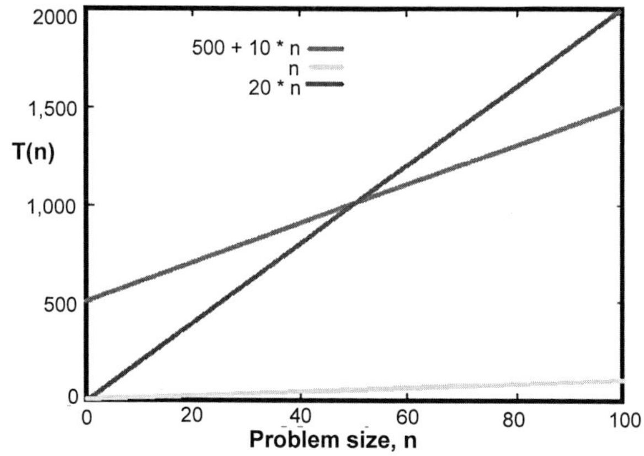

Fig. 1.8: Growth of some functions

If you observe the figure, you will find that the function n will never be larger than the function 500 + 10 n. However, there are constants c and n0 such that 500 + 10n <= cn when n >= n_0 . One choice for these constants is c >= 20 and n_0 >= 50. Therefore, T(n) = 500 + 10n = O(n). That is, this data reading problem is of order O(n). Of course, there can be other choices for c and n_0 to arrive in big-O order. By the way, what is the big-O order of the algorithm whose T(n) is 20n?. What are c, and n_0 values?

Example 17: Consider the following two algorithms A, B.

```
Algorithm A: {
set up the algorithm, taking 50 time units;
read in n elements into array A; /* 3 units per element */
for (i = 0; i < n; i++) {
do operation that  takes 10 units
do operation that takes 5 units
do operation that takes 15 units
}
}
```

```
Algorithm B: {
set up the algorithm, taking 200 time units;
read in n elements into array A; /* 3 units per element */
for (i = 0; i < n; i++) {
do operation that takes 10 units
do operation that takes 5 units
}
}
```

Algorithm A sets up faster than B, but does more operations on the data. The execution time of A and B will be TA(n) = 50 + 3*n + (10 + 5 + 15)*n = 50 + 33*n and TB(n) =200 + 3*n + (10 + 5)*n = 200 + 18*n respectively. The above graph shows the execution time for the two algorithms as a function of n. Algorithm A is the better choice for small values of n. For values of n > 10, algorithm B is the better choice. Remember that both algorithms have time complexity O(n). The reason is that asymptotic analysis ignores constants of proportionality (see Fig. 1.9). In the following figure, if you can draw another line for T(n) = n, you will find that it will be smaller than both the curves for all problem sizes. Thus, these both algorithms are of the same order O(n) though they have different constant multiplication factors(33,18) in their time complexities.

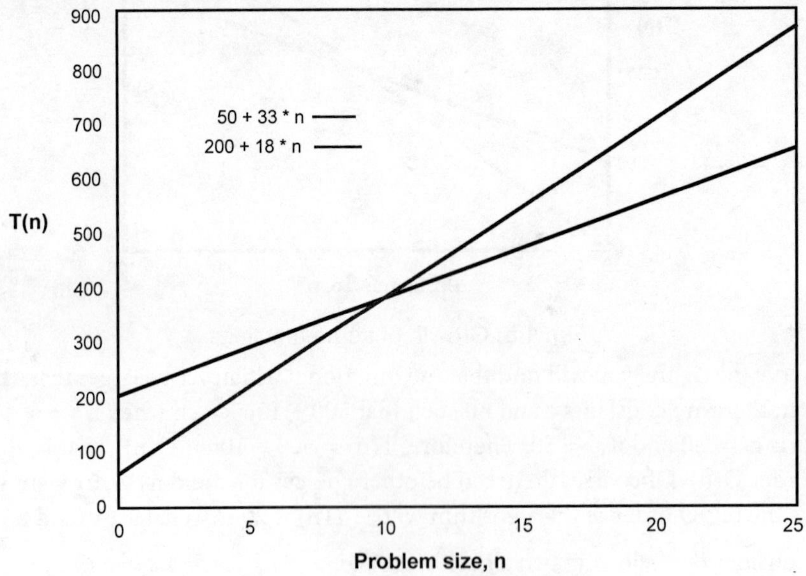

Fig. 1.9: Growth of some functions and constants of proportionality

Relatives of the Big-Oh

Big-Omega and Big-Theta

Recall that f(n) is O(g(n)) if for large n, f is not much bigger than g. That is, g is some sort of upper bound on f. How about a definition for the case when g is (in the same sense) a lower bound for f?

Definition: Let f(n) and g(n) be real valued functions of an integer value. Then **f(n) is Ω(g(n))** if g(n) is O(f(n)).

Definition: We write **f(n) is Θ(g(n))** if **both** f(n) is O(g(n)) **and** f(n) is Ω(g(n)).

Remarks We pronounce f(n) is Θ(g(n)) as "f(n) is big-Theta of g(n)"

Little-Oh and Little-Omega

Definition: Let f(n) and g(n) be real valued functions of an integer variable. We say **f(n) is o(g(n))** if for **any** $c > 0$, there is an n_0 such that $f(n) \leq g(n)$ for all $n > n_0$. This is pronounced as "f(n) is little-oh of g(n)".

Definition: Let f(n) and g(n) be real valued functions of an integer variable. We say f(n) is ω(g(n)) if g(n) is o(f(n)). This is pronounced as "f(n) is little-omega of g(n)".

Examples: log(n) is o(n) and x^2 is ω(nlog(n)).

As this book is an introductory level book, we are not discussing the Importance of Asymptotics analysis of algorithms.

1.3.2.3 Space Complexity

We know that space complexity of an algorithm is also an important criterion while comparing and selecting the algorithms for practical problems. Also, it is vital to reduce the space requirements of algorithms. In a nutshell, we may employ some alternative physical storage schemas to reduce memory space requirements of an algorithm. However, it poses another difficulty. That is, if we propose another schema of storage; then we also need to propose (new) mechanisms (data structures) to do the operations.

For example, if we propose to store a 2D matrix in a 1-D array, then implementations of all the operations such as additions, subtractions, etc. which we normally carry on a 2-D matrix have to be modified such that they assume the matrix is in a 1-D array.

Compared to the 1970's, today the unit cost of RAM is cheap. However, revolutionary developments that are taking place under the name of Internet of Things(IOT) are employing trillions of trillions internet enabled tiny inexpensive processors with tiny memory. These tiny memory devices continue to demand programs that consume less memory. Otherwise also, reducing memory requirements is a classic activity on its own.

In the following, we propose some examples which illuminate the reader about reducing memory space requirements of algorithms.

Example 18: Propose a method to map a symmetric matrix into a 1 D array along with methods to add, subtract, multiply symmetric matrices which are in the 1-D array fashion.

We know that symmetric matrices will have their upper and lower triangular portion elements the same. Thus, to conserve memory, we propose to store only the lower triangular part of the matrix including main diagonal elements. If one observes, we can find that ith row jth column element of the symmetric matrix is stored in location i*(i+1)/2+j of 1-D array. For example, 2nd row 2nd column element, i.e., x5 will be available at: 2*(2+1)/2+2=3+2=5.

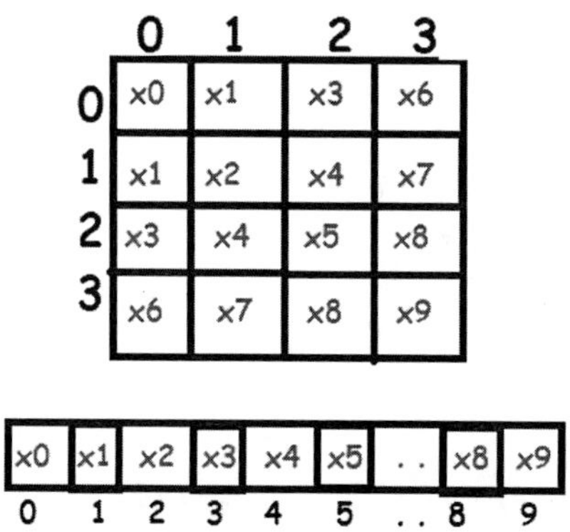

Total number of elements in the 2-D symmetric matrix = n^2

Number of elements needed in the 1-D representation= $1+2+\ldots+n = n(n+1)/2$

Thus, a saving of almost 50%.

If we want i^{th} row j^{th} column element of the symmetric matrix, its location in the 1-D array can be calculated as: i*(i+1)/2+j. However, this will not work for upper triangular portion elements. Thus, if we want upper triangular portion elements of the 2-D array, we simply exchange their row (i) and column(j) indexes and then apply the above formula to get the required element. This became possible because of symmetry.

The following program demonstrates the storage of a symmetric matrix in a 1-D array and accessing the same. Remember, really 2-D array information is in 1-D fashion. However, users can still work at 2-D notation by using the above mapping function.

```
#include<stdio.h>
int Element(int s[], int i, int j){
        return s[i*(i+1)/2+j];
  }
int main(){
int i,j,k,s[200],n,a[10][10];
printf("Enter Size of the matrix\n");
scanf("%d", &n);
for(i=0;i<n;i++)
for(j=0;j<n;j++) scanf("%d", &a[i][j]);

for(i=0,k=0;i<n;i++)
for(j=0;j<=i;j++) s[k++]=a[i][j];

/* here k becomes the total elements of 1-D array */
printf("Symmetric Matrix Data From 1-D Array\n");
for(i=0;i<k;i++)printf("%d\n", s[i]);

printf("Enter Row and Column Element of Any element\n");
scanf("%d%d", &i, &j);
if(j>i) {

            int t=i;
            i=j;
            j=t;
           }
printf("Element Value=%d\n", Element(s,i,j));
      return 0;
}
```

Now, let us discuss how to add two symmetric matrices which are represented in 1-D array fashion as explained above.

Consider First matrix A and its 1-D array representations are:

1	9	1	9
0	2	2	8
1	2	3	1
9	4	4	1

1	9	2	1	2	3	9	8	4	1

Consider Second symmetric matrix and its 1-D representation:

1	7	1	9
7	2	7	4
1	7	3	1
9	8	4	1

1	7	2	1	7	3	9	4	4	1

Now their sum matrix and its 1-D representations are:

1 + 1	9+ 7	1+ 1	9+ 9
9+ 7	2+ 2	2+ 7	8+ 4
1+ 1	2+ 7	3+ 3	1+ 1
9+ 9	8+ 4	4+ 4	1+ 1

1+ 1	9+ 7	2+ 2	1+ 1	2+ 7	3+ 3	9+ 9	8+ 4	4+ 4	1+ 1

By observing the above workout, we can say that adding two 2-D symmetric matrices in this representation is the same as adding their resective 1-D representations element by element. It is true with the subtraction of two symmetric matrices. The following function allows us to do addition of two symmetric matrices which are in their 1-D representation.

We know that in nxn elements, total n*(n+1)/2 elements are stored in the 1-D array. Thus, in the function, we allocate a dynamic array to store n*(n+1)/2 elements. The address of this array is returned as the resultant matrix in 1-D representation.

```
int * AddSymMat(int a[], int b[], int n){
int i, *c;
C=(int*) malloc( n*(n+1)/2*sizeof(int));

for(i=0; i< n*(n+1)/2; i++) C[i]=a[i]+b[i];
return C;
}
```

We can carry the subtraction also in the same fashion. For multiplication, we propose the following function. Verify whether it will give the expected results are not. Remember, we need to calculate only the lower triangular portion of the product of two symmetric matrices.

```
int * ProdSymMat(int a[], int b[], int n){
int i, j,k,l,*c;
C=(int*) malloc( n*(n+1)/2*sizeof(int));

l=0;
for(i=0; i<n; i++)
for(j=0;j<=i;j++){
C[l]=0;
for(k=0;k<n;k++) C[l] += Element(a, i,k) * Element(b,k,j);
l++;
}
return C;
}
```

Example 19: Now consider storing two symmetric matrices of same size (nxn) in a 2-D array to conserve space.

A

1	9	1	9
9	2	2	8
1	2	3	1
9	4	4	1

B

1	7	1	9
9	2	9	4
1	9	3	1
9	4	4	1

1	1	4	4	1
9	2	3	9	1
1	2	3	2	7
9	8	4	1	1

Resultant matrix

Fig. 1.10: Two symmetric matrices together to conserve space

As we know that the symmetric matrices will be having redundancy, we proposed to store two nxn symmetric matrices lower triangular portions in a nx(n+1) matrix. Here, we may find a savings of almost 50%. That is, as such for both the matrices A and B together we need $2n^2$ elements. If we store both in a 2-D array like C, we need n^2+n elements. This is 2-D array to 2-D array mapping (see Fig. 1.10).

Probable mapping steps are:

```
for(i=0;i<n;i++)
for(j=0;j<=I;j++) {
        C[i][j]=A[i][j];
        C[n-1-i][n-j]=B[i][j];
    }
```

Of course, if we want to i^{th} row j^{th} column element of Matrix A, it can be accessed simply as i^{th} row j^{th} column element of C as it is stored like that way. Similarly, if we want i^{th} row j^{th} column element of matrix B, the same can be accessed as C[n-1-i][n-j] as it is stored like that as shown in the above code fragment. That is, whatever way we have stored the element, the same way we can access. However, with both the matrices A and B, if we want upper triangular portion elements, then we can exchange their row and column elements and then access from C.

An algorithm is said to be "in-place[23]" if the amount of additional memory required by the algorithm does not grow with increase in the input size. For example, algorithms like Insertion Sort and Bubble Sort are in place because the amount of additional memory (like the use of temporary variables) needed by these algorithms does not grow with input size.

- In-place algorithms are said to have $\Theta(1)$ space complexity.
- An algorithm is said to be "out-of-place" if the amount of additional memory required by the algorithm grows with increase in input size. – For example, if an algorithm copies the contents of the input array to another new array, then the amount of additional memory (to be allocated for the new array) grows with increase in the size of the input array. E.g., Merge Sort.

We welcome readers to refer to the following video to get littlemore enlightenment of this theme. https://www.youtube.com/watch?v=5Fjmbm-Pguc&list=PLXX7XiUxnzzWoLDfgad4s4dwleb4NMtVN &index=75

A simple tool to estimate time.

https://csfieldguide.org.nz/en/interactives/algorithm-timer/

1.3.3 A note on abstract data types

Elsewhere you might have come across the statement that C language has primitive data types(char,int,float,double), derived type(strings, 1-D, 2-D, multidimensional arrays, user defined types(structs, unions, and enumerators). In order to explain ADT (abstract data type), we feel it is wiser to open a little more theoretical background of computing also.

In Mathematics, Integers are said to be a set of all positive numbers without any fractional parts. They are abstracted in C and other languages as **int type**. In similar lines, real numbers are a set of all possible numbers including integers. They are abstracted in C and other languages as **float or double or long double types**. We are sure that you are already familiar with these words. In the computing point of view, **A type can be said as a collection of values.** For example, the boolean type (available in C++, Java, Python, R but not in C) consists of the possible values true or false. The integers also form a type.

An integer is a **simple type** because its values can be any number from the universe of integers from Mathematics.

A student record will have name, address, account number, age, and marks. Such a record is an example of an **aggregate type** or **composite type**. A **data item** is a piece of information or a record whose value is drawn from a type. A data item is said to be a **member** of a type.

Also, a **data type** is a type along with a set of permissible operations to process the type. For example, an integer variable is a member of the integer data type. Addition, subtraction, multiplication are example operations on the two integer data types.

23 in-place, in-situ, in-core, in-memory are synonyms.

An **abstract data type** (ADT) is the specification of a data type within some language, independent of an implementation. The interface for the ADT is defined in terms of a type and a set of operations on that type. The behavior of each operation is determined by its inputs and outputs. An ADT does not specify *how* the data type is implemented. These implementation details are hidden from the user of the ADT and protected from outside access, a concept referred to as **encapsulation**.

Let us consider an example. Assume you are the richest person and you love cars. You have purchased every model of the car from every car company. Also, assume that you have some number of licensed drivers. You can call any driver and ask him to drive any car of your interest on any day. The chance of a driver telling you that I cannot drive this car as the primary activities such as steering, accelerating, and braking are the same for all passenger cars. He can steer any car by turning the steering wheel, accelerate any car by pushing the accelerator pedal through his leg, and slow any car by applying brakes by pushing the brake pedal through his leg. This design for cars can be viewed as an ADT with operations "steer", "accelerate", and "brake". However, each car might implement these operations in radically different ways, say with different types of engine, or front- versus rear-wheel drive. Brakes can be realized in one car through hydraulic means; while in some other cars by some other means. Nowadays, everyone is able to drive cars by just knowing the functionalities of steering, accelerating, and breaking. Thus, any driver can operate many different cars because the ADT presents a uniform method of operation that does not require the driver to understand the specifics of any particular engine, breaking system, or drive design. In fact, these specifics of important parts (engine, break, drive system) of the car are deliberately hidden (data hiding, one of the concepts of object oriented systems and languages).

A **data structure** is the realization for an ADT. We have already understood that the term **data structure** connotes data stored in a computer's main memory, RAM. The related term **file structure** refers to data on secondary memory devices.

The **int** variable type (say in languages such as C, C++, Java), along with the operations that act on an **int** variable, form an ADT. Unfortunately, the int implementation is not completely true to the abstract integer, as there are limitations on the range of values an int variable can store because of the finiteness of computers. If these limitations prove unacceptable, then some other representation for the ADT "integer" must be devised, and a new implementation must be used for the associated operations (Do recollect the example discussed in the first pages on Python in which we understood that Python will be using Bignum data structure to have overflow free integer additions).

Also, some programming languages such as Python, R, MATLAB, Wolfram, did **abstract** the Mathematical quantity, complex number. Majority of the operations that we can do on complex numbers in Mathematics can be happily carried out in these languages. For example, if we add two complex numbers we will get a complex number in Mathematics and this is very possible in the above programming languages also. This is applicable to other operations such as subtraction, multiplication, division with complex type quantities. For example, the following R code demonstrates the same. How it is (abstraction) implemented is transparent to the user of complex objects.

https://tinyurl.com/AICTEDSBOOK8

Do remember that complex type variable type is not available in C language. However, of course we can realize complex type through structures. Python language also **abstracts** the Mathematical concept of complex numbers. We welcome the readers to visit the following link to experiment with a sample Python code involving complex objects.

https://tinyurl.com/AICTEDSBOOK11

The following picture (Fig. 1.11) is the snapshot of the above code. The code that is available in the link declares two complex type objects(variables) x and y. It shows how one can use x+y, x-y, x*y, x/y operators between x and y like Mathematics.

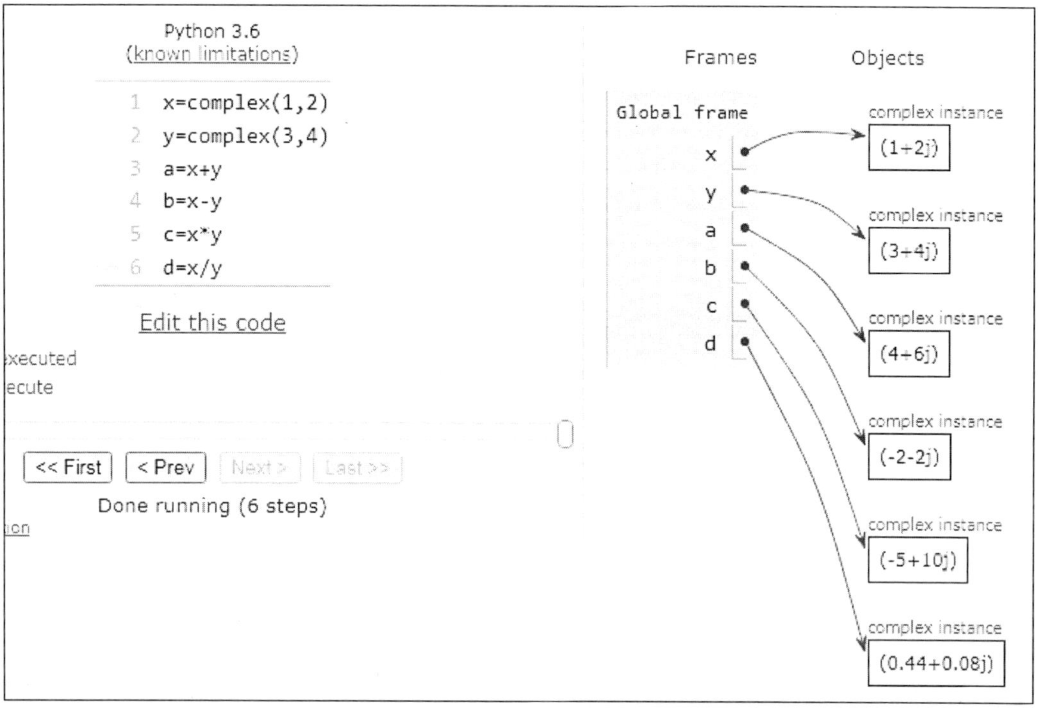

Fig. 1.11: Operations on Complex type in Python

Also, we know that in Mathematics, we can add, subtract, multiply two vectors. This is abstracted in R language such that a Mathematical expression involving vectors can be directly executed in R language. The same if we want in C language, we need to put more effort such as using loops etc. The following examples demonstrate the Vector operations in R language.

https://tinyurl.com/AICTEDSBOOK9

In the following link, you find how two matrices can be multiplied in R language with a simple operator. Do you remember our discussion elsewhere in the book that we need three nested for loops to achieve the same in C language.

https://tinyurl.com/AICTEDSBOOK10

This became very much possible as the R programming language has nicely abstracted the Mathematical quantity matrix. This is true with MATLAB language also. You may visit the following link to explore matrix multiplication in MATLAB.

https://in.mathworks.com/help/matlab/ref/mtimes.html

Do remember that MATLAB abstracted complex numbers, vectors very nicely.

Data types will have **logical forms** and **physical forms**. The ADT specification of a data type is its logical form while its realization using a data structure is its physical form(see Fig. 1.12).

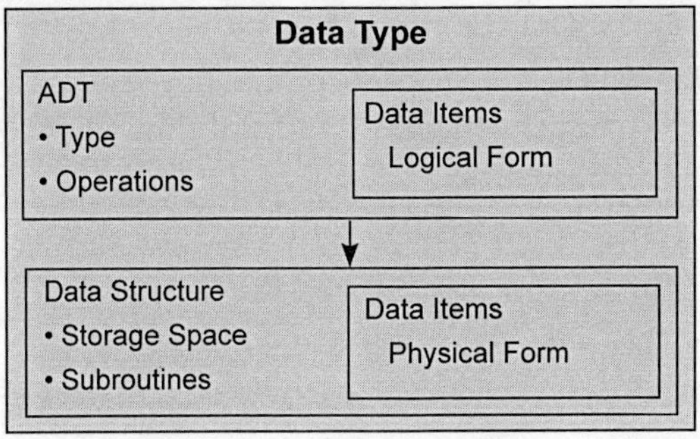

Fig. 1.12: The relationship between data items, abstract data types, and data structures. (Courtesy: https://opendsa-server.cs.vt.edu/ODSA/Books/CS3/html/ADT.html Last accessed: 10th Aug 2022)

The following picture (Fig. 1.13) illustrates the relationships between type, ADT, data structures, etc., terms which are explained in the above pages.

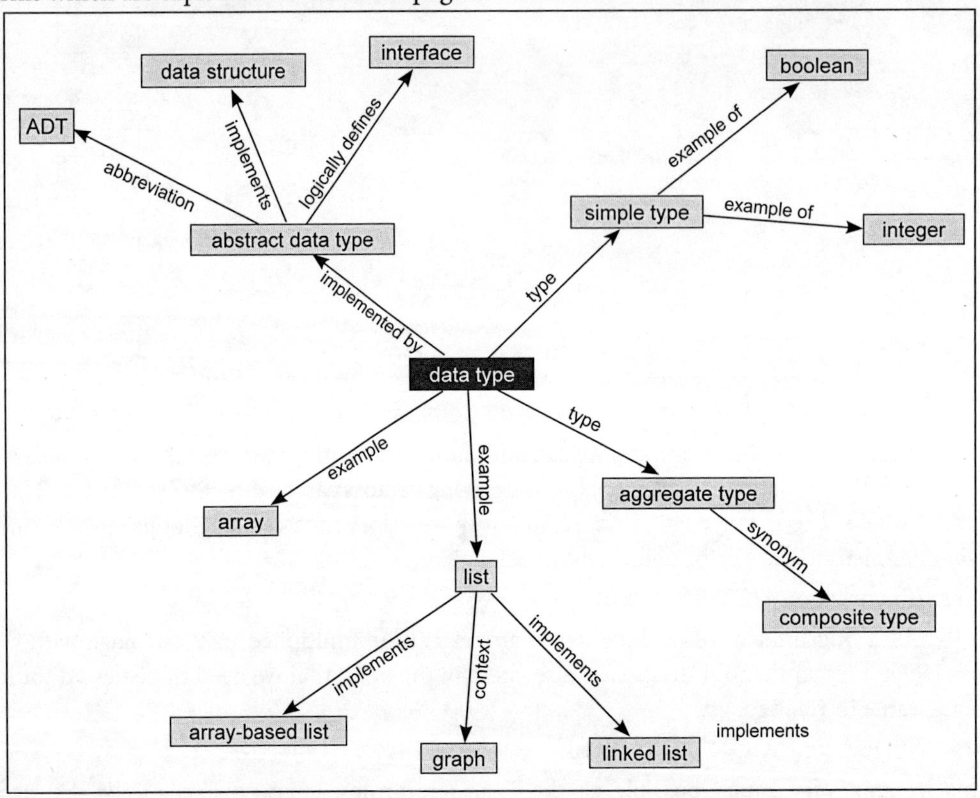

Fig. 1.13: Relationships between type, ADT, data structures, etc

(Source: https://opendsa-server.cs.vt.edu/ODSA/Books/CS3/html/ADT.html Last accessed: 10th Aug 2022)

Let me take one more example which you are already exposed to in your C programming course. You might have certainly used "FILE *" type variables while reading and writing data into a file. Do you know what the contents of the FILE structure are? It is given below.

```
typedef struct _iobuf{
char*_ptr;
```

```
int_cnt;
/* indicates how much space is still available in the buffer*/
char*_base;
int_flag; /* mode of opening*/
int_file; /* A unique number associated with the file*/
int_charbuf; /* The I/O buffer*/
int_bufsiz; /* The buffer size*/
char*_tmpfname;
} FILE;
```

We can say the above as ADT for FILE*. And the standard I/O library[24] that implemented functions(operations) such as fopen(), fclose(), fread(), fwrite(), fprintf(), fscanf(), ftell(), fseek(), feof(), fgetc(), fputc(), fputs(), fgets() is the data structure of this ADT.

1.3.4 Common Algorithm Design Paradigms

We do require to know about common program design paradigms that are prominently used in the literature. They are:

- Divide-and-conquer
- Iterative
- Recursive
- Back tracking
- Dynamic programming
- Greedy algorithms
- Randomized/probabilistic

Already, we have got exposure to iterative, and recursive solutions in C programming. We will explore divide-and-conquer based solutions in the coming chapters. Other paradigms are beyond the scope of this book.

In the following example, we have included a simple example of permutations of a string using both iterative and recursive means. In practice, we may need to study which is better in terms of time, space, scalability, and ease of implementation.

Example 20: Printing permutations of a string.

```
#include < stdio.h >
#define SIZE 3
int main(char *argv[],int argc){
	char list[3]={'a','b','c'};
	int i,j,k;

	for(i=0;i < SIZE;i++)
	for(j=0;j < SIZE;j++)
	for(k=0;k < SIZE;k++)
	if(i!=j && j!=k && i!=k)
	printf("%c%c%c\n",list[i],list[j],list[k]);

	return(0);
}
```

24 A collection functions is called as library or package

The following link contains the above code for readers for their experimentation.

https://tinyurl.com/AICTEDSBOOK13

Example 21: Recursive permutations

```
#include < stdio.h >
#define N 5
int main(char *argv[],int argc){
        char list[5]={'a','b','c','d','e'};
        permute(list,0,N);
        return(0);
}
void permute(char list[],int k, int m){
        int i;
        char temp;

        if(k==m){
        /* PRINT A FROM k to m! */
        for(i=0;i < N;i++){printf("%c",list[i]);}
        printf("\n");
        }
        else{
        for(i=k;i < m;i++){
        /* swap(a[i],a[m-1]); */
        temp=list[i];
        list[i]=list[m-1];
        list[m-1]=temp;

        permute(list,k,m-1);

        /* swap(a[m-1],a[i]); */

        temp=list[m-1];
        list[m-1]=list[i];
        list[i]=temp;
        }
        }
}
```

The following link contains the above code for readers for their experimentation.

https://tinyurl.com/AICTEDSBOOK14

If we observe, the recursive version has better scalability.

Example 22: Some algorithms will have best case and worst case behaviors. For example, let us assume that we wanted to a function to check whether a square matrix is symmetric or not. We have already given solution in previous chapters. Here, we compare ij'th element with ji'th element by traversing the matrix in lower triangular portion. If the first pair itself are not same, we can say with one comparison that the matrix is not symmetric. Only after comparing all the pairs, we can say it is a symmetric matrix (worst case situation).

```
int issymmetric(int a[][10],int n){
        int i,j;
        for(i=1;i<n;i+=)
        for(j=0;j<i;j++) if (a[i][j] != a[j][i]) return 0;

        return 1;
}
```

Best Case= 1 pair of comparisons.

Worst Case= 1+2+….n-1= n(n-1)/2 pairs of comparisons. That is O(n^2) complexity.

The following link contains the above code on a visualization server that shows both best and worst case scenarios of this algorithm.

https://tinyurl.com/AICTEDSBOOK12

Question 7: How to transpose a square matrix in-place?

Hint: Think of exchanging a[i][j], a[j][i] of the above issymmteric() function.

EXERCISES

Multiple Choice Questions

1. Minimum how many comparisons are needed to find the minimum of three integers?
   (a) 1 (b) 2
   (c) 3 (d) 4
2. Minimum how many comparisons are needed to find both the maximum and minimum of three integers?
   (a) 1 (b) 2
   (c) 3 (d) 4
3. How many bytes of memory is allocated for int type variables in C language?
   (a) 2 (b) 4
   (c) 6 (d) 8
4. Assume a, b, c are the variables having three sides of a triangle. The following expression is written to check whether a, b, c form an equilateral triangle or not.

   (expr)?printf("Equilateral\n"):printf("Not equilateral\n");

   How many minimum number of comparisons that "expr" can be made of?
   (a) 2 (b) 3
   (c) 4 (d) 5
5. Minimum how many comparisons and logical operators are needed to check the uniqueness of given three numbers a, b, and c?
   (a) 2 (b) 2 comparisons and one logical AND
   (c) 4 (d) None

6. Minimum how many exchanges are needed to reverse elements of a 1-D array with n elements? (You may look at the following before answering https://tinyurl.com/THANKYOUVASU3)
   (a) n (b) 1
   (c) n/2 (d) None
7. Minimum how many comparisons are needed to check whether a given nxn square matrix is symmetric or not?
   (a) 1 (b) n/2
   (c) n(n–1)/2 (d) None
8. Worst case, how many comparisons are needed to check whether a given nxn square matrix is symmetric or not?
   (a) 1 (b) n/2
   (c) n(n–1)/2 (d) 1+2+3+...+(n–1)
9. Minimum how many comparisons are needed to check whether a given n element array is unique or not?
   (a) 1 (b) n/2
   (c) n(n–1)/2 (d) None
10. Worst case, how many comparisons are needed to check whether a given n element array is unique or not?
    (a) 1 (b) n/2
    (c) n(n–1)/2 (d) 1+2+3+...+(n–1)
11. In which programming language, vectors are abstracted aptly like Mathematical vectors?
    (a) MATLAB (b) R
    (c) C++ (d) C
12. How many multiplications are needed to multiply two nxn matrices?
    (a) n^2 (b) n^3
    (c) n (d) n^4
13. Declaration of an array in C language with the statement "int a[10]" is:
    (a) Linear data structure (b) Static data structure
    (c) Homogeneous data structure (d) Mutable data structure
    (e) All are valid data structure
14. How many comparisons are needed in the best case to check whether a given n element 1-D array is having all the same valued elements or not?
    (a) 1 (b) n–1
    (c) n^2 (d) None
15. How many comparisons are needed in the worst case to check whether a given n element 1-D array is having all the same valued elements or not?
    (a) 1 (b) n–1
    (c) n^2 (d) None

16. A compiler can compile source codes into executable programs. But what compiles the compiler (which is a program itself)? Of course we would need a compiler for this job.

    Source code A is the source code of Compiler A. When we compile Source code A by Compiler A, we will get back Compiler A. Source code B is the source code of Compiler B. When we compile Source code B by Compiler A, we will get Compiler B. Which of the followings must be true? Note that we call two files identical if they are bit-by-bit identical.

    i. Compiler A and Compiler B are compilers for the same programming language.
    ii. If we compile Source code A by Compiler B, the output is identical to Compiler A.
    iii. If we compile Source code B by Compiler B, the output is identical to Compiler B.

    (a) None of the statements (b) i only
    (c) ii only (d) iii only

17. We now modify Source code A to a new version -- Source code C. When we compile Source code C by Compiler A, we get Compiler C. Compiler A and Compiler C are compilers for the same programming language, and Compiler C always give faster programs compared to Compiler A, which means that when the same source code is compiled by the two compilers (and no compilation error occurs), and then the same input are fed to the two programs, the outputs of the two programs are the same (if no runtime error occurs), and the program compiled by Compiler C runs faster than that compiled by Compiler A (if both programs terminates) for any input. When we compile Source code A by Compiler C, we get Compiler A2. When we compile Source code C by Compiler C, we get Compiler C2. Which of the following must be true?

    i. Compiler A2 runs faster than Compiler A (it needs a shorter time to compile any source code).
    ii. Compiler A2 runs faster than Compiler C (it needs a shorter time to compile any source code).
    iii. Compiler C2 runs faster than Compiler A (it needs a shorter time to compile any source code).

    (a) i only (b) iii only
    (c) i and iii only (d) i, ii and iii

ANSWERS															
1.	(a)	2.	(c)	3.	(b)	4.	(a)	5.	(b)	6.	(c)	7.	(a)	8.	(c) & (d)
9.	(a)	10.	(c)	11.	(a) & (b)	12.	(b)	13.	(e)	14.	(a)	15.	(b)	16.	(a)
17.	(a)														

Descriptive Questions

1. What do you know about the time-space tradeoff?
2. Support with examples that data structures are instrumental high level language design.
3. Consider this Unit's summary and content (whole text, images, figures, tables). Which is ADT and which is data structure?
4. What are the uses of data structures?
5. Why study algorithms?

6. What is in-place computing?
7. Explain how data structures and DBMS are related?
8. What did you understand by data abstraction?
9. What do you know about problem size?
10. Explain about the data types supported in C language.

Laboratory Programming Tasks

Task 1: Assume that x^n calculation is represented in the following equation.

$$x^n = x^{n/2}\, x^{n-n/2} \text{ if } n>1$$

That is, calculation of xn for n>1 is divided into two subproblems (divide and conquer method); computing xn and xn-n/2. The following C program is implemented using the above recursive relationship. This program also computes the height of the call tree.

```
#include<stdio.h>
static int times=0;
static int callTreeHeight=0;
int power(int x, int p,int h){
  times++;
  if(h>callTreeHeight)
  callTreeHeight=h;

  if(p==1) return x;
  else return(power(x,p/2,h+1)*power(x,p-p/2,h+1));
}
int main() {
  printf("%d\n",power(2,8,1));
  printf("%d\n",times);
  printf("Call trees maximum height=%d\n",callTreeHeight);
  return 0;
}
```

The above code is available on a visualization server. We have modified the above repeatedSquaring1() function such that it counts how many recursive calls it has made and also what is the recursion tree height. The code is written in C language.

https://tinyurl.com/ychju2f5

The above method's complexity is $O(2^n)$. The following is the call tree (Fig. 1.14) for x^43. The red marked nodes are once which are calculated first[25].

25 If you observe the figure, you will find some powers of x are computed more than once. In fact, we can store them in an array and use them as and when needed so as to speed up the function. Wow, this is the essence of dynamic programming, another algorithm design paradigm

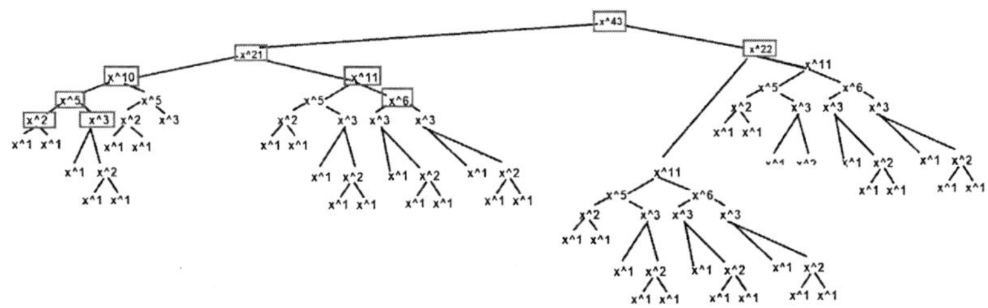

Fig. 1.14: Call tree for the exponentiation algorithm

Task 2: You are asked to write a C program to compute the product of two integers without using any multiplication and any loop.

May be, you can get inspiration from the following link https://tinyurl.com/y3jdgdcs

Task 3: For example, if x1, x2, ...xN are a set of students marks of a class and we are interested to find standard deviation of their marks, then we need to use the following statistical formula

$$\sigma = \sqrt{\frac{\sum_{i-1}^{N}(x_i - \mu)^2}{N}}$$

where μ is the mean of the students marks which can be calculated using $\frac{x1 + x2 + x3 + ...xN}{N}$.

However, if we want to implement the above equation to compute standard deviation in a selected programming language, we first need to compute for which we need to use students marks once(probably using a loop) and then only can be calculated using the students marks again and calculating their deviations from the class mean(this may need another loop). Thus, it forces us to go through all the students' marks more than once and also demands two iterations or loops to be used in the language. See the following solution that is implemented in C language.

```
#include<stdio.h>
#include<math.h>
int main(){
        int N,xi,i;
        float mu=0,sigma=0;
        scanf("%d",&N);
        for(i=0;i<N;i++){
                scanf("%d",&xi);
                mu=mu+xi;
        }
        mu/=N;
        for(i=0;i<N;i++){
                scanf("%d",&xi);
                sigma+=pow((xi-mu),2);
        }
        sigma=sqrt(sigma/N);
        printf("Standard deviation=%f\n",sigma);
        return 0;
}
```

The above code is available at https://ideone.com/ET7V3O for experimentation.

With some mathematical manipulations, standard deviation calculation can be represented as:

$$\sigma = \sqrt{\frac{\Sigma x_i^2}{N} - \mu^2}$$

This form allows us to calculate with one pass of students marks. That is, with one loop we can find the required salutation. That is, in the loop itself, we can compute sum of the students marks () and sum of the squares of the students marks(). Also, this equation alleviates the need for an array. After exiting from the loop, we first calculate and then . The following is the C language solution using this approach which we call a tractable form. The following is a video that elucidates the standard deviation calculation using this tractable form. https://www.youtube.com/watch?v=NFcUU9d8XFs&list=PLXX7XiUxnzzUILTy1F68tpk7FZ56nJrOg&index=40

```
#include<stdio.h>
#include<math.h>
int main(){
        int N,xi,i;
        float mu=0,sigma=0;
        scanf("%d",&N);
        for(i=0;i<N;i++){
                scanf("%d",&xi);
                mu=mu+xi;
                sigma+=xi*xi;
        }
        mu/=N;
        sigma=sqrt(sigma/N-mu*mu);
        printf("Standard deviation=%f\n",sigma);
        return 0;
}
```

The above code is available at https://ideone.com/UC0TOi.

Task 4: Let us explore another example to elucidate the concept of tractability. We are given a sequence a1, . . . , aN numbers. Give an algorithm that computes the value of

$$F = \sum_{j=1}^{n} \frac{\sum_{i=1}^{j} a_i^2 - \sum_{i=1}^{j} i a_i}{j(j+1)}$$

The following implements the above function calculation through a C language. You may play with it at https://ideone.com/JSsmmo.

```
#include<math.h>
int main(){
        int N,a[100],i,j;
        float F=0,s1,s2;
        scanf("%d",&N);
```

```
        for(i=0;i<N;i++)
                scanf("%d",&a[i]);
    for(j=0;j<N;j++){
        s1=0;
        s2=0;
        for(i=0;i<=j;i++){
                s1+=a[i]*a[i];
                s2+=(i+1)*a[i];
        }
        F+=(s1-s2)/((j+1)*(j+2));
    }
        printf("F=%f\n",F);
        return 0;
}
```

The above code is available on a visualization server also. We welcome readers to trace the same at https://tinyurl.com/y9okpu48.

In the above program, we find that we have used two nested for loops to compute F. Let us expand the above mathematical equation to identify for possible tractable for,

Let us take N=4 and expand the above equation. We get the following. We find that $a_1^2 - a_1$, $a_1^2 - a_1 + a_2^2 - 2a_2$, , etc., terms are seen in all the subsequent terms. That is, once these terms are calculated, they can be used in subsequent terms also.

$$\frac{a_1^2 - a_1}{2} + \frac{a_1^2 - a_1 + a_2^2 - 2a_2}{2*3} + \frac{a_1^2 - a_1 + a_2^2 - 2a_2 + a_3^2 - 3a_3}{3*4} + \frac{a_1^2 - a_1 + a_2^2 - 2a_2 + a_3^2 - 3a_3 + a_4^2 - 4a_4}{4*5}$$

By exploiting this property, we propose the following solution that uses a single loop.

```
#include <stdio.h>
int main(void) {
        int N,a[100],i,j;
        float F=0,prefixsum=0;
        scanf("%d",&N);
        for(i=0;i<N;i++)
                scanf("%d",&a[i]);
  for(j=0;j<N;j++){
                prefixsum+=a[j]*a[j]-(j+1)*a[j];
            F+=prefixsum/((j+1)*(j+2));
  }
        printf("F=%f\n",F);
        return 0;
}
```

The above code is available at https://ideone.com/gNcbe4

Also, the above code is available on a visualization server to trace its working. https://tinyurl.com/y7kzfh56

For this problem, the computational complexity of the first solution is O(n2) while the second one is O(n).

Task 5: Sum of a 1-D array

Majority of us most commonly employ an iterative solution[26] to calculate the sum of the elements of a 1-D array with time complexity O(n).

Sum of a 1-D array using Exclude & Conquer approach.

That is, we want to use the following recurrence relation:

Sum_of_n_element_array=Sum_of_first_n-1_elements+last element if n>1

Sum_of_the_array_with_one_element=that_element_or_zeroth_element_itself if n=1

That is, to find the sum of an n-element array, somehow we find the sum of the elements of the first n-1 elements and add the last element. This, we apply recursively. That is, to find the sum of an (n-1)-element array, somehow we find the sum of the elements of the first n-2 elements and add the last but one element. We reach the base case when n becomes 1. The following recursive function is written that exploits the above recurrence.

```
int sum(int a[], int n){
  if(n==1) return a[0];
  else
  return sum(a,n-1)+a[n-1];
  }
int main(){
  int x[10]={10,20,10,20,30,20,30};
  printf("%d\n",sum(x,7));
  return 0;
  }
```

You can visit the following sites to test the above code.

https://tinyurl.com/sum1D

https://tinyurl.com/y3ygy519?fbclid=IwAR3XcV1i-Ri75Guwc_u5_h5clLsMTWt268NSejtedfIFS7e3ZHLvRzSvAao

The following uses the following recurrence that is different from previous.

Sum_of_n_element_array=first_element + Sum_of_last_n-1_elements if n>1

Sum_of_the_array_with_one_element=that_element_itself if n=1

```
int sum(int a[], int b,int e){
  if(b==e) return a[b];
  else
```

26 int sum(int a[], int n){
int i, sum=0;
for(i=0;i<n;i++)sum+a[i];
return sum;
}

```
    return sum(a,b+1,e)+a[b];
    }
int main(){
    int x[10]={10,20,10,20,30,20,30};
    printf("%d\n",sum(x,0,6));
    return 0;
    }
```

https://tinyurl.com/y22t4hyy?fbclid=IwAR34q10UdBW1Mdn7DzYJNY2AYDX5YqWM0XW8vop0jVuPtAB4p0p4e5A2ELg

Divide & Conquer approach

The following is divide conquer based solution like binary searching.

Sum_of_n_elements=Sum_of_left_half+Sum_of_right_half

Base case:

If any subarray becomes of size one then that element itself becomes that subarray sum.

```
int sum(int a[],int b, int n){
 int sum1,sum2;
  if(n==1) return a[b];
  else {
   sum1=sum(a,b,n/2)
   sum2=sum(a,b+n/2,n-n/2);
  return sum1+sum2;
  }
  }
int main(){
  int x[10]={10,20,10,20,31,20,30};
  printf("%d\n",sum(x,0,7));
  return 0;
  }
```

https://tinyurl.com/y3jfczf6

Welcome to participate in the online competition

We are hosting a competition so as to encourage students to build their competence in coding. This will be very useful for placements also in the coming years. Thus, welcome students to attempt the competition at the following link.

https://www.hackerrank.com/aictedsbook

Programming puzzles

Some programming puzzles along with their solutions around this chaper's concepts are made available at the following link.

https://docs.google.com/document/d/1QtNTk0riNJjuHpsbrTCOMly9CT79GmGVJKN0DPu8K4A/edit?usp=sharing

REFERENCES

1. Fundamentals of Data Structure in C, Horowitz, Ellis, Sahni, Sartaj, Anderson-Freed, Susan, University Press, India.
2. Data Structures: A Pseudocode approach with C, Richard F. Gilberg, Behrouz A. Forouzan, CENGAGE Learning, India.
3. My class notes on Algorithmic Complexity, now a refresher for craving teachers and knowledge greedy students: A must primer for GATE(India), Adv. GRE appearing students. https://www.amazon.com/dp/B09DJCW78T
4. C and Data Structures, NB Venkateswarlu & EV Prasad, 2010, S Chand & Co, New Delhi.

2 Stacks and Queues

UNIT COVERAGE

Linear Data Structures- Stacks: Introduction to Stacks, Array Representation of Stacks, Operations on a Stack, Applications of Stacks - Infix-to-Postfix Transformation, evaluating Postfix Expressions.

Queues: Introduction to Queues, Array Representation of Queues, Operations on a Queue, Types of Queues-Deque, Circular Queue, Applications of Queues - Round Robin Algorithm

OBJECTIVES OF THE UNIT

By the end of this unit, student will be able to:

- describe and use the stack and queue **abstract data types.**
- explain the **relevance of data structures such as stack and queue** in practical SW development such as operating systems, compilers.
- describe and use stacks for validations of expressions.
- describe and use stacks for evaluation of expressions programming languages.
- explain the relevance of data structures in **programming language design.**
- give typical examples of **overflow**, **underflow** conditions with stack and queue ADTs

LEARNING OUTCOMES OF THE UNIT

After completing the Unit, the student

- has detailed knowledge of **stack abstract data type (U2-01).**
- has detailed knowledge of **queue abstract data type (U2-02).**
- is familiar with the basic concepts **overflow, underflow (U2-03) with stack and queue ADTs.**
- has detailed knowledge of how stacks **are instrumental** in programming language design **and especially while evaluating expressions(U2-04).**
- is familiar with priority queues, round robm scheduling of processes in operating systems **(U2-05).**

Unit-2 Outcome	EXPECTED MAPPING WITH COURSE OUTCOMES (1 - Weak Correlation; 2 - Medium Correlation; 3 - Strong Correlation)				
	CO-1	CO-2	CO-3	CO-4	CO-5
U2-O1	1	3		-	
U2-O2	1	3			
U2-O3		1			
U2-O4	1	1			
U2-O5	1	1			

2.1 LINEAR DATA STRUCTURES

Linear data structures are the ones in which elements are organized in a sequential fashion (either physically in memory or logically) so that they can be accessed in a linear fashion (one after another). In this chapter, we will be exploring two linear data structures to name stacks and queues. In the next chapter, another linear data structure, known as linked lists will be discussed.

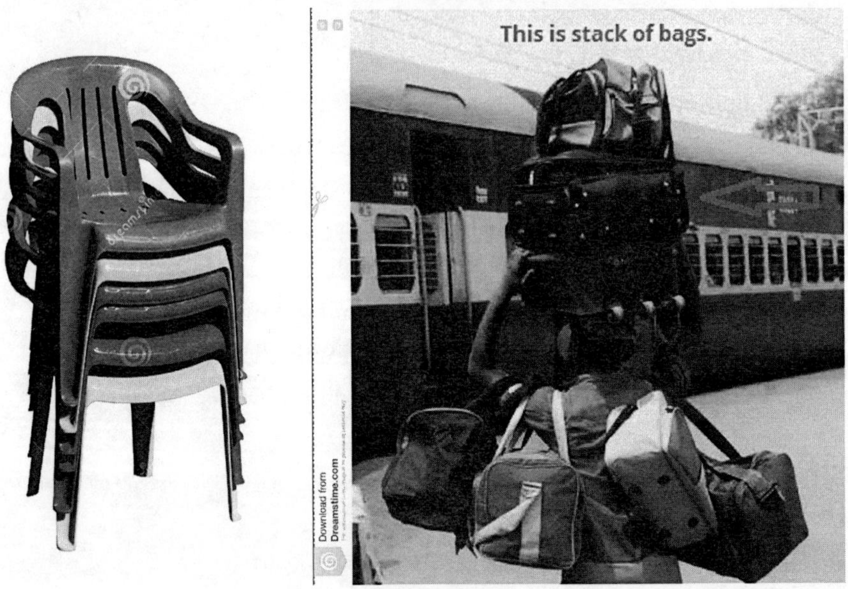

Fig. 2.1: Stack of chairs

(Courtesy: https://www.dreamstime.com/stock-photo-stack-plastic-chairs-isolation-white-background-image76425428 Last Accessed: 15th Aug 2022)

2.1.1 Stack

Let us assume we have a set of moulded (plastic) chairs. When we have visitors to our home, we take chairs one after another (from top) and allow the visitors to sit. When they leave, in order to tidy up the house, we put all the chairs one–by-one, i.e., one on top of the other. Is it possible to pull the middle chair?. **No**. Is it possible to insert a chair in between two chairs?. **No**. We can insert a new chair at the top only. Also, we can remove a chair from the top only. This type of thing is called a **stack**. In fact, we refer to these chairs as a **stack of chairs** (See Fig. 2.1). Of course, we will have many of these types of things in our daily life, for instance a railway porter carrying a **stack of bags** on the right side of Fig. 2.1.

You may love to see the following Facebook post that shows how a skilled labour carries that many number of bricks as a stack.

https://www.facebook.com/watch/?ref=saved&v=658368031847687

Also think of spring loaded plate dispensers (Fig. 2.2). Whenever we press the top lever, we get a plate ejected from the stack of plates. Here, also, we cannot take plates that are in the middle. Also, some dispensers will have freedom to insert some more plates on the top but not in the middle.

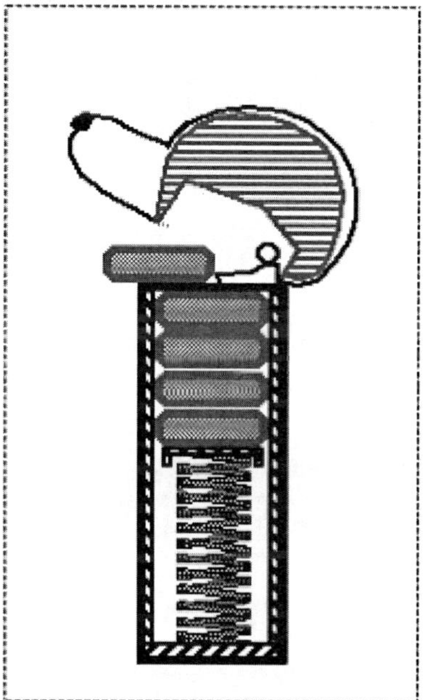

Fig. 2.2: Plate dispenser

One of the 21st century challenges is providing safe drinkable water for masses. There are hundreds of innovations that are aimed at producing safe water from various sources such as ground water, river water, water from air through dehumidification. The following is an indigeneous design proposed by authors from Nigeria[27] for producing potable water from the ground water. If you observe, you find a series (stack) of filters (pebbles, sand, a mesh, charcoal) in the tank. Pebbles, sand layers control suspended matter from the ground water; while the charcoal layer takes care of bacteria, odour (see Fig. 2.3).

27 Performance evaluation of a locally developed domestic drinking water filter, Bolaji, B. O. , Bolaji, G. A. and Ismaila, S. O., October 2010, International Journal of Environmental Studies 67(5):763-771.

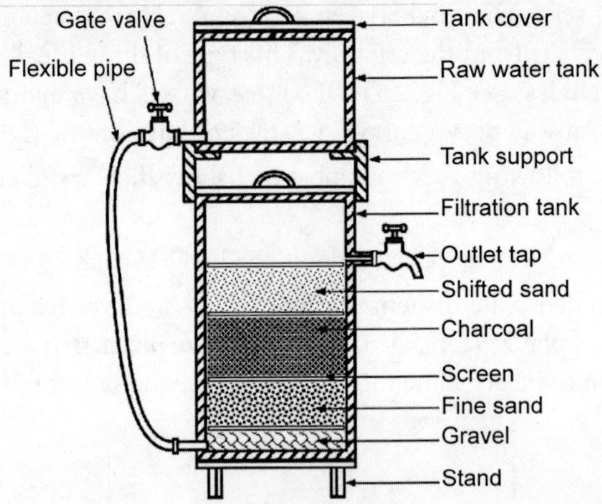

Fig. 2.3: A water filter wit a stack of filtering layers

All of you will agree with me that the performance of these filtering layers will decay as time progresses and we may certainly need to replenish them. Actually, this replenishment is carried all layers at once. If we want to replenish only a certain filter layer, it is not possibly easy. Probably, we may replenish the top layer without disturbing other layers. This example shows that we cannot replenish bottom layers without removing other layers.

Also, in recent years the Government of India and all the state governments are encouraging people to replenish groundwater (rain water harvesting) by digging rainwater discharge ponds which are also designed with a series of layers as explained above. See the following figures (Fig. 2.4).

Fig. 2.4: Rainwater harvesting pits with a stack of filters.

(Source: https://rain-water-harvesting-in-hyderabad.blogspot.com/2019/06/ Last accessed: 27th Aug, 202)

For all Hindu's Lord Krishna's birthday (Krishnashtami) is a very very auspicious day. One prominent program which is celebrated on that day is "Utti Kottu (or Utti Kottadam or Dahi Handi[28])". In this program, a clay pot filled with yogurt (dahi), butter, or any other milk-based foods at a convenient or tall height. Young men and boys form teams, make a human pyramid (one layer of standing people, on the

28 https://en.wikipedia.org/wiki/Dahi_Handi

top of them another layer of standing people, like this on the top one person will be seen), and attempt to reach or break the pot. The following picture (Fig. 2.5) shows the stack of people breaking the clay pot.

Fig. 2.5: Stack of people (Courtesy of www.alamy.com Last Accessed: 15th Aug 2022)

In the human pyramid, new people will be added on the top only while forming the human pyramid. After breaking the clay pot, the top layer people come down; this is repeated for all the layers of the people. That is, while adding people to the pyramid they get added at the top only, while removing the people from the human pyramid, people on the top will be asked to come down.

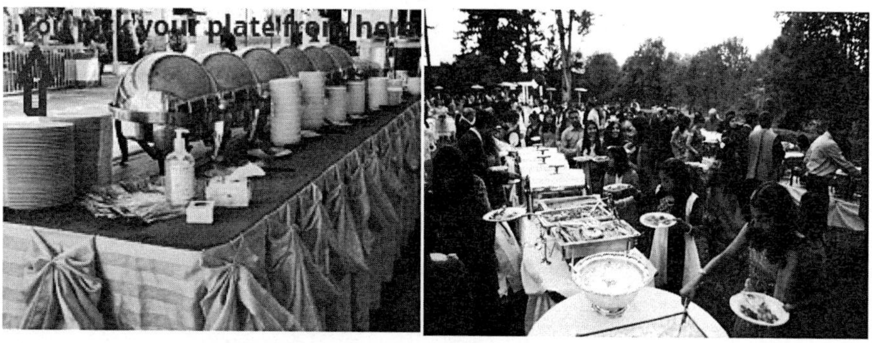

Fig. 2.6: Stack of plates and we take a plate from the top

Let us have one more example. Consider that we are in a buffet. Obviously, on the first table we may find a pile of plates (a.k.a stack of plates). We go along with other people in the queue and take the top plate when our turn comes (See Fig. 2.6).

Once we finish our dinner, we leave our plate on the top of another pile of plates which are meant for cleaning (see Fig. 2.7). Do you dare to push your used plate in between two plates of the pile of plates that are meant for cleaning? No. No. Not at all. You will keep on the top of the existing pile of plates only. Here, we can say that the pile of plates is a stack of plates.

Fig. 2.7: stack of plates to be washed

Let us explore another example where stack is involved. A busy office executive maintains two trays, "in" tray and "out" trays. When a file arrives at his desk, it will be left in the "in" tray(see Fig. 2.8). Thus files pile up in the "in" tray. Whenever the executive has time to clear the files, he/she takes one file from the top. That is, files are added to the "in" tray at the top, and removed from the "in" tray also from the top. Therefore stacks are sometimes referred to as **LIFO (Last in First Out)structures**. Stacks are also referred to as ***pushdown lists as the previous items go down when a new item is pushed***.

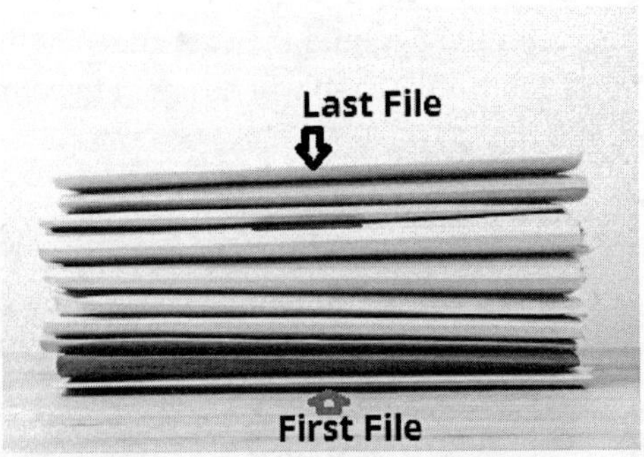

Fig. 2.8: An executives "in" Tray

Let us take one more example related to our daily life which is none other than browsing the Internet using our browsers such as Google Chrome, Firefox, etc.,. See the following Fig. 2.9 where you see left and right arrows with which we can browse through the web pages which we have visited (already).

Fig. 2.9: Browsers left and right navigation arrows

In the above figure, if we click the left arrow then the browser gets loaded with the web site that is visited before the present web page. If we click the left arrow further, it makes the browser load the site that is earlier to the recent one. OK. OK. Are you catching my point? Here, the web pages visited are in the stack fashion[29]. (see Fig. 2.10)

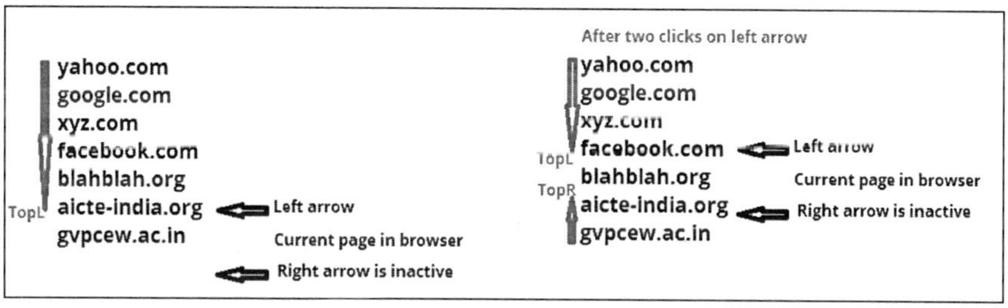

Fig. 2.10: Navigation of web pages visited

Let us explore some high school level competition examples that appeared in Bebras[30] challenges.

ICE Cream (UK Bebras, 2015, Australia Bebras 2015)

(Source: https://www.bebras.edu.au/wp-content/uploads/2016/10/2015-Bebras-Solution-Guide.pdf Last Accessed: 15th Aug 2022)

At an ice cream parlour, cones will be filled(stacked) with one scoop after another according to your specification.

Question 1: If you want ice cream as shown in the picture, you specify __

A... Chocolate, Smurf and strawberry!

B... Strawberry, Smurf and Chocolate!

C... Chocolate, Strawberry and Smurf!

D... Strawberry, Chocolate and Smurf!

29 In fact, two stacks. This in principle can be called deque

30 Courtesy of bebras.org

Answer: B. Strawberry, Smurf and Chocolate! The actual order used in this task is stack order. In particular **"Last in, First out" or LIFO(LIFO)**[31].

Stack of plates (2010, Germany)

(Source: http://www.ict-21.ch/com-ict/IMG/pptx/Promoting-Inclusive-Informatics-Education-Through-the-Bebras-Challenge-G.S..pptx Last Accessed: 15th Aug 2022)

In Beavers hostel, two kinds of plates are used. The high green ones for the small beavers whereas the flat brown ones for the big beavers. One day, due to building activities, there is only room for one stack of plates. Beavers will be standing in a queue for their lunch. The kitchen beavers need to put the plates on the stack in the right order to make the stack match to the queue as shown in the following figure.

Question 2: In the following pictures, we are supplied four types of Beavers queues and an associated stack of plates. In which one exists a mismatch between queue and stack?

Answer: B. First two Beavers are larger ones, while the top plates on the stack are green ones. Remaining all three pairs are in correct form.

How can we solve this? Let us use some coding. Assume big Beaver as 1 and small one as 0. In the same fashion, brown plate as 1 and green as 0. Now, code bevers from left to right while plates from top to bottom.

31 While traversing trees, graphs using stacks, we use this concept or order. That is, the nodes which are to be processed later are pushed into the stack.

Option A:
Beavers (Left to right): 10010110
Plates(top to bottom): 10010110
Both are matching. This is a valid one.

Option B:
Beavers (Left to right): 1101100
Plates(top to bottom): 0011011
Both are not matching. This is not a valid one. This is the answer for our question.

Option C:
Beavers (Left to right): 011100
Plates(top to bottom): 011100
Both are matching. This is a valid one.

Option D:
Beavers (Left to right): 101010
Plates(top to bottom): 101010
Both are matching. This is a valid one.

We do have image stacks[32] (see Fig. 2.11) which are collections of images. They are also referred to as layers or slices. Assume that you want to analyze how the coast of your town is changing year by year. By stacking the satellite images of your town of various years, and displaying them one after another, we can understand how the coast is changing in that city.

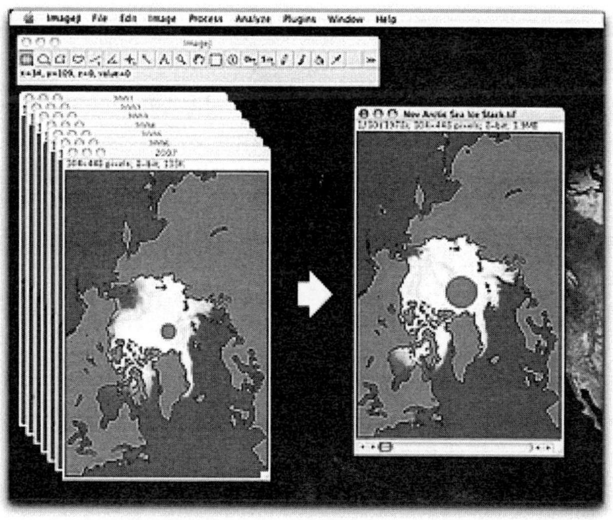

Fig. 2.11: An example image stack

In addition, while running programs which are having functions, functions that are calling other functions, the computer system inherently maintains a special structure known as **program stack** where return addresses are stored. See the following example program that contains a set of functions that are called from other functions as a chain fashion.

32 https://serc.carleton.edu/earth_analysis/image_analysis/introduction/day_2_part_2.html

```
void FUNCT1(){

  }
 void FUNCT2(){

    FUNCT1();
    Address 3 ______

  }
 void FUNCT3(){
    FUNCT2();
   Address 2 ______
}
int main(){
FUNCT3();
Address 1 ________
return 0;
}
```

Whenever a function is called, the address of the next instruction (of the function call instruction) is stored in the program stack and then program execution will be switched to the function that is called. Whenever either a return statement is encountered or the last statement of the function has reached, program execution will be continued from the address which is on the top of the program stack. For example, consider the above set of functions and the main. Program execution starts from main. Thus, when FUNCT3() is called, the next instruction address (i.e., Address1) is stored in the program stack and then control switches to FUNCT3(). While running FUNCT3(), when FUNCT2() is called, the next instruction address (Address 2) is stored in the program stack before jumping to FUNCT2(). Like this functions are executed. Thus, the program stack maintains the return addresses. An address is added at the top when a function is called and also an address is removed from the top of the program stack when the program control returns from the function. The following figure illustrates this concept (Fig. 2.12).

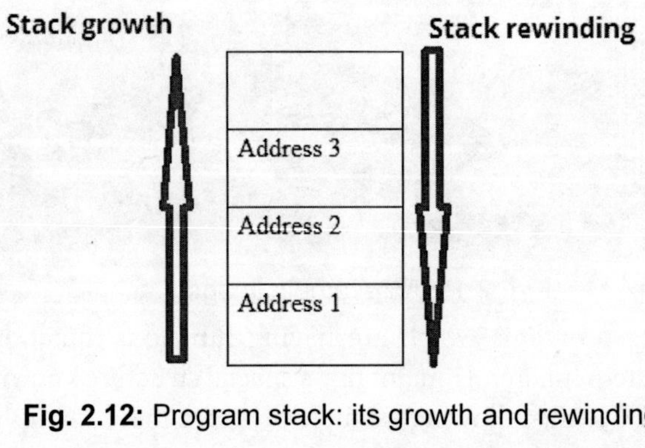

Fig. 2.12: Program stack: its growth and rewinding

We welcome readers to visit the following link. Here, we are trying to print the Program Counter (PC[33]) value before and after the function calls. Identify which addresses are the ones that goes to program stack[34].

https://tinyurl.com/AICTEDSBOOK19

https://ideone.com/cZC9hA

The ***insertion operation*** into the stack is called **PUSH;** while the ***deletion operation*** is called **POP**. The ***most accessible element in a stack*** is known as the **TOP of the stack (TOS).**

As insertion and deletion operations are performed at the same end of the stack, if elements are removed one after another, their order becomes the opposite order of their addition to the stack. That is, the most recently added item will be the one removed first. Thus, this type of structure is called the **LIFO (Last In First Out)** queue.

Thus, theoretically, we can have any type of stacks such as: stack of chairs, stack of plates, stack of documents, stack of addresses, stack of tables, stack of people, etc.,.

In practice, we can realize stack of characters, stack of integers, stack of structures, etc.,.

In practical implementations, we can realize stacks either using arrays or using linked lists[35]. From the examples, we are sure that you might have also got a feeling that stack is a **linear data structure** like array.

The following guy (see Fig. 2.13) made a rare Guiness record of wearing 35 T-shirts one above the other within 1 minute[36]. Wow. That is, **a stack of shirts**. Is it possible to remove a 10th T-shirt without removing the T-shirts above it? No way. Is it possible to wear another (insert) T-shirt above the 10th T-shirt of the present stack of 36 T-shirts? No way it is possible. He can put a new T-shirt on the top of the current T-shirt and also he can remove the T-shirt which is on the top. Just trying to kid with you. Can he remove all the T-shirts(stack) in one go?. If so, he can wear all the 35 T-shirts much before 60 seconds. Ha. Ha.

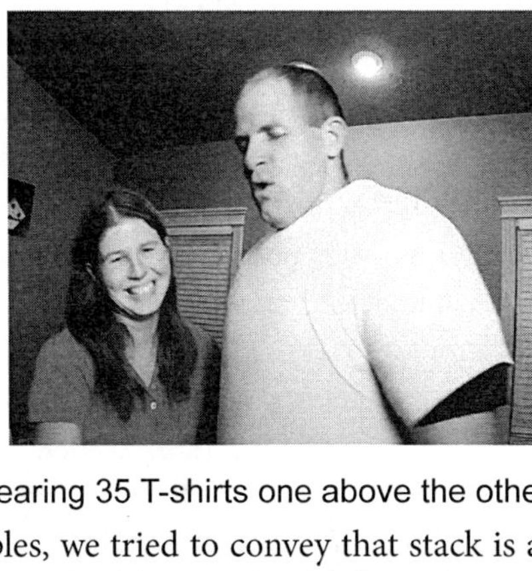

Fig. 2.13: A guy wearing 35 T-shirts one above the other(**stack of shirts!!**)

From our illustrative examples, we tried to convey that stack is a generic concept. That is, we can have a stack of moulded chairs, a stack of filters, a stack of people, a stack of ice cream snoops, etc.,.

---

33 Not even, the famous bollywood heroine Priyanka Chopra or Personal Computer

34 We have tested on 8086 machine

35 We will be implementing this in the next chapter.

36 https://www.youtube.com/watch?v=RosxpIGnRC0

2.1.2 Operations on Stacks

According to Wikipedia[37]:

In computer science, a **stack** is an abstract data type that serves as a collection of elements, with two main principal operations:

- **Push**, which adds an element to the collection, and
- **Pop**, which removes the most recently added element that was not yet removed.

We do have some other operations on stacks such as as **peek**(also known as **top**), **isempty**, **isfull**. We shall deal with this along with stack's implementation in the C programming language.

The following video illustrates the operations on stacks.

https://www.youtube.com/watch?v=V1voux_sU5M&list=PLXX7XiUxnzzWoLDfgad4s4dwleb4NMtVN&index=2&t=7s

2.1.3 Realization of Stacks Using Arrays

We use a pointer TOP or index variable that is used to show or point the top of the stack at any time. That is, the TOP value will be the index of the array element which was inserted recently. We assume that the array has sz elements. We are sure that you will accept with us that an array in C language (for that matter in any language) is a consecutive sequence of memory locations which is thus considered as linear in accessing the same. As we are using this for realising our stack and elements are also manipulated in a sequential manner, the stack also becomes linear one.

That is, a pointer or index variable TOP keeps track of the top element in the stack or top of stack(TOS). When the stack is empty, TOP value is set to **–1.** This is done when a stack object or variable is created or instantiated. When the stack contains a single element, TOP will be made to have a value of **0** (Zero) and so on. Each time a new element is inserted in the stack (called as PUSH operation); the pointer (TOP) is incremented by **1**. The pointer (TOP) is decremented by **1** whenever an element is deleted from the stack.

How long can we continue this PUSH operation?. The answer is till there are some free elements in the array (which is used for realizing the stack). An attempt to PUSH an element into a stack which is already full is said to be **over flow** condition.

Similarly as briefed above, we have another operation which we can do on a stack known as POP. When this is executed, the top most element is removed from the stack and TOP is adjusted (reduced) to point to one element below the current one.

Obviously, we may get a doubt about how long or how many times we can do POP operation?. The answer is we can do it till the array elements are exhausted. Rather, whenever POP operation is done; TOP value will be reduced by one. When this becomes -1, then no elements are there in the stack. Any attempt to POP from an empty stack will be said to be **under flow**.

37 https://en.wikipedia.org/wiki/Stack_(abstract_data_type)

Steps in PUSH operation

```
STEP 1 : [Check for stack underflow]
         If (TOP>=sz-1)
         then declare the stack has encountered a stack overflow
              return
STEP 2 : [Increment TOP]
         TOP =TOP+1
STEP 3 : [Insert element]
         S[TOP] =X
```

In the above algorithm for PUSH, the 1st step checks for an overflow condition. If such a condition exists (that is the array used is fully occupied), the insertion can't be performed and instead an appropriate error message will be displayed. If the stack is not full, then insertion takes place and TOP is adjusted accordingly.

The following figure (Fig. 2.14) demonstrates a series of PUSH and POP operations on a stack.

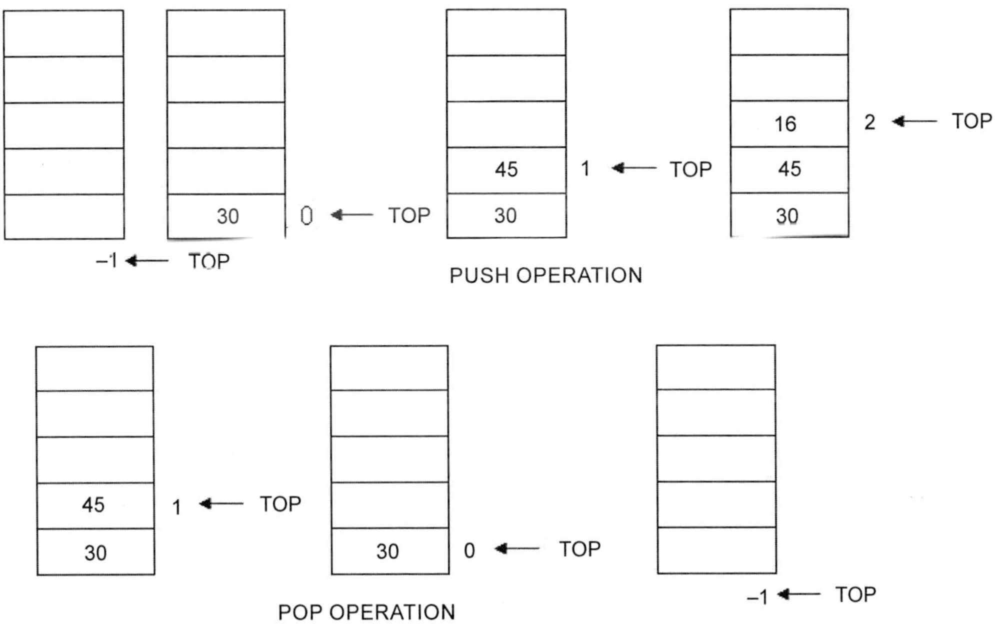

Fig. 2.14: Pop and Push operations on stacks

Steps in POP operation:

```
STEP 1 : [Check for the underflow on stack]
         If (TOP<0)
         then declare the stack is encountered an underflow
              return
STEP 2 : [Hold the former top element of stack into X]
         X= S[TOP]
STEP 3 : [Decrement the TOP pointer or index by 1]
         TOP= TOP-1
STEP 4 : [finished-Return the popped item from the stack]
         return(X)
```

In the above algorithm for POP operation, an underflow condition is checked in the first step of the algorithm. If such a condition exists(i.e TOP value is less than 0), then the deletion cannot be performed and instead an appropriate error message will be displayed.

We do have another operation known as **PEEK**, which is used on stacks in many applications. It returns the element on the top of the stack but not removed. That is, the top element is returned but the TOP value is not reduced. That is, if we call PEEK followed by POP, we get the same output.

Example 1: The following program realizes the stack using arrays in C language. All the functions are implemented with the above background.

Just to show how to use this stack, we have used a simple example. Elements of a string are pushed into the stack and printed the same by popping one after another.

```
#include<stdio.h>
#include<stdlib.h>
#define sz 10
struct stack{
    char a[sz];
    int top;
};
void INITSTACK(struct stack *A){
  A->top=-1;
}
int isempty(struct stack *A){
  return (A->top <0);
}
int isfull(struct stack *A){
  return (A->top == (sz-1));
}

void push(struct stack *A, char v){
  if(isfull(A)){
        printf("Stack full\n");
        exit(-1);
  }
  A->a[++A->top]=v;
}

char pop(struct stack *A){
            if(isempty(A)){
                  printf("Stack Empty\n");
                  exit(-1);
            }
            return ( A->a[A->top--]);
}

char peek(struct stack *A){
             if(isempty(A)){
                   printf("Stack Empty\n");
                   exit(-1);
             }
             return ( A->a[A->top]);
}
```

```
int main(){
    struct stack A, *p;
    char x[20]="rama";
    int i;
    p=&A;
    INITSTACK(p);
    for(i=0; x[i]!='\0'; i++) push(p,x[i]);
    while(!isempty(p)) printf("%c", pop(p) );
    return(0);
}
```

Output:

amar

The following link contains the above code on a visualization server. We welcome readers to visit the link and execute the same.

https://tinyurl.com/AICTEDSBOOK16

The following video explains the above code.

https://www.youtube.com/watch?v=2GElnTKyi3E&list=PLXX7XiUxnzzWoLDfgad4s4dwleb4NMtVN&index=6

Question 3: See the following code that is available at https://ideone.com/qwGjjw for experimentation[38]. Is this implementation of stack better or the above one?

```
#include <stdio.h>
#include<stdlib.h>
#define sz 10
void push();
void pop();
void display();
int stack[sz], top=-1, item;

void push(){
if(top == sz-1)
printf("Stack is full");
else{
printf("Enter item:");
scanf("%d",&item);
top++;
stack[top] = item;
printf("Item pushed = %d", item);
}
}
```

38 These types of programs are taught by many teachers in many colleges. Thus, we are of the opinion that it is our responsibility to address whether such implementations are good or bad. Thus, we have framed this question. We welcome teachers and students to compare in terms of reusability and abstraction.

```
void pop(){
if(top == -1)
printf("Stack is empty");
else{
item = stack[top];
top--;
printf("Item popped = %d", item);
}
}

void display(){
int i;
if(top == -1)
printf("Stack is empty");
else{
for(i=top; i>=0; i--)
printf("\n %d", stack[i]);
}
}

int main(){
int opt;
while(1){
//printf("Enter 1 for pushing one element\nEnter 2 for popping\nEnter 3 to
display stack contents\nEnter any integer to exit\n");
scanf("%d",&opt);
switch(opt){
case 1:push();break;
case 2:pop();break;
case 3: display();break;
default:exit(-1);
}
}
return 0;
}
```

Question 4: Why is the initial value of top taken as -1 in the above program?

Question 5: Assume that in some programming language array's first element is at location 1 instead of 0 like in C language. Then, what will be the initial value of top?

Question 6: Assume that in some programming language array's first element is at location 1 instead of 0 in C language. Identify what modifications you need to apply to the functions used in the above implementation?

Question 7: Assume that we want the stack (in the array) to grow in the opposite direction that is used in our implementation. What is the initial value of TOP if you plan to do so? Identify what modifications you need to apply to all the functions used in the above implementation?

Question 8: Assume that we want to implement the stack in a language in which array elements are indexed as n:m, where n<m and lowest indexed element is at location n and higher indexed element is at the location m in the array. What is the initial value of TOP if you plan to implement the stack in this language? Identify what modifications you need to apply to all the functions used in the above implementation?

Question 9: We welcome readers to visit the following link. Here, we are trying to maintain students in a stack. Here, 'stud' is defined with his roll number (RNO) and name. For ease of explanation, we have used only two data members; in reality we can have any number of data members to define the student.

```
struct stud{
  int RNO;
  char name[9];
};
```

The following link contains our code on a visualization server. We welcome readers to visit the link and execute the same and understand how generic is the concept of stack.

https://tinyurl.com/AICTEDSBOOK15

Example 2: An example to simulate the operations on the stack. A menu is given to the user, with which he can do operations on the stacks and see the effect.

```
#include<stdio.h>
#include<stdlib.h>
#define sz 10
/* Use the stack structure and other functions of the previous program*/
main(){
        int item,choice;
        struct stack A, *p;
        p=&A;
        INITSTACK(p);
        while(1){
printf("\nMENU\n1.PUSH\n2.POP\n3.PEEK\n4.DISPLAY\n5.EXIT\n");
                printf("Enter your choice\n");
                scanf("%d",&choice);
                switch(choice){
                        case 1:
                                        if(isfull(p))
                                                printf("stack overflow\n");
                                        else{

                        printf("Enter a character to be inserted\n");
                                                push(p,(char)fgetc(stdin));
                                }
                                break;

                case 2:
                                if(isempty(p))
                        printf("stack underflow\n");
                                else
                        printf("The deleted item is %c\n",pop(p));
                                break;

        case 3:
                                if(isempty(p))
                                        printf("stack underflow\n");
                                else
                        printf("The deleted item is %c\n",peek(p));
                                break;
```

```
                case 4:
                        if(isempty(p))
                                printf("stack is empty\n");
                        else
                        while(!isempty(p))printf("%c", pop(p));
                        break;
                case 5:
                        exit(-1);
                default:
                        printf("Invalid choice\n");
            }
        }
    return 0;
    }
```

The following link contains the code that demonstrates the stack overflow, stack empty conditions. https://tinyurl.com/NBVstackusingarray

Question 10: Name the data structure that keeps items in order and only allows to add or remove the elements at one side only?

Answer: The stack

Question 11: Assuming that "A", "B", "C" elements are pushed in order into a stack. After one pop operation, which elements will be left in the stack?

Answer: "A" and "B".

2.1.4 Applications of stacks

2.1.4.1 An application of stack for checking expression validity

See the following C language statement.

```
printf("%d\n", 2+3*( 2 - 3* (2-3)*6 + 3*1-(3*3-4            );
```

If we try to compile the program using the above line, we get the following errors in the Dev C/C++ compiler.

```
C:\Users\Administrator\Desktop\AICTEBOOK\Untitled1.cpp    In function 'int main()':
4     63   C:\Users\Administrator\Desktop\AICTEBOOK\Untitled1.cpp   [Error] expected ')' before ';' token
4     63   C:\Users\Administrator\Desktop\AICTEBOOK\Untitled1.cpp   [Error] expected ')' before ';' token
```

If we observe the above printf statement, we find that the statement is invalid in terms of parentheses. That is, the statement is missing one ')'. The above compiler error messages are also conveying the same.

```
#include<stdio.h>
int main(){
    printf("%d\n,2+3*(2-3*  (2-3)*6 + 3*1-(3*3-4 ));
    return 0;
}
```

Line	Col	File	Message
3	9	C:\Users\Administrator\Desktop\AICTEBOOK\Untitled1....	[Warning] missing terminating " character
3	2	C:\Users\Administrator\Desktop\AICTEBOOK\Untitled1....	[Error] missing terminating " character
		C:\Users\Administrator\Desktop\AICTEBOOK\Untitle...	In function 'int main()':
4	2	C:\Users\Administrator\Desktop\AICTEBOOK\Untitled1....	[Error] expected primary-expression before 'return'

See the above code where we have used beginning **double quotes** but forgot **closing double quotes** in a C language statement. The above compiler error messages are reporting this. The compiler is showing "missing " character" on the line in which a mistake is made. Also, it is considering the next line is also an error as it could not find closing double quotes in that line also!.

See the following code where we have declared a five dimensional array. On statement 4, we have purposefully missed a "(" and thus that statement is identified by an erroneous statement by the compiler. The compiler reports that it is expecting "(" before "]" which of course is very much valid also.

```
#include<stdio.h>
int main(){
    int a[10][10][10][10][10];
    a[2][(1*(2+2))][2][2][1]=10;
    a[2][(1*(2+2)][2][2][1]=10;
    return 0;
}
```

Line	Col	File	Message
		C:\Users\Administrator\Desktop\AICTEBOOK\Untitle...	In function 'int main()':
5	15	C:\Users\Administrator\Desktop\AICTEBOOK\Untitled1....	[Error] expected ')' before ']' token
5	28	C:\Users\Administrator\Desktop\AICTEBOOK\Untitled1....	[Error] expected ']' before ';' token

We have used all these examples to show that compilers are supposed to validate statements in terms of brackets, double or single quotes and vice versa. Here, we propose an ad hoc method for this type of validation.

We traverse the given expression element by element. Whenever, we find an opening type bracket such as '(', '[', and '{', the same will be pushed into the stack. When we find a closing type bracket such as ')', '}', and ']', we pop the character from the stack and compare the current closing bracket. If they are matching of type, the expression is valid till that element. Otherwise, we can out rightly say that the expression is invalid. We proceed like this till we encounter the null character in the given input string or statement. After that we check whether the stack is empty or not. If the stack is empty, it means all the opened brackets are closed and that too with correct matching type brackets. Thus, the given expression is valid; otherwise, the expression is invalid as some brackets which are closed did not get closed.

Example 3: Evaluating the expression for their parenthesis.

Solution: We will be using the above stack structure and related functions here. In addition, we will be using the following functions.

```
int isopen(char v){
  return (  (v=='(') || (v =='{') || ( v =='[' ));
}
int isclose(char v){
  return (  (v==')') || (v =='}') || ( v ==']' ));
}
int match(char a, char b){
        if( ( a== '(') && (b == ')')) return 1;
        else if( ( a== '{') && (b == '}')) return 1;
        else if( ( a== '[') && (b == ']')) return 1;
        else return 0;
}
```

```
int main(){
        char x[132];
        int i;
        struct stack A, *p;
        p=&A;
        INITSTACK(p);
        printf("Enter an expression\n");
        scanf("%[^\n]", x);
        i=0;
        while(x[i]!='\0'){
            if(isopen(x[i]))push(p, x[i]);
            else if(isclose(x[i])){
                char v=pop(p);
                if(!match(v,x[i])){
                        printf("Mismatched Parentheses\n");
                        break;
                }
            }
        i++;
        }
        (isempty(p))? printf("Valid Expr\n"): printf("Invalid Expr\n");
        return 0;
}
```

Output:

Enter an expression

2+3*(2 - 3* [2-3]*6 + 3*{1-3*3}-4

Invalid Expr

Enter an expression

2+3*(4+3*[2-3]*6-{2*3-4}+4)-3

Valid Expr

The following link contains the above code on a visualization server. We welcome readers to visit the link and execute the same.

https://tinyurl.com/NBVparenthesisvalidation

Question 12: See the following type of expression which have some spurious (extra) closing brackets. What happens if we input this type of expressions to the above program? Do we get "invalid expression" message? If not, what changes you need to do for the above code?

2+3*(4+3*[2-3]])*6-{2*3-4}+4)-3

Example 4: We wanted to realize two stacks in the same array. First stack, we call A and second one B. We assume, stack A will grow from bottom to top locations of the array (like previous stack) while stack B grows from top to bottom. **This is proposed to utilize the array in a better way. It is possible in practical applications, some stacks will grow very much compared to others. To increase the utility of array memory we want both the stacks to be using the same array.**

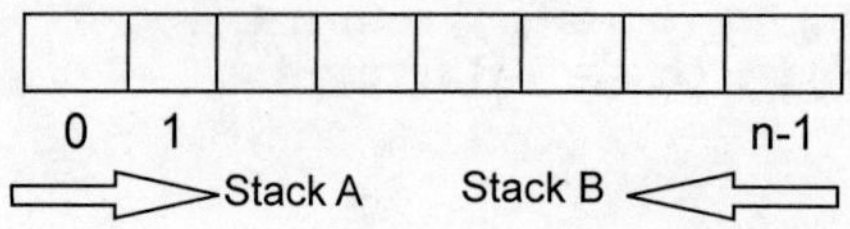

We take two indexes known as topA and topB. They will be initialized to -1 and sz respectively as array elements indexes are 0 to sz-1. When an element is pushed into stack A, topA is incremented at that location element is inserted. While an element is pushed into stack B, topB is reduced and then element is inserted in element pointed by topB. When we pop from stack A, topA is reduced after returning the element. While an element is popped from stack B, topB is increased after returning the element.

We can go on inserting elements into stack A or B till the array has some space. That is, if topA+1 is the same topB, then we can conclude that the stack is full. Stack A will be empty if topA value is -1. While stack B is empty if topB is the same as sz.

```
#include<stdio.h>
#include<stdlib.h>
#define sz 10
struct dstack{
     char a[sz];
     int topA;
     int topB;
};
void INITDSTACK(struct dstack *A){
   A->topA=-1;
   A->topB=sz;
}
int isemptyA(struct dstack *A){
   return  (A->topA <0);
}
int isfull(struct dstack *A){
   return ((A->topA+1) == A->topB);
}
void pushA(struct dstack *A, char v){
        if(isfull(A)){
            printf("Stack full\n");
            exit(-1);
        }
        A->a[++A->topA]=v;
}
char peekA(struct dstack *A){
        if(isemptyA(A)){
             printf("A Stack Empty\n");
             exit(-1);
             }
           return ( A->a[A->topA]);
}
int isemptyB(struct dstack *A){
   return  (A->topB >=sz);
}
```

```
void pushB(struct dstack *A, char v){
        if(isfull(A)){
            printf("Stack full\n");
            exit(-1);
        }
        A->a[--A->topB]=v;
}
char popB(struct dstack *A){
        if(isemptyB(A)){
             printf("A Stack Empty\n");
             exit(-1);
             }
           return ( A->a[A->topB++]);
}

char peekB(struct dstack *A){
        if(isemptyB(A)){
             printf("B Stack Empty\n");
             exit(-1);
             }
           return ( A->a[A->topB]);
}

int main(){
        struct dstack A, *p;
        char x[20]="rama";
        int i;
        p=&A;
        INITDSTACK(p);
        for(i=0; x[i]!='\0'; i++){
         pushA(p,x[i]);
         pushB(p,toupper(x[i]));
         }

        while(!isemptyA(p)) printf("%c%c",  popA(p), popB(p) );
        return(0);
}
```

Output:

aAmMaArR

The following link contains the above code on a visualization server. We welcome readers to visit the link and execute the same.

https://tinyurl.com/AICTEDSBOOK17

The following link contains a video that explains the above double stack implementation.

https://www.youtube.com/watch?v=WLpRLIhWZ8Q&list=PLXX7XiUxnzzWoLDfgad4s4dwleb4NMtVN&index=17

Question 13: Assume that we want to implement two stacks in the same array like the previous example with the exception that both the stack grows as shown below.

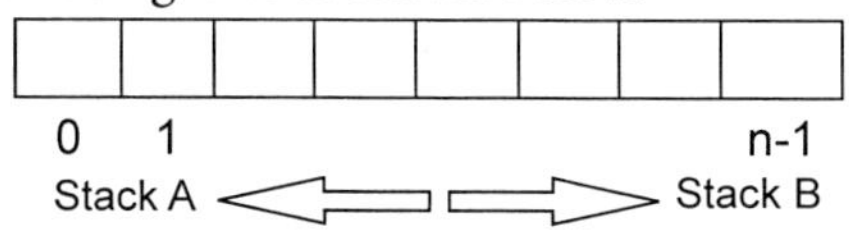

That is, the left half of the array used for stack for stack A, while the right half of the array for growing stack B. You plan what you are going to do if the array size is even and similarly if it is odd. Modify the whole code given above for implementing the two stacks in this fashion.

2.1.4.2 Infix, Postfix and Prefix Expressions

We are usually taught mathematical operations such as addition, subtractions etc.. during our school days. Adding two quantities A, B is mentioned as A+B. That is, the operator + is placed in between the two operands A, B and this representation is called an infix representation. We do have other representations of mathematical operations. These are

+ A B	***Prefix notation***
A B +	***Postfix notation***
A+B	***Infix Notation***

The three prefixes "pre-", "post-" and "in-" convey the relative position of the operator in relation to the two operands. I

In ***Prefix notation*** (also known as polish notation) the operator will be before (***precedes)*** the two operands.

In ***Postfix notation*** (also called reverse polish notation, RPN) the operator will be after (***follows***) the two operands.

In ***Infix notation*** the operator is in ***between*** the two operands.

Do you remember the BODMAS rule that would have been taught during your school days? BTW, does BODMAS stand for person or acronym? Ha. Ha. It is an acronym. The following table in support of this rule says while evaluating expressions, one needs to evaluate brackets, powers, division, multiplication, addition, subtraction in the order left to right.

Order of Operations

B	Brackets	$10 \times (4 + 2) = 10 \times 6 = 60$
O	Order	$5 + 2^2 = 5 + 4 = 9$
D	Division	$10 + 6 \div 2 = 10 + 3 = 13$
M	Multiplication	$10 - 4 \times 2 = 10 - 8 = 2$
A	Addition	$10 \times 4 + 7 = 40 + 7 = 47$
S	Subtraction	$10 \div 2 - 3 = 5 - 3 = 2$

Consider the evaluation of the expression infix expression A + B * C. We "know" that multiplication is to be done before addition). That is, **A+B*C** can be interpreted as **A + (B * C)**.

How to write **A + B * C** in postfix or reverse polish notation?. This can be done by applying the rules of precedence. That is, we first convert the portion of the infix expression that is evaluated first into postfix, namely here the multiplication. Then, we convert the + operation as it is done after *. That is :

A + (B * C)	***Parentheses for emphasis***
A + (BC*)	***Convert the multiplication***
A (BC*) +	***Convert the addition***
ABC*+	***Postfix form***

Let us carry the similar conversion operation on the infix expression (A+B)*C.

(A + B) * C	***Infix form***
(AB+) * C	***Convert the addition***
(AB+) C *	***Convert the multiplication***
AB+C*	***Postfix form***

In the above example the addition is converted before the multiplication because of the parenthesis. In going from (A + B) * C to (AB+) * C, A and B are the operands and + is the operator. In going from (AB+) * C to (AB+) C *, (AB+) and C are the operands and * is the operator. The rules for converting from infix to postfix are simple. The following figure (Fig. 2.15) provides the order of precedence.

Usual	Precedence	Binary
+	L R	Addition
–	L R	Subtraction
*	L R	Multiplication

Fig. 2.15: Operators and their precedence

2.1.4.2.1 Algorithm : Evaluation of a Postfix or Suffix expression

Here, we assume operands in the given expression are single digit operands. Thus, we can use the stack explained in the first examples. Also, we assume our postfix string will contain only digits and operators.

STEP 1: Read the given postfix expression into a string.

STEP 2: Read one character at a time & perform the following operations:

1. If the read character is an operand, then convert it to push it onto the stack (here, this stack is called an operand stack as we are pushing the operands into it).
2. If the character is not an operand, then pop the operator from stack and assign to OP2. Similarly, pop one more operator from stack and assign to OP1. Subtract 48 to get the digit values.
3. Evaluate the result based on operator x.
4. Push the result (based operator x) onto the stack after adding 48.

STEP 3: Repeat STE 2 till all characters are processed from the input string.

STEP 4: Return the result as the last value which is left in the stack. Pop the stack and remove 48 and print the result.

A snapshot of evaluating a postfix expression: **236*+42/+**

	6 3 2	18 2	20	2 4 20	2 20	22
	TOP=2	TOP=1	TOP=0	TOP=2	TOP=1	TOP=0
Initially the stack is empty.	Now, 2,3,6 are pushed into the stack.	As, we have encountered * operator, we pop 6,3 and calculate their product and push the same into the stack.	As we have now encountered + operator, we pop 18, 2 and calculate their sum and push the result into the stack.	Now, 4,2 are pushed into the stack.	As we have now encountered /, we pop 2,4 and calculate their division and push the same into the stack.	As we have encountered +, we pop 2,20 and calculate their sum and push the same into the stack.

Readers are welcome to run the following program on a visualization tool to verify the above table.
https://tinyurl.com/AICTEDSBOOK28

Example 5: Evaluating Postfix expression

Solution: We propose to take the same stack structure as discussed in previous examples. Also, we assume operands are simple single digit operands. As the stack is character stack, we are pushing the operands as characters. However, once we pop the same from the stack, we are subtracting 48 to get digit value before evaluating the operator. Also, 48 is added to the result before pushing into the stack. At the end, 48 is subtracted from the popped item to get the integer result.

```
int expr(int a, int b, char opr){
   switch(opr){
          case '+': return a+b;
          case '-': return a-b;
          case '*': return a*b;
          case '/': return a/b;
          case '%': return a%b;
   }
}

int main(){
        char x[132];
        int i,a,b;
        struct stack A, *p;
        p=&A;
        initstack(p);
        printf("Enter a Postfix expression\n");
        scanf("%[^\n]", x);
        i=0;
        while(x[i]!='\0'){
                if(isdigit(x[i]))push(p, x[i]);
                else{
                        b=pop(p)-48;
```

```
                a=pop(p)-48;
                push(p, expr(a,b,x[i])+48);
            }
        i++;
        }
        printf("%d\n", pop(p)-48);
        return 0;
    }
```

Output:

Enter a Postfix expression

234*+ 42/–6 + 18

The following link contains the above code on a visualization server. We welcome readers to visit the link and execute the same.

https://tinyurl.com/AICTEDSBOOK18

The following link contains a video that explains infix to postfix conversion using a stack.

https://www.youtube.com/watch?v=cDGtjfz3kmk&list=PLXX7XiUxnzzWoLDfgad4s4dwleb4NMtVN&index=28

Question 14a: In the expr() function of the above code, we are not using any break statement after return statements. By chance if we insert break after each of the return statements of switch construct, what compilation error are you going to get. Please experiment on a variety of compilers instead of one compiler.

Answer: You will get unreachable code.

Question 14b: In our stack, we have used character array, x in the stack structures. Assume that we have modified the stack structure to have an integer array instead of character array as shown below.

```
struct stack{
  int a[sz];
  int top;
};
```

What modifications one has to do for the above code so as to use for expression evaluation.

Hint: You may look at the following link after your initial thought process.

https://tinyurl.com/AICTEDSBOOK20

Question 15: What is the postfix expression whose evaluation changes the stack content as shown in the following figure?

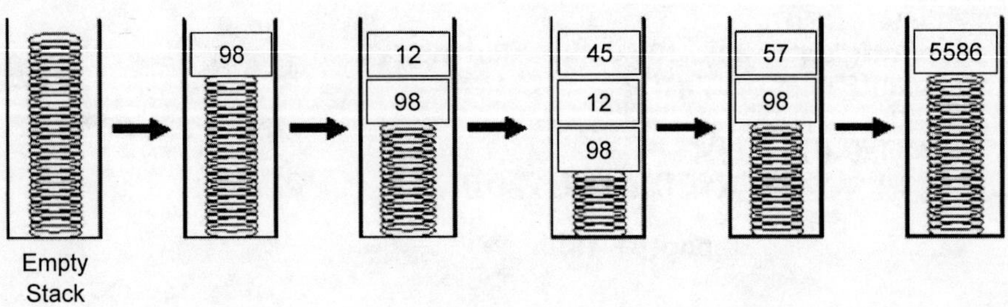

2.1.4.2.2 Stack based computers

We do have stack based computers[39]; we mean HW which internally uses the operations push and pop in HW. Also, we do have some freely available SW to simulate them[40]. We request teachers to use them during their classes.

Conventional processors of contemporary design will have a finite set of named registers. However, in a stack machine CPU, the registers are arranged in a stack fashion. It supports the usual range of arithmetic operators and stack manipulation instructions push, pop. Do remember that we are referring to HW aspects. That is, these push, pop are of that stack processor's machine language or level instructions.

As usual, any expression can be converted to RPN and a stack computer can be used to evaluate that expression without. For example, if we want to evaluate **X + Y - Z**, its postfix form **XY + Z -** is computed.

Now, we can give instructions: push val X, push val Y, add, push val Z, sub.

Of course, in this machine also, to execute an operation like add or sub, top two items from stack are used and the result will be pushed back to stack. We welcome readers to visit the following site for more details.

https://www.cs.csustan.edu/~xliang/Courses/SimulatorWeb/Examples/StackMachine/Expr_0a

Stack machine code for computing expression (X+Y)*(W-Y)

```
PUSH X        //X will be on top
PUSH Y        //Y will be on top
ADD           //X, Y are popped X+Y is calculated and pushed on to top
PUSH W        //W will be on top
PUSH Y        //Y  will be on top
SUB           //W,Y are popped W-Y is calculated and pushed on to top
MUL           //(X+Y)*(W-Y) is calculated and pushed
POP Z         //Z = (X+Y)*(W-Y)   Popped
PUSH Z        //Z
PRNT          //Print Z
STOP          //Terminate
```

Question 16: In order to evaluate an expression 5+(((9+8)*(4*6))+7), the following steps are taken by a stack based computer. Are they valid steps?

```
push(5);
push(9);
push(8);
push(pop+pop);
push(4);
push(6);
push(pop*pop);
push(pop*pop);
push(7);
push(pop+pop);
push(pop*pop);
printf("%d", pop);
```

39 https://people.ece.cornell.edu/land/courses/ece5760/DE2/Stack_cpu_2011.html

40 https://www.cs.csustan.edu/~xliang/Courses/SimulatorWeb/index.htm

Question 17: The following pictures illustrate the evaluation of a RPN expression. Is there any mistake in it? (Source: http://ds.nathanielgmartin.com Last Accessed: 15th Aug 2022)

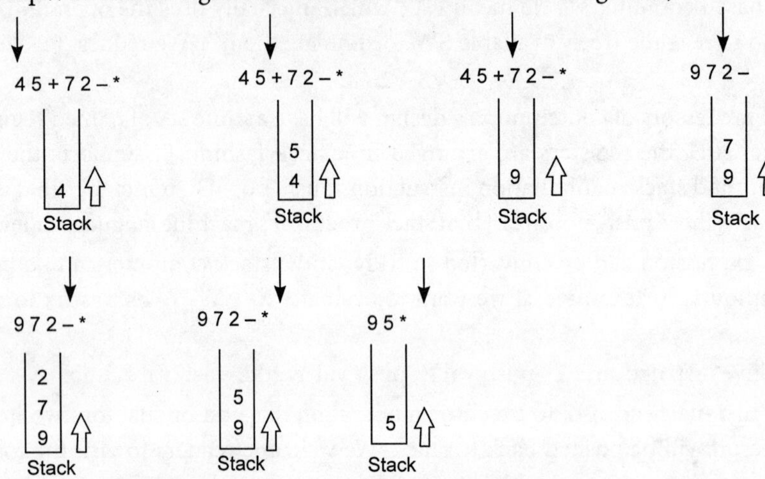

Answer: Yes. There is a mistake at the end. That is, the stack is supposed to have 45 instead of 5 as 9*6 is 45. You are welcome to visit the following visulaization to verify the above.

https://tinyurl.com/AICTEDSBOOK27

2.1.4.2.3 Converting Infix Expressions to Postfix

We have discussed in the previous example about evaluating a postfix expression. Now, we have to know how to convert an infix expression to postfix.

We know that the postfix expression contains the operands which have high precedence before to operands whose precedence is lower. Thus, we traverse the given string (we assume here also the operands are single digit operands for our convenience sake) character by character. If we encounter an operand, we simply output. When we encounter an operator we will check the stack if it is free simply we can push into it. Else, we compare the operator at TOS, if TOS character precedence is higher we will pop and print. (here, this stack is called an operator stack as we are pushing the operators into it).This, we repeat till the stack is empty or till we encounter an operator whose precedence is lesser than the current operator. Then, we push the current character into the stack. Once after processing all the elements of the expression, we pop the all operators from the stack and print.

We have demonstrated in our examples that the postfix expression does not contain parenthesis. Without them also, evaluation will be carried out correctly. Thus, we propose to push a bracket of opening type into the stack. Any operator will be having high precedence (this we have assumed for our programming convenience). When a closing bracket is encountered, we go on pop and print operators from the stack till we encounter the opening bracket from the stack. However, we will not print popped bracket in the postfix string.

Example 6: To convert an infix expression to postfix.

```
int isopen(char v){
   return (  (v=='(') || (v =='{') || ( v =='[' ));
}
int isclose(char v){
   return (  (v==')') || (v =='}') || ( v ==']' ));
}
```

```
/* The following function returns 1 if operator 1 has higher precedence than b*/
int PRECED( char a, char b){
   char opr[]="+-*/";
   int i=0, j=3;
   if(isopen(b)) return 1;
   while( opr[i] !=a)i++;
   while( opr[j] !=b) j--;
   return (i/2 >j/2);
}

int main(){
        char x[132];
        int i,a,b;
        struct stack A, *p;
        p=&A;
        INITSTACK(p);
        printf("Enter an  InFix expression\n");
        scanf("%[^\n]", x);
        printf("Post Fix Expression=");
        i=0;
        while(x[i]!='\0'){
                if(isdigit(x[i]))printf("%c",x[i]);
                else if(isopen(x[i]))push(p,x[i]);
                else  if(isclose(x[i])){
                 while(!isopen(peek(p)))printf("%c", pop(p));
                 char v=pop(p);
                }
                else{
                        while( (!isempty(p)) && (!PRECED(x[i],peek(p))) )
                           printf("%c", pop(p));

                        push(p,x[i]);
                        }
        i++;
        }
        while(!isempty(p))
                printf("%c", pop(p));
        printf("\n");
        return 0;
}
```

Output:

Enter an InFix expression

2+3*6+4/2+6

Post Fix Expression = 236*+42/+6+

A snapshot of the program which converts an infix expression to postfix is given below.

Input String: 2+3*6+4/2+6

TOP=1	+ TOP=0	* + TOP=2	+ TOP=0	/ + TOP=2	+ TOP=0	TOP=1
Output	Output: 2	Output: 22	Output: 236*+	Output: 236*+42	Output: 236*+42/+	Output: 236*+42/+6
	Digit 2 is printed, + is pushed into the stack	3 is printed As * as higher precedence than TOS character +, the same is pushed into stack.	When, second + is encountered the elements of the stack are popped and printd till we find stack is free or we find or we find TOS charactrer whose precedence is less. Then, push + into stack	The operands 4, 2 are printed. The operator / is pushed into the stack.	When we encounter last +, we pop and print operators and then push + into stack.	Pop and print all operators in the stack, when we find trhe end of the expression.

The following link contains the above code on a visualization server. We welcome readers to visit the link and execute the same.

https://tinyurl.com/NBVinfixtopostfix

Question 18: Reverse polish notation of an infix expression 5+(((9+8)*(4*6))+7) is given as : 5 9 8+4 6 * * 7 + * (for clarity reasons, we have used spaces). Is this a valid equivalent?

Question 19: Analyse the working of PRECED() function defined above by filling the returned value of this function in the following table for various values of arguments a, b.

Argument a	Argument b	The value that will be returned by PRECED() function.
Any value(operator)	‘(‘	
+	+	
+	-	
-	-	
-	+	
+	*	
*	+	
+	/	
/	+	
-	*	
*	-	
-	/	
/	-	
*	/	
/	*	

Question 20: In the above program, we have assumed that our expressions are having only +, -, * and / operators. According to the logic of PRECED() function is developed. What is we want to consider another operand \$, which can be assumed as exponentiation whose precedence is considered to be more than * and /. Do remember that this operator is also a binary operator (that is, it will also have two operands). That is, A\$B is equivalent to A^{B}. Explore what modification you need to apply for PRECED() function.

The following figure illustrate how the infix expression A + B * C - D / E is converted to postfix.

Infix expression	Stack content(bot->top)	Partial postfix expression
A+B*C-D/E		
+B*C-D/E		A
B*C-D/E	+	A
*C-D/E	+	AB
C-D/E	+*	AB
-D/E	+*	ABC
D/E	+-	ABC*
/E	+-	ABC*D
E	+-/	ABC*DE
	+-/	ABCD*DE/-+

Readers are welcome to visit the following link to visualize the conversion.

https://tinyurl.com/AICTEDSBOOK29

The following figure illustrate how the infix expression A*B-(C-D)+E is converted to infix to postfix. Do observe that the previous one is free from any brackets compared to this example.

Infix Expression	Stack contents (bot->top)	Postfix expression
A*B-(C-D)+E		
*B-(C-D)+E		A
B-(C-D)+E	*	A
-(C-D)+E		AB
(C-D)+E	-	AB*
C-D)+E	-(	AB*
-D)+E	-(	AB*C
D)+E	-(-	AB*C
)+E	-(-	AB*CD
+E	-	AB*CD-
E	+	AB*CD--
	+	AB*CD- -
		AB*CD- - +

The following link contains the code to verify the above table.

https://tinyurl.com/AICTEDSBOOK30

Example 7: You are given the daily stock price of a company for some number of consecutive market days. You need to compute the span value for all the given days. Span value of a day i (si) is the maximum number of consecutive days (up to the day i) for which the stock price of the stock is <= stock price of day i.

(Courtesy: https://www.heppenstall.ca - /academics/doc/242/ Last Accessed: 15th Aug 2022)

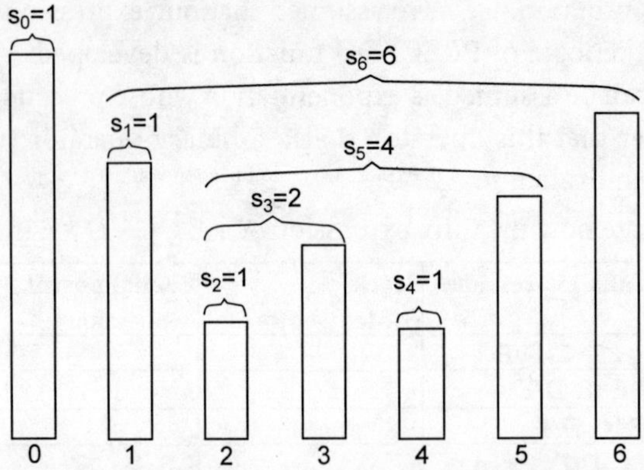

Assuming P is a 1-D array having stock's daily price values. Let us take another 1-D array S to store the span of the stock for every ith day. The following is a little crude procedure with time complexity O(n2) where n is the number of consecutive days for which stock's price is given.

```
for i ← 0 to n – 1 do
  k ←0
  done ← false
  repeat
    if P[i – k] ≤ P[i] then
      k ← k + 1
    else
      done ← true
  until (k = i) or done
  S[i] ← k
return S
```

The author of this problem has suggested the following algorithm that uses a stack. Take here the function top() as our peek(). Also, the pseudo language what the algorithm is little inspired by object oriented languages such as Java.

```
Algorithm computeSpan2(P):
  Input: An n-element array P of numbers representing
         stock prices
  Output: An n-element array S of numbers such that
         S[i] is the span of the stock on day i
  Let D be an empty stack
  for i ← 0 to n – 1 do
    done ← false
    while not(D.isEmpty() or done) do
      if P[i] ≥ P[D.top()] then
        D.pop()
      else
        done ← true
      if D.isEmpty() then
        h ← –1
```

```
        else
          h ← D.top()
        S[i] ← i − h
        D.push(i)
    return S
```

We have made a solution and it is made available at the following link. Explore how time complexity of this method is compared to the crude approach given above.

https://tinyurl.com/AICTEDSBOOK21

Question 21: What is the complexity of push(), pop(), peek() operations on a stack implementation that uses an array?

Question 22: Assume that we want to design a growable stack in C language by using functions such as realloc(), malloc(). Maybe, initially you can create a dynamic array in the stack structure that was proposed earlier. Also, the initstack function can be made to create a dynamic array, x. See the possible stack structure.

```
struct stack{
char *x;
int top;
};
void INITSTACK(struct stack *A){
x=(char*)malloc(sz);
---
-
}
```

Assume that whenever we find the available space of the array x becomes full, then by calling malloc() function create a new dynamic array with twice the size of the current array, x, and then copy the present stack content into it then make that new dynamic array as x. Like this, we want you to implement a growable stack using the array.

Question 23: The following table illustrates conversion of the infix expression a - (b + c * d)/e to postfix form. Is there any mistake in this trace?

Infix expression character	Stack contents(bot->top)	Postfix expression
a		a
-	-	a
(	-(	a
b	-(+	ab
+	-(+	ab
c	-(+	abc
*	-(+*	abc
d	-(+*	abcd
)	-	abcd*+
/	-/	abcd*+
e	-/	abcd*+e
		abcd*+e/-

Readers are welcome to visit the following link to visualize the conversion.

https://tinyurl.com/AICTEDSBOOK35

Answer: No

Question 24: Is there any mistake in the following infix to postfix conversion table of the expression 2*3/(2-1)+5*3?

Next character from the given expression	Contents of the stack (bottom to top) ⇨	Postfix expression or output string
2	Empty	2
*	*	2
3	*	23
/	/	23*
(	/(	23*
2	/(	23*2
-	/(-	23*2
1	/(-	23*21
)	/	23*21-
+	+	23*21-/
5	+	23*21-/5
*	+*	23*21-/53
3	+*	23*21-/53
	Empty	23*21-/53*+

Readers are welcome to visit the following link to visualize the conversion.

https://tinyurl.com/AICTEDSBOOK36

Answer: No

2.2 INTRODUCTION TO QUEUES

We will find queues very commonly in our daily life where we will find people will be waiting in the queue for some service (see Fig. 2.16)

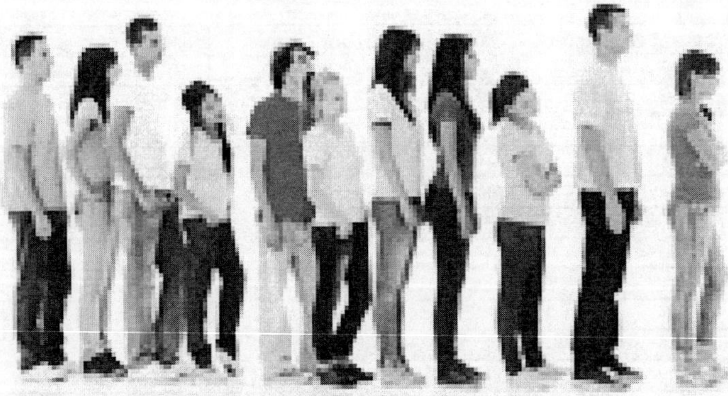

Fig. 2.16: People in the queue

Courtesy: https://depositphotos.com/stock-photos/queue.html Last Accessed: 15th Aug 2022

Fig. 2.17: Vehicle in queue

The above Fig. 2.17(left) shows vehicles at a toll gate. Fig. 2.17 (right) shows how orderly the traffic is in Aizawl, State of Mizoram, India. **Hats off to the Mizoram people.** The following is a figure (Fig. 2.18) where childrens will be standing in a queue to get their turn of ice cream.

Fig. 2.18: Children queuing in front of an ice cream van

The following figure (Fig. 2.19) shows packets in a queue at a router.

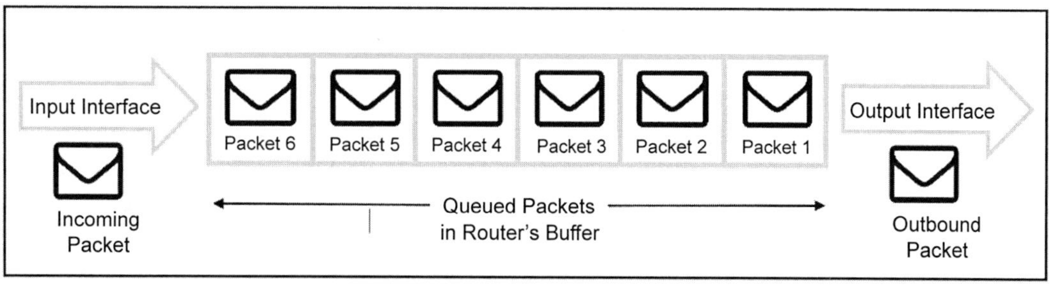

Fig. 2.19: Packets in a queue at a router

Courtesy: https://www.geeksforgeeks.org/packet-queuing-and-dropping-in-routers/ Last Accessed: 15th Aug 2022

Keyboard buffering

Queues are even used in keyboard management. Here, our key presses are maintained in a buffer which is often called a keyboard buffer. Sometimes whatever we have typed will not immediately appear on the screen; but appear with some delay. This may be due to the processor busyness with some other task. That means, whatever we have typed, that key presses will be temporarily stored in a queue, till the processor becomes free and reads it. Once the processor becomes free, all the keystrokes that are in the queue are read in the sequence of their key presses and displayed on the screen at once. Have you ever experienced this?. Similarly, mouse events are also maintained in special buffers.

Let us consider that we went to a ration shop. We will stand in a place where already some people are waiting. People who come after us, will be standing after us. Ration will be given first to the people who are before us then we will get our turn. People who joined after us will be getting their turn only after we get our turn. Thus, people who come first to the shop will be given service first. Thus, this type of structure is called the First in First Out (FIFO) queue. Evidently, items (here people) will be added at one end, while people will be leaving from the other end after getting service. The end, where people are added is referred to as the rear end; the end from which people will be served (and will leave the queue) is called the front end. That is, at the rear end items will be added; while at the rear end service will be given and removed from the queue.

2.2.1 Operations on Queues

Evidently, we have the following operations which are carried out on queues.

Insert: An item is added at the rear end. The **REAR** pointer will be changing (This operation is also called an **enqueue**).

Remove: An item is removed from the front end. The **FRONT** pointer will be changed to show the effect (This operation is also called **dequeue**).

Isempty: This will indicate whether the queue is empty or not. If empty, it returns true else false.

Isfull: This is used with only array based queue realizations. It is to check whether the space available in the array is full or not. If full, it returns true else false.

Theoretically, we can have a queue of any living things or non living things. That is, this is also a generic concept. Also, queues can be realized either using arrays or linked lists. In the following pages, we will first explain how to realize a queue using arrays and then using linked lists. The following Fig. 2.20 shows FRONT, REAR[41] etc.

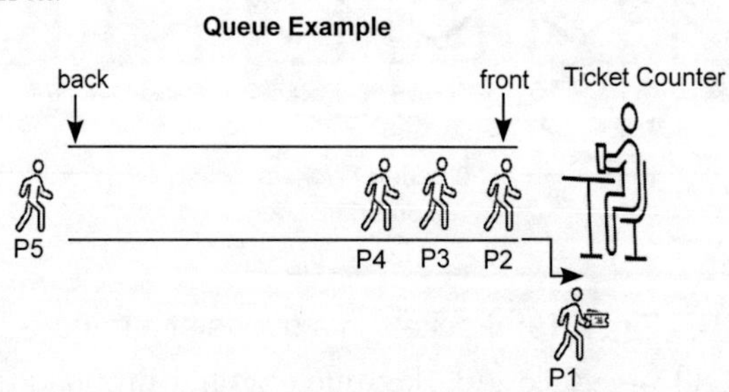

Fig. 2.20: A typical queue with where some service is provided at the front

41 Rear is sometimes referred to as tail, back, end also.

The following video introduces queues in practice.

https://www.youtube.com/watch?v=pGjMwP-r8LU&list=PLXX7XiUxnzzWoLDfgad4s4dwleb4NMtVN&index=32

Question 25: Assuming that "A", "B", "C" elements are inserted in order into a queue. After one remove operation, which elements will be left in the queue?

Answer: "B" and "C".

2.2.2 Array Representation of Queues

Linear Queues

Let us consider that we propose to use arrays to realize queues. Rather, we want to realize queue to store characters. We assume that initially FRONT and REAR to be pointing to an imaginary cell before the 0th element.

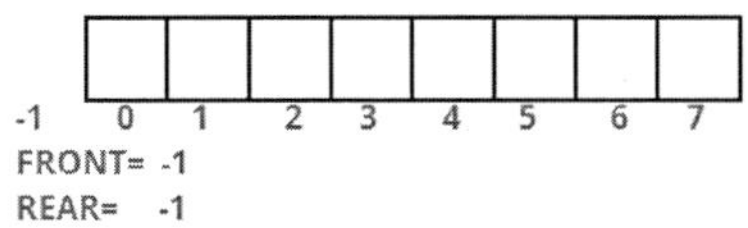

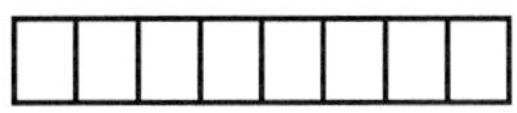

When we insert a first element, we assume we will adjust both FRONT and REAR to 0 as shown below.

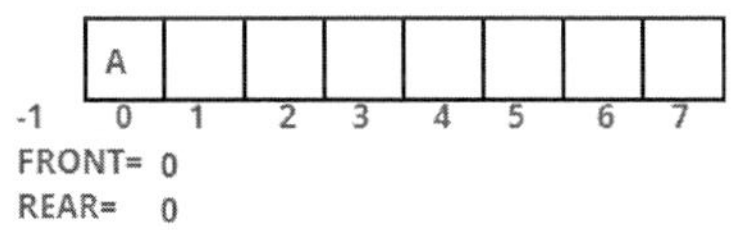

Now, if we insert some more elements (say X,Y,Z,T,U,B), only REAR will be changing.

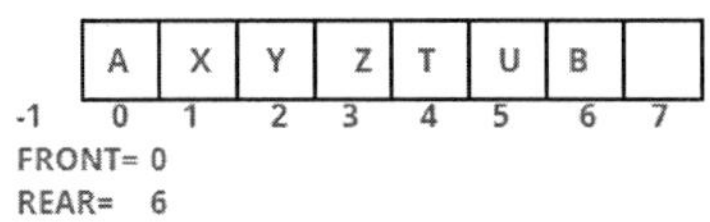

Now, let us assume that we have removed the first three elements. Thus, FRONT will be adjusted. Thus, the queue looks like:

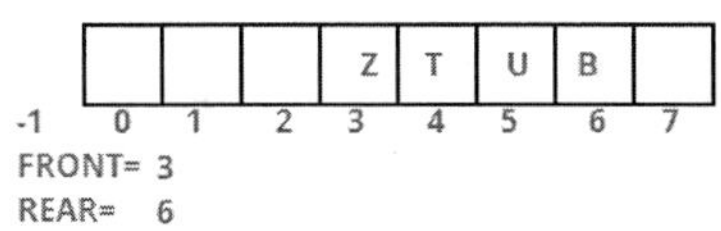

The following link demonstrates the implementation of stack using the above concepts. We welcome readers to explore this without fail.

https://tinyurl.com/AICTEDSBOOK33

Circular Queue

Now, if we think of doing insertion and deletion operations like this, in the above example, we may have one more element that can be inserted. However, if we observe some free elements or locations are available at the beginning which are previously allocated to some elements. If we want to utilize them, we can think of moving all the elements towards the left such that we can maintain some more elements in the queue. However, this demands memory movements. **Thus, in the following program we have proposed a solution which utilizes the free elements by considering the array as a cyclic array(This can be also called as wrap-around).**

Initially, we assume both FRONT and REAR (often called as **back** also) will be set to size-1 as shown below.

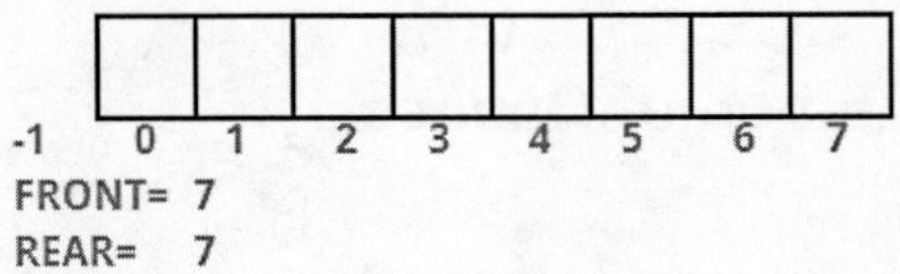

Thus, we consider when FRONT is REAR then the queue is empty.

If we insert an item first, REAR will be set to zero if it is sz-1 else REAR is incremented by one. Then, we insert the at the index referred by REAR. For instance like:

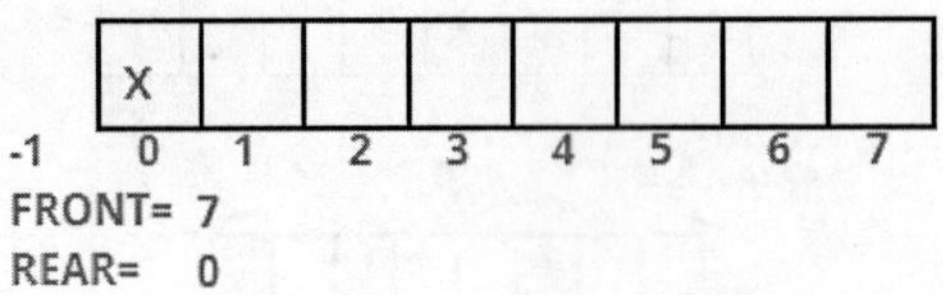

Now, if we call remove, we want to return the first element 'X'. Thus, we have to adjust FRONT. When remove is called FRONT is adjusted. If FRONT is sz-1 it will be made as 0, else it will be incremented by one. Then, we return the element which is referred to by FRONT. In this case it is 'X'. However, one important point we are missing here. Before changing FRONT, we have to check whether the queue is empty or not. If not, then only FRONT has to be adjusted. Thus, the queue becomes:

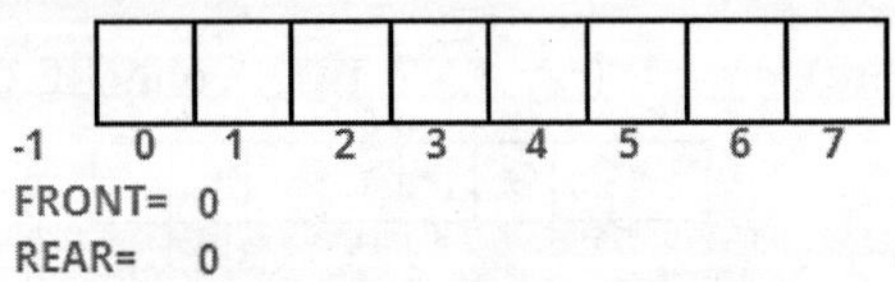

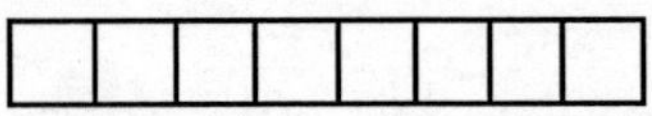

Now, is it possible to call remove?. As FRONT is same as REAR no elements are there. Thus, remove fails.

Let us proceed our discussion assuming the state of the queue as:

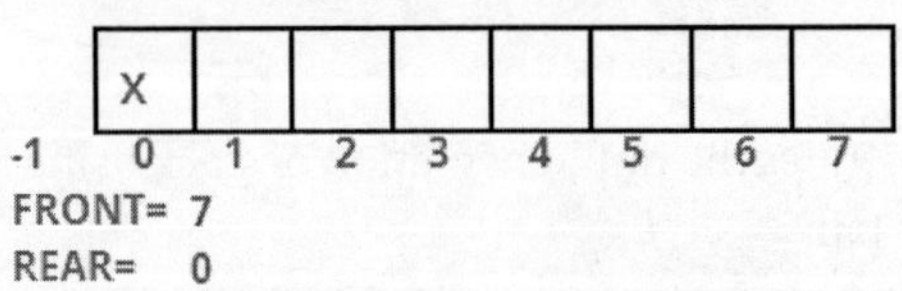

Now, let we have inserted items 'P','N','R'. Whenever we insert, we change REAR and at that modified position, the new element is inserted. Thus, queue now becomes

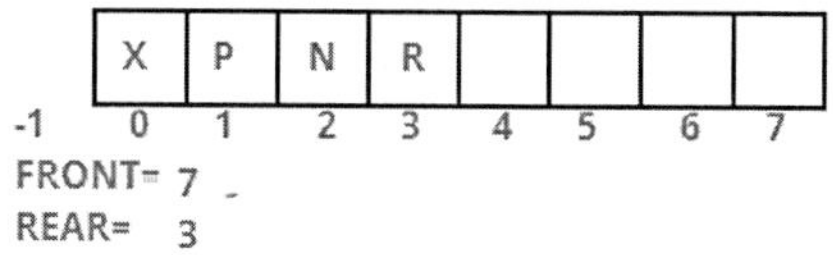

How long insertion can be carried out?. If we insert till (including) 7th element also then REAR becomes 7. As we are assuming if FRONT is the same as REAR, the queue is empty. Thus, if we insert till 7th location we may come to the wrong conclusion that the queue is empty. So, we will insert till sixth only. Rather, when we call insertion, we will change the REAR value and check whether it is the same as FRONT or not. If the same, we rise as "overflow" or full and terminate the operation. Otherwise, we continue the insertion operation.

Thus, if we assume some more elements 'M', 'N', and 'L' are inserted and the queue looks like:

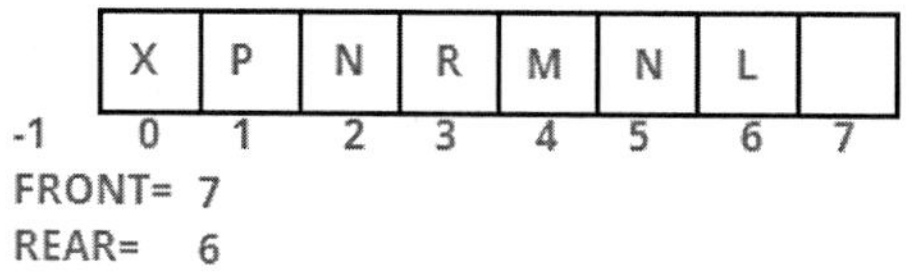

If we try to insert another element, it becomes an illegal operation. However, if we remove one element, the queue looks like:

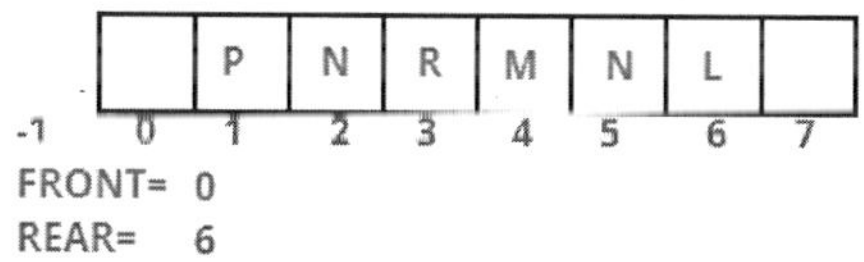

Now, we can insert another element (say 'U'). The queue looks like:

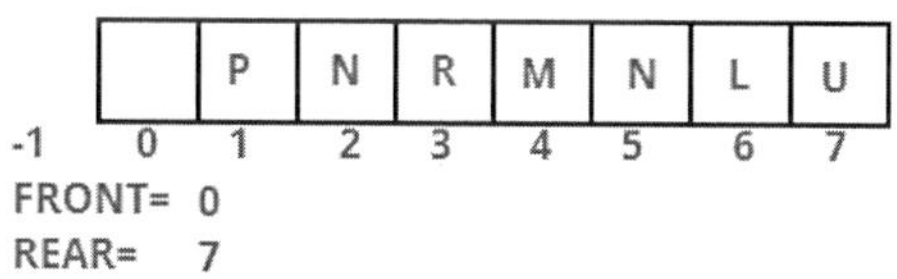

Is it possible to insert another element? No. When we try to insert, REAR becomes 0. Thus, REAR becomes FRONT. So, we don't insert.

Let, two more elements are removed. Thus, queue looks like:

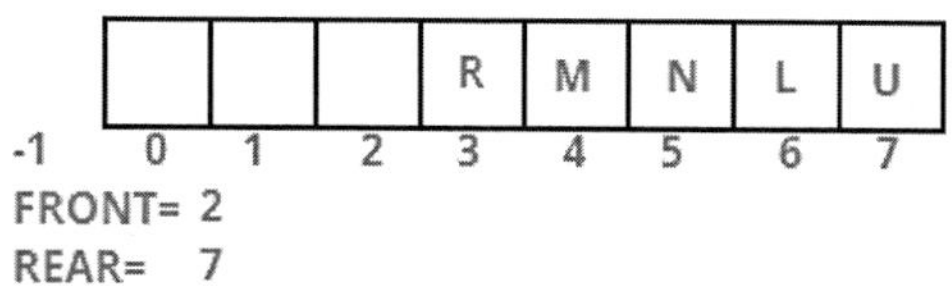

Now, we have space at the beginning to insert two more elements only. If we assume that we have inserted 'O' and 'Y', the queue looks like:

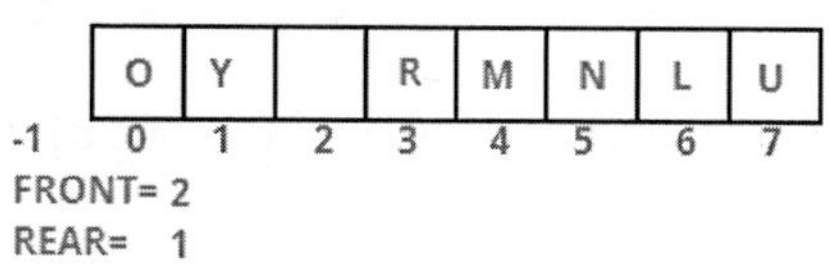

Thus, by moving REAR and FRONT cyclically, we can utilize the array space in a better manner. The following code fragment implements the above steps.

We consider the given array as a circular array. We are using a circle with equal annular portions. Just like a linear array, we did number these annular parts starting from 0. Initially, we kept front and back(read) at size-1. Here, they are initialized to 7 as we have eight annular parts along the periphery of the circle. If the annular part is grey, it is not occupied; otherwise it is occupied with some element. The following figure indicates that the queue is empty.

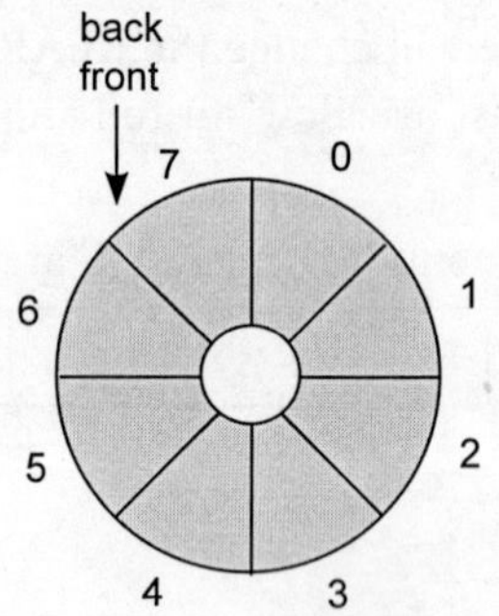

Assuming that we have inserted 2, 4, 1, and 7 into the queue. Thus, queue looks like the following figure.

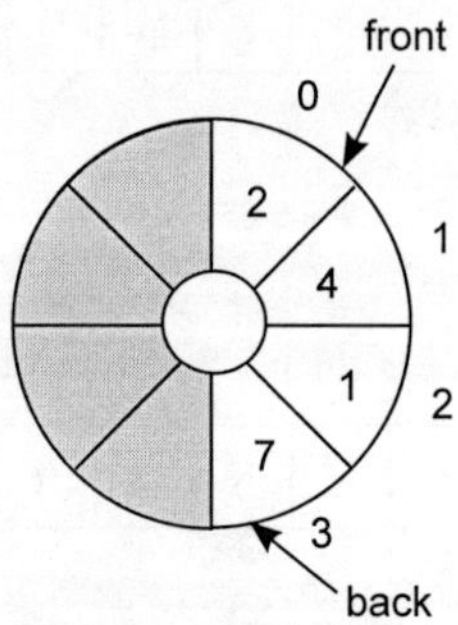

If we remove one element, that is 2 then the queue becomes as shown below.

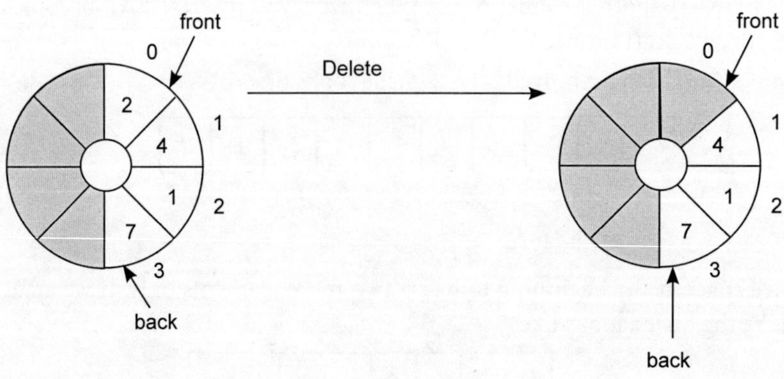

Assuming that we remove (4) and then add 9 then the queue becomes as shown below.

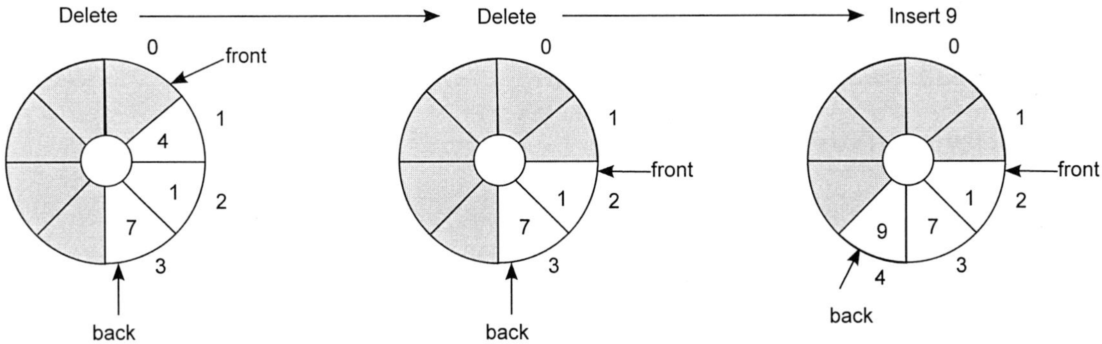

If we remove 1 and 7 in sequence then the queue looks like the following.

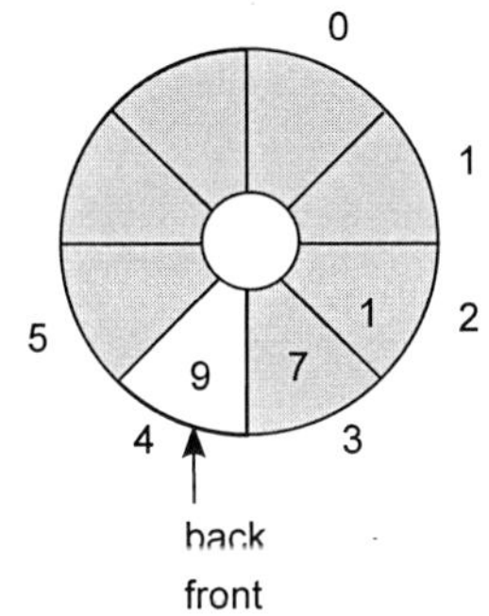

The following picture shows the queue in full condition. Do remember that we want to waste one location. If we try to insert any element, it should raise a queue full error.

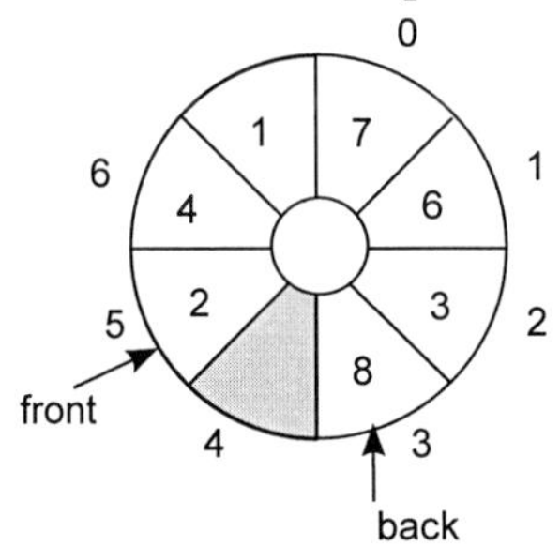

Example 8: Realizing queue using arrays.

```
#include<stdio.h>
#include<stdlib.h>
#define sz 10
struct queue{
    char a[sz];
    int front;
    int rear;
};
```

```
void INITQUEUE(struct queue *A){
   A->rear=sz-1;
   A->front=sz-1;
}
int isempty(struct queue *A){
   return  (A->rear == A->front);
}
int isfull(struct queue *A){
   return (A->front == A->rear);
}

void insert(struct queue *A, char v){
    if(A->rear==(sz-1))A->rear=0;
    else
      A->rear++;
    if(isfull(A)){
              printf("Stack full\n");
              exit(-1);
    }
  A->a[A->rear]=v;
}

char remove(struct queue *A){
   if(isempty(A)){
              printf("Queue Empty\n");
              exit(-1);
              }
   if(A->front==(sz-1)) A->front=0;
   else
   A->front++;
            return ( A->a[A->front]);
}
int main(){
   struct queue A, *p;
   char x[20]="rama";

   int i;
   p=&A;
   INITQUEUE(p);
   for(i=0; x[i]!='\0';  i++) insert(p,x[i]);
   printf("Output from the queue\n");
   while(!isempty(p)) printf("%c",  remove(p) );
   return(0);
}
```

Output:

Output from the queue

rama

The following link contains the above code hosted on a visualization server. We welcome readers to experiment with the same.

https://tinyurl.com/NBVQueueusingarray

The following video explains about queue realization in C language using an array.

https://www.youtube.com/watch?v=8ClFbAxtKB0&list=PLXX7XiUxnzzWoLDfgad4s4dwleb4NMtVN&index=3

Question 26: In the above implementation of Queue, we want to implement some change.

The following lines

```
if(A->rear==(sz-1))A->rear=0;
else
 A->rear++;
```

to be replaced with

```
A->rear=(A->rear+1)%sz;
```

Similarly, the following lines

```
if(A->front==(sz-1)) A->front=0;
else
A->front++;
```

to be replaced with

```
A->front=(A->front+1)%sz;
```

The following link contains the modified code.

https://tinyurl.com/AICTEDSBOOK23

Explore whether this works in the same fashion as that of the previous implementation of queue or not.

Question 27: If you observe the above implementation of the queue, you find it is inserting elements at 0, 1, 2,.....size - 1, 0, 1, 2,....size-1, and vice versa in the cyclic fashion as long as one empty slot is available (see the following figure).

Can you plan to realize the same in the opposite direction? That is, first element to go to the location size-1, that next to size - 2, ... 2.1.0 then again from the location size-1, size-2,...,2,1,0, and vice versa?

Question 28: In the queue implemented above, we plan to use another variable Count representing the current number of elements in the queue.

```
#define sz 10
struct queue{
        char a[sz];
        int front;
        int rear;
        int count;
};
```

We have modified all the functions taking the new variable count into account. Also, unlike our previous implementation, we were wasting one element of the array, this uses all the elements of the array to realize the queue. Is there any advantage of this method in relation to our previous implementation? The following link contains the code that is using Count data members in our implementation.

https://tinyurl.com/AICTEDSBOOK24

Question 29: In the lines of Question 28, we plan to use another variable Count representing the current number of elements in the queue. Assume that the array is of size 25. We initialise Rear, Front and Count to 0.

(a) What is the value of Front, Count and Rear after we have inserted 15 elements?

Answer: 0,15,15

(b) What is the value of Front, Count and Rear when we have subsequently taken 8 elements out?

Answer: 8,15,7

(c) What is the value of Front, Count and Rear when we insert another 15 elements?

Answer: 8,5,22

(d) What is the relation between Count, Front and Rear? Do you need to maintain all the three?

Answer: Rear = (Front + Count) mod 25. No, you don't need all three, you can drop one and compute the value from the other two

Question 30: If one observes all the functions such as insert(), remove(), isfull(), iseempty(), INITQUEUE() all are designed to take the address of the queue as an argument as shown like INITQUEUE function.

```
void INITQUEUE(struct queue *A){
        A->rear=sz-1;
        A->front=sz-1;
        A->count=0;
}
```

Is it possible to send a queue as a passing by value style (not passing by address fashion) to all the functions? Maybe, you may look at the following link to guess the answer.

https://tinyurl.com/AICTEDSBOOK25

Question 31: What is meant by the False-Overflow Issue in linear queue?

Answer: There are some free elements in the queue but the rear reaches the end of the queue. In order to use those free spaces, elements will be moved.

2.2.2.1 Comparison of Circular queues and Linear queues

- Linear queue consumes more memory as compared to circular queue.
- A circular queue is an efficient way for memory utilization.
- In a circular queue, new data can be inserted again at a particular position after deleting previous data on that position which is not the same in the case of a linear queue.
- In a linear queue, if the rear pointer reaches last and the front pointer deletes all data from the queue, it continues to show the message of "Overflow", which is the main drawback of the linear queue. Whereas in a circular queue, an overflow message is shown when the queue is full.
- Easy to perform dequeue operation and enqueue operation in linear queue.

2.2.3 Deque

A double-ended queue or deque[42] is a double-ended linear data structure that is more general than stack and queue. A deque has four major operations: insertFront(), insertRear(), removeFront(), removeRear(). There are two types of deques based on the restrictions put to perform either the insertions or deletions only at one end. They are:

(i) Input-restricted deque

(ii) Output-restricted deque.

42 It is also often called a head-tail linked list

Input-restricted deque: In input-restricted deque, insertion can be made only at one end while deletions can be carried out at both ends.

Output-restricted deque: In output-restricted deque deletion can be made only at one end while insertions can be carried out at both ends.

A deque can be also realized using either arrays or linked lists. In this section we will use an array based deque. Do recall why we have implemented our queue in a wrap-around manner. For the same reasons, we continue to employ wrap-around approach(circular buffer) on the selected array[43] to realize deque.

Assume that we have a 10-element array to realize a deque of characters. Assume the array is initially empty. Now, assume that we have added six elements to it by calling insertRear() function and passing A, then B, C, D, E, and then F as its arguments.

0	1	2	3	4	5	6	7	8	9
A	B	C	D	E	F				

Front=9
Rear=5

After this, we have called removeFront()function three times. Then the queue status is shown below.

0	1	2	3	4	5	6	7	8	9
A	B	C	D	E	F				
3		front	3						

Front=2
Rear=5

To use all available array space, a circular buffer (wrap-around) to its other end if needed. Suppose the client calls removeFront on D, then calls insertRear() six more times, adding G, H, I, J, K, and L. The deque's state is now becomes:

0	1	2	3	4	5	6	7	8	9
K	L			E	F	G	H	I	J

Front=3
Rear=1

We want wrapping to occur in both directions. Suppose the queue is currently having D-F in indexes 3-5, and we have called insertFront() five more times to add M, N, O, P, and Q. The deque's state will be:

0	1	2	3	4	5	6	7	8	9
O	n	M	D	E	F			Q	P

Front=7
Rear=5

Assume that we have inserted 'R' at the front by insertFront(). The queue status becomes as shown in the following figure.

0	1	2	3	4	5	6	7	8	9
O	N	M	D	E	F		R	Q	P

Front=6
Rear=5

Can we insert one more element either at the front or rear? No. We want to take this situation as the deque full condition. We want this to raise as an error. Do remember we have followed the same approach in our queue implementation.

43 https://courses.cs.washington.edu/courses/cse373/13wi/homework/3/spec.pdf

Assume that we want to remove all the elements from front by calling removeFront(). That is, R, Q, P, O, N, M, D, E, F to be removed in the order. After that front value and rear values are as shown below and now deque is empty.

0	1	2	3	4	5	6	7	8	9
O	N	M	D	E	F		R	Q	P

Front=5
Rear=5

Instead, if we call removeRear() and remove F, E, D, M, N, O, P, Q, R then front and rear values will be as shown below.

0	1	2	3	4	5	6	7	8	9
O	N	M	D	E	F		R	Q	P

Front=5
Rear=5

Do remember that when we say we are removing, we are simply adjusting Front, Rear values; we are not clearing the array element values. OK.

Example 9: The following code is our implementation of deque.

```
#define sz 10
struct queue{
        char a[sz];

        int front;
        int rear;
};

void INITQUEUE(struct queue *A){
        A->rear=sz-1;
        A->front=sz-1;
}
int isempty(struct queue *A){
        return  (A->rear == A->front);
}
int isfull(struct queue *A){
        return (A->front == A->rear);
}
void insertRear(struct queue *A, char v){
        A->rear=(A->rear+1)%sz;
        if(isfull(A)){
                printf("Queue full\n");
                exit(-1);
        }
  A->a[A->rear]=v;
}

char removeFront(struct queue *A){
        if(isempty(A)){
                printf("Queue Empty\n");
                exit(-1);
                }
        A->front=(A->front+1)%sz;
                return ( A->a[A->front]);
}
```

```
void insertFront(struct queue *A, char v){
        int l=A->front;
        if(A->front==0)A->front=sz-1;
        else A->front--;
        if(isfull(A)){
                printf("Queue full\n");
                exit(-1);
        }
        A->a[l]=v;
}

char removeRear(struct queue *A){
char v;
        if(isempty(A)){
                printf("Queue Empty\n");
                exit(-1);
                }
                v=A->a[A->rear];
                if(A->rear==0)A->rear=sz-1;
                else A->rear--;
                return(v);
}

int main(){
        struct queue A, *p;
        char x[20]="ramanaao";
        int i;
        p=&A;
        INITQUEUE(p);
        insertRear(p,'r');
        insertRear(p,'a');
        insertRear(p,'m');
        insertFront(p,'r');
        insertFront(p,'a');
        insertFront(p,'m');

        while(!isempty(p)) printf("%c",  removeFront(p) );
        removeFront(p);
        for(i=0; x[i]!='\0';  i++) {
        insertRear(p,x[i]);
        insertFront(p,x[i]);
        }
        printf("Output from the queue\n");
        while(!isempty(p)) printf("%c",  removeFront(p) );
        return(0);
}
```

We have made a solution and it is made available at the following link. Explore the same.
https://tinyurl.com/AICTEDSBOOK26

Question 32: You have to implement a deque that is growable. First, assume you are using a dynamic array that is created through malloc() to realize deque. Initially it will be having some size. If the deque becomes full, first create another dynamic array with malloc() whose size is twice the size of the current array. Then, copy the current array content into the newly created. Do remember that one cannot simply copy the contents such that ith element of the old array will become the ith element in the new array, because of the wrapping that affects Front and Rear values a lot. If we start from the 10-element array just shown below.

0	1	2	3	4	5	6	7	8	9
O	P	O	N	M	D		F	R	S

Front=6
Rear=5

You have observed that the deque is full. Now, we create a new array as shown below and copy elements and adjust Front and Rear values as shown below.

0	1	2	3	4	5	6	7	8	9	10	11	12	13	14	15	16	17	18	19
O	P	O	N	M	D												F	R	S

Front=16
Rear=5

Modify the above deque implementation of ours so as to accommodate this enlarging concept.

Question 33: Assume that we want to realize deque using the same circular array concept. The following things are proposed as the changes to front and rear whose initial values are taken as sz-1 where sz is the size of the zero indexed array.

```
removeFront: front = (front + 1) % sz
removeRear: No change to front
insertRear: rear = (front + sz) % sz
insertFront: rear = (front – 1 + sz) % sz
```

Are they going to give correct deque implementation?

Question 34: Assume that we want to implement a deque using the following structure where we are using number elements in the deque as an argument instead of rear.

```
#define sz 10
struct queue{
        char a[sz];
        int front;  //front of the queue
        int nelms;  //number of elements in the deque
};
```

We have provided below (see the link below) one cooked up program for implementing the deque using the above structure. Explore its working in relation to our previous solution above. Identify the advantage of this over the above if any advantage is existing.

https://tinyurl.com/AICTEDSBOOK32

2.2.4 Circular Queues for Round-Robin Scheduling

See the figure (Fig. 2.21) having traffic signals at a four road junction. Here, traffic lights will be controlling the traffic using circular fashion or round robin fashion. Maybe, green light will be issued for north bound traffic, then west bound, south bound, and east bound traffic in a cyclic manner. This is a good example for round robin scheduling.

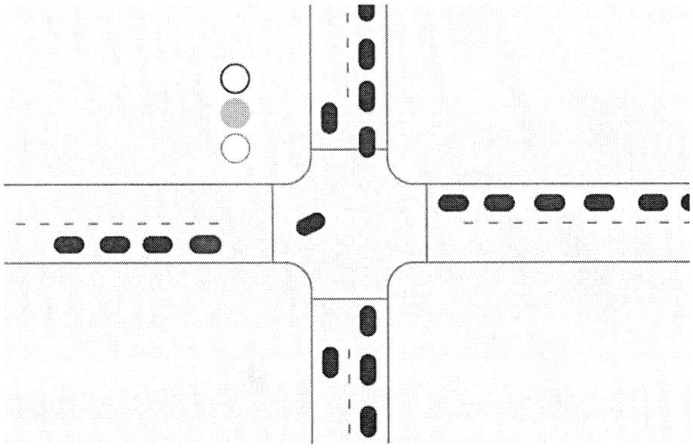

Fig. 2.21: Traffic lights at a four road junction

A program under execution is called a **process.** In order to **run** or **execute** a process, it needs CPU (central processing unit or simply processor). Scheduler of operating systems decides to which process the CPU has to be attached. When a CPU is attached to a process, it(process) is said to be in running state. The processes that are waiting for the scheduler's attention (or service) are in the **ready queue.** When a process is running, it (process) may ask the OS for some resource(such as printer or plotter) which makes the scheduler put this process in another queue known as **waiting queue.** Thus, queues are used in many SW systems in addition to operating systems, compilers, network monitors. The following picture (Fig. 2.22) shows how processes changes their states in an operating system.

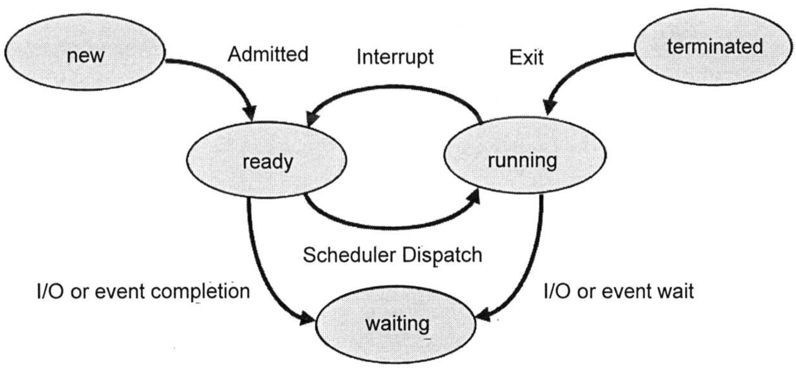

Fig. 2.22: Ready Queue, Waiting Queue in operating systems

Courtesy: https://www.researchgate.net/figure/Process-state-transition-diagram_fig3_332546783 Last Accessed: 15th Aug 2022

As mentioned above, in a multitasking operating system, the available CPU time is shared between competing processes. In order to run or execute, CPU has to be given to a program. On uni-processor machines, at any given instant of time, only one process is running, all the others are in 'sleeping' or waiting state. The CPU allocation/deallocation is administered by the scheduler. The scheduler keeps all the current processes in a queue(ready queue) with the active process at the front of the queue (Fig. 2.23).

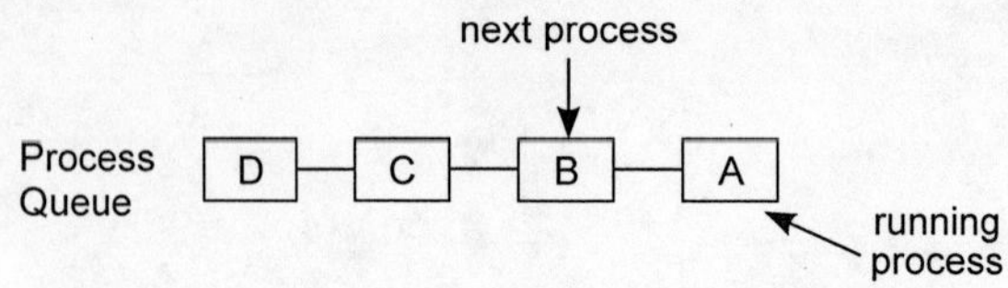

Fig. 2.23: Ready queue

In Round-Robin Scheduling, every process is granted a specific amount of CPU time called the time slice or time 'quantum'. That is, for that duration of the time, CPU is allocated for that process. If the process is still not completed even after its allocated time quantum, it is suspended and put towards the end of the queue[44]. See the following figure (Fig. 2.24). Assume that process "A" is selected by the scheduler for execution and it runs for a given amount of time slice then it will be suspended if not completed) and kept at the end of the ready queue then the next process in the ready queue, that is "B" is selected for execution. Thus, processes may change their states ready, running, ready. Also, they may change their states ready, running, waiting, ready.

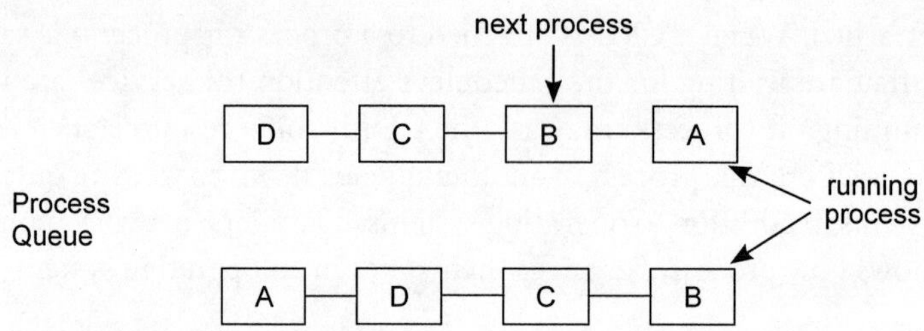

Fig. 2.24: Scheduling processes in round robin fashion

We can implement a round robin scheduler using a queue, Q. That is, the current process that is at the head will be allocated a time slot, after its expiry this process will be put at the rear of the queue. The same can be represented as: (Fig. 2.25):

1. e = remove()
2. Run e for the duration equivalent to time quantum.
3. Insert the process.

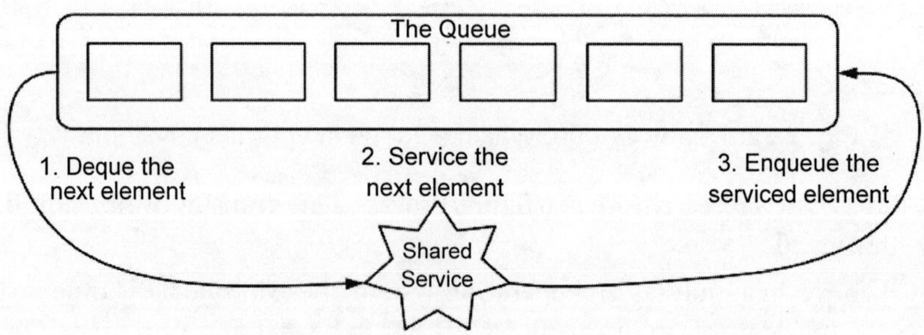

Fig. 2.25: Operations on a ready queue

44 This is known as context switching in operating systems terminology. Of course, context switching may take place because of many reasons.

In fact, current Unix/Linux uses priority oriented round robin scheduling where the processes will be having some priority which may even change with time and the number of time slices it has already consumed. That is, in the ready queue processes may be maintained in some order; which indirectly indicates removal, insertion of the processes into such a queue may not be necessarily at front or rear always. More discussion on this theme is beyond the scope of the book.

Question 35: Algebraic expression to call a function of two variables "X" and "Y" which is the sum operators "+" and the product "." and as delimiters to parentheses "(" and ")". Write a program which reads an algebraic expression and values for X and Y then evaluates the expression for the given values of X and Y.

Examples:

If the expression is: XYX + X + Y + Y.Y and X = 1 and Y = 2, the evaluation result is 9.

If the expression is: (Y + (X + YX)). X + X + YY and X = 3 and Y = 1 then the evaluation result is 25.

The input format has to be the algebraic expression and the values of X and Y prepended with a slash "\":

Example Inputs:

Y.Y XYX + X + + Y \ 1 \ 2

(Y + (X + YX)). X + X + YY \ 3 \ 5

X + Y \ 10 \ 11

Question 36: Translate and evaluate an expression using the following specifications.

(Source: Data Structures, Assignment 3, April 13, 2001, The University of Texas at San Antonio)

- The input source will be made up of the following elements:
- single-digit integer constants, 0, 1, 2, 3, 4, 5, 6, 7, 8, or 9.
- single-letter variables, like a or X.
- operators: , * /, +, or - ,= .
- parentheses: '(' and ')'.
- the special symbols: # to terminate the whole input (and ; to terminate an expression).

To make things easier you are allowed to assume operands as single-digits or single alphabetic characters in any case. As usual all whitespace (space, newline, tab, etc.) should be ignored while processing the input. Always, assume the given input will terminate with a '#'; also you need to output a '#' after your processing results.

While converting the infix expression to postfix expression the following operator associativity and precedence has to be used. Certainly this is not too different from our discussions with the exception of extra operators to be considered in this assignment.

Operator	Precedence	Associativity
∧	5	R
*	4	L
/	4	L
+	3	L
-	3	L
=	2	R
(	1	R
)	1	R

For example, assume that we want to compute one root of the quadratic equation $y=x^2+3x+2$. We know a=1, b=3, c=2 are the coefficients of the quadratic equation in a casual Mathematical sense. We also know that one of the root is

$$\frac{\sqrt{b^2-4ac}-b}{2a}$$ which can be also written as ((b^2 - 4*a*c)^(1/2) - b)/(2*a).

Your program has to do two things. First it has to convert the expression into postfix. Always, assume that all the variables of an expression will be specified in advance before the expression. Of course, users may directly give expressions with only digits, no variables. For example, if the following is the input ending with a '#' character:

a=1; b=3; c=2; ((b^2 - 4*a*c)^(1/2) - b)/(2*a)#

After the first step, we have to get the following expression as output:

a1=b3=c2=b2^4a*c*-12/^b-2a*/#.

The final value to be outputted as:

0.50000#

Do remember that the arithmetic should be carried in double precision. The output should be also in double precision.You may use the function pow(x, y) of the math library.

One more sample input for reasons of understanding of the problem is given below.

```
a = 1; b = –3; c = 2;
d = (b^2 – 4*a*c)^(1/2);
r = (0 – b + d)/(2*a);
s = (0 – b - d)/(2*a);
r; s;#
```

For the above input, the final result is:

-2.0000 -1.0000#

The intermediate reverse Polish form would be:

a1=b03-=c2=db2^4a*c*-12/^=r0b-d+2a*/=s0b-d-2a*/=rs#

Develop a program for the above specified problem.

Question 37: Assume that we want one more nonrecursive algorithm to check whether a given string is palindrome or not. Traverse the given string from till you encounter a null character, insert each character into both a queue and a stack. Now compare the characters at the front of the queue and the top of the stack. If both of them are the same then pop a character from the stack and remove one character from the queue; otherwise declare the given string is not a palindrome. If either stack or queue are empty, declare the given string as palindrome.

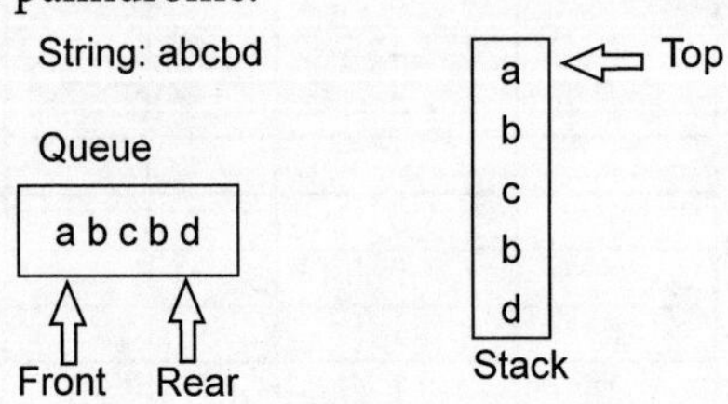

What is the complexity of this approach in relation to an iterative solution whose code is given below?.

https://tinyurl.com/THANKYOUVASU2

https://tinyurl.com/THANKYOUVASU1

Question 38: Implement a decimal to binary conversion algorithm with the following pseudocode as inspiration.

```
Read (number)
Loop (number > 0)
   1) digit = number modulo 2
   2) print (digit)
   3) number = number / 2
```

If you observe the pseudocode, you will find that it will be giving binary digits of the **number backwards**. (ex: if the number value is 19, we get 11001 instead of 10011). To remedy this problem, instead of printing the digit right away, we will push it into a stack. At the end, we pop the digit out of the stack and print it till the stack is empty. Maybe, the following pseudocode may be of use while developing your code.

```
Read(number)
stack s
Loop(number>0):
        digit=number%2
        push digit to stack s
        number=number/2

Loop(! stack is empty):
        pop an item from s and print
```

Note: Linked list implementation of stacks and queues are discussed in the forthcoming chapters.

EXERCISES

Multiple Choice Questions

1. Stacks can be realized using
   (a) Arrays (b) Linked lists
   (c) Both a & b (d) None
2. Stack is also called as
   (a) MEMO (b) FIFO
   (c) LIFO (d) none
3. Postfix equivalent of 2+3*4
   (a) 3*4+2 (b) 2+*34
   (c) 234*+ (d) None
4. Prefix equivalent of 2+3*4
   (a) 3*4+2 (b) 234*+
   (c) +2*34 (d) None

5. In evaluating a postfix expression using a stack, the stack is called as
   (a) Program stack (b) LIFO
   (c) Operand stack (d) Operator stack
6. While converting an infix expression to a postfix expression using a stack, the stack is called as
   (a) Program stack (b) LIFO
   (c) Operator stack (c) Operand stack
7. While executing program with functions, compiler uses the stack which is called as
   (a) operand stack (b) LIFO
   (c) program stack (d) Operator stack
8. Assume that we have a series of n number of character stacks. We take a string and push all the characters of the string from beginning to till null ('\0', excluding null) are pushed into the first stack of the chain of stacks. Then, we go on pop() from the first stack and push to the next stack of the chain of stacks. This, we repeat for each of the stacks except the last stack. Whatever we get from the last stack when we apply pop() operations and simply display the popped characters from it. Assume none gives any overflow errors. If we are getting the original string then n is
   (a) 1 (b) Even
   (c) Odd (d) None
9. Assume that we have a series of n (even) numbers of character stacks and queues (that is stack, queue, stack, queue, and vice versa). We take a string and push all the characters of the string from beginning to till null ('\0', excluding null) are pushed into the first stack of the chain of stacks. Then, we go on pop() from the first stack and insert to the next available queue. This, we repeat for each of the stacks/queues except the last stack/queue. Whatever we get from the last stack/queue when we apply pop()/remove operations, we simply display the popped/removed characters from it. Assume none gives any overflow errors. What do we get on the screen?
   (a) Given string itself (b) Reverse of the given string
   (c) A series of characters (d) None
10. Assume that we have a series of n (n is divisible with 3) numbers of character stacks and queues (that is stack, queue, queue, stack, queue, queue, and vice versa). We take a string and push all the characters of the string from beginning to till null ('\0', excluding null) are pushed into the first stack of the chain of stacks. Then, we go on pop() from the first stack and insert to the next available queue. This, we repeat for each of the stacks/queues except the last stack/queue. Whatever we get from the last stack/queue when we apply pop()/remove operations, we simply display the popped/removed characters from it. Assume none gives any overflow errors. What do we get on the screen?
    (a) Given string itself (b) Reverse of the given string
    (c) A series of characters (d) None
11. Queue is also called as
    (a) MEMO (b) FIFO
    (c) LIFO (d) None
12. The ADT which can be used both as a stack and queue is
    (a) Circular queue (b) Double stack in a array
    (c) Deque (d) None

13. The ADT which can allows insertion and removal at both the ends is
    (a) Circular queue
    (b) Double stack in a array
    (c) Deque
    (d) Dequeue
14. In our RPN expression evaluation code, we are using 48, why?
    (a) Every author uses this, so
    (b) 48 is ASCII code of symbol 0
    (c) We are using char stack and RPN expression is processed character by character while the operands are considered as single digit operands. To get digit value, we are subtracting 48.
    (d) None
15. Assume that we have an ADT stack of character stacks. Assume A is such a type of variable. Assume both stack of stacks and character stacks are realized using an array. Do we need to take the same size (sz) for both types of stacks?
    (a) Yes
    (b) No
    (c) Not necessary
    (d) I don't know
16. Assume that we have a stack that uses an n element array where n can be an even or odd positive integer. Assume that n/2 push and n/2 pop operations have taken place. Here, order of push or pop operations are not specified and n/2 value is taken in integer mode. Which of the following are invalid statements? We are assuming here that the operations will continue even after underflow or overflow errors also.
    (a) Overflow will never take place.
    (b) Underflow can take place.
    (c) Underflow take place more than once
    (d) Overflow take place guaranteedly
17. Assume that we have a queue that uses an n element array where n can be an even or odd positive integer. Assume that n/2 insert and n/2 remove operations have taken place. Here, order of insert or remove operations are not specified and n/2 value is taken in integer mode. Which of the following are invalid statements? We are assuming here that the operations will continue even after underflow or overflow errors also.
    (a) Overflow will never take place.
    (b) Underflow never takes place.
    (c) rear value will be n/2
    (d) Overflow take place guaranteedly
18. Assume that we have an empty stack which is realised using an array of size 10. The following operations are applied on it in sequence: one pop, two push operations, one pop,four push operations, two pop operations. How many elements are in the stack? We are assuming here that the operations will continue even after underflow or overflow errors also.
    (a) 4
    (b) 3
    (c) 8
    (d) 2
19. Assume that we have an empty stack which is realised using an array of size 10. The following operations are applied on it in sequence: one pop, two push operations, one peek, four push operations, two peek operations. How many elements are in the stack? We are assuming here that the operations will continue even after underflow or overflow errors also.
    (a) 4
    (b) 3
    (c) 6
    (d) 2

20. Assume that we have an empty queue which is realised using an array of size 10. The following operations are applied on it in sequence: one remove, two insert operations, one remove, four insert operations, two remove operations. How many elements are in the queue? We are assuming here that the operations will continue even after underflow or overflow errors also.
    (a) 4 (b) 3
    (c) 8 (d) 2
21. Assume that we have an empty stack which is realised using an array of size 10. The following operations are applied on it in sequence: one pop, two push operations, one pop, four push operations, two pop operations. What is the value of the TOP of the stack assuming the initial value of the TOP is -1? We are assuming here that the operations will continue even after underflow or overflow errors also.
    (a) 4 (b) 3
    (c) 8 (d) 2
22. Assume that we have an empty stack which is realised using an array of size 10. The following operations are applied on it in sequence: one pop, two push operations, one peek, four push operations, two peek operations. What is the value of the TOP of the stack assuming the initial value of the TOP is 10? We are assuming here that the operations will continue even after underflow or overflow errors also.
    (a) 4 (b) 5
    (c) 6 (d) 2
23. Assume that we have an empty stack which is realised using an array of size 10. The following operations are applied on it in sequence: one pop, two push operations, one pop, four push operations, two pop operations. What is the value of the TOP of the stack assuming the initial value of the TOP is 10? We are assuming here that the operations will continue even after underflow or overflow errors also.
    (a) 4 (b) 3
    (c) 8 (d) 5
24. Assume that we have an empty stack which is realised using an array of size 10. The following operations are applied on it in sequence: one pop, two push operations, one peek, four push operations, two peek operations. What is the value of the TOP of the stack assuming the initial value of the TOP is -1? We are assuming here that the operations will continue even after underflow or overflow errors also.
    (a) 4 (b) 5
    (c) 6 (d) 2
25. Assume that we have an empty queue which is realised using an array of size 10. The following operations are applied on it in sequence: one remove, two insert operations, one remove, four insert operations, two remove operations. What is the value of the front of the queue assuming the initial value of the front is -1, rear is -1? We are assuming here that the operations will continue even after underflow or overflow errors also.
    (a) 4 (b) 3
    (c) 8 (d) 2

ANSWERS															
1.	(c)	2.	(c)	3.	(c)	4.	(c)	5.	(c)	6.	(c)	7.	(c)	8.	(b)
9.	(b)	10.	(b)	11.	(b)	12.	(c)	13.	(c)	14.	(c)	15.	(c)	16.	(d)
17.	(d)	18.	(b)	19.	(c)	20.	(b)	21.	(d)	22.	(b)	23.	(d)	24.	(c)
25.	(d)														

Descriptive Questions

1. Question: Assume that we have used a five element array (zero indexed) for realizing the queue. Also, initial values of Front=-1 and Rear=-1. Assume that the following operations are carried out on the queue one after another.

```
insert(7)
insert(188)
insert(7)
remove()
insert(10)
insert(15)
remove()
```

What is the status of the queue?

Answer:

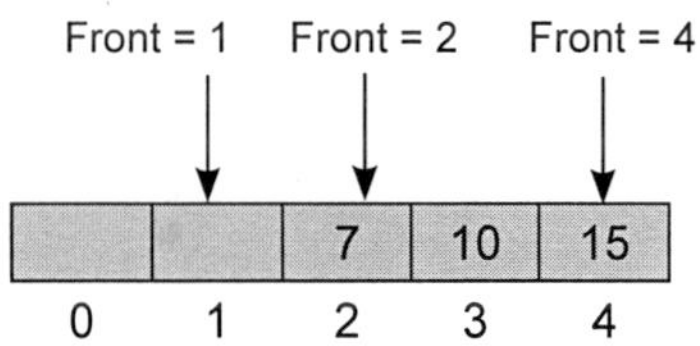

2. See the following implementation of insert function of a queue. What modifications one need to apply if the language uses 1-D arrays with valid array indices starting from 1?

```
FRONT = -1, REAR = -1,  TO REPRESENT QUEUE IS EMPTY
Algorithm INSERT(QUEUE[N],FRONT,REAR,ITEM)
{
//QUEUE  is an array of  size N ,ITEM is element to be inserted.
1. if (REAR == N-1)
        1.1 Print "OVERFLOW"
   else
        1.1 if (FRONT  == -1)
                1.1.1 FRONT = 0
        1.2 REAR = REAR+1
        1.3 QUEUE[REAR] = ITEM
}
```

Answer: See the following figure with modifications.

```
FRONT = -1, REAR = -1 TO REPRESENT QUEUE IS EMPTY
Algorithm INSERT(QUEUE[N],FRONT,REAR,ITEM)
{
//QUEUE is an array of size N ,ITEM is element to be inserted.
1. if (REAR == N-1)
        1.1 Print "OVERFLOW"
   else
        1.1 if (FRONT == -1)
                1.1.1 FRONT = 0
        1.2 REAR = REAR+1
        1.3 QUEUE[REAR] = ITEM
}
```

3. See the following method for removing an element from the queue. Assume FRONT=-1, REAR=-1 initially and the array size is N.

```
Algorithm REMOVE(QUEUE[N],ITEM,FRONT,REAR) {
1. if ( FRONT == - 1 )
       1.1 Print "QUEUE EMPTY"
2. else
       2.1 ITEM = QUEUE[FRONT]
       2.2 FRONT = FRONT +1
}
```

Is it going to work correctly?

Answer: No.

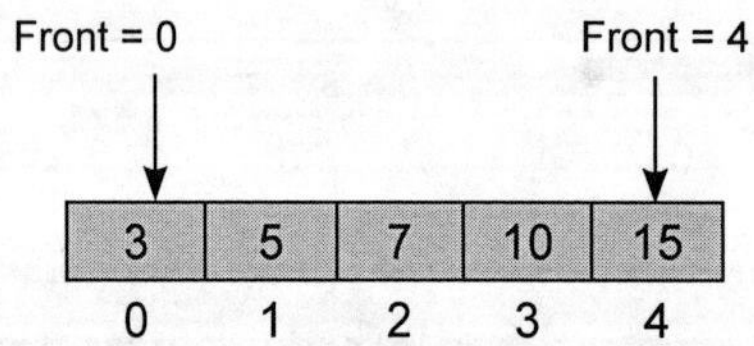

With the above queue, after five calls to the REMOVE() function the given queue becomes empty and if we continue to call REMOVE() we need to get a "QUEUE EMPTY" error which the above code will not give. Similarly, in the following queue also the fourth successive call to the REMOVE() function will not give a "QUEUE EMPTY" message.

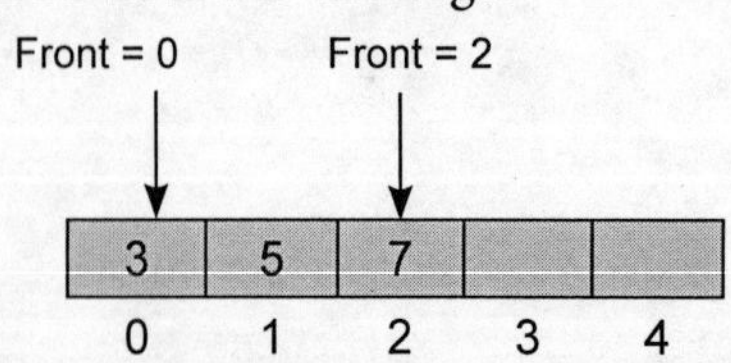

4. See the following implementations of INSERT() and REMOVE() functions to implement a circular queue using an array. Compare this with our solution discussed in the book. (Source: http://ds.nathanielgmartin.com/wk09/W9L1-Queues.pdf Last Accessed: 15th Aug 2022)

```
FRONT = -1, REAR = -1, TO REPRESENT QUEUE IS EMPTY
Algorithm INSERT(QUEUE[N],FRONT,REAR,ITEM){
//QUEUE is an array of size N ,ITEM is an element to be inserted.
1. if ((FRONT == REAR+1) || ((FRONT == 0) && (REAR == N-1)))
   1.1 DISPLAY "QUEUE OVERFLOW"
   1.2 exit
2. else
   2.1 if(FRONT == -1)
         2.1.1 FRONT = 0
         2.1.2 REAR = 0
   2.1 else if ( REAR == N-1 )
         2.1.1 REAR = 0
   2.1 else
         2.1.1 REAR = REAR + 1
2.2 QUEUE[REAR] = ITEM
}

Algorithm REMOVE(QUEUE[N],FRONT,REAR,ITEM){
//QUEUE is an array of size N ,ITEM is element to be inserted.
1. if (FRONT == -1)
   1.1 DISPLAY "QUEUE UNDERFLOW"
2. else
   2.1 ITEM = QUEUE[FRONT]
   2.2 if(FRONT== REAR)
         2.2.1 FRONT = -1
         2.2.2 REAR =-1
         2.2.3 EXIT
   2.2 else if ( FRONT == N-1 )
         2.2.1 FRONT = 0
   2.2.2 EXIT
   2.2 else
         2.4.1 FRONT = FRONT + 1
}
```

5. Compare our realization of deque in the book with the following from http://ds.nathanielgmartin.com/wk09/W9L1-Queues.pdf .

```
Algorithm to Insert / enqueue from rear
FRONT = -1, REAR = -1, TO REPRESENT DEQUEUE IS EMPTY
Algorithm INSERTREAR(QUEUE[N],FRONT,REAR,ITEM){
//QUEUE is an array of size N , ITEM is the element to be inserted.
1. if (REAR == N-1)
      1.1 PRINT "OVERFLOW"
2. Else
      2.1 IF(FRONT==-1)
            2.1.1 FRONT = 0
      2.2. REAR = REAR+1
      2.3 QUEUE[REAR] = ITEM
}
```

```
Algorithm to Insert / enqueue from front
FRONT = -1, REAR = -1, TO REPRESENT DEQUEUE IS EMPTY
Algorithm INSERTFRONT(QUEUE[N],FRONT,REAR,ITEM){
//QUEUE is an array of size N ,ITEM is the element to be inserted.
1. if( FRONT == 0)
        1.1 Print "CAN NOT INSERT"
2. else
        2.1 if (FRONT == -1)
                2.1.1 FRONT = 0
                2.1.2 REAR = 0
        2.1 else
                2.1.1 FRONT = FRONT-1
        2.3 QUEUE[FRONT] = ITEM
}
```

```
Algorithm to Delete / dequeue from front
FRONT = -1, REAR = -1, TO REPRESENT DEQUEUE IS EMPTY
Algorithm DELETE(QUEUE[N],ITEM,FRONT,REAR){
1. if (( FRONT == - 1 ) || (FRONT == REAR+1))
        1.1 Print "QUEUE EMPTY"
2. Else
        2.1 ITEM = QUEUE[FRONT]
        2.2 FRONT = FRONT +1
}
```

```
Algorithm to Delete / dequeue from rear
FRONT = -1, REAR = -1, TO REPRESENT DEQUEUE IS EMPTY
Algorithm DELETE(QUEUE[N],ITEM,FRONT,REAR)
{
1. if (( FRONT == - 1 ) || (FRONT == REAR+1))
        1.1 Print "QUEUE EMPTY"
2. Else
        2.1 ITEM = QUEUE[REAR]
        2.2 REAR = REAR - 1
}
```

6. A deque can be used as either a stack or a queue. Do you think that it is faster or slower in execution time than either a dynamic array stack or a linked list stack? Can you design an exercise to test your hypothesis? In using a Deque as a stack there are two choices; you can either add and remove from the front, or add and remove from the back. Is there a measurable difference in execution time between these two alternatives? (Source: http://web.engr.oregonstate.edu/~sinisa/courses/OSU/CS261/CS261_Textbook/Chapter07.pdf Last Accessed: 15th Aug 2022) Note: You may attempt once the linked lists chapter is read by you.

7. Assume that you want to realize a stack and a queue in an array of size sz(=8) as shown below. That is, the stack is supposed to grow from left to right while the queue grows from right to left. It is possible that sometimes the stack may grow faster while some other times the queue may grow faster. Total available space for both is sz number of elements.

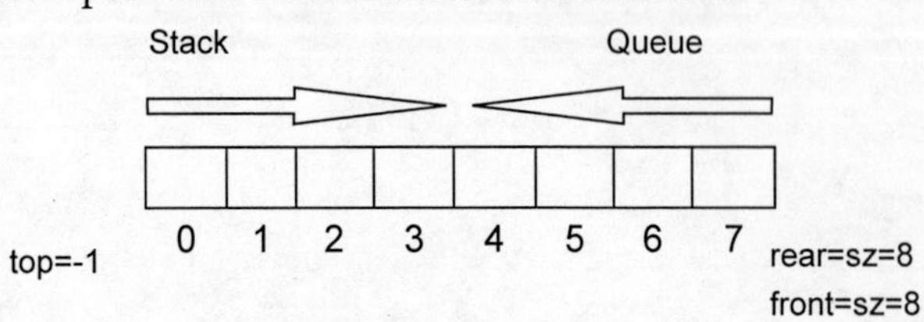

For example, stack is having there elements while queue is having five elements as shown below. There are no free elements available in which case both stack and queue insertion/push operations raise "overflow error".

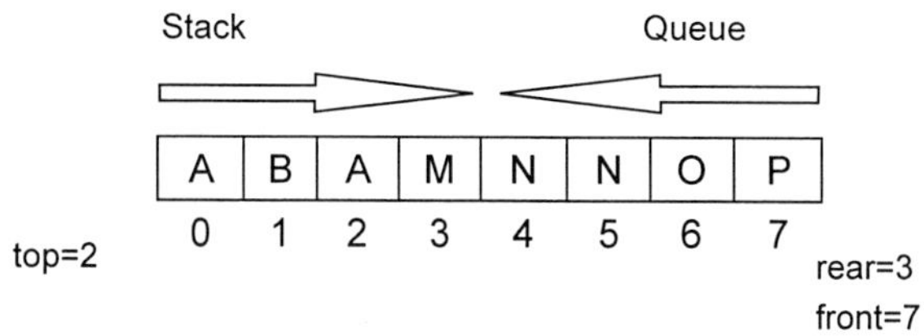

However, consider the following situation in which there are some free elements in the queue.

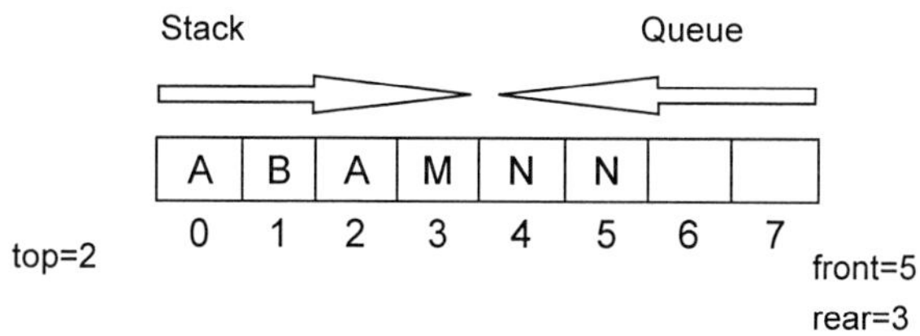

Now, we propose to move the elements towards the right and create space for both stack and queue to grow. This can be done either by operations of stack or queue.

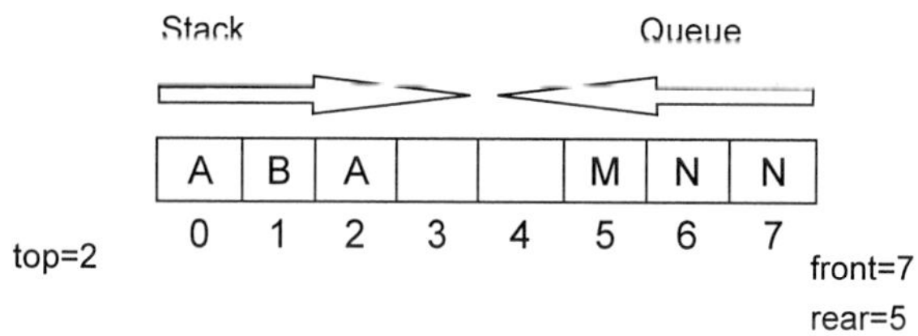

Do remember your design should be such that stack alone can occupy all the sz elements or queue alone can occupy all the sz elements. However, do remember that some free elements are available in the queue at any time then the elements of the queue have to be moved to the right side to create space for further growth of stack/queue.

8. Implement two queues (A & B) in a single array as shown below. Both the queues can occupy the whole array. Also, whenever an "overflow" situation arises, think of moving elements either to left or right to create space to grow.

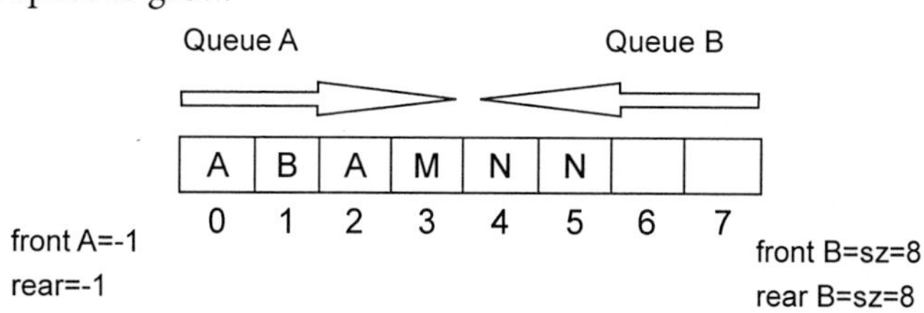

9. Implement two queues (A & B) in a single array as shown below. Both the queues can occupy the whole array. Also, assume both the queues can move their elements to use free spaces.

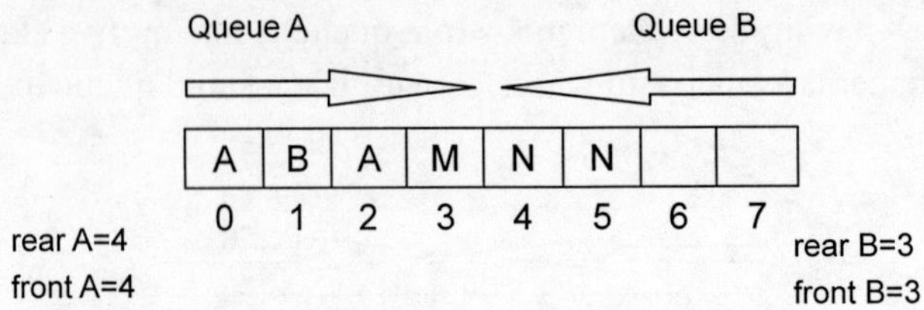

10. Verify whether the following code is working fine to realize a stack or not. Compare this with our original stack implementation. This code is already available on the visualization server at https://tinyurl.com/AICTEDSBOOK34 . You are welcome to test and then compare.

```
#define sz 10
struct stack{
  char a[sz];
  int top;
};
void initstack(struct stack *A){
  A->top=sz;
}

int isEmpty(struct stack *A){
  return (A->top>=sz);
}
void push(struct stack *A, char V){
  if(A->top==0){
        printf("Stack Full\n");
        return;
  }
  else
  A->a[--A->top]=V;
}

char pop(struct stack *A){
  if(isEmpty(A)){
        printf("Sorry. Stack is empty\n");
        return;
  }
  else
  return (A->a[A->top++]);
}
char peek(struct stack *A){
  if(isEmpty(A)){
        printf("Sorry. Stack is empty\n");
        return;
  }
  else
  return (A->a[A->top]);
}

int main() {
  struct stack A,*p;
  int i;
  char x[20]="rama";
  p=&A;
  initstack(p);
  for(i=0;i<4;i++)push(p,x[i]);
  while(!isEmpty(p))
        printf("%c",pop(p));
  return 0;
}
```

11. Write a program that takes a prefix expression and evaluates the expression value. For example, +3*45 should be evaluated as 23. Do remember that the operands in the given prefix expression are single digit operands (0-9). Hint: Process the given prefix expression string from the last character to first character.

12. Polish Notation (Source: https://egr.vcu.edu/media/engineering/documents/cs/VCU_HSContest_2016_Problems.pdf Last Accessed: 15th Aug 2022)

    Computer scientists have a strange way of looking at arithmetic expressions. What a regular person sees as 3+4*5 looks like + 3 * 4 5 to a computer scientist. The former is called the infix notation, while the latter is called the prefix notation, or the Polish notation. In the Polish notation, the operator (e.g. +) comes first, followed by the left-hand side sub-expression, followed by a right-hand side subexpression. Each of the subexpressions again is in the prefix notation. One benefit is that no brackets are needed, they can be inferred: + 3 * 4 5 can be unambiguously understood as + 3 (* 4 5), that is, as 3+(4*5).

    You task is to write a converter from prefix notation to infix notation for expressions that involve numbers in the range 0-9 (that is, every number is a single digit, there won't be numbers such as 123), as well as two binary operators: + and *. The converter should preserve the left-right order, that is, + 3 4 is translated to 3+4 and not to 4+3. To simplify things, every binary operation should be enclosed in brackets: instead of 3+4*5 you should print (3+(4*5)).

    Input A string of length up to 100 characters representing an expression in prefix notation. The string will contain only the following characters: 0123456789+* and each character will be separated from the next by a single white space.

    Output A string representing the expression in infix notation. Do not use any white spaces.

    Sample Input

    + * 3 + + 4 5 6 7

    Sample Output

    ((3*((4+5)+6))+7

Laboratory programming tasks

1. Implement stack using array as explained in this chapter.
2. Implement reverse polish notation(RPN) or postfix expression evaluator.
3. Implement infix to postfix expression converter.
4. Implement double stack in an array.
5. Implement a queue using an array
6. Implement input-restricted deque.
7. Implement output-restricted deque.

Welcome to participate in the online competition

We are hosting a competition so as to encourage students to build their competence in coding. This will be very useful for placements also in the coming years. Thus, welcome students to attempt the competition at the following link.

https://www.hackerrank.com/aictedsbook

Programming puzzles

Some programming puzzles along with their solution around stacks and queues are made available at the following link.

https://docs.google.com/document/d/1oMC1DctCaWYWO9L5hvdTuYQsUczT_RgAgM6_Hk92spM/edit?usp=sharing

REFERENCES

1. Fundamentals of Data Structure in C, Horowitz, Ellis, Sahni, Sartaj, Anderson-Freed, Susan, University Press, India.
2. Data Structures: A Pseudocode approach with C, Richard F. Gilberg, Behrouz A. Forouzan, CENGAGE Learning, India.
3. My class notes on Algorithmic Complexity, now a refresher for craving teachers and knowledge greedy students: A must primer for GATE(India), Adv. GRE appearing students. https://www.amazon.com/dp/B09DJCW78T
4. C and Data Structures, NB Venkateswarlu & EV Prasad, 2010, S Chand & Co, New Delhi
5. http://web.engr.oregonstate.edu/~sinisa/courses/OSU/CS261/CS261_Textbook/Chapter07.pdf
6. https://visualgo.net/en

3 Linked Lists

UNIT COVERAGE

Linked Lists: Singly Linked List, Representation in Memory, Operations on a Single Linked List, Circular Linked Lists, Doubly Linked Lists, Linked List Representation and Operations of Stack, Linked List Representation and Operations of Queue.

OBJECTIVES OF THE UNIT

By the end of this unit, student will be able to:

- describe and use the linked list based stack and queue abstract data types.
- explain single linked lists, circular lists, double linked lists in practical SW development such as operating systems, compilers.
- describe and use single linked lists, doubly linked lists, circular lists.
- explain the relevance of data structures **in operating systems design aspects such as free data blocks management, garbage collection**.
- give typical examples of **null pointer exception** conditions with various linked list based ADTS.

LEARNING OUTCOMES OF THE UNIT

After completing the Unit, the student

- has detailed knowledge of linked list based **stack abstract data type, queue (U3-01).**
- has detailed knowledge of **single linked lists, doubly linked lists, circular lists (U3-02).**
- is familiar with the basic concepts null pointer exception in various **ADTs (U3-03).**
- has detailed knowledge of how linked lists, doubly linked lists, circular lists are used in practical SW systems such as operating systems, networks, etc. **(U3-04).**
- is familiar with processes scheduling in operating systems **(U3-05).**
- **is** familiar with recursive implementations of various operations on single linked lists, circular lists, doubly linked lists.**(U3-06).**
- has knowledge of implementing multiply linked lists which contains more than two links **(U3-07).**

Unit-3 Outcomes	EXPECTED MAPPING WITH COURSE OUTCOMES (1- Weak Correlation; 2- Medium correlation; 3- Strong Correlation)				
	CO-1	CO-2	CO-3	CO-4	CO-5
U3-O1	3	3		-	
U3-O2	3	3			
U3-O3		1			
U3-O4		1			
U3-O5	1	1			
U3-06		1			
U3-07		1			

3.1 LINKED LISTS

Why do we need linked lists?

Let us assume that you are asked to write a program that takes ID numbers of people who are visiting a busy airport. Maybe, you can assume that the airport has only one way!.

Fig. 3.1: One of the busiest airport Chek Lap Kok (Hongkong)
(Source: https://www.frommers.com/slideshows/820279-the-10-best-business-friendly-airports
Last Accessed: 1st Sep 2022)

An immediate idea people usually get is using an array (either static or dynamic through malloc). We are sure you are all aware that either to declare a static array or to create a dynamic array, one needs to supply the required number of elements of the array. Of course, we want to store one visitor ID in one element of the array. To do this, we need to know how many visitors are going to visit the airport today(see Fig. 3.1). Oh. my God. Does anyone know this in advance to either declare or create an array? **Not at all.** Today, maybe 100000 people may visit the airport, tomorrow 120202 people may visit. Thus, an **array based solution** is not an apt one in this problem. That is, the number of people who visit the airport is a **dynamic quantity**. It may vary from day to day. Whereas an array based solution tries to solve using a statically sized(fixed sizes) array. Somedays, it (array) may be sufficient to store visitors IDs while on some other days it may not be sufficient to store visitors IDs. This is where **linked list** based solutions rescue us. They can **grow** to any extent and they can **shrink** to any extent also. Thus, **we can say that linked list based solutions are vital in solving dynamic systems.**

Linked Lists

The data structure singly linked list consists a sequence of data records[45] (not physically in memory but logically) with a data member whose value can be an address or reference (i.e., a link) to the next record in the sequence (see Fig. 3.2).

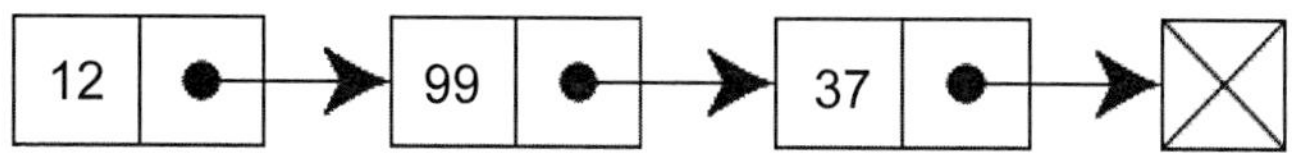

Fig. 3.2: A Sample linked list with an integer and a link to the next node as its members (source www.wikipedia.com Last Accessed: 1st Sep 2022)

We have a variety of linked lists known as single linked lists (as shown above in Fig.3.2), circular lists (Fig. 3.3), and double linked lists (Fig. 3.4).

Circular lists

In a single linked list, the last node of a list will be a null[46] link[47] field; a special value that is interpreted by programs as "there is no such node/records/elements or no more nodes further". Instead of null in the last node, we let it point to the first node of the list; thus the list is said to be **circular** or **circularly linked**[48]. Without this link to the first node, the list is said to be open or linear (see Fig. 3.3).

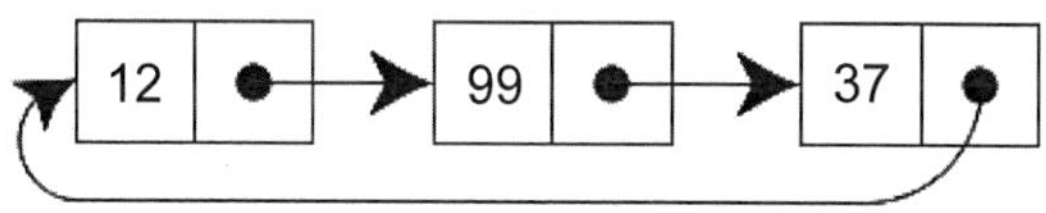

Fig. 3.3: A circular linked list (source www.wikidpedia.com Last Accessed: 1st Sep 2022)

Doubly linked lists

Unlike a single linked list, in a **doubly-linked list**, each node/record contains two links; one to the next-node in the sequence, the other to the *previous* node in the sequence (see Fig. 3.4). These two links may also be referred to **forward(s)** and **backward(s)** respectively.

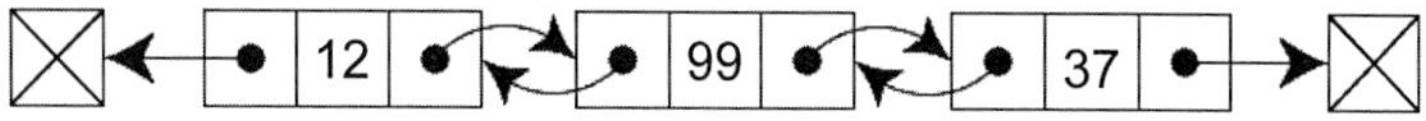

Fig. 3.4: A doubly-linked list with an integer, the link to the next node, and the link to the previous node (www.wikepedia.com Last Accessed: 1st Sep 2022)

45 also referred to nodes or elements

46 null has different meanings. Please refer to the following for more understanding. However, we follow to use 0 as null in our book. https://stackoverflow.com/questions/1296843/what-is-the-difference-between-null-0-and-0 ,https://www.open-std.org/JTC1/SC22/WG14/www/docs/n1124.pdf

47 null link means it is not pointing to any more record/node/element

48 it is also referred to closed list

If the nodes of the sequences are designed to be having more than two or more links they are called **multiply-linked list** as **multiply-linked list,**

Treasure hunt: A lively example

Fig. 3.5: A simple treasure hunt box

(Source: https://www.wikihow.com/Make-a-Treasure-Hunt Last Accessed: 1st Sep 2022)

Linked list is more similar to a treasure hunt game(Fig. 3.5) that is organized in schools or in some kitty parties. You will find a **clue** for the next one. That next one will be having a clue for the following one, and vice versa Here, the clue can be considered as the **link** of the linked list.

The following is the problem statement of a problem that appeared in the Australian Bebras competition.

Secret Recipe (Australia, Bebras, 2017)

(Source: https://www.bebras.edu.au/wp-content/uploads/2018/01/2017_Bebras_Solution_Guide_AU.pdf Last Accessed: 1st Sep 2022)

Assume that you are asked to cook a special cake made of five ingredients out of the ones that are placed in the garden. For some items, you will find labels which convey which is the next ingredient to be added. Here, labels are the links with which you will identify the next ingredient to be added to the cake. By the way, what is data here? Data are the ingredients.

Question 1: Which ingredient should be added first?

Answer: B

All the five ingredients in the right order gets added if we start with the flower. Of course, the first added ingredient will be the one with no label. If you choose the strawberry, you can not select any more ingredients as there is no label along with it. If you start with the apple, you will be missing the red flower. If you would have started with the pine cone, you would be skipping the apple and red flower. Like this, to reach one goal there will be hints (clues or links) to the next goal.

Here, the linked list is the recipe. The ingredients are the node's data items with the label being the pointer to the valid next item of the recipe. The first ingredient is that ingredient with a label and is not referred to by any label

The following is a link to an online treasure hunt game. My request to teachers is to encourage children to play this game.

https://brainchase.com/the-treasure-hunt/

The following link contains a GPS treasure hunt that is spread across the world.

https://www.nationalgeographic.com/travel/article/gps_treasure_hunting#:~:text=So%20why%20not%20try%20taking,located%20all%20over%20the%20world.

We welcome teachers to have a glance at the following videos that explain about linked lists.

https://www.youtube.com/watch?v=-3G-K51h2oA

https://www.youtube.com/watch?v=Ujf9q3mbjrY&t=61s

The following link contains a linked list visualization tool.

https://visualgo.net/en/list

Wow. A train is nothing but a Linked List!!

Fig. 3.6: Two train coaches along with their couplings

Let us take one real life example which is none other than trains (both passenger and goods trains). If you see the above picture(Fig. 3.6) you will find two coaches are connected to each other (by a special thing known as coupler which we can consider as our link which connects a node with another node of our SW linked list)[49]. In reality a train is formed by an engine (an electric engine or loco engine), a series of coaches connected one after another and at the end a special coach known as Guard's coach. Here, engine and Guard coaches are different from normal coaches. We may also have some special coaches such as Railway Mail Service coaches, refreshment coaches(pantry coach), etc., on the trains. Also, in the case of goods trains we may have special types of coaches such as open type or closed type, A/C type to carry perishable goods, water tankers, oil tankers, special units to ship cars/vehicles etc. Many operations are possible on trains(or goods trains), we can remove the engine, we can add new coaches either at the end or at the front, we can break a train into two small trains, etc. In the same fashion, we may find operations on linked lists also. BTW, in this example point of view, which is the data? Here, data is nothing but people who will be transported in passenger coaches or items that are transported in good vagons.

Humanity cherish for long

Fig. 3.7: Blind people crossing the road one after another with the help of a volunteer.

Let us have one more example that has a closest analogy with linked lists. We are sure you might have seen a group of blind people crossing a road or walking on the road with the help of a person. Sometimes, a trained dog will also help the group of blind to walk. See the picture Fig. 3.7. Who is head here? The starting person who is incidentally not blind. Who are coaches (or data) here? The blind people who formed as a chain (one after another see Fig. 3.7). Which is the link here? One blind person's on the shoulder of a blind person before him is the link.

A necklace(see Fig. 3.8) can be also considered as akin to a linked list. If we don't like that blue jewel anymore, we can remove it from the sequence and tie the resulting two ends together.

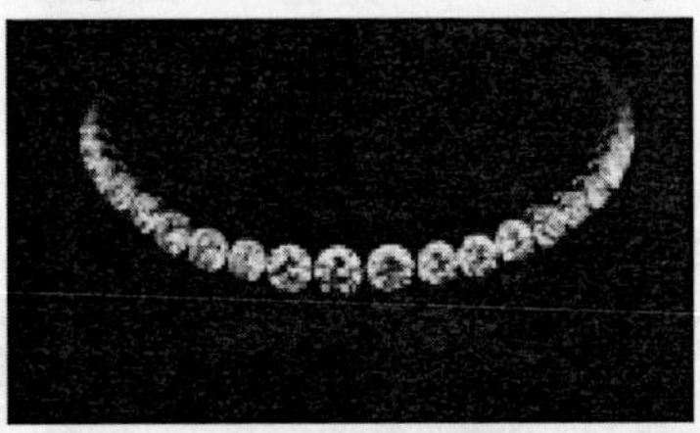

Fig. 3.8: A necklace

Source: iStock.com Last Accessed: 1st Sep 2022

49 In terms of programming, one may consider the coach body as the data (value) node and coupler (connector) as a reference pointer.

A roller chain is also another marvelous example to links. Also, a cycle chain is another one (see Fig. 3.9).

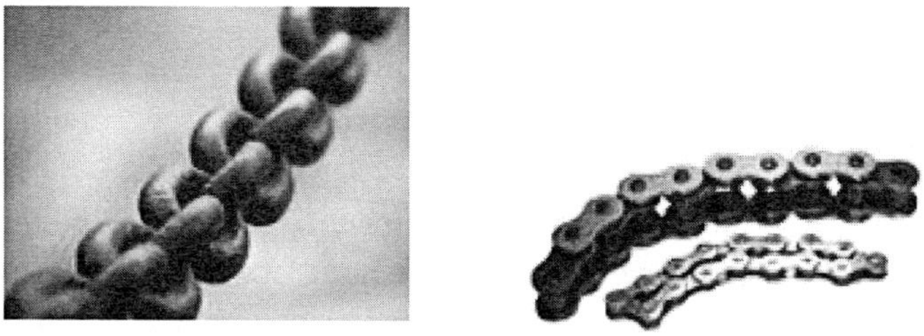

Fig. 3.9: Practical links of our daily life

We all know that each of the chain parts is connected to two chains as shown above. We can break any spoiled chain and insert a new one easily.

Want to be a 21st century Sherlock Holmes?

Let us take one more example. When a crime takes place, police will start their investigations from some number of suspects. They will get clues from these investigations about the real culprits. BTW, have you read Sherlock Holmes novels? Wow. They are mostly around criminals and clues!. Nowadays, phone call data is also helping police officers to catch the criminal. Ofcourse, sometimes criminals are more sophisticated than police; while some other times they are innocent enough to leave clues. Think, here in this example where are the links and what is data?

Document registration

Also, we would like to share one more practical example that uses the concept of link and of course the example may be specific to India. Say, you want to take a loan from a Bank by pledging your property. Bank people ask the registered document or sale deed of the property in addition to all link documents. That is, from whom I have purchased, from whom that person(my seller) has purchased, and vice versa. Every document will have its associated link document number. That is, my registered document(a set of printed pages) contains the document number of my seller. If I get a copy of my seller's document from that number, it contains the document number of his seller, and vice versa. Here, document numbers that are maintained in the registry are linked.

URL

Let us bring another lively example which we presume that the majority of people know. That is, none other than WWW(world wide web) which is a collection of hyper documents. A hyper document contains some text, images, videos, sound, along with hyper links such as the link http://bit.ly/BEBRASTELUGUBOOK. We see hyperlinks or Uniform Resource Locators (URL's) in web pages. If we click on one URL, then the page pointed by that URL will be displayed. That URL may have some more links, which may be pointing to other pages on the Internet. Thus, we use links very commonly in our daily life. BTW, is WWW is SW or HW? Oh. Yes. It is SW. What is the Internet? Yes. Yes. I know, you know it. Yes. It is HW.

Index pages of a book

To have a real feeling of what is meant by links, let us recollect some practical applications. Consider index pages of any book like ours. Index pages contain the most important key words of the book and in which pages they are used. If we are in a hurry to know about a topic which is not listed in the content pages, we often open index pages and then find the pages where that topic would have been discussed. Thus, we can say that keywords and the page numbers associated with them can be considered as links.

Consider another situation. Let us consider we are reading a book and authors have referred to another book for more details about a concept. To know more, we will try to get that book and read. Probably, that second book might refer to another book or journal. That is, the first book is referring to the second book; the second book may be referring to the third, and vice versa. Like this, in real life also, we may use links commonly.

Files & Directories

Let us also consider another practical example which is related to storing files/directories in secondary memory devices such as hard disks. Smallest addressable entity in secondary memory devices such as hard disks is usually called a **block** (physical **block**) or a **cluster** (a group of sectors is called a block).

There are various data block allocation policies for storing files. One such approach is called **linked allocation**, which is of course a very very old one. Here, files (we mean a file's content) are stored as linked lists, with the expense of the storage space consumed by each link. Assume that block size 512 and **block addresses are 4 bytes**. That is, any data block number is 4 bytes long. For example, a file size 1500 bytes and data blocks 50, 56 and 57 are allocated to store these 1500 bytes. That is, in the data block 50, 508 bytes of the file is stored and then the next file data block number (i.e., 56) is stored in the remaining four bytes of the block 56. This is carried for the remaining blocks of the file also (see Fig. 310.).

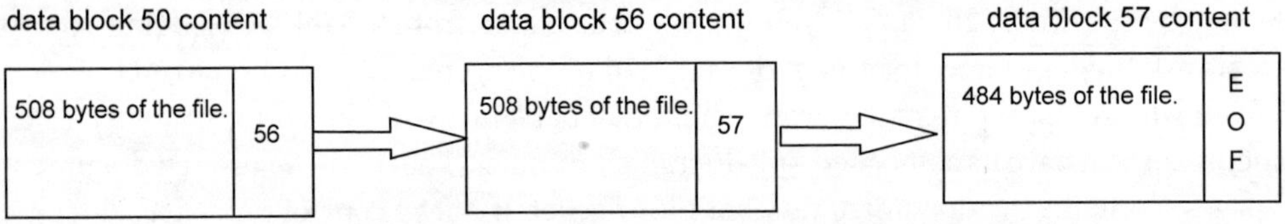

Fig. 3.10: How a file is stored in linked allocation method

This can be also shown with the following figure Fig. 3.11 in disk point of view.

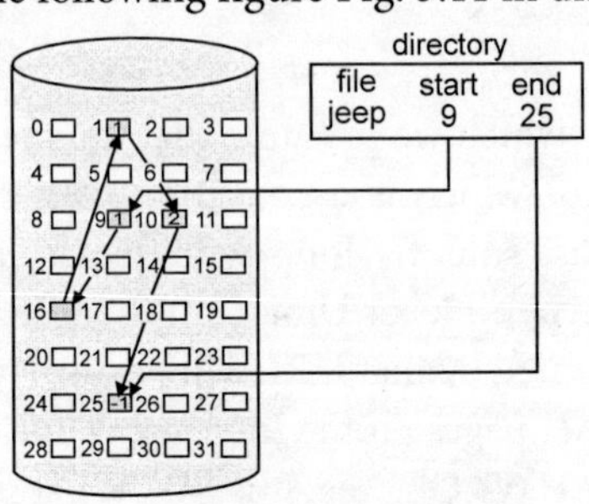

Fig. 3.11: Linked allocation

(Source: https://www.cs.uic.edu/~jbell/CourseNotes/OperatingSystems/12_FileSystemImplementation.html Last Accessed: 17th Aug 2022)

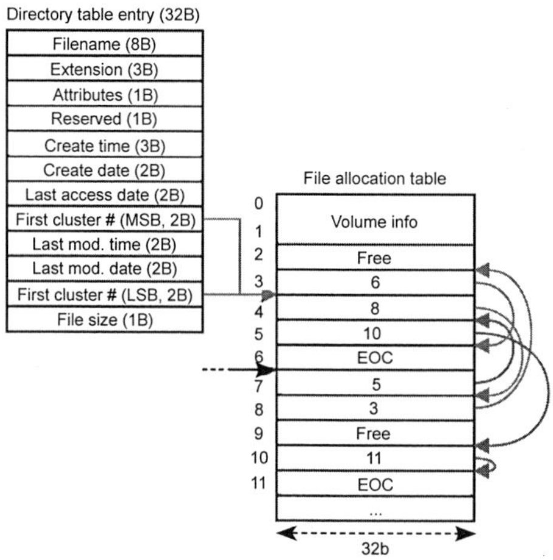

Fig. 3.12: How a file blocks are linked

Whenever we save a new file in the disk, a group of free blocks[50] (or clusters) and in them file content will be saved. Also, that file's first cluster is saved or added to the directory in which the file is located. In the following figure, we have details of a directory and associated **FAT**(file allocation table). FAT is used in **DOS**[51] based file systems. For example, if the first cluster/block number is 4 in which file content is available then we can find remaining data blocks in which file content is available can be found using FAT as shown below. Next data block is 8, the next data block is 3, and the next data block is 6. That is, the file content is available in data blocks (clusters) 4,8,3, and 6. **Did you observe links here?.** Similarly, if a file is starting from the 7th cluster then the following data blocks are 5, 10, 11(see Fig. 3.12) in which file content is available .

Free-Space Management is an important aspect of disk management that keeps track of free space and allocates free data blocks whenever needed. There are many methods in realizing the same. One of them is using a Linked List. The FAT table shown in figure 3.13 displays how a free data blocks list is maintained as a linked list.

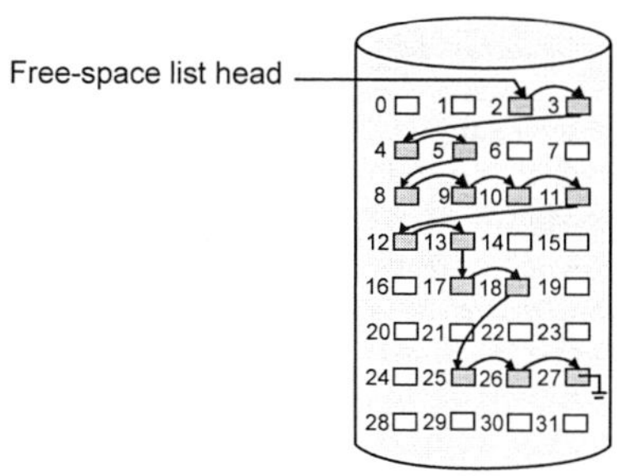

Fig. 3.13: Free space blocks links

(Source: https://www.cs.uic.edu/~jbell/CourseNotes/OperatingSystems/12_FileSystemImplementation.html Last Accessed on 17th Aug 2022)

50 Here a block is called a physical data block whereas in database management systems(DBMS), a record (one row of a table or relation) is called a logical record.

51 DOS stands for disk operating system. Of course, it can be also denial of service(DOS) attack or distributed operating system(DOS)

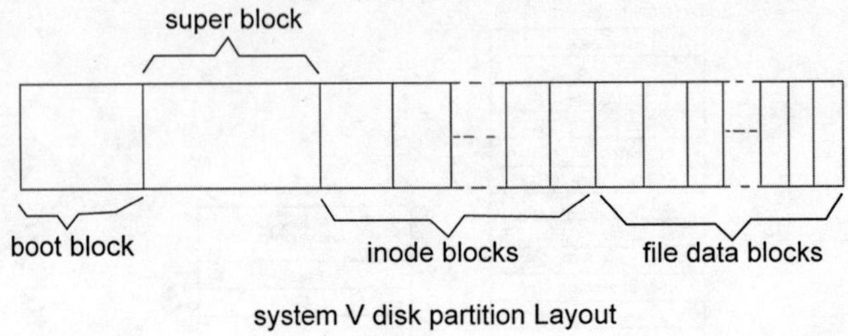

Fig. 3.14: A Unix system disk partition and its pertinent parts

Let us also understand another free data block management that is used in the original Unix V. A disk partition in a Unix system is considered to be having boot block, super block, inode blocks and data blocks as shown below(see Fig. 3.14).

Free list here is a form of linked list and the filesystem's superblock contains the first part of the same. When the filesystem is first created, all data blocks appear on the free list as obviously they are free by then. By the way, do you know the technical name of this operation? Did you ever install any operating system on a fresh hard disk? The operation is known as formatting. During the formatting time, the above logical structure of the disk partition(Fig 3.14) will be created.

However, as the space in the super block is limited, only a small part of the free list will be maintained in the superblock while the most of free list information is really stored in free data blocks. The data block number(for example 200) of which is arranged to be the last block number in the super block list points to the remaining free list details. This idea is repeated, using free data blocks to store free lists block numbers. That is, the last free block number in each free list segment is the data block that is having the next list of free block numbers. This idea is shown in Fig. 3.15.

For example, in the following figure you will find in the super block that block numbers 171-200 as free. If we want the next free block numbers, simply we need to read the data block whose number is 200. If we find in data block 200 that free data blocks are 201 to 230 then the next portion of the free list can be found by reading data block whose number is 230.

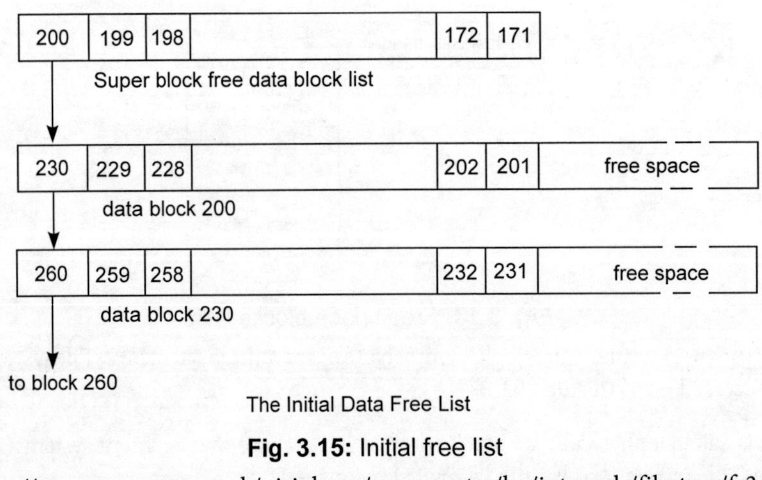

Fig. 3.15: Initial free list

(Source: https://www.cems.uwe.ac.uk/~irjohnso/coursenotes/lrc/internals/filestore/fs3.htm Last Accessed: 1st Sep 2022)

If a request is made for a new data block to store a file's content, the next free one on the super block list will be allocated first (blocks will be allocated right to left in the above diagram). That is, data block 171 will be allocated. Which means, the file's content is stored in the data block whose number or address is 171. As more data blocks are requested, required free data block numbers can be taken from the super block (next 172, that next 173, and vice versa) until the super block free list has only one entry left in it. Why is that one entry cannot be removed? That last block number in the super block list is the data block that contains the block numbers of the remaining part of the system's free block list. By reading that data block, we fetch the block numbers of the remaining free list into the super block (see Fig. 3.16).

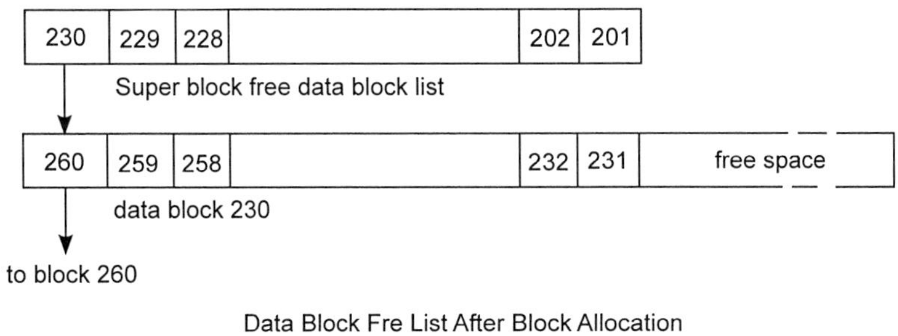

Fig. 3.16: Free list after allocating some data blocks

(Source: https://www.cems.uwe.ac.uk/~irjohnso/coursenotes/lrc/internals/filestore/fs3.htm Last Accessed: 1st Sep 2022)

Fig. 3.16 shows the situation after all the initial list of free block numbers in the super block have been allocated to a request and then the contents of the data block number whose address is 200 is fetched into the super block. Of course, after that data block whose address is 200 will be declared as free and added to the free list. In the same lines, when files are deleted and their data blocks become free, their block numbers are just added to the free list and accordingly super block content will be updated. We are afraid, detailed discussion on this theme further makes this book bulky.

Linked lists in memory management

Linked lists are extensively used in memory (RAM) management also. Every piece of memory used by a process (a running program) is allocated from one of three different areas:

- **Static area**: The static area is used to store global variables and constants. Its requirements such as size (and layout) is computed during compilation time and allocated when the program starts.
- **Stack**: This area stores the arguments of the function call, variables declared inside the function(called as scratch variables). The data structure that stores all these things is known as stack frame or activation record[52]. From the stack area memory is allocated (when a function is called) and freed(when you return from the function) dynamically, in LIFO order. Also, in most of the programming languages including C language, a function call's arguments are pushed into stack in right to left fashion, that is in LIFO order.

52 Do remember that nothing is infinite including the memory allocated for the program stack. Because of this finiteness of program stack, usually recursive functions encounter a serious runtime error known as "stack overflow" problem where because of repeated creation of activation records, the available program stack gets exhausted and thus we face this situation. Of course, do remember this word "stack overflow" is used with some issues regarding databases and their online form fill data.

- **Heap:** From heap dynamic memory is allocated and freed, in any order. The heap is used to store objects that are supposed to outlive after the function that created them. To make things easy, when we call malloc() memory will be allocated from the heap and when we call free() it will be deallocated.

For example, in the following C program, we have commented the variables along with their type(static type, stack type, heap type) for ease of understanding.

```
int x=122;  //this variables memory belongs to static area as it is a global
variable
int *all(int n){ //the argument n's memory is in the stack
int p;
//the argument p's memory is also in the stack. This is also called the scratch
variable.
int *x;
p=4*n;
x=(int*) malloc(100); //this 100 bytes of memory is from heap
}
int main(){
int a=10, b=17, *c;
c=(int *)malloc(100); //this 100 bytes of memory is from heap
all(5);
return 0;
}
```

The above program is available on a visualization server. Readers are welcome to execute the same to understand the theme of static, stack, heap type variables or objects.

https://tinyurl.com/AICTEDSBOOK43

The following picture (Fig. 3.17) illustrates these concepts while the above program is getting executed on the visualization server. The variable a will be having its memory allocated much before the main program is started. Similarly, memory for a, b, c are allocated from stack while the dynamic memory (through malloc) is allocated from heap.

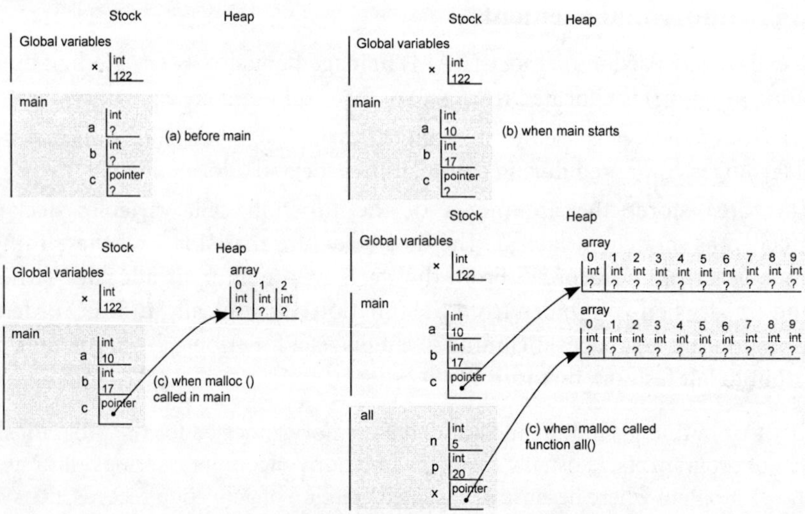

Fig. 3.17: Static, stack and heap variables

Advantages and disadvantages of each of static, automatic(stack), and dynamic(heap) are presented in the following table 3.1.

Table. 3.1: Comparison of static, stack and heap variables or objects.

STATIC (globals)	AUTOMATIC (locals, stack)	DYNAMIC (heap)
+ simple	- simple	- complicated
+ managed by compiler	+ managed by compiler	- managed by programmer (much easier to have memory errors)
+ cheap	+ cheap	- nameless objects, require pointers
+ lifetime is program execution (no memory errors!)	- lifetime bounded by function	+ flexible lifetime determined by code
- fixed size determined at compile time, not dependent on input	- number of stack frames dependent on input (e.g. recursion) - individual frame is fixed size	+ size can be totally input dependent

Garbage Collection or Heap Management

We have explained that the dynamic memory is allocated from the heap area. In order to give a real feeling of execution of a program, we will try to explain tersely how memory is managed during the execution of a program.

The three areas (stack, heap etc) just described above can be organised as follows in the address space of a running program in primary memory or virtual memory. By the way, if someone asks you what an executable file contains, what is your answer? Typically an executable file contains two important areas to name: text segment or area (which is also called code segment) and data segment. When we run the executable file its code or text segment and data segment are mapped onto the address space in RAM as shown below (Fig. 3.18, 3.19). Only when this structure is created, that program is said to be a process.

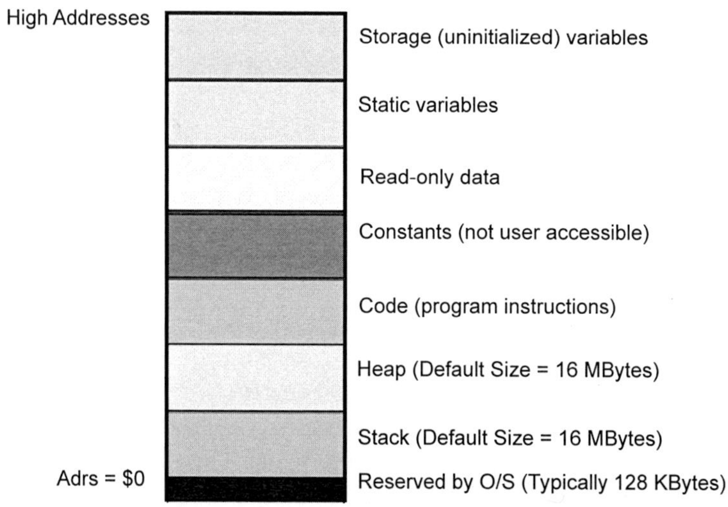

Fig. 3.18: Process address space in Windows

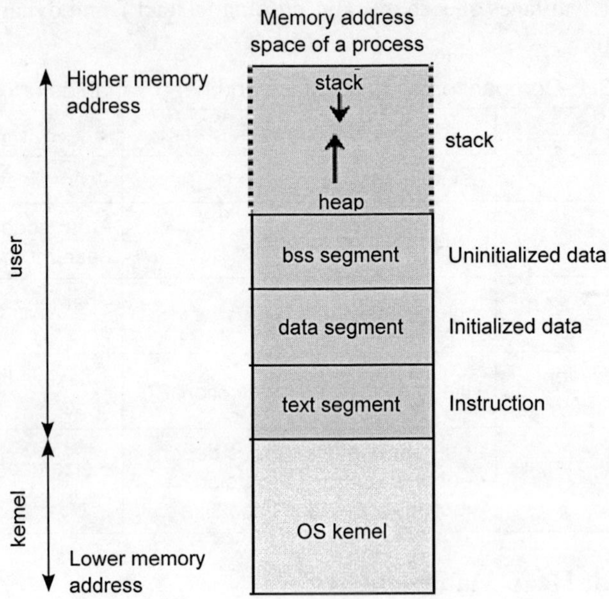

Fig. 3.19: Process address space in Linux

(Source: https://www.tenouk.com/Bufferoverflowc/Bufferoverflow1c.html Last Accessed: 1st Sep 2022)

What is Garbage Collection?

1. track every dynamic object
2. find all accessible objects (difficult process!)
3. free all inaccessible objects

See the following example.

```
int main() {
int *x, *y, *z;
x=(int *)malloc(4);
z=x;
y=(int *)malloc(10);
x = 0;
free(y);
z=0;
 return 0;
}
```

We welcome readers to visualize the above code here at the following link.

https://tinyurl.com/AICTEDSBOOK42

In this example, we would like to show that if the memory allocated is now no longer referenced by any pointers in the program that will be taken back by garbage collector in automatic garbage collectors. In the above program, we are creating a dynamic memory with 4 bytes and making it to be referenced by two pointers x and z. Also, another pointer y is made to point to another 10 bytes dynamic memory. That is, once we set x to 0, we no longer have two pointers referring to the allocated 4 bytes of memory. Also, when we call free() function with pointer y as argument, that 10 bytes also disappeared or deallocated (of course now y is called a dangling pointer. see the difference between x and y in the visualization tool). When the z=0; statement got executed then only that four bytes memory got deallocated.

Managing the static area and the stack is trivial and beyond the scope of this book because of book size limitations. Managing the heap which is also called as garbage collection is much more difficult because of the irregular lifetimes of the blocks(that are hosting objects or variables) it contains. It prominently involves satisfying: 1. memory allocation requests (which consist in finding a free block of memory big enough to satisfy the request, remove it from the set of free blocks, and return it to the program), 2. memory deallocation requests, which consist in returning a previously-allocated block to the set of free blocks, to make it available for further allocation requests.

Which area of the heap is free and which is in use is tracked by the memory manager. For this purpose, free memory blocks details are maintained in a special data structure known as the **free list.** Notice that the term free list is used even when the data-structure used to track free memory is not a list. There is no need to keep a list of allocated blocks, as it can be computed using the free list – all blocks that are not in the free list are allocated.

Since the blocks stored in the free list are by definition not used by the program, the memory manager can store information in them! For example, if the free list is represented as a singly linked list(see Fig. 3.20), then the pointer to the next free block can be stored in the blocks themselves:

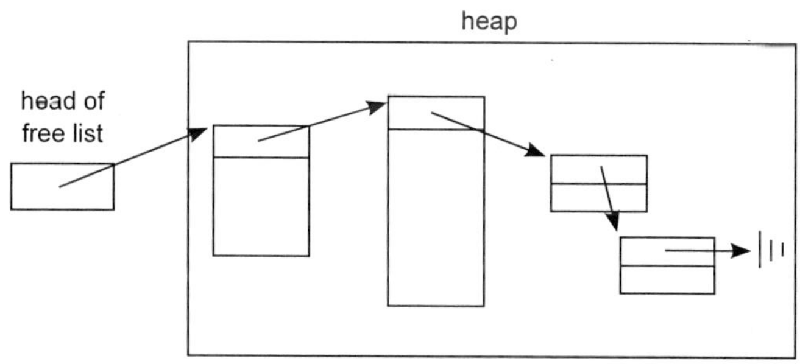

Fig. 3.20: Free list in heap management

Apart from the link to their successor and/or to their predecessor, free blocks must contain their size. Allocated blocks do not require links to other blocks, but must also contain their size (Fig. 3.21). This information is stored in the block's header, situated just before the area used by the client, and invisible to it.

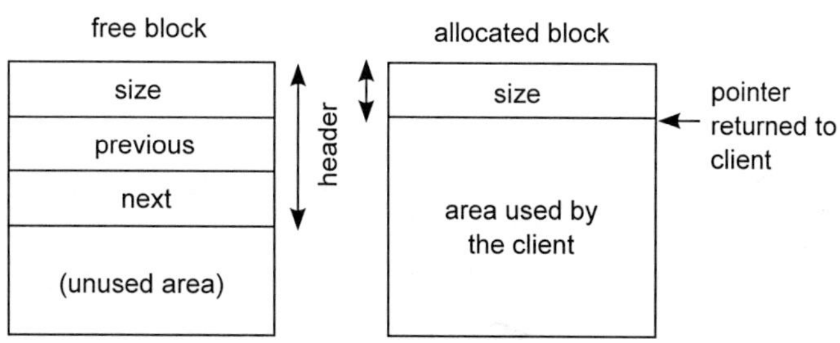

Fig. 3.21: Free and allocated blocks that are used in heap management

Data structures are extensively used for heap management. Here, we shall explain how heap memory can be managed using a circular linked list. Here, we maintain a circular linked list of allocated blocks. Each block contains its used size, the size of the free space after it, and a pointer to the next block as shown in Figure 3.22. The block at the top of the heap points to the block with some free space after it (see Figure). Every node points to the next used block. In the sample figure, heap memory is assumed to be having 60 bytes. The following steps are needed while allocating memory for a malloc() call:

- search for a block with enough free space after it
- Go to the end of that blocks used space
- Insert the new block into the heap
- Calculate the remaining free space
- Assign the previous block's free space to 0
- Update the list

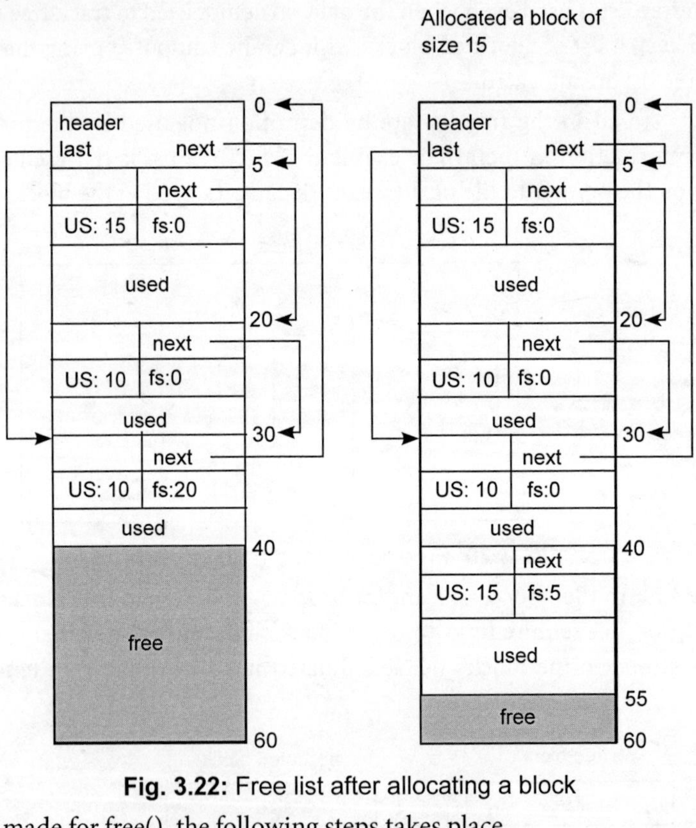

Fig. 3.22: Free list after allocating a block

When a call is made for free(), the following steps takes place

- Start from the top block of heap
- Traverse the list till we find the block to be removed
- Adjust the previous block such that this free area will be considered as free or un-allocated (see Fig. 3.23)

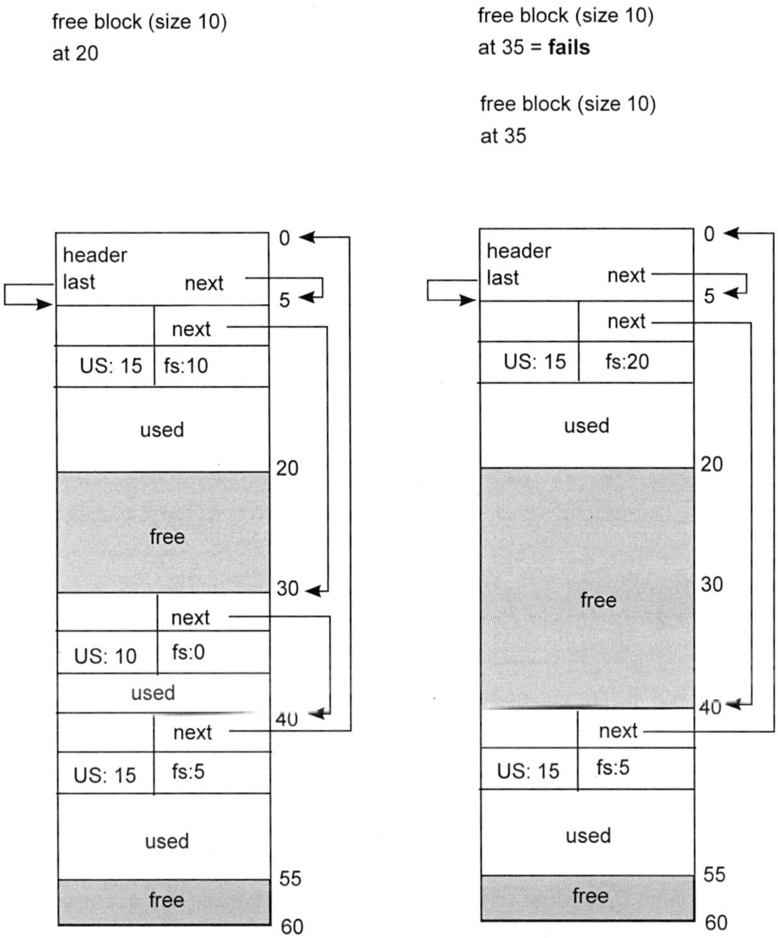

Fig. 3.23: Free list after deleting an object

Process Management

In the previous chapter we did introduce process scheduling in operating systems using circular queues, ready queues. In fact, in process control block (PCB[53, 54]) OS maintains all the information it needs to know about a process such as: opened files, memory, process identification number, owner, priorities of the process, process group, etc.

These PCBs are maintained as a ready queue and device queues[55] as shown in the following figure 3.24.

53 https://www.cs.auckland.ac.nz/courses/compsci340s2c/lectures/lecture06.pdf
54 PCB stands for printed circuit board also. Ha. Ha. This is also related to computers!
55 http://www.cs.fsu.edu/~zwang/files/cop4610/Fall2016/chapter3.pdf

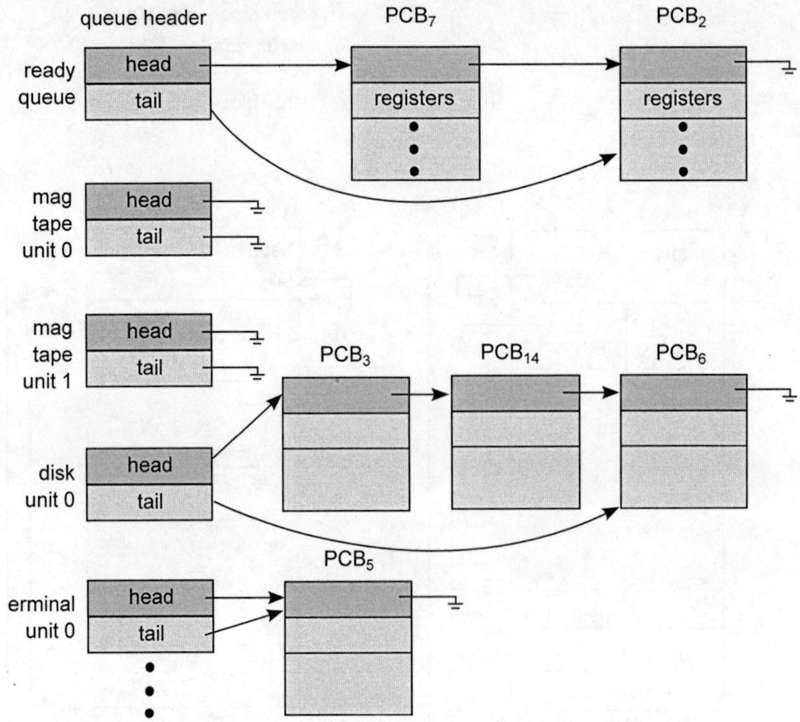

Fig. 3.24: PCB's as a linked list in process management

In Networks too linked lists are in demand!

Let's consider you are asked to write code for a firewall. Is it not obvious for you to monitor Internet Protocol (IP) addresses such that some to be allowed and some other to be blocked? Your machine IP, your jobs IPs, and some other testing IP's need to be whitelisted as you want to use them; while a list of known IP's that may harm you to be blacklisted.You may get a doubt why might I use LinkedList for this? The operation is fast for adding/removing an item from the list. Also, You do not know how many IP's are going to be blocked/whitelisted.

In summary

The principal benefit of a linked list over a conventional array is that the order of the linked items may be different from the order that the data items are stored in physical memory(RAM) or on disk. For that reason, linked lists allow insertion and removal of nodes(records) at any point in the list, with a constant number of operations, that is with complexity of O(1). Usually, language supported arrays will allow us to have their size fixed during their declaration itself. This may make some practical problems lose flexibility. Here, the linked list will come to rescue us. We can add and remove at any time.

In an array we can access any element by directly specifying its index. That is, they allow the random accessing of the data. However, in the case of linked lists this random accessing to the data is not possible or demanding more CPU time. Thus, many basic operations such as obtaining the last but one node of the list, or finding a node(s) that contains a given data, or locating the place where a new node should be inserted, etc., in linked list may require scanning most of the list elements and becomes comparatively computationally costly.

The following table 3.2 contains the comparison between arrays and linked lists.

Table 3.2: Comparison of arrays and lists

Array	Linked List
Size or number of elements of the data which we can store at most is fixed at the size of the array.	Size or the number of data elements which we can store in a linked list is not fixed. It can grow to any extent with the limitations from available memory for our process.
Required memory is allocated from the stack area of our process.	Required memory is allocated from the heap area of our process.
It takes less memory to store n elements.	It takes more memory to store n elements as here we will be storing the next element or node's address also.
You cannot remove an element in the middle.	You can happily remove any element from anywhere.
If an array is full and we want to add some more elements at the front of the array. This demands a lot of effort as we need to create another bigger array, copy the current elements, etc	This is very easy here.
Insertion of a new element may demand movement of some elements. Thus, It takes more effort.	The insertion operation is also very easily here.

The following table 3.3 shows the tradeoff between arrays and linked lists in terms of various parameters.

Table 3.3: Performance comparison of arrays and lists

Parameter	Arrays	Linked Lists
Sequential access	Efficient	Efficient
Random access	Efficient with complexity of O(1)	Inefficient with complexity of O(n) where n is the number of elements in the linked list.
Overhead	None	1 address for ea h element in the case of single linked lists, 2 addresses for each element in the double linked lists.
Growing/shrinking	Not possible at all.	In accordance with our wish it can grow and shrink also.
Ease of arranging elements	Inefficient	Efficient

The following video introduces linked lists.

https://www.youtube.com/watch?v=45-fO24-iv4&list=PLXX7XiUxnzzWoLDfgad4s4dwleb4NMtVN&index=40

3.1.1 Single Linked Lists

In the following example, we want to introduce the creation of a linked list in the simplest possible manner. Do remember that we can maintain anything in a linked list. But, for ease of understanding we proposed to create a linked list of integers. For this, we have proposed the following structure, a user defined variable in C language. Do recollect from our examples in the introductory section, a linked list's node essentially contains data and a link (or a pointer or a reference) to the next item(node) in the list. Thus, we have used the following structure with two data members, **n** (an integer) and **next**(a pointer) as we want to maintain integers as a linked list. Do remember that n is referred to as data of the linked list node[56]. As all the nodes are of the same type, the next data member will be a pointer of the node type, that is whatever name we are going to give to the node(structure), the next will be a pointer of that type. That is, we will be using **self referencing** structures in building the linked lists.

3.1.1.1 Linked List representation in Memory

```
struct lst{
 int n;
 struct lst* next;
};
int main() {
struct lst A, B, C, *H;
//assigning data to nodes
A.n=10;
B.n=109;
C.n=22;
//creating links
A.next=&B;
B.next=&C;
C.next=0;
//pointer to the head of the linked list
H=&A;
//traversing the linked list
while(H){
printf("%d\n", H->n);
H=H->next;
}
 return 0;
}
```

The above code is available on the visualization server. We advise readers to visualize the same before processing further.

https://tinyurl.com/nbvstruct11

https://tinyurl.com/NBVsimplesinglelinkedlist

In the above program, we are declaring struct lst type variables A, B and C along with struct lst type pointer type variable H. Then, we are storing integer numbers in each of the objects A, B and C with the following three instructions.

A.n = 10;

B.n = 109;

C.n = 22;

56 Do remember we can maintain in a node/item/record of a linked list any number data members of any type. However, for ease of explanation we are taking only one integer data member and a pointer.

We are then assigning the a lst object to the next data member of each of the variables A, B and C. Now, a linked list is formed among A, B and C. At the end, we are assigning the address of A to H. This H can be called as the **head** of the linked list.

A.next = &B;

B.next = &C;

C.next = 0;

H = &A;

The following picture is a snap-shot of the above steps.

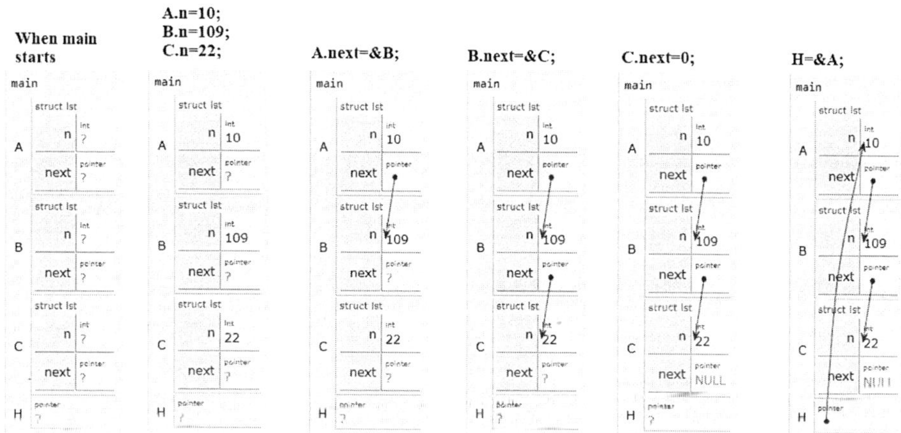

The following picture is a snap-shot of the while loop that is used to traverse[57] the linked list from head to bottom (or top to end). Do remember that pointer values will be other than zero if they are pointing to some object (or memory of an object).Thus, while(H) will be true whenever H is pointing to an object like either A or B or C. When H value becomes null, while(H) becomes false and we exit from the loop.

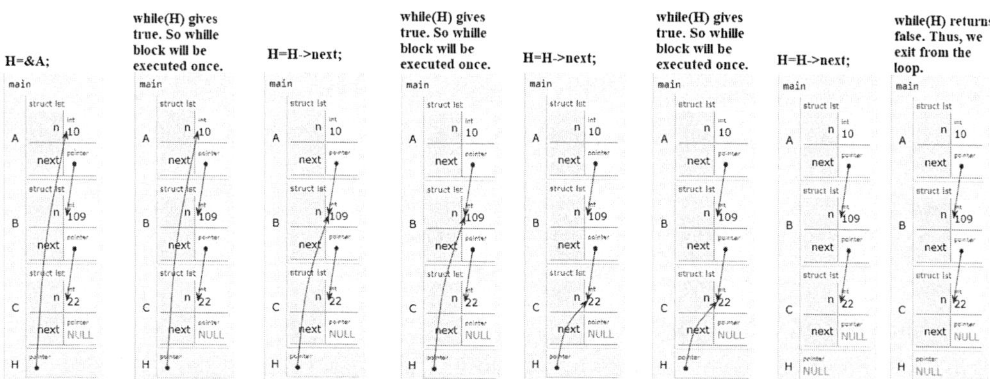

The following video explains the linked list creation.

https://www.youtube.com/watch?v=-3G-K51h2oA&list=PLXX7XiUxnzzUILTy1F68tpk7FZ56nJrOg&index=131&t=192s

57 Traversing (moving from one node to another) in a linked list is called link hopping or pointer hopping.

https://www.youtube.com/watch?v=Ujf9q3mbjrY&list=PLXX7XiUxnzzUILTy1F68tpk7FZ56nJrOg&index=132&t=8s

Question 2: Assuming A, B are struct lst type(whose definition is given above) variables. Is the memory(amount) allocated for A and B the same?

Answer: Yes. Very much the same. You may use the sizeof() function like the following.

```
printf("%d %d\n", sizeof(A), sizeof(B));
```

Question 3: Assuming A, B are struct lst type(whose definition is given above) variables. Is the memory allocated for A is same as B?

Answer: No. The memory allocated for A is different from memory allocated for B. You may check their addresses like the following. Both of them will be having different addresses.

```
printf("%X %X\n", &A, &B);
```

Question 4: How much memory is assigned for struct lst type object or variable?

Answer: On my machine, pointers are taking four bytes. The amount of memory for data member **n** plus the amount of memory for the pointer type data member **next**. In my machine, it is 4 + 4 = 8 bytes. You can happily call the **sizeof**() function to find the answer on your machine with instructions such as:

```
struct lst A; printf("%d\n", sizeof(A));
```

Question 5: How much memory is allocated for struct lst type of pointer variable?

Answer: For any pointer irrespective of its type, memory allocated will be the same. Thus, to know the amount of memory allocated for struct lst type pointer, simply one can call **sizeof(struct lst** *). On my machine, I am getting 4 bytes. Of course, you may get 8 bytes indicating that your compiler/computer is a 64 bit compiler.

Question 6: Does the following code give 19 on the standard output?

```
struct lst A={19,0};
printf("%d\n",     (&(*(&A)))->n);
```

Answer: Yes. You may verify the same at https://tinyurl.com/AICTEDSBOOK104

Question 7: Is the following code statement valid?

```
struct lst *A={19,0};
```

Answer: No. You may verify the same at https://tinyurl.com/AICTEDSBOOK105

Question 8: Assuming that the while loop in the above program is modified as follows. Do you get the same results?

```
H=&A;
while(H&&printf("%d\n", H->n),H=H->next);
```

You are welcome to explore the following link before answering.

https://tinyurl.com/AICTEDSBOOK50

Question 9: Assuming that the while loop in the above program is modified as follows. Do you get the same results?

```
H=&A;
while(H,printf("%d\n", H->n),H=H->next);
```

You are welcome to explore the following link before answering.

https://tinyurl.com/AICTEDSBOOK51

Question 10: Assuming that the while loop in the above program is modified as follows. Do you get the same results?

```
H=&A;
while(H,H=H->next);
printf("%d\n", H->n);
```

You are welcome to explore the following link before answering.

https://tinyurl.com/AICTEDSBOOK52

Question 11: Assuming that the while loop in the above program is modified as follows. Do you get the same results?

```
H=&A;
while(H&&(H=H->next));
printf("%d\n", H->n);
```

You are welcome to explore the following link before answering.

https://tinyurl.com/AICTEDSBOOK53

Question 12: Assuming that the while loop in the above program is modified as follows. Do you get the same results?

```
H=&A;
while(H,H=H->next);
printf("%d\n", H->n);
```

You are welcome to explore the following link before answering.

https://tinyurl.com/AICTEDSBOOK54

Question 13: Assuming that the while loop in the above program is modified as follows. Do you get the same results?

```
H=&A;
while(H,H->next)H=H->next;
printf("%d\n", H->n);
```

You are welcome to explore the following link before answering.

https://tinyurl.com/AICTEDSBOOK55

Question 14: Assuming that the while loop in the above program is modified as follows. Do you get the same results?

```
H=&A;
while(H&&H->next)H=H->next;
printf("%d\n", H->n);
```

You are welcome to explore the following link before answering.

https://tinyurl.com/AICTEDSBOOK56

Question 15: Assuming that the while loop in the above program is modified as follows. Do you get the same results?

```
H=&A;
while(H*H->next)H=H->next;
printf("%d\n", H->n);
```

You are welcome to explore the following link before answering.

https://tinyurl.com/AICTEDSBOOK57

Question 16: Assuming that the while loop in the above program is modified as follows. Do you get the same results? That is, is it going to print all the elements of the linked list? Is it going to encounter any runtime errors?

```
H=&A;
while(printf("%d\n", H->n))H=H->next;
```

You are welcome to explore the following link before answering.

https://tinyurl.com/AICTEDSBOOK58

Question 17: Does this piece of code display all the node's values? Here, H is the head of a linked list?

```
while(H&&H->next)H=H->next;
 printf("%d\n", H->n);
```

You are welcome to explore the following link before answering.

https://tinyurl.com/AICTEDSBOOK65

Question 18: Does this piece of code display the last node's value? Here, H is the head of a linked list?

```
while(H&&H->next)H=H->next;
 printf("%d\n", H->n);
```

You are welcome to explore the following link before answering.

https://tinyurl.com/AICTEDSBOOK65

Question 19: Assume that H is the head of a linked list. After executing the while loop, to which node H will be pointing?

```
while(H&&H->next)H=H->next;
 printf("%d\n", H->n);
```

You are welcome to explore the following link before answering.

https://tinyurl.com/AICTEDSBOOK65

Question 20: Assume that H is the head of a linked list. After executing the while loop, to which node H will be pointing?

```
while(H&&H->next)H=H->next->next;
 printf("%d\n", H->n);
```

You are welcome to explore the following link before answering.

https://tinyurl.com/AICTEDSBOOK66

Question 21: Assume that H is the head of a linked list. After executing the while loop, which node's values are displayed?

```
while(H&&H->next){ printf("%d\n", H->n);
        H=H->next->next;
}
```

You are welcome to explore the following link before answering.

https://tinyurl.com/AICTEDSBOOK67

Question 22: Assume that H is the head of a linked list. After executing the while loop, which node's values are displayed?

```
do{ printf("%d\n", H->n);
      H=H->next->next;
}while(H&&H->next);
```

You are welcome to explore the following link before answering.

https://tinyurl.com/AICTEDSBOOK68

Question 23: Assume that H is the head of a linked list. After executing the while loop, which node's values are displayed?

```
while(H){ printf("%d\n", H->n);
        H=H->next->next;
 }
```

You are welcome to explore the following link before answering.

https://tinyurl.com/AICTEDSBOOK69

Question 24: Assume that H is the head of a linked list. After executing the while loop, which node's values are displayed?

```
do{ printf("%d\n", H->n);
        H=H->next->next;
 }while(H||H->next);
```

You are welcome to explore the following link before answering.

https://tinyurl.com/AICTEDSBOOK70

Question 25: Does the following program behave in the same fashion as that of the above program?

```
struct lst{
  int n;
  struct lst* next;
};
int main() {
struct lst C={22,0}, B={109,&C},A={10,&B},  *H=&A;
while(H){
printf("%d\n", H->n);
H=H->next;
}
  return 0;
}
```

You are welcome to explore the following link before answering.

https://tinyurl.com/AICTEDSBOOK83

Answer: Yes. It also creates a linked list with three nodes and prints the same.

Question 26: Does the following statement create a linked list for which H is a pointer? Of course, the definition for struct lst is the same as above.

```
struct lst C={22,0}, B={109,&C},A={10,&B},  *H=&A;
```

Answer: Yes

Question 27: What will you get on the screen? Of course, the definition for struct lst is the same as above.

```
struct lst C={22,0}, B={109,&C},A={10,&B},  *H=&A;
printf("%d\n", H->n + H->next->n + H->next->next->n);
```

Answer: 141

You may experiment the code at the following link before answering

https://tinyurl.com/AICTEDSBOOK88

Question 28: What will you get on the screen? Of course, the definition for struct lst is the same as above.

```
struct lst C={22,0}, B={109,&C},A={10,&B}, *H=&A;
printf("%d\n", H->next->next->n);
```

Answer: 22

You may experiment the code at the following link before answering

https://tinyurl.com/AICTEDSBOOK84

Question 29: What will you get on the screen? Of course, the definition for struct lst is the same as above.

```
struct lst C={22,0}, B={109,&C},A={10,&B}, *H=&A;
printf("%d\n", A.next->next->n);
```

Answer: 22

You may experiment the code at the following link before answering

https://tinyurl.com/AICTEDSBOOK85

Question 30: What will you get on the screen? Of course, the definition for struct lst is the same as above.

```
struct lst C={22,0}, B={109,&C},A={10,&B}, *H=&A;
printf("%d\n", (&(*(H)))->next->next->n);
```

Answer: 22

You may experiment the code at the following link before answering

https://tinyurl.com/AICTEDSBOOK86

Question 31: What will you get on the screen? Of course, the definition for struct lst is the same as above.

```
struct lst C={22,0}, B={109,&C},A={10,&B}, *H=&A;
printf("%d\n", (&(*((&(*((&(*(H)))->next)))->next)))->n);
```

Answer: 22

You may experiment the code at the following link before answering

https://tinyurl.com/AICTEDSBOOK87

We know you might find the following definition of the structure is used by many people to maintain a set of integers as a linked list. I am sure you are able to identify the difference in our structure and this. After all, variable name n is taken as data.

```
struct Node{
 int data;
 struct Node * next;
};
typedef struct Node Node;
```

We can declare variables and pointers of Node type as:

Node A, B, C, *H;

The above program using this structure definition is available for readers experemination at:

https://tinyurl.com/AICTEDBOOK40

This type of structure is also used by many people.

```
typedef struct lst{
 int data;
 struct lst * next;
}Node;
```

We can declare variables and pointers of Node type as:

Node A, B, C, *H;

The above program using this structure definition is available for readers experemination at:

https://tinyurl.com/AICTEDSBOOK44

During the last thirty years of my lecturing I have used the above structure lst with data member names as n and next. I love to follow the same in this book also.

Question 32: Is this type of structure valid to use?

```
struct lst{
 int n;
 struct lst next;
};
```

You are welcome to explore the following link before answering.

https://tinyurl.com/AICTEDSBOOK93

Question 33: Does the following program work?

```
struct lst{
 int n;
 struct lst *next;
}C={10,0},B={101,&C},A={122,&B},*H=&A;
int main() {
while(H){
 printf("%d\n",H->n);
 H=H->next;
}
 return 0;
}
```

You are welcome to explore the following link before answering.

https://tinyurl.com/AICTEDSBOOK94

Question 34: Does the following program work? What will be the output of this program?

```
struct lst{
 int n;
 struct lst *next;
}C={10,0},B={101,&C},A={122,&B},*H=&A;
int main() {
struct lst C={101,0},B={1021,&C},A={1212,&B},*H=&A;
while(H){
 printf("%d\n",H->n);
 H=H->next;
}
 return 0;
}
```

We welcome readers to experiment with the following link where the above code is hosted. Evidently, this shows how two linked lists are created, one in the global area and the other in stack space.

https://tinyurl.com/AICTEDSBOOK95

Question 35: Are there any mistakes in the following program? First of all, does this program get compiled?

```
struct _{
  int _;
  struct _ *__;
};
int main() {
  struct _ _, __, ___, *____;
  _._=10;
  __._=50;
  ___._=190;
  _.__=&__;
  __.__=&___;
  ___.__=0;
  ____=&_;
  while(____&&printf("%d\n", ____->_),____=____->__);
  return 0;
}
```

You are welcome to explore the following link before answering.

https://tinyurl.com/AICTEDSBOOK110

Question 36: In a cryptic single linked list if the following refers to an integer, what will be the structure members in the most pessimistic manner?

____->__->__->_

Answer:
```
struct xxx{
  int _;
  struct xxx *__;
};
```

You are welcome to explore the following link before answering.

https://tinyurl.com/AICTEDSBOOK111

3.1.1.2 Operations on a Single Linked List

Displaying Linked List content or data

Assume that we want to convert the above while loop that traverses the linked lists and displays each node's data as a function. The following is our solution. If you observe, we have made that while block inside the function. This function can be used to display the contents of a linked list.

```
void display(struct lst *B){
        printf("Items in the Single Linked List:\n");
        while(B){
            printf("%d\t", B->n);
            B=B->next;
        }
        printf("\n");
}
```

We welcome readers to visit the following link to test the above function.

https://tinyurl.com/AICTEDSBOOK45

Time complexity of this function is O(n) as every node of the list has to be visited.

Question 37: Assume that we want to write a function that takes the head of a linked list having numbers in it and returns the sum of the integers of each node of the linked list. The following solution is proposed by us. Verify the same with the following link given below.

```
int sum(struct lst *B){
        int s=0;
        while(B){ s=s+B->n;
            B=B->next;
        }
        return(s);
}
```

You are welcome to explore the following link before answering.

https://tinyurl.com/AICTEDSBOOK47

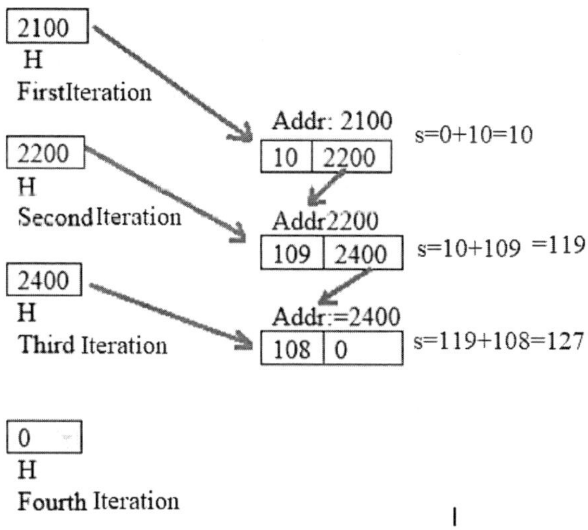

Time complexity of this function is O(n) as every node of the list has to be visited.

Question 38: The following is the recursive version of the above function.

```
int rsum(struct lst *H){
        if(H)return(H->n+rsum(H->next));
        else
        return(0);
}
```

We welcome the readers to experiment the above code that is available on the visualization server at:

You are welcome to explore the following link before answering.

https://tinyurl.com/AICTEDSBOOK48

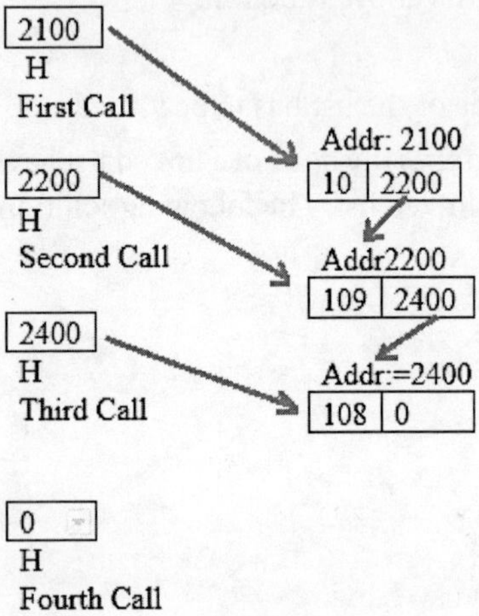

Let us assume that the first time when this function is called, H will be pointing to the head node of the linked list. As H is true, another recursive call is made. Thus, during the second call, H will be pointing to the second node in the list. In that call also, as H is true another recursive call is made to the same function. In the third call, H will be pointing to the last (third node here). Logic behind this is that the sum of the linked list nodes with n elements is the same as the sum of the element in the first node plus sum of node elements of remaining n-1 nodes. To find out the sum of the n-1 node elements, the function is called again. This is repeated till H becomes 0 in a recursive call. At this junction (here in the fourth call), the function returns 0. That and the value of the node in the previous call, i.e., 108 is returned to its previous call and vice versa.

Time complexity of this function is O(n) as every node of the list has to be visited.

Also, explore the following two links and identify the complexity of each of them. Which one is iterative and which one is a recursive approach to find a node having a given value?

https://tinyurl.com/findlist

https://tinyurl.com/recursivefind

Question 39: Explain what will be the output of the following function.

```
int xyz(struct lst *H, int x){
if(H)return ( (H->n ==x) + xyz(H->next,x) );
else
return 0;
}
```

You are welcome to explore the following link before answering.

https://tinyurl.com/AICTEDSBOOK77

Example 1: A simple example to explain the creation of a simple linked list dynamically. This program reads a set of integers till we enter 0 and maintains them in a single linked list and prints the same. This allows us to insert the integers in a stack fashion. That is, the most recent integer will be pointed by the head pointer, H.

```
//please do include structure def, functions def from previous pages
int main(){
        int m;
        struct lst *A *H=0;
        while(1){
                printf("Enter an integer\n");
                scanf("%d", &m)
                if(m==0)break;
                A=(struct lst*) malloc(sizeof(struct lst));
                /* A lst type of object is created dynamically*/
                A->n=m;
                A->next=0;
                H=A;
        }
        printf("Numbers in single linked list are:");
        while(H){
                        printf("%d\t", H->n);
                        H=H->next;
        }
        return(0);
}
```

Output: Enter an integer

10

Enter an integer

19

Enter an integer

79

Enter an integer

0

Numbers in Single linked list are: 10 19 79

The following pages we have used two tables to demonstrate how the above program works. Table 3.4 explains about the creation of a linked list. Because of the space limitations, we have explained the linked list with three numbers only. However, it can work with any number of integers. How many numbers we can maintain in a linked list very much depends on the available virtual memory for our program.

Table. 3.4: A snapshot of Linked List Creation

Statements and their effect	
struct lst *A,*H=0; Two lst type pointers are created and for H initial value is given as 0.	H: 0 A: (empty)
Assume that user has entered 11. Thus, a new lst object is created (with address 2222) and 11 is assigned to A->n. That is, **A->n=m;** **A->next=H;** **H=A;** are executed.	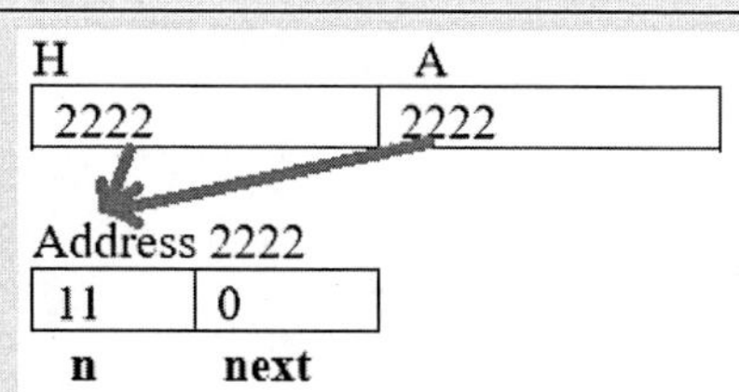

<table>
<tr>
<td>

Assume that the user has entered 190 now. Thus, a new lst object is created (with address 2122) and 100 is stored in A->n.
A->n=m;
A->next=H;
H=A; are executed.

</td>
<td>

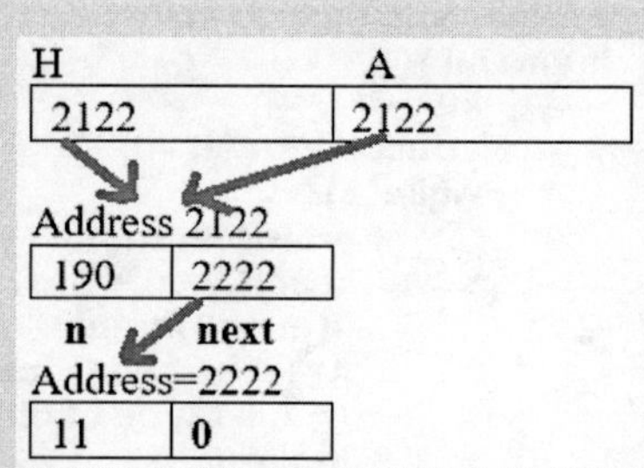

</td>
</tr>
<tr>
<td>

Assume that user has entered 100. Thus, a new lst object is created (with Address 2004) and 100 is assigned to A->n.
A->n=m;
A->next=H;
H=A;

</td>
<td>

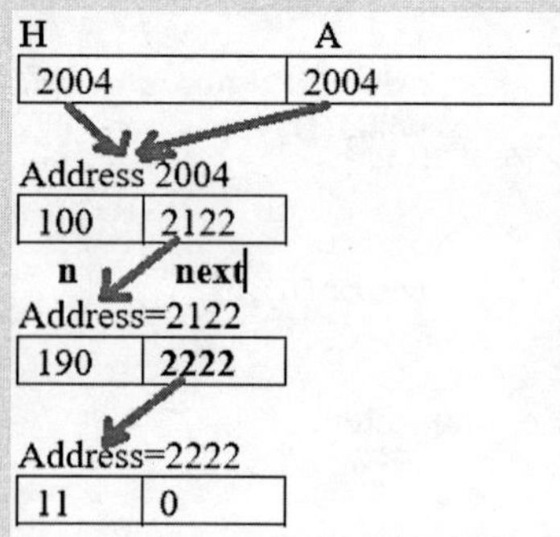

</td>
</tr>
</table>

Table 3.5 explains about the traversal of a linked list from the top node (which is often referred as head node). As long as the head pointer, H, is positive (we know acceptable addresses are always positive numbers) we can traverse the linked list and print the information available (in this case integer number) in each node.

Table. 3.5: Traversing a Singly Linked List

<table>
<tr>
<td>

while(H) is tested.

As H value is 2004, the loop condition becomes true. Thus, while Block will be executed once. Thus, H->n, i.e. 100 is printed and H=H->next statement gets executed. Thus H value becomes 2122. That is H points to B.

</td>
<td>

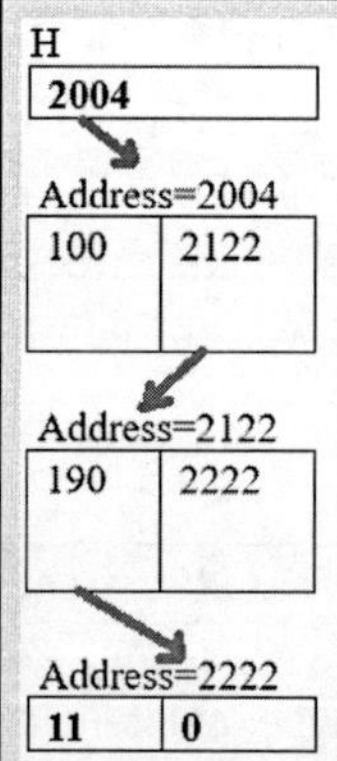

</td>
</tr>
</table>

while(H) is tested. As H value is 2122, the loop condition becomes true. Thus, while block will be executed once. Thus, H->n, i.e. 190 is printed and H=H->next statement gets executed. Thus H value becomes 2222. That is H points to C.	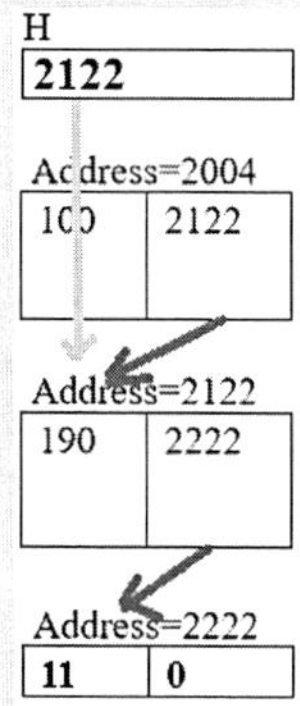
while(H) is tested. As H value is 2222, the loop condition becomes true. Thus, the while block will be executed once. Thus, H->n, i.e. 11 is printed and H=H->next statement gets executed. Thus H value becomes 0. That is H points to nothing.	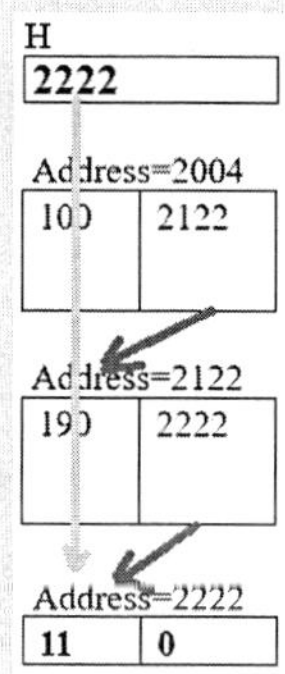
while(H) is tested. As H value is zero, we will come out from the while loop. This is how we can traverse a linked list and visit each node.	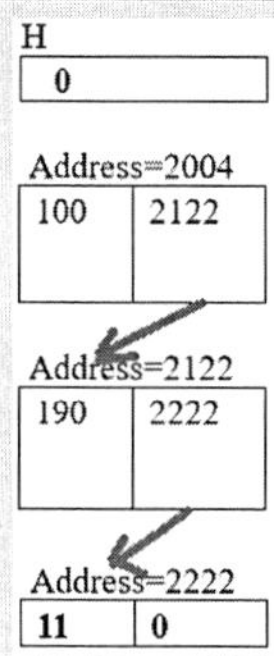

The following link contains a little variant of the above code on a visualization server. Please do observe the addresses that this code displays. Also, as this Visualization server does not support interactive input, we have supplied a function that emulates scanf function by returning a random number.

https://tinyurl.com/dynamiclinkedlist

We have converted the above main program into a function and called from the main as shown below.

```
struct lst * createlist() {
  struct lst *A, *H=0;
  int m;
  while(1){
        SCANF("%d", &m);
        if(m==0)break;
        A=createNode(m);
        A->n=m;
        A->next=H;
        H=A;
  }
  return A;
}
int main(){
  struct lst *list;
  list=createlist();
  display(list);
  return 0;
}
```

We welcome readers to experiment with the above function at the following link.
https://tinyurl.com/dynamiclinkedlistusingfunct

Question 40: Consider the following two statements of the above createlist() function.

```
A->next=A;
H=A;
```

Explore what happens if we replace the above two statements with the following lines.

```
if(H==0){
        H=A;
        B=A;
        }
else{
 B->next=A;
 B=A;
}
```

Here, A,B,C are lst type of pointers and the initial value of H is 0.

Creating a node dynamically

The following function takes an integer as an argument and creates an lst type object dynamically by invoking malloc() function then it assigns x to n and 0 to next of the object created. At the end it returns the address of the node created.

```
struct lst* createnode(int x){
     struct lst *c;
     c=(struct lst*) malloc(sizeof(struct lst));
     c->n=x;
     c->next=0;
    return c;
}
```

The following link contains the above function and associated main program for experimentation sake.

https://tinyurl.com/AICTEDSBOOK46

```
while(H){
        if(H->n%2==0){
        if(Even)A->next=H;
        else Even=H;
        A=H;
        }
        else{
        if(Odd)B->next=H;
        else Odd=H;
        B=H;
        }
        H=H->next;
}
A->next=0;
B->next=0;
```

Question 41: Assume H, Even, Odd, A, B are struct lst type pointers. Also assume H is pointing to the head of a linked list. What happens if we execute the right side code fragment? What Even and Odd pointers will be pointing?

The following link contains the right side and associated main program for experimentation sake. You are welcome to experiment with this code before answering.

https://tinyurl.com/AICTEDSBOOK71

```
while(H){
        if(i++n%2==0){
        if(Even)A->next=H;
        else Even=H;
        A=H;
        }
        else{
        if(Odd)B->next=H;
        else Odd=H;
        B=H;
        }
        H=H->next;
}
A->next=0;
B->next=0;
```

Question 42: Assume H, Even, Odd, A, B are struct lst type pointers. Also assume H is pointing to the head of a linked list. In addition, the value of the variable i before this while loop is zero. What happens if we execute the right side code segment? What Even and Odd pointers will be pointing?

The following link contains the right side code and associated main program for experimentation sake. You are welcome to experiment with this code before answering.

https://tinyurl.com/AICTEDSBOOK73

```
while(H){
        if(i++n%2==0){
        if(Even)A->next=H;
        else Even=H;
        A=H;
        }
        else{
        if(Odd)B->next=H;
        else Odd=H;
        B=H;
        }
        H=H->next;
}
A->next=0;
B->next=0;
```

Example 2: Creating a linked list with elements in descending order.

Here also, we assume users will be asked to enter integers. They will be taken and kept in the linked list in descending order till 0 is entered by them. The last number 0 will not be kept in the linked list. If one wants, they can change this while loop according to their wish. For example, a user can be asked to enter how many numbers he wanted to maintain in the linked list. He/she can write a loop (while or for loop) which runs for n times and reads each time a number and maintains them in the linked list.

When the first number is entered, the same will be kept in a dynamically allocated lst type of node while initializing its next member as 0. This node will be made as the head for the linked list. Next number on wards the following actions will be taken

If the new number is larger than the number in the head node then a new node will be added before the current head and it will be made as new head.

If the new number is smaller than the number in the head node then we will traverse the linked list from the second node onwards till we find a node whose value is smaller than the new number. A new node is created with this new number and inserted before the node whose value is less than the new number. It may happen that the new node might be inserted either at the end of the linked list or in between the available list of nodes.

```
int main(){
        int m;
        struct lst *A,*B, *C, *H=0;
        printf("Enter Numbers\n");
        while(1){
                scanf("%d", &m); if(m==0)break;
                A=createnode(m);
                if(H==0)H=A;    /* Considering this as the head of the list*/
                else if(H->n<m){
                        /* Adding before the current head*/
                A->next=H;
                H=A;
                }
```

```
                else{         /* Adding after the current head*/
                        B=H;
                        C=H->next;
                        while(C && C->n > m){
                        B=C;
                        C=C->next;
                        }
                        B->next=A;
                        if(C){
                                A->next=C;
                        }
                }
        }
        display(H);
        return 0;
}
```

Output: Enter Numbers

11

100

190

10

0

Items in the Single Linked List:

190 100 11 10

A little variant of the above program that suits the visualization server is available at the following link. We recommend readers to explore this code.

https://tinyurl.com/sortedlinkedlist

In the following link you will find how we have converted the above main program into a function (**createsortlist**) and invoked the same from another main program in creating a sorted linked list.

https://tinyurl.com/insertionlistfunction

A Snapshot of Linked List Creation

Initially, assume that we have taken head of the list, H as 0.	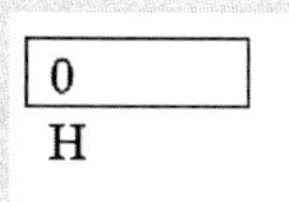
Inserting at the front: Now, let us assume that the user has entered 11. A new node will be created with its n =11 and next data member as 0. The head, H, will be made to point to this new node.	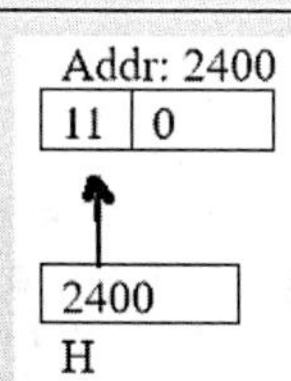

Inserting at the front:
Now, let us assume that the user has entered 100. As 100 is larger than 11 (which is currently in the head node), a new node has to be inserted before the current head and it has to be made as the next current head.

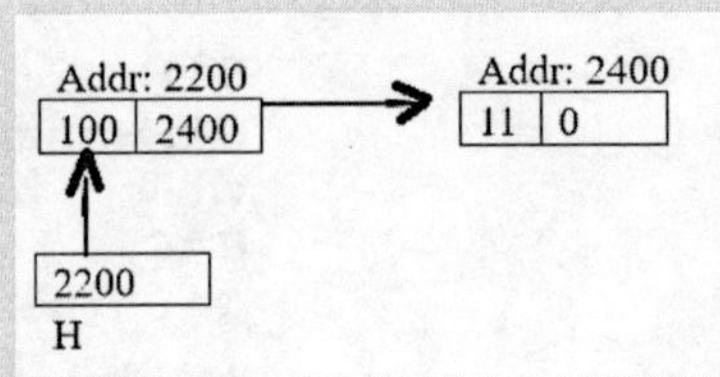

Inserting at the front:
Now, let us consider that the user has entered 190. As 190 is larger than 100 (which is currently in the head node), a new node will be inserted before the current head and it will be made as the next current head of the linked list.

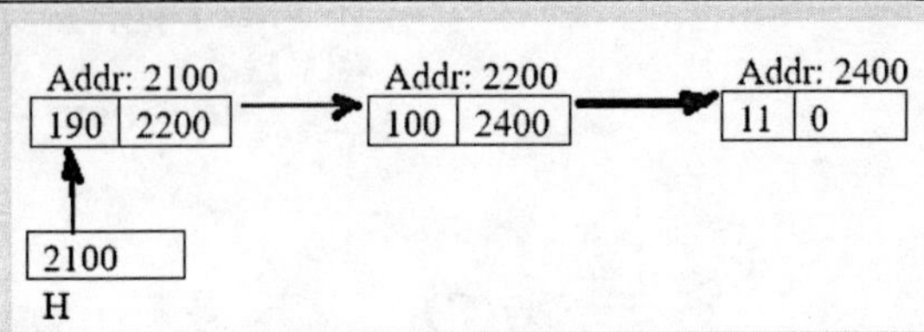

Inserting at the last:
Now, consider that the user has entered a number 10 . As it is smaller than the head value, i.e., 190, it has to be inserted to the right hand side of the head node. Rather, we have to traverse the linked list and find a node whose value is less than 10, before that the new node will be inserted with its value as 10. Here also we may have two possibilities. A new node might be added at the end if the given number is smaller than the values in all the nodes of the current linked list; otherwise, a new node will be added in between two nodes in the existing linked list.

To carry out this operation, we take two pointers B and C which point to head and next node to head respectively. As we have already checked with the head node, we continue the checking from the next node onwards.

As the value in the node pointed by the pointer C, i.e., 11 is more than 10, B is adjusted to point current C and C is made as C->next. Thus, C becomes zero. Control comes out of the while loop. This indicates that the new node has to be added at the end, that is after B.

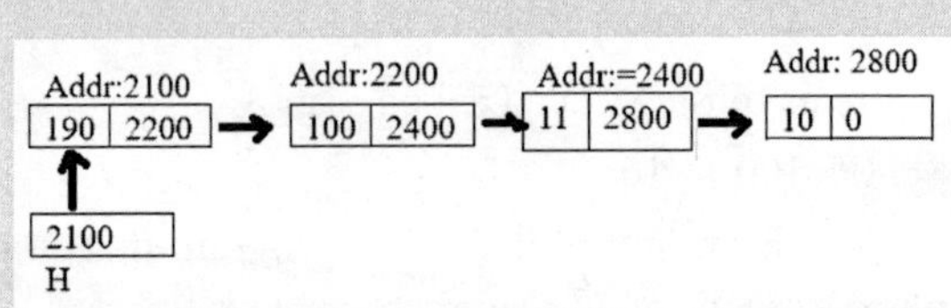

Inserting in the middle:
Now, consider that the user has given a number 15. We assume that the current list contains numbers 190, 100 and 11 in descending order. This 15 is not more than 190, which is the number in the head node. Thus, we will have to traverse the list as explained above and find the node having value less than 15. While traversing the list, when C is pointing to the node having 11, the loop condition becomes false. That is, the new node has to be inserted before it (C). That is, in between B and C as shown in the figure.

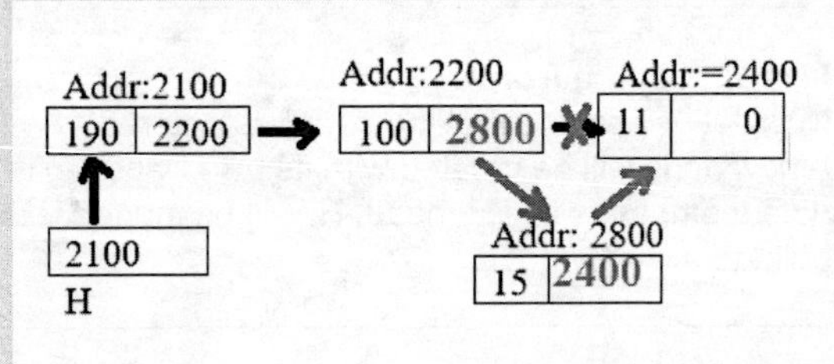

Question 43: We want a recursive version of the above insertion sort function. The following is our proposal. Test whether it is going to work as expected or not.

```
struct lst *insert(struct lst *H, int x){
  struct lst *A, *P,*Q;
  if(H==0 || H->n<=x){
        A=createNode(x);
        A->next=H;
        return A;
  }
  else{ H->next=insert(H->next,x);
        return H;
  }
}
```

We made a fully functional program that calls the above function on a visualization server at the following link. We welcome readers to experiment with it before answering.

https://tinyurl.com/AICTEDSBOOK59

Question 44: Is iterative solution simpler than recursive solution for a problem? What is the problem with recursive solutions?

Answer: No. Not at all. It depends on the problem.

Question 45: What will be the result of the following function?

```
int xyz(struct lst *H, int x){
int s=0;
while(H){ s+=(H->n ==x);
H=H->next;
}
return s;
}
```

You are welcome to explore the following link before answering.

https://tinyurl.com/AICTEDSBOOK78

Question 46: What will be the result of the following function?

```
int xyz(struct lst *H){
while(H&&H->next)H=H->next;
return ((H )?H->n:0);
}
```

You are welcome to explore the following link before answering.

https://tinyurl.com/AICTEDSBOOK79

Question 47: What will be the result of the following function?

```
struct lst * xyz(struct lst *H){
while(H&&H->next)H=H->next;
return ((H )?H:0);
}
```

You are welcome to explore the following link before answering.

https://tinyurl.com/AICTEDSBOOK80

BTW, what does the following statement convey? Assume H is the head of a linked list.

xyz(H)->n

Question 48: What will be the result of the following function?

```
struct lst* xyz(struct lst *H){
while(H&&H->next&&H->next->next)H=H->next;
return ((H&&H ->next)?H->next:0);
}
```

You are welcome to explore the following link before answering.

https://tinyurl.com/AICTEDSBOOK81

Example 3: Explain how the following function works.

```
void print(struct lst *H)
{
if(H->next)print(H->next);
printf("%d\n",H->n);
}
```

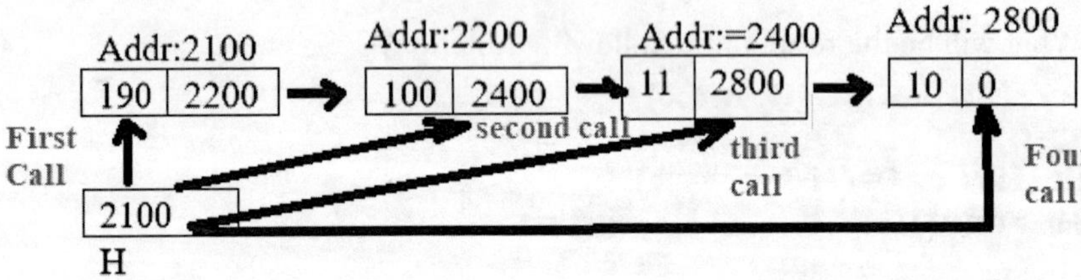

Let us assume that the first time when this function is called, H will be pointing to the head node of the linked list. As it is having the next node, a recursive call is made further. Thus, during the second call, H will be pointing to the second node in the list. As this is also having its next node (i.e. H->next is true), another recursive call is made to this function. Thus, H in the third call will be pointing to the next node (third node here). This recursive calls will continue a node without any next node. In each recursive call, the printf statement will be executed. Thus, 10 will be printed. Then, control comes back to the previous function call. Here again, printf statement is executed. Thus, 11 will be printed. Then, control returns to the previous function call. Thus, we get 100 when printf is executed. Here, we understand that the first last node is processed (last node element is printed), then last but one, and vice versa. We get the elements of the linked list in reverse fashion.

Question 49: What will be the result from this function if we send the address of a linked list which is created through creatsortlist() function.

Question 50: What will be the error if H becomes 0 in the first call itself.

Example 4: Function that takes head of a linked list and an integer x and deletes the first node having x.

Also, the function to delete all the nodes having a given number from the linked list. We have written a function which takes head of a linked list having integers and an integer number which has to be removed from the list as arguments and removes all the occurrences of the nodes having given number and returns the head of the modified linked list.

The node(s) that can be deleted can be either at the front (head) or in the middle or even the last node also.

If we want to remove the head node as it is having x then we move H to point to the next node then free the head node.

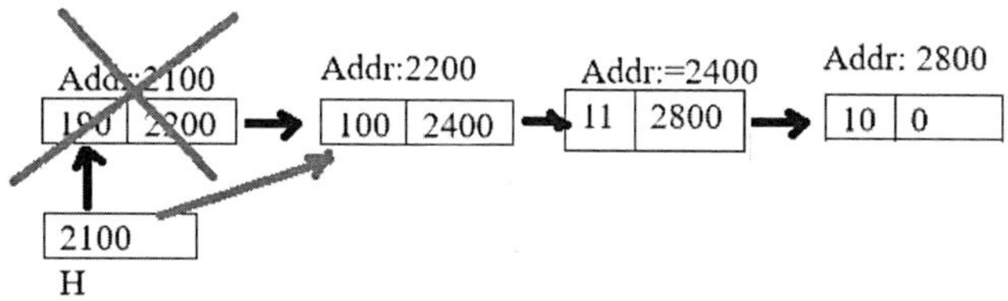

If we want to remove the node which is in the middle of the link then we need to adjust links before removing the node having x.

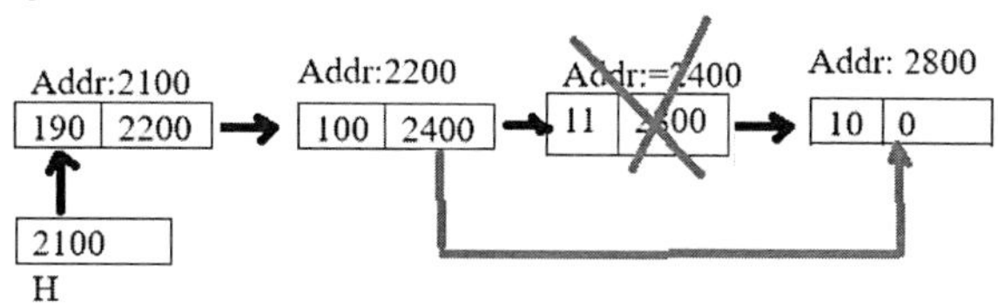

//this removes single node

```
struct lst * delete(struct lst *H, int x){
  struct lst *P,*Q;
  if(H==0)return H;
  //case That is in the head node itself.
  if(H->n==x){
        P=H;
  H=H->next;
  free(P);
  return H;
  }
 //other than head node
  P=H;
  Q=H->next;
  while(Q){
        if(Q->n==x){
        P->next=Q->next;
        free(Q);
        return H;
        }
        P=Q;
        Q=Q->next;
  }
  return H;
}
```

This removes all the nodes having x

```
struct lst * Delete(struct lst *A, int x){
    struct lst *B, *C;
    while(A&&A->n==x){
            B=A;
            A=A->next;
            free(B);
            }
    if(A==0)return 0;
    B=A;
    C=A->next;
    while(C)
    {
        if(C->n==x){
            B->next=C->next;
            free(C);
            C=B->next;
            continue;
            }
    B=C;
    C=C->next;
    }
    return A;
}
```

The following link contains a working program loaded on a visualization server.We welcome readers to experiment the same.

https://tinyurl.com/AICTEDSBOOK60

https://tinyurl.com/deleteanodefromlist1

https://tinyurl.com/deletenodeinalist

Example 5: Program to delete all nodes with a given number from a descending ordered single linked list.

This is almost the same as the above example. As the linked list is in descending ordered one, we can make a better algorithm. For example, if the number which we have to remove is larger than the number in the head node, then we can simply return the head of the linked list without traversing the list at all as all the nodes will be having numbers less than the given number. Similarly, we can stop searching if we find a node whose value is less than the given number. See the changes we made.

We have also written a function createsortlist() which reads a set of numbers and maintains them in descending order. This is used in the main program to test our Delete() function.

```
struct lst * Delete(struct lst *A, int x){
    struct lst *B, *C;
    while(A->n==x){
            B=A;
            A=A->next;
            free(B);
            }
```

```
    if(A==0 || A->n < x)return A;
    B=A;
    C=A->next;
    while(C&&C->n >=x){
        if(C->n==x){
            B->next=C->next;
            free(C);
            C=B->next;
            continue;
            }
    B=C;
    C=C->next;
    }
    return A;
    }
struct lst* createsortlst(){
      int m;
      struct lst *A,*B, *C, *H=0;
      printf("Enter Numbers\n");
      while(1){
      scanf("%d", &m); if(m==0)break;
      A=createnode(m);
      if(H==0)H=A;
      else if(H->n<m){

          A->next=H;
        H=A;
      }
      else{
       B=H;
       C=H->next;
       while(C && C->n > m){
           B=C;
           C=C->next;
       }
       B->next=A;
         if(C){
          A->next=C;
          }
        }
    }
    return(H);
  }
```

```
int main(){
        int m;
        struct lst *H;
        printf("Creating List\n");
        H=createsortlst();
        display(H);
        printf("Enter Number whose all the occurrences to be removed \n");
        scanf("%d", &m);
        H=Delete(H,m);
        printf("List after deleting %d\n", m);
        display(H);
        return 0;
}
```

Output: Creating List

Enter Numbers

12 1 20 20 12 20 90 28 10 10 89 21 10 0

Items in the Single Linked List:

90 89 28 21 20 20 20 12 12 10

10 10 1

Enter Number whose all the occurrences to be removed

10

List after deleting 10

Items in the Single Linked List:

90 89 28 21 20 20 20 12 12 1

Best case time complexity of this function is O(1) and the worst case complexity is O(n) as every node of the list has to be visited if the element required to be deleted is not in the linked list at all.

Question 51: Modify the above Delete() function assuming that the linked list contains numbers in ascending order.

Question 52: Modify the above Delete() function such that it contains only a single while loop.

Question 53: What is the return value of the following function?

```
int compare(struct lst *A, struct lst *B){
  if(A==0&&B==0) return 1;
  else if( A==0 || B==0) return 0;
  else if(A->n<B->n)
  return(compare(A->next,B->next));
  else return 0;
}
```

Question 54: What is the return value of the following function?

```
int compare1(struct lst *A, struct lst *B){
  if(A==0&&B==0) return 1;
  else if( A==0 || B==0) return 0;
  else
  return(compare(A->next,B->next));
}
```

Example 6: Write a function to insert a node at the end of a linked list.

Solution: If the linked list is null (H==0), then the new node itself is returned as itself becomes the first and last element of the list. Otherwise, we take a pointer B which points to H (top most node) and will be made to traverse one by one till the last node. Then, new node A is made next to the node B and then H is returned.

```
struct lst * insertlast(struct lst *H, int x){
     struct lst *A, *B;
     A=createnode(x);
     if(H==0)return A;
     else{
      B=H;
      while(B->next)B=B->next;
      B->next=A;
      return H;
     }
     }

int main(){
         int i,m;
         struct lst *H;
         printf("Creating List\n");
         H=createlist();
         display(H);

            printf("Enter Number \n");
            scanf("%d", &m);

            H=insertlast(H,m);
            printf("List after inserting %d\n", m);
            display(H);
            return 0;
}
```

Output: Case 1: Already Linked list is available:

Creating List

Enter Numbers

20 30 30 21 0

Items in the Single Linked List:

20 30 30 21

Enter Number 34

List after inserting 34

Items in the Single Linked List:

20 30 30 31 34

Case 2: No linked list is existing

Creating List

Enter Numbers

0

Items in the Single Linked List:

Enter Number 34

List after inserting 34

Items in the Single Linked List:

34

See the following picture for more understanding

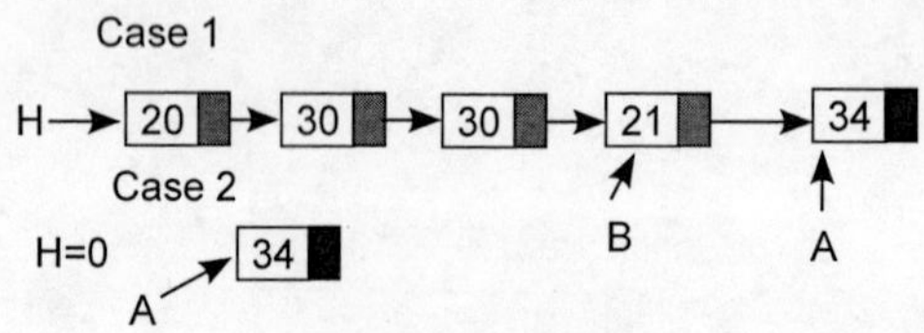

You are welcome to explore the following link before answering.

https://tinyurl.com/AICTEDSBOOK61

Example 7: Insert a node with a given value, x, after nth node.

Solution: If the linked list is null, the new node itself is the resultant linked list. If the linked list is not having n nodes, no insertion takes place. Otherwise, insertion takes place.

```
struct lst * insertafter(struct lst *H, int n, int x){
    struct lst *A, *B;
    A=createnode(x);
    if(H==0)return A;
    else {
     B=H;
     while(B&&n--)B=B->next;
     if(B){A->next=B->next;
        B->next=A;
        }
     else
   printf("Not that many nodes are there. No insertion has taken place\n");
     return H;
    }
    }
int main(){
        int m;
        struct lst *H;
        printf("Creating List\n");
        H=createlist();
        display(H);
        printf("Enter Number whose  occurrences to be removed \n");
```

```
        scanf("%d", &m);
        H=insertafter(H,5,m);  /*insert after 5th node*/
        printf("List after inserting %d\n", m);
        display(H);
        return 0;
}
```

Output: Creating List

Enter Numbers

20 30 12 22 89 77 12 22 0

Items in the Single Linked List:

22 12 77 89 22 12 30 20

Enter Number whose occurrences to be removed

7

List after inserting 7

Items in the Single Linked List:

22 12 77 89 22 12 7 30 20

You are welcome to explore the following link to test the above code..

https://tinyurl.com/AICTEDSBOOK62

Question 55: Create a new node with a given value x, after the nth node in the descending ordered list. The following code is proposed. Will it work?.

```
struct lst * insertafter(struct lst *H, int n, int x){
    struct lst *A, *B;
    if(H==0||H->n<x)return H;
    else {
    A=createnode(x);
     B=H;
     while(B&&--n&&B->n>x)B=B->next;
     if(B){A->next=B->next;
        B->next=A;
        }
     else
  printf("Not that many nodes are there. No insertion has taken place\n");
     return H;
     }
     }
```

You are welcome to explore the following link before answering.

https://tinyurl.com/AICTEDSBOOK82

Example 8: Merging Two Linked Lists having numbers in descending order. We wanted to adjust their links such that all the nodes of both the lists forms as a singled linked list with all the numbers in descending order.

```
struct lst * merge(struct lst *A, struct lst *B){
  struct lst *C, *D, *H;
  if(A==0) return B;
  if(B==0) return A;
     if(A->n <B->n) {
              H=B;
              B=B->next;
              }
     else{
       H=A;
       A=A->next;
     }
     C=H;
     while(A&&B){
          if(A->n < B->n) {
                  C->next=B;
                  C=B;
                  B=B->next;
                  }
          else{
             C->next=A;
             C=A;
             A=A->next;
             }
     }
     if(A) C->next=A;
     if(B) C->next=B;
  return (H);
}
int main(){
      struct lst *A,*B, *C;
 A=createsortlst();
 B=createsortlst();
   printf("First List\n");
   display(A);
   printf("Second List\n");
   display(B);
   printf("Merged List\n");
   C=merge(A,B);
   display(C);
   return 0;
}
```

Output: Enter Numbers

```
10
2
33
80
4
0
Enter Numbers
12
44
123
41
92
32
21
0
First List
Items in the  Linked List:
80   33   10   4   2
Second List
Items in the  Linked List:
123   92   44   41   32   21   12
Merged List
Items in the  Linked List:
123   92   80   44   41   33   32   21   12   10       4   2
```

Explanation: Two lists are given below. If any of the lists are null lists, the other list becomes a merged list.

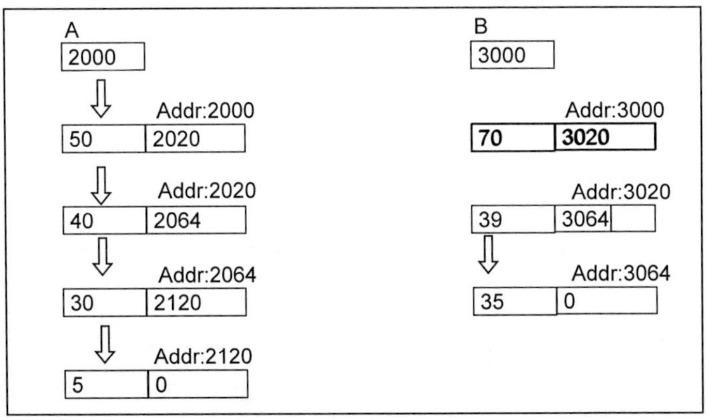

First, we compare the values of both the heads of both the lists and we assign two pointers H and C to point to the largest one as shown below. Also, A or B adjusted to point to the next node in its list. In this example, list B's head node is larger, thus H and C will be made pointed to it. While B is adjusted to point to the next node.

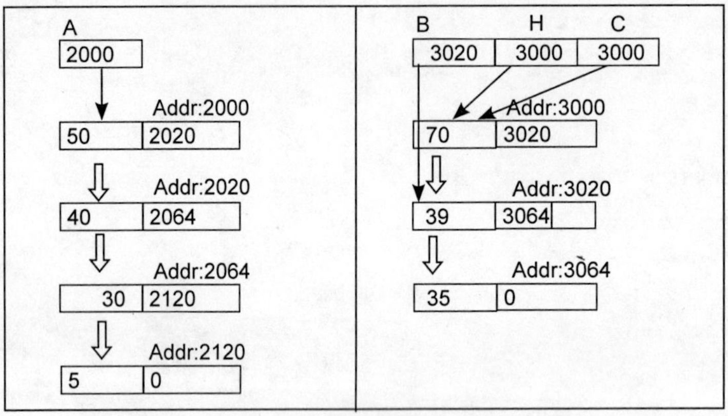

Now, we enter into the while loop and compare values of the nodes pointed by A and B. C will be adjusted to point to the largest of them. After that A (or B) is adjusted to point to the next node.

For example, currently A is pointing to 50 while B is pointing to 35. Thus, we make C's next as A, C as A and then A is made a pointer to the next node (i.e., the node with 40).

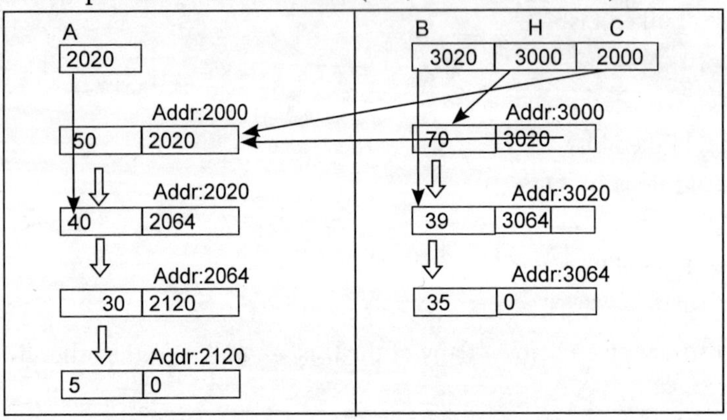

Similarly, the next pointer adjustment takes place as shown below.

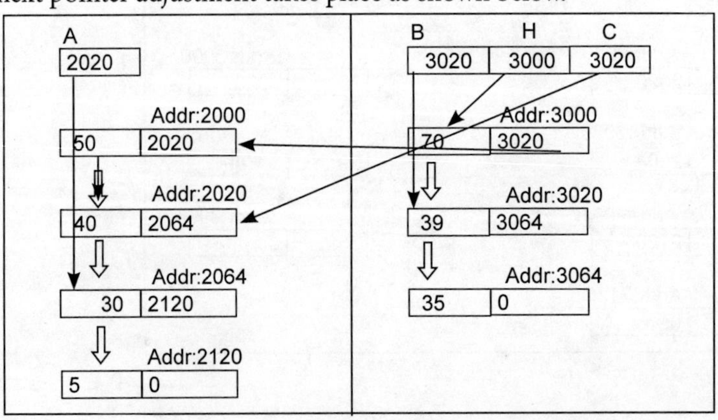

Finally, the merged linked list is as follows.

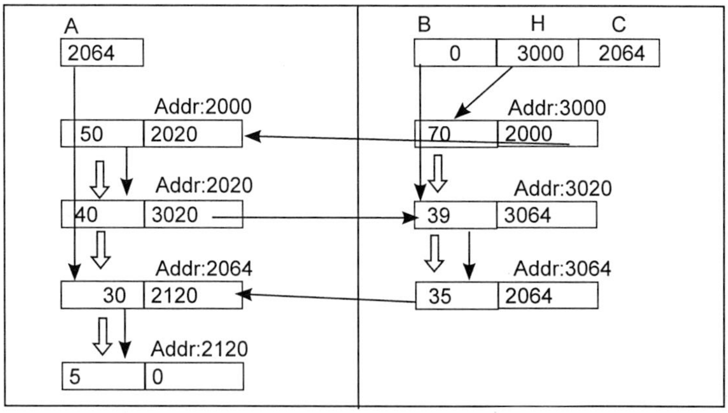

Thus, if we traverse from H, we may get all the node values of both the lists in descending order.

You are welcome to explore the following links to understand things further.

https://tinyurl.com/mergingtwolists

https://tinyurl.com/mergesortedlists

Question 56: What do we get if we send A and B to display() function after merging. Verify the figure and check.

Example 9: The following program merges two Linked Lists having numbers in descending order and creates a resultant linked list such that elements of both the lists will be in descending order. Whatever memory is needed for the resultant list will be allocated dynamically. Original lists should not get modified.

```
struct lst * merge(struct lst *A, struct lst *B){
 struct lst *C, *D, *H, *E;
 if(A==0) return B;
 if(B==0) return A;
   if(A->n <B->n) {E=createnode(B->n);
              H=B;
              B=B->next;
              }
   else{
     E=createnode(A->n);
      H=A;
      A=A->next;
   }
   C=H;
   while(A&&B){
          if(A->n < B->n) { E=createnode(B->n);
                      C->next=E;
                          C=E;
                      B=B->next;
                      }
```

```
            else
            {  E=createnode(A->n);
               C->next=E;
                   C=E;
               A=A->next;
               }
        }

        while(A) {
            E=createnode(A->n);
            C->next=E;
                A=A->next;
            }
            while(B) {
            E=createnode(B->n);
            C->next=E;
                B=B->next;
            }
    return (H);
    }

    int main(){
     struct lst *A,*B, *C;
     A=createsortlst();
     B=createsortlst();
       printf("First List\n");
       display(A);
       printf("Second List\n");
       display(B);
       printf("Merged List\n");
       C=merge(A,B);
       display(C);
    return 0;
    }
```

Output: Enter Numbers

12

2

33

22

12

2

0

Enter Numbers

44

12

90

2

12

44

45

0

First List

Items in the Linked List:

33 22 12 12 2 2

Second List

Items in the Linked List:

90 45 44 44 12 12 2

Merged List

Items in the Linked List:

90 45 44 44 33 22 12 12 12 12

2 2 2

Example 10: The following function which takes the address of a single linked list with descending ordered elements, an integer, n, and lst type pointer to pointer. It splits the list into such that numbers less than or equal to n will be in the second list and others will be in the first linked list. Second link list addressed is stored in the third pointer which is sent arguments.

Solution: If list is null or the value if top most node is less than or equal to n, then the second linked list becomes null and returns H value. Otherwise, we traverse the linked list for the node whose value is less than or equal to n. That node address is stored in the memory location pointer by **second** while making the first list ending is till this node.

```
struct lst * split(struct lst *H, int n, struct lst **second){
    struct lst *A, *B;
    if(H==0||H->n<=n){ *second=0;
              return H;
              }
    A=H;
    B=H->next;
    while(B){
         if(B->n <=n) break;
         A=B;
         B=B->next;
         }
    if(B==0){ *second=0;
         return H;
         }
    else{
       A->next=0;
       *second=B;
       return H;
       }
}
```

```
int main(){
        int i,m;
        struct lst *H, *B;
        printf("Creating List\n");
        H=createlist(); /* we call also call createsortlist() */
       display(H);

        printf("Enter Number from which second list has to be created\n");
        scanf("%d", &m);
        H=split(H,m,&B);
        printf("First List after splitting %d\n");
        display(H);
        printf("Second List after splitting %d\n");
        display(B);
        return 0;
}
```

Output: Creating List

Enter Numbers

10 20 30 40 50 60 70 90 0

Items in the Single Linked List:

90 70 60 50 40 30 20 10

Enter Number from which second list has to be created

45

First List after splitting 45

Items in the Single Linked List:

90 70 60 50

Second List after splitting 45

Items in the Single Linked List:

40 30 20 10

You are welcome to explore the following link to verify the above code.

https://tinyurl.com/AICTEDSBOOK74

Question 57: See the following function which takes the address of a single linked list having numbers in descending order, an integer, n, and address of the dlst type of pointer as arguments. Identify it correctly splits the single linked list such that all the first n nodes will be in the first single linked list and others are in the second single linked list its address is stored in the memory pointed by the second pointer. Address of the first list will be returned.

```
struct lst * splitfromnthnode(struct lst *H, int n, struct lst **second){
    struct lst *A, *B;
    if(H==0||n<=0){ *second=0;
            return H;
            }
```

```
        A=H;
        B=H->next;
        while(B&&--n){
              A=B;
              B=B->next;
              }
        if(B==0){ *second=0;
              return H;
              }
        else
        {
           A->next=0;
           *second=B;
         return H;
           }
    }
```

You are welcome to explore the following link before answering.

https://tinyurl.com/AICTEDSBOOK75

Example 11: The following program shows how a structure can be defined to maintain a union type object in the linked list.

```
struct lst{
 int type;
 union Item{
        int lrno;
        char *desc;
 }abc;
 struct lst *next;
};
int main() {
 struct lst C={0,122,0},B={1,"Ram",&C},A={1,"Abhi",&B},*H=&A;

while(H){
 if(H->type==0)printf("%d\n",H->abc.lrno);
 else printf("%s\n",H->abc.desc);
 H=H->next;
}
 return 0;
}
```

You are welcome to explore the following link before answering.

https://tinyurl.com/AICTEDSBOOK97

The following picture shows a variety(different) types of elements as a list! Ha. Ha.

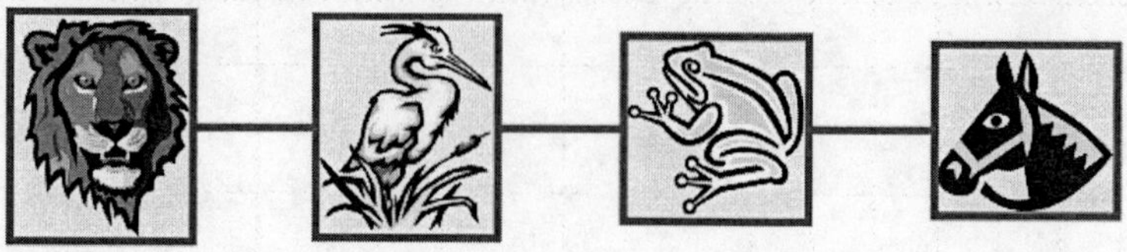

Example 12: The following program shows how a structure can be defined to maintain a chain of functions in the linked list.

```
void f(int n){
 int i;
 for(i=0;i<n;i++)printf("One\t");
}
void ff(int n){
 int i;
 for(i=0;i<2*n;i++)printf("Two\t");
}
void fff(int n){
 int i;
 for(i=0;i<3*n;i++)printf("Three\t");
}

struct lst{
 int n;
 void (*abc)(int);
 struct lst *next;
}C={2,f,0},B={3,ff,&C},A={1,fff,&B},*H=&A;

int main() {
while(H){
 H->abc(H->n);
 H=H->next;
}
 return 0;
}
```

You are welcome to explore the following link before answering.
https://tinyurl.com/AICTEDSBOOK96

3.1.2 Circular Linked Lists

This is a simple variant of a single linked list. Unlike a single linked list, here there is no node which can be called as head or tail node. In a single linked list, tail node will be having null as its next. Here, we don't have such a node at all. All the nodes will be having their next. To create this type list, we may first create a singly linked list then head of it will be assigned to the last node's next. The following code fragment demonstrates how the same can be done in practice.

```
struct lst{int n; struct lst *next}A,B,C,D;
int main() {
struct lst *P, *H=0;
A.n=10;B.n=5;C.n=3, D.n=100;
A.next=&B;B.next=&C; C.next=&D; D.next=&A; P=&A;
H=P;
do{
  printf("%d\n",H->n);
  H=H->next;
}while(H!=P);
  return 0;
}
```

Readers may play with the above code on the visualization server given below.

https://tinyurl.com/circularlists

The following snapshot shows the circular list creation. Especially when D.next=&A is executed, the circular list is getting created.

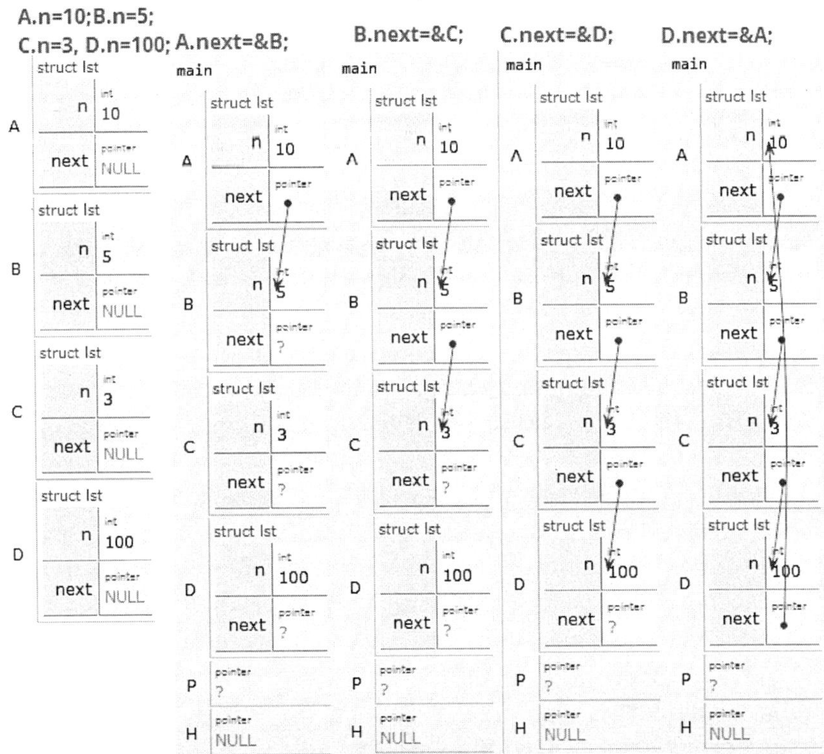

The following is the snapshot that explains how we can traverse a circular list. Initially, P and H are pointers to A. The pointer P stays at A only while H moves till it reaches again P. In the following picture you may find how H is changing.

First Iteration Second Iteration Third Iteration Fourth Iteration Last Iteration

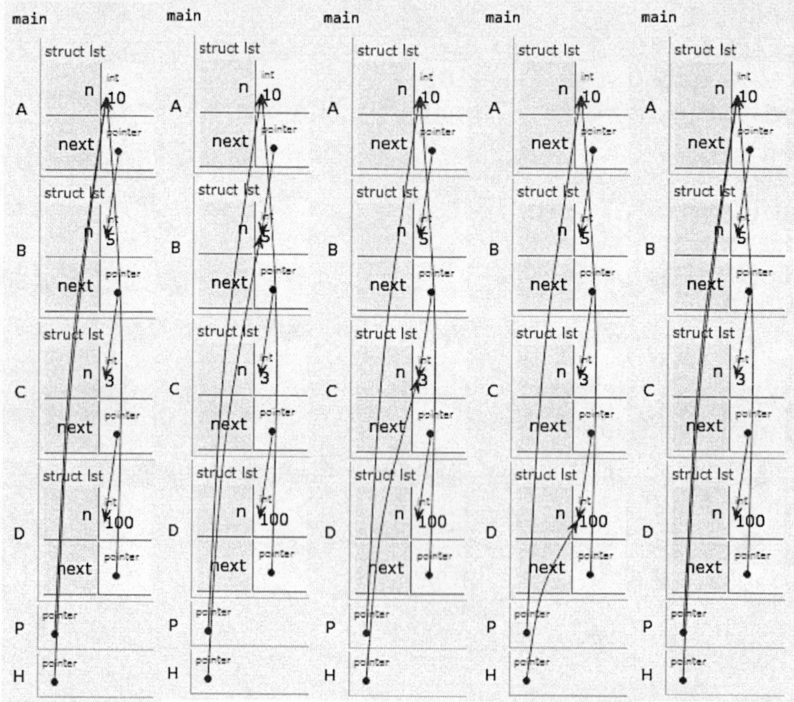

This type of list is useful for having priority queues. It is not uncommon to call in circular lists also a node as head node, Though, every node is equally eligible to be called head node. Usually, from the priority queue point of view a node whose value is high is called a head node such that whenever we carry insertions or deletions from the priority queue, we shall with the help of this head node.

In the following example, we have the function createcirlist(), which takes the head of a circular list and an integer to be inserted and inserts a new node in the circular list at its appropriate place and returns the head of the modified circular list. This is more similar to creating a sorted linked list with simple modification.

First time, circular list is assumed as null list. When we send this and a new number to createcirlist() function, then a new node will be created with the given number and its address itself is assigned to its next data member of itself such that a circular list of single node is formed. This node's address is returned from the function. Next time onwards, the returned address of the function createcirlist() and new number will be sent to the function createcirlist(). Thus, circular list will be created.

Example 13: Program to create single circular lists.

```
/* Circular single list*/
struct lst* createcirlst(struct lst*H, int m){
        struct lst *A,*B, *C;
        A=createnode(m);
        if(H==0){ A->next=A;
                return A;
                }
```

```
            else if(H->n<m){
               B=H;
               while(B->next !=H) B=B->next;
               B->next=A;
               A->next=H;
               return A;
            }
            else{
             B=H;
             C=H->next;
             while((C!=H) && (C->n > m)){
                   B=C;
                   C=C->next;
             }
             B->next=A;
             A->next=C;
             return H;
            }
      }

   int main(){
            int i,m;
            struct lst *H=0, *A;
            printf("Enter Numbers\n");
            while(1){
            scanf("%d", &m); if(m==0)break;
            H=createcirlst(H,m);
            }
            printf("Numbers in circular list are\n");
            A=H;
            do{
                  printf("%d\n", A->n);
                  A=A->next;
            }while(A !=H);
            return 0;
   }
```

Output: Enter Numbers

12 3 2 29 8 78 21 0

Numbers in circular list are

78

29

21

12

8

3

2

Question 58: In the following link we have code loaded on to the visualization server. Check whether it is deleting a given node from the circular linked list or not.

https://tinyurl.com/deletingcircularlist

Example 14: The following function takes the head of a circular linked list and an integer n as arguments then adds a new node with n as its data and then returns the head of the modified circular linked list.

```
struct lst *createCircularlist(struct lst *H, int n){
  struct lst *A=createNode(n);
  struct lst *P;
  if(H==0) {
        A->next=A;
        return A;
  }
        P=H->next;
        do{
        P=P->next;
        }while(P->next!=H);

        A->next=H;
        P->next=A;
        return A;
}
```

We welcome readers to visit the following link to check the working of the above function.

https://tinyurl.com/insertcircularlist

Question 59: What is the output of the following code fragment?

```
struct lst{  int n;      struct lst* next;    };
int main() {
struct lst A={19,0};
int i;
A.next=&A;
for(i=0;i<10;){A=*(A.next);
 i++;
}
printf("%d\n",       A.n);
 return 0;
}
```

You are welcome to explore the following link before answering.

https://tinyurl.com/AICTEDSBOOK106

3.1.3 Doubly Linked Lists

Here in the double linked list(DLL)[58], for each node, we will be having two pointers (next, prev) which are pointing to next and previous nodes of the double linked list. In addition to pointers, we can maintain

58 DLL also stands for dynamic link library. Ever did you come across with an error window in windows such as "This application cannot run, so and so DLL is missing" etc?

any information in each node. For example, the following structure is used to store integer numbers in a double linked list.

Example 15: The following programming example defines a structure to realize a double linked list. Also, three such variables are declared and links are created to show how a double linked list can be created. Also, a while loop is written to show the traversal of the double linked list using the next link.

```
struct dlst{
      int n;
      struct dlst *next;
      struct dlst *prev;
};
void display(struct dlst *B){
    printf("Items in the Double Linked List:\n");
    while(B){
            printf("%d\t", B->n);
            B=B->next;
    }
    printf("\n");
}
 int main(){
        struct dlst A,B,C, *H;
        A.n=10;
        B.n=90;
        C.n=78;
        A.next=&B;
        A.prev=0;
        B.next=&C;
        B.prev=&A;
        C.next=0;
        C.prev=&B;
        H=&A;
        while(H){
        printf("%d\n", H->n);
        H=H->next;
        }
        return 0;
 }
```

Analysis of the above Program

When struct dlst A, B, C, *H; statement is executed, memory for them will be allocated as shown below.

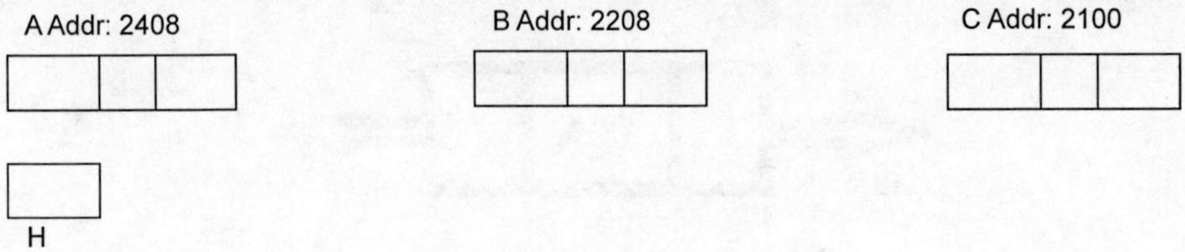

When the following statements are executed, the variables A,B,C may contain members like this.

A.n = 10;

B.n = 90;

C.n = 78;

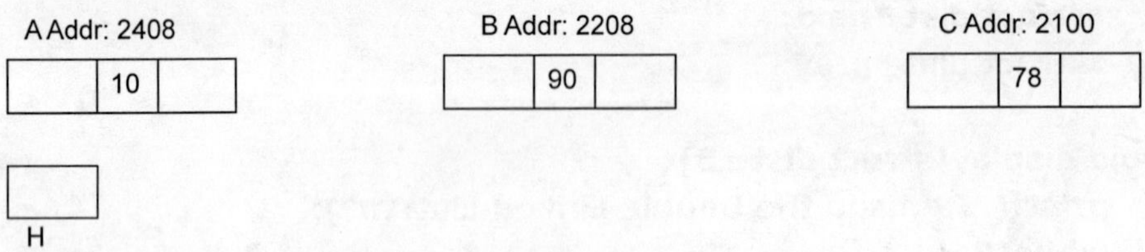

When the statements **A.next=&B** and **A.prev=0** executed, the following actions take place.

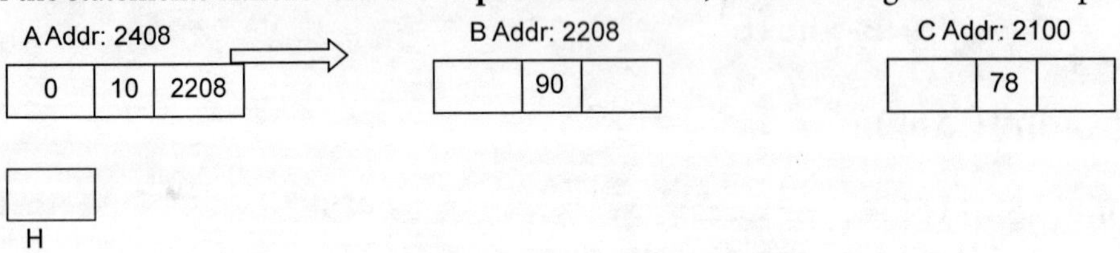

Similarly, when **B.next=&C and B.prev=&A** is executed the following actions take place.

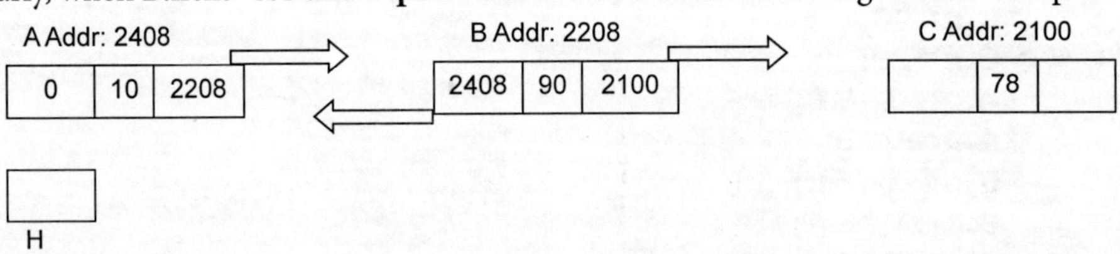

Similarly, when **C.next=0 and C.prev=&B** is executed, the following actions take place.

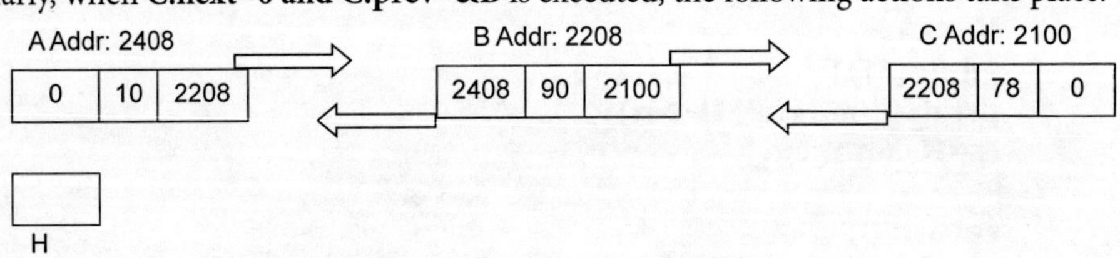

When the H=&A statement is executed, the address of A is assigned to H as shown below.

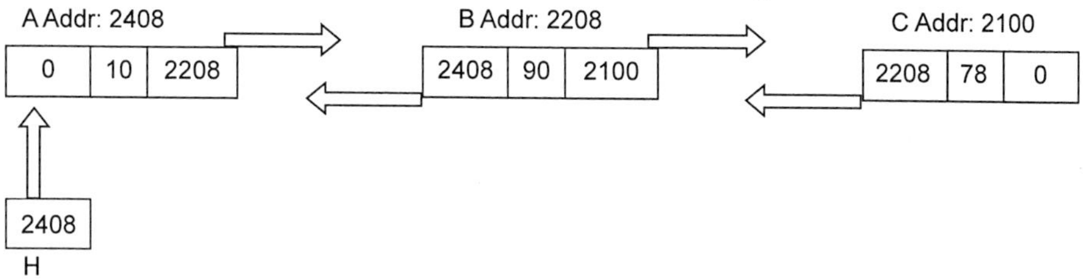

The above structure is called a double linked list.

Now, analyze the while loop which traverses the double linked list and prints elements in it. Initially, H value is the address of A, i.e. 2408, thus the while loop condition becomes true. Thus, control goes to the while(H) block and **H->n**, i.e., 10 is printed and then **H->next**, i.e., 2208 is assigned to H, which is the address of B. Thus, H now will be pointing to B.

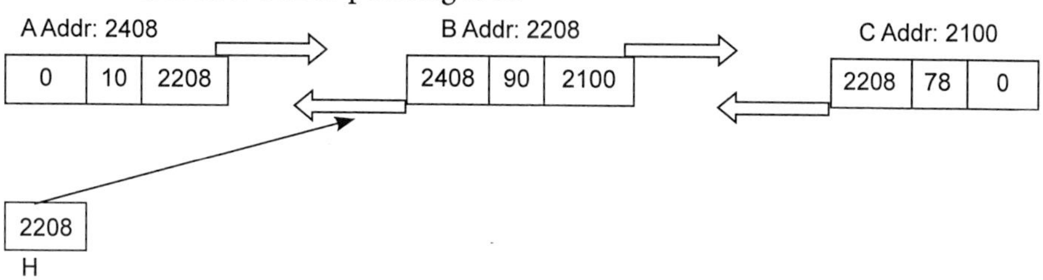

Again, while(H) is executed. As, current value of H is 2208, loop control goes to the loop block. Thus, **H->n**, i.e., 90 will be printed. Then, **H->next**, i.e., 2100 is assigned to H. Thus, H now points to C.

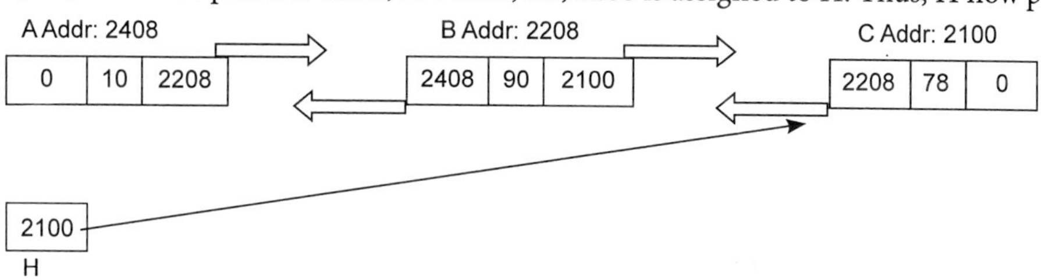

Now, again while(H) condition becomes true. Thus, loop control enters into the while loop block. The H->n value, i.e. 78 is printed. Then, H->next value, i.e., 0, is assigned to 0. Thus, in the next iteration while(H) condition becomes false. Control comes out of the while loop. Like this, double linked lists can be traversed.

https://tinyurl.com/AICTEDSBOOK89

Question 60: Assuming that H, rH are struct dlst type of pointers and H is currently pointing to the head of the double linked list. What happens if the following code gets executed?

```
while(H){
 printf("%d\n",H->n);
 rH=H;
 H=H->next;
}
H=rH;
while(H){
 printf("%d\n",H->n);
 H=H->prev;
}
```

You are welcome to explore the following link before answering.

https://tinyurl.com/doublelinkedlist

Question 61: Assuming that H is struct dlst type of pointer and H is currently pointing to the head of the double linked list. What happens if the following code gets executed?

```
H=&A;
do{
 printf("%d\n",H->n);
 H=H->next;
}while(H->next);
while(H){
 printf("%d\n",H->n);
 H=H->prev;
}
```

You are welcome to explore the following link before answering.

https://tinyurl.com/AICTEDSBOOK90

Question 62: What does the following code fragment do?

```
struct dlst A={10,0,0},B={90,0,&A},
C={199,0,&B},D={111,0,&C},*H=&A,*rH; A.next=&B;B.next=&C;C.next=&D;
```

You are welcome to explore the following link before answering.

https://tinyurl.com/AICTEDSBOOK98

In the above example, a double linked list is created with static objects. Let us assume that we want to create a doubly linked list with dynamically created nodes. For that, we have written the following function that takes an integer as argument and creates a dynamic node by calling malloc function then stores this integer while setting next, prev members of the nade as zero.

```
struct dlst *createNode(int n){
 struct dlst *A;
 A=(struct dlst *)malloc(sizeof(struct dlst));
 A->n=n;
 A->prev=0;
 A->next=0;
 return A;
 }
```

You are welcome to explore the following links before answering.

https://tinyurl.com/doublelinkedlists1

https://tinyurl.com/doublelinkelists2

Question 63: For the above working double linked list program, can we use the following structure? Then, can we declare this structure type objects and pointers as Node A, B, *C?

```
typedef struct dlst{
  int n;
  struct dlst *next;
  struct dlst *prev;
}Node;
```

You are welcome to explore the following link before answering.

https://tinyurl.com/AICTEDSBOOK99

Question 64: For the above working double linked list program, can we use the following structure? Then, can we declare this structure type objects and pointers as Node A, B, *C?

```
struct dlst{
  int n;
  struct dlst *next;
  struct dlst *prev;
};
typedef struct dlst Node;
```

You are welcome to explore the following link before answering.

https://tinyurl.com/AICTEDSBOOK100

Question 65: Assuming that H, rH are struct dlst type of pointers and H is currently pointing to the head of the double linked list. What happens if the following code gets executed?

```
for(i=0;i<5;i++){
  printf("Iteration %d\n",i+1);
while(H){ printf("%d\n",H->n);
  rH=H;
  H=H->next;
}
H=rH;
while(H){ printf("%d\n",H->n);
  rH=H;
  H=H->prev;
}
H=rH;
}
```

You are welcome to explore the following link before answering.

https://tinyurl.com/AICTEDSBOOK103

Example 16: The following function takes head of a linked list, an integer n as arguments then adds a new node with n as its data at the front of the linked list. At the end, returns the head of the modified linked list.

```
struct dlst *insert(struct dlst *H, int n){
  struct dlst *A;
  A=createNode(n);
  if(H==0)H=A;
  else{
   H->prev=A;
        A->next=H;
        H=A;
  }
  return H;
 }
```

You are welcome to explore the following link before answering.

https://tinyurl.com/doublelinkedlistinsert

Assume that we want to create a doubly linked list in the sorted fashion. For this purpose, the following function takes head of a linked list having numbers in descending order, an integer n as arguments then adds a new node with n as its data at its appropriate place in the doubly linked list. At the end, it returns the head of the modified linked list. As usual, like singly linked lists, here also the new node may be added before the front, after the last node or in between the doubly linked list.

```
struct dlst *insertSort(struct dlst *H, int n){
  struct dlst *A,*B,*C;
  A=createNode(n);
  if(H==0)return A; //the new node itself becomes the double list
  else if(H->n<n){  //adding at the front
   H->prev=A;
        A->next=H;
        H=A;
        return H;
  }

  else{
        B=H;
        C=H->next;
        while(C&&C->n>n){
        B=C;
        C=C->next;
        }
        if(C){ //adding in the middle of the doubly linked list
        B->next=A;
        A->prev=B;
        A->next=C;
        C->prev=A;
        }
        else{//adding at the end of the existing doubly linked list
        B->next=A;
        A->prev=B;
        }
  return H;
  }
 }
```

You are welcome to explore the following link to understand the concepts further.

https://tinyurl.com/doublelinkedlistsorteddes

Question 66: Do visit the following link that is having a main program which shows how a node can be deleted from a doubly linked list. After exploring that main program, convert the main program into a function to delete a node with a given value x from the given double linked list.

You are welcome to explore the following link before answering.

https://tinyurl.com/doublelinkedlistdeletion

Example 17: The following code will add a new number at the end of the double linked list.

```
struct dlst * insertlast(struct dlst *H, int x){
    struct dlst *A, *B;
    A=(struct dlst *) malloc(sizeof(struct dlst));
    A->n=x;
    A->next=0;
    A->prev=0;
    if(H==0)return A;
    else{
     B=H;
     while(B->next)B=B->next;
     B->next=A;
     A->prev=B;
     return H;
    }
    }
```

You are welcome to explore the following link before answering.

https://tinyurl.com/AICTEDSBOOK91

Question 67: We wanted to insert a new node to the double linked list with value x and after nth node. The following function takes the address of the double linked list, n, and x arguments and returns the head of the modified double linked list. Verify if it works or not.

```
struct dlst * insertafter(struct dlst *H, int n, int x){
    struct dlst *A, *B;
    A=(struct dlst *) malloc(sizeof(struct dlst));
    A->n=x;
    A->next=0;
    A->prev=0;
    if(H==0)return A;
    else{
     B=H;
     while(B&&n--)B=B->next;
     if(B){A->next=B->next;
        B->next=A;
        }
     else
       printf("Not that many nodes are there. No insertion has taken place\n")
     return H;
    }
      }
```

Before answering the question, please do explore the following link.

https://tinyurl.com/AICTEDSBOOK92

Question 68: In the following, we have a function, display which takes a dlst type pointer. Is it acceptable to send a lst type pointer as an argument?

```
struct dlst{
 int n;
 struct dlst *next;
 struct dlst *prev;
};
struct lst{
 int n;
 struct lst *next;
};
void display(struct dlst *A){
 while(A){printf("%d\n",A->n);
 A=A->next;
 }
}
int main() {
struct lst C={10,0},B={11,&C},A={122,&B}, *H=&A;
display(H);
 return 0;
}
```

You are welcome to explore the following link before answering.

https://tinyurl.com/AICTEDSBOOK101

Question 69: In the following, we have a function, display which takes a lst type pointer. Is it acceptable to send a dlst type pointer as an argument?

```
struct dlst{
 int n;
 struct dlst *next;
 struct dlst *prev;
};
struct lst{
 int n;
 struct lst *next;
};
void display(struct lst *A){
 while(A){printf("%d\n",A->n);
 A=A->next;
 }
}
int main() {
struct      dlst      C={10,0,0},B={11,&C,0},A={122,&B,0},      *H=&A;
C.prev=&B;B.prev=&A;
display(H);
 return 0;
}
```

You are welcome to explore the following link before answering.

https://tinyurl.com/AICTEDSBOOK102

3.1.4 Linked List Representation and Operations of Stack

Example 18: The following example demonstrates the use of linked lists in realizing stacks. As we will be creating nodes dynamically, we may not find a need for isfull() function. Remaining all functions that are discussed in the previous chapter are implemented below. We are taking a struct lst type of data member with the TOP in the stack structure. When the stack type object or variable is initiated this TOP value will be set to 0 to indicate that the stack is empty. Whenever a new object is pushed, a new struct lst type object is created and current TOP is made as next to this new object then TOP is made to point to this new object. Whenever pop is called the object which TOP is pointing to will be removed and TOP is adjusted to point to the next object.

```
struct stack{
     struct lst* top;
};
void INITSTACK(struct stack *A){
   A->top=0;
}
int isempty(struct stack *A){
   return  (A->top ==0);
}
void push(struct stack *A, int v){
    struct lst *B;
    B=(struct lst*) malloc(sizeof(struct lst));
    B->n=v;
    B->next=A->top;
    A->top=B;
}

int pop(struct stack *A){
   struct lst *B;
   int x;
    if(isempty(A)){
              printf("Stack Empty\n");
              exit(-1);
              }
   B=A->top;
   x=B->n;
   A->top=B->next;
   free(B);
   return (x);
}
int peek(struct stack *A){
    if(isempty(A)){
              printf("Stack Empty\n");
              exit(-1);
              }
      return (A->top->n);
}
```

```
int main(){
        int m;
        struct stack A, *p;
        p=&A;
        INITSTACK(p);
        while(1){
                scanf("%d", &m); if(m==0)break;
                push(p,m);
        }
        while(!isempty(p))printf("%d\n", pop(p));
        return 0;
}
```

A Snapshot of stack operations on linked list based stack. Now, a new number 10 is pushed. Thus, TOP points to the node having 10.

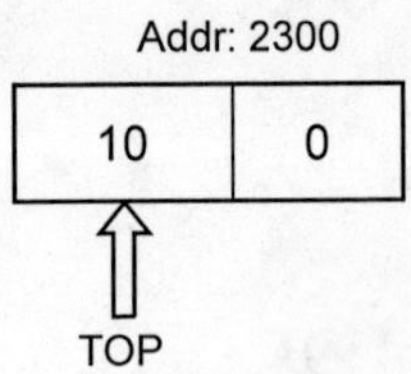

Now, a new number 19 is pushed. Thus, TOP points to the node having 19 while the previous node will be next to this.

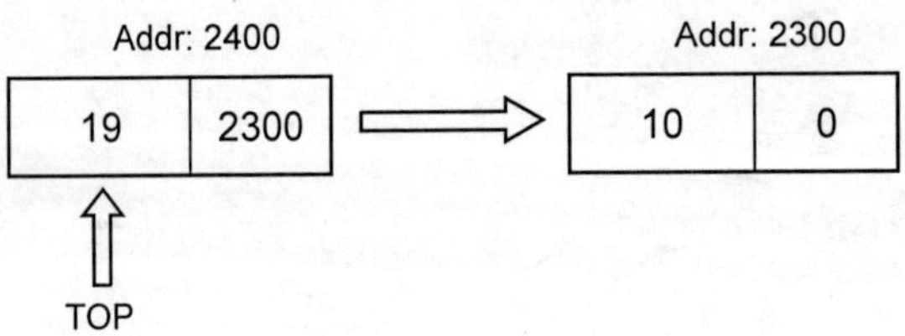

Now, a new number 91 is pushed. Thus, TOP points to the node having 91 while the previous node will be next to this.

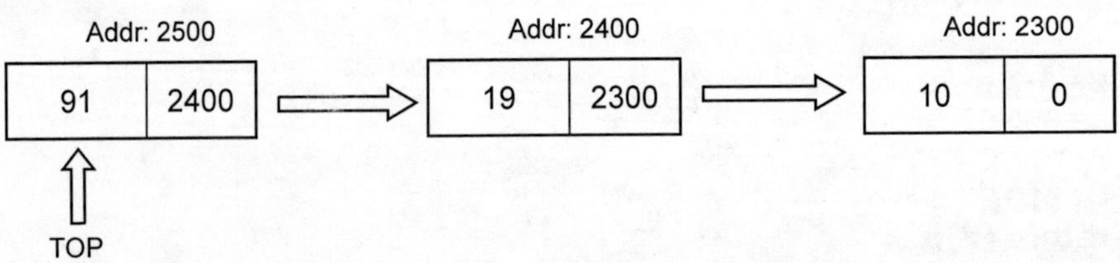

If we assume that pop is called. Which means 91 will be printed and the node having 91 will be freed after making TOP to point to the next node, i.e. the node having 19. State of the stack will be as shown next.

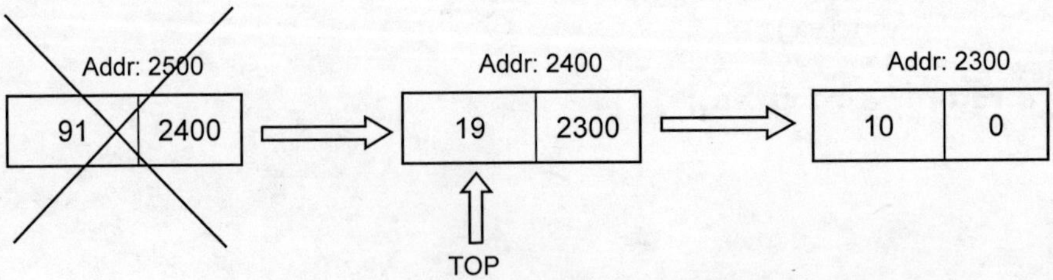

If we assume that pop is called. Which means 19 will be printed and the node having 19 will be freed after making TOP to point to the next node, i.e. the node having 10. State of the stack will be as shown next.

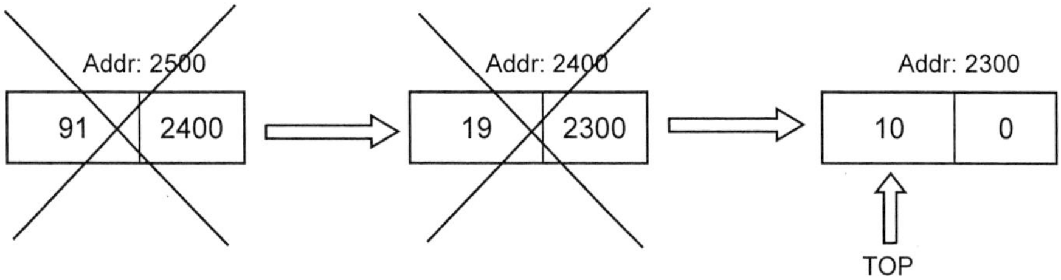

If we assume that pop is called. Which means 10 will be printed and the node having 10 will be freed after making TOP to point to the next node, i.e. null node now.

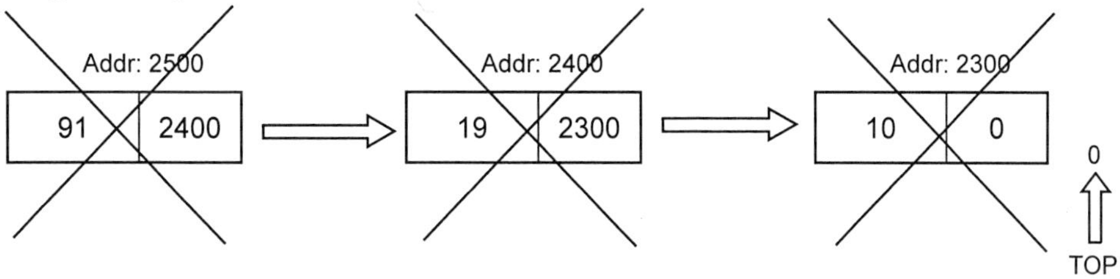

You are welcome to explore the following link to understand the things further.

https://tinyurl.com/NBVstackusinglinkedlists

The following video explains how a stack can be realized using a linked list.

https://www.youtube.com/watch?v=L0hTOwXC5yU&list=PLXX7XiUxnzzWoLDfgad4s4dwleb4NMtVN&index=39

3.1.5 Linked List Representation and Operations of Queue

Example 19: Realizing the queues using a single linked list. As we will be creating nodes dynamically, we may not find a need for isfull() function. Remaining all functions that are discussed in the previous chapter are implemented below. We are taking a struct lst type of data members FRONT, REAR in the queue structure. When this type object or variable is initiated this FRONT, REAR values will be set to 0 to indicate that the queue is empty. Whenever a new object is inserted, a new struct lst type object is created and current REAR is made as next to this new object then REAR is made to point to this new object. Also, when the first object is inserted FRONT is made to point to it. Whenever we call remove, the object which FRONT is pointing to will be removed and FRONT is adjusted to point to the next object. Also, when FRONT becomes zero, REAR also initialized to zero.

```
struct queue{
    struct lst* rear;
    struct lst *front;
};
void INITQUEUE(struct queue *A){
   A->rear=0;
   A->front=0;
}
```

```
int isempty(struct queue *A){
   return  (A->rear ==0);
}
void insert(struct queue *A, int v){
    struct lst *B;
    B=(struct lst*) malloc(sizeof(struct lst));
    B->n=v;
    B->next=0;
    if(isempty(A)){ A->front=B;
              A->rear=B;
              }

    else{
    A->rear->next=B;
    A->rear=B;
    }
}
int remove(struct queue *A){
   struct lst *B;
   int x;
    if(isempty(A)){
             printf("Queue Empty\n");
             exit(-1);
             }
   B=A->front;
   x=B->n;
   A->front=B->next;
   if(A->front==0)A->rear=0;
   free(B);
   return (x);
}
int main(){
        int i,m;
        struct queue A, *p;
        p=&A;
        INITQUEUE(p);
        while(1){
         scanf("%d", &m); if(m==0)break;
         insert(p,m);
         }
   printf("Elements from the queue\n");
         while(!isempty(p))printf("%d\n", remove(p));
return 0;
}
```

Output:

90

12

22

3

23

22

0

Elements from the queue

90

12

22

3

23

22

The following is an explanation of how a queue is realized using linked lists.

When a new number 10 is inserted into an empty queue, a new node of lst type is created. Its n data member is assigned to 10 and the next data member to 0. Then, both FRONT and REAR are made point to this node.

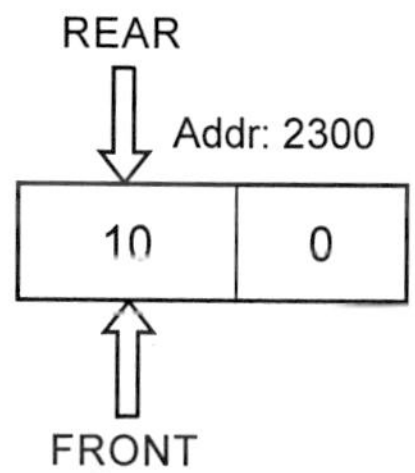

When another number 19 is inserted in the queue, a new lst type of object is created (its n and next values are initialized to 19 and 0) and it is linked as next node to current last node. Then, REAR is made to point to this new node. That is, whenever a new node is inserted, REAR will be changed to point to that.

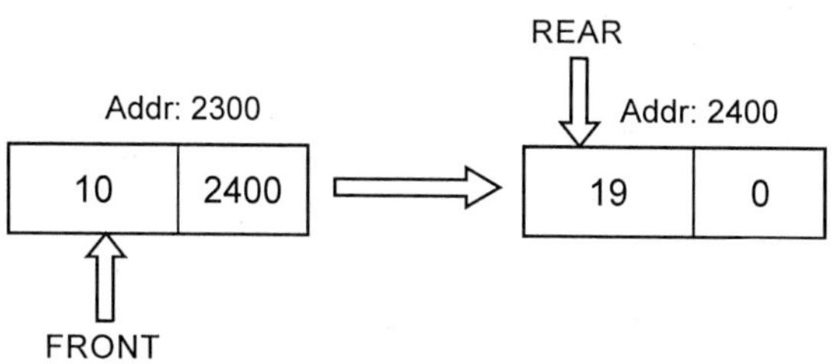

When another number 91 is inserted in the queue, a new lst type of object is created (its n and next values are initialized to 91 and 0) and it is linked as next node to current last node. Then, REAR is made to point to this new node. That is, whenever a new node is inserted, REAR will be changed to point to that. We can see this change in the figure.

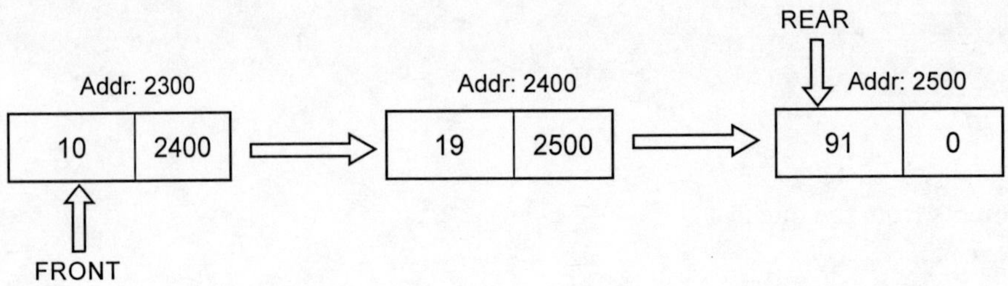

Now, let's remove an item from the queue. When we remove an item from the queue from the above queue, 10 will be returned and FRONT will be made pointer to the next node in the queue. The node having 10 will be removed. The modified queue will be as shown in figure.

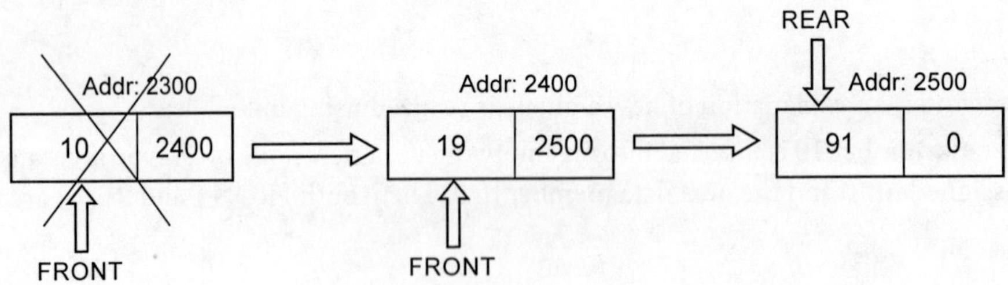

Now, let us assume that we wanted to remove one more item from the queue. Currently FRONT is pointing to the node having 19. Thus, 19 will be returned. Then, FRONT is adjusted to point to the next node in the queue. Then, the node having 19 will be removed. Thus, when remove is called, the FRONT pointer will be adjusted. The resultant queue is shown in the next Figure.

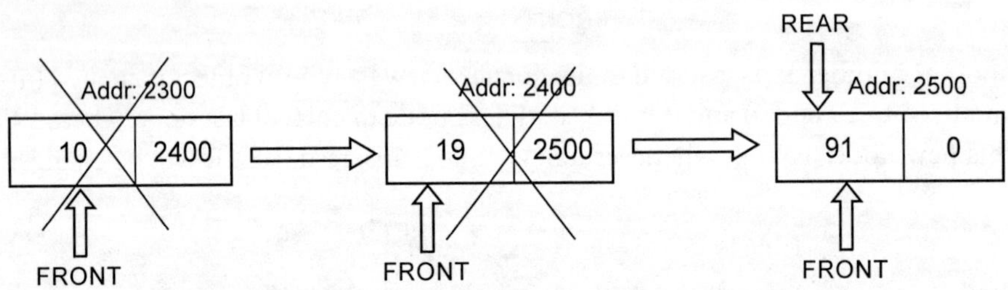

Now, let us assume that we wanted to remove one more item from the queue. Currently FRONT is pointing to the node having 91. Thus, 91 will be returned. Then, FRONT is adjusted to point to the next node in the queue. Then, the node having 91 will be removed. Thus, when remove is called, the FRONT pointer will be adjusted. However, the resultant queue is null here, as 91 is the last item in the queue. When FRONT becomes null (0), REAR also will be made as 0.

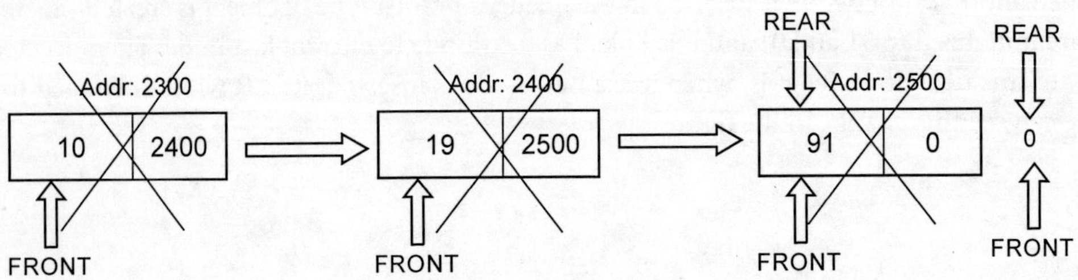

You are welcome to explore the following links to understand the things further.

https://tinyurl.com/AICTEDSBOOK76

https://tinyurl.com/NBVpriorityqueueusinglists

The following video explains how queues can be realized using linked lists.

https://www.youtube.com/watch?v=uZLLh4wApuA&list=PLXX7XiUxnzzWoLDfgad4s4dwleb4NMtVN&index=57

3.1.6 Sentinel Nodes

Oftentimes we add sentinel (a.k.a. dummy) nodes to the beginning and end of a doubly linked list which are called the header and the trailer. Of course, we do add a header node(sentinel node) to a single linked list. Use of sentinels simplify programming. A real list node contains data, whereas sentinels are not.

These sentinel or dummy nodes eliminate null pointer problems. They ensure that next and prev references exist for every data node. Instead of checking current.next == null, check if current.next == trailer or current.prev == header etc., makes programming a little convenient. However, for many short lists, sentinel nodes use up extra space. The following figure shows a DLL with sentinel nodes.

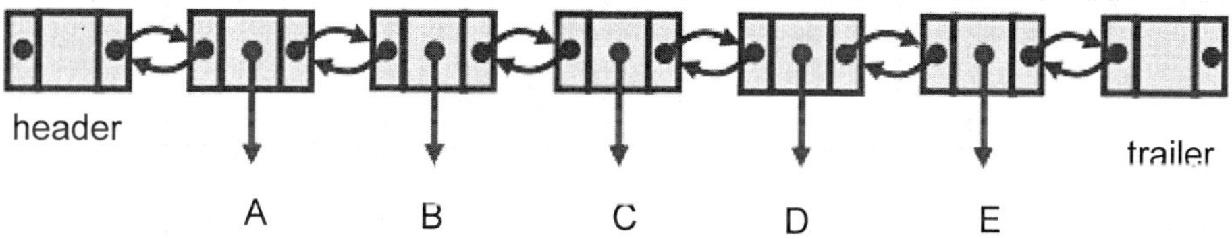

EXERCISES

Multiple Choice Questions

1. Best suitable one for realizing dequeue is
   (a) Single linked list (b) Doubly linked list
   (c) Circular linked list (d) None
2. The head of a list concept is not applicable for
   (a) Single linked list (b) Doubly linked list
   (c) Circular linked list (d) a & b
3. The memory that is consecutive in
   (a) Single linked list (b) Doubly linked list
   (c) Circular linked list (d) Array
4. Link overhead is more in
   (a) double circular list (b) single linked list
   (c) doubly linked list (d) circular linked list
   (e) a & c

5. Assuming H is a pointer to a node in a list. After the execution of H=H->next; statement also H is pointing to the same node then the list is
   (a) double circular list
   (b) single linked list
   (c) doubly linked list
   (d) circular linked list
   (e) a & d
6. Assuming H is a pointer to a node in a list. After the execution of H=H->next; statement also H is pointing to the same node then the list is having ______ number of nodes.
   (a) 0
   (b) 1
   (c) 2
   (c) n
7. Assuming H is a pointer to a node in a list. After the execution of H=H->next; statement for 5 times also H is pointing to the same node then the circular list is having ______ number of nodes.
   (a) 5
   (b) 4
   (c) 2
   (d) 6
8. Assuming H is a pointer to a node in a list. After the execution of H=H->next; statement for 5 times H value becomes null then the list is having ______ number of nodes.
   (a) 5
   (b) at least five nodes
   (c) 2
   (d) n
9. Assuming H is a pointer to a node in a list. After the execution of H=H->next; statement for 5 times also H value is not null then the list is having ______ number of nodes.
   (a) 5
   (b) at least five nodes
   (c) 2
   (d) n
10. Assuming H is a pointer to a node in a list. When we try to execute the H=H->next; statement in a loop, after the fifth iteration we have encountered a runtime error then the list is having ______ number of nodes.
   (a) 5
   (b) at least five nodes
   (c) more than five nodes
   (d) n
11. The average time complexity of removing an element from a single linked list
   (a) O(0)
   (b) O(1)
   (c) O(n)
   (d) None
12. Assuming that on your machine pointer takes 4 bytes then the amount of memory needed for a node of a circular doubly linked list whose node's data is a character is
   (a) 5
   (b) 8
   (c) 9
   (d) 32
13. Assuming that on your machine pointer takes 8 bytes then the amount of memory needed for a node of a circular doubly linked list whose node's data is a also a pointer i
   (a) 15
   (b) 24
   (c) 19
   (d) 32
14. Assuming that on your machine pointer takes 8 bytes then the amount of memory needed for a node of a circular doubly linked list whose node's data is a 1-D static character array of size 10 is
   (a) 26
   (b) 24
   (c) 19
   (d) 32

15. Linked lists are not used in
    (a) RAM fabrication (b) Operating Systems
    (c) Networks (d) Compilers
16. _______ is the linear structure which needs O(1) time to access i^{th} element out of available n elements, where i<n
    (a) single linked list (b) circular list
    (c) array (d) double linked list
17. The operation on a singly linked list whose time complexity is not O(1).
    (a) adding new element before the head
    (b) adding new element soon after the head
    (c) inserting a new node
    (d) deleting head node
18. The operation on a singly linked list whose time complexity is not O(1).
    (a) adding new element before the head
    (b) adding a new element after a given node
    (c) inserting a new node
    (d) deleting a node
19. The data structure in which we can not traverse the elements in both the directions.
    (a) array (b) double linked list
    (c) single circular list (d) double circular list
20. The data structure that takes exactly n*sizeof(node type) to store n elements is
    (a) singly linked list (b) doubly linked list
    (c) circular lists (d) arrays
21. Total number of null pointers in a single circular list are
    (a) 0 (b) 1
    (c) 2 (d) 3
22. Total number of null pointers in a double circular list are
    (a) 0 (b) 1
    (c) 2 (d) 3
23. Total number of null pointers in a doubly linked list are
    (a) 0 (b) 1
    (c) 2 (d) 3
24. At most how many null pointers will you have in any of the linked lists, single, double, circular etc.,?
    (a) 0 (b) 1
    (c) 2 (d) 3
25. It is possible to create linked lists in _____ area(s) of the process address space.
    (a) stack (b) heap
    (c) static or BSS (d) all three areas

26. Data structure that is easiest to access the ith element.
    (a) singly linked list
    (b) doubly linked list
    (c) array
    (d) circular list
27. The operation of a singly linked list that very much depends on the length of the list is
    (a) Deleting the last element of the list
    (b) Adding a new element before the head
    (c) Deleting the first node of the list
    (d) checking whether the list is empty or not
28. Assume that the address of an object of type struct dlst{int n;struct dlst next, struct dlst prev;} is 34412 and both pointers and int are of 4 bytes size. Then, what is the address of its data member, prev?
    (a) 34412
    (b) 34416
    (c) 34420
    (d) We can't say
29. Assume that at present H is pointing to a node in a double linked list. We observed while(H)H=H->next; and while(H)H=H->prev; loops are iterating same number of times, then
    (a) double linked list is having only one node
    (b) a double linked list has an odd number of nodes.
    (c) a & b
    (d) None
30. Assume that at present H, P are pointing to a node in a circular double linked list. We observed do{H=H->next;}while(H!=P); and do{H=H->prev;}while(H!=P); loops are iterating same number of times, then
    (a) double linked list is having only one node
    (b) a double linked list may be having an even or odd number of nodes..
    (c) a & b
    (d) None
31. When inserting a new node in a double linked list, worst number of link adjustments needed are
    (a) 0
    (b) 1
    (c) 2
    (d) 4
32. While inserting a new node either at front/rear in a double linked list, the worst number of link adjustments needed are assuming that when a new node is created by calling a function, it sets the nodes next, prev to zero before returning its address.
    (a) 0
    (b) 1
    (c) 2
    (d) 4
33. When inserting a new node in an existing double circular linked list, we always need _____ number of link adjustments.
    (a) 0
    (b) 1
    (c) 2
    (d) 4

34. Assume that X is pointing to a node in a single linked list. X is not the last node in the list. Assume that we want to delete the node after X. Which of the following statements can be used?

    a. X->next=0; free(X);
    b. A=X->next; free(A);
    c. A=X->next;X->next=A->next;free(A);
    d. A=X->next;free(A);X->next=0;

35. To delete the head of a single linked list, which of the following statements can be used?

    a. X->next=0; free(X);
    b. A=X->next; free(A);
    c. A=X;X=A->next;free(A);
    d. A=X->next;free(A);X->next=0;

36. Assume that X is pointing to the last node in a double linked list. Assume that we want to delete the node X. Which of the following statements can be used?

    a. X->next=0; free(X);
    b. X->prev->next=0;free(X);
    c. A=X->next;X->next=A->next;free(A);
    d. A=X->next;free(A);X->next=0;

37. Assume that X is pointing to the head node in a double linked list. Assume that we want to delete the node X. Which of the following statements can be used?

    a. X->next=0; free(X);
    b. X->next->prev=0;A=X; X=A->next;free(A);
    c. A=X->next;X->next=A->next;free(A);
    d. A=X->next;free(A);X->next=0;

38. Assuming that H is the head of a single linked list, which code places H on the last node?

    a. while(H)H=H->next;
    b. do{H=H->next}while(H);
    c. while(H&&H->next)H=H->next;
    d. None

39. Assuming that H is the tail of a double linked list, which code places H on the head node?

    a. while(H)H=H->prev;
    b. do{H=H->prev}while(H);
    c. while(H&&H->prev)H=H->prev;
    d. None

40. Assuming that H is a pointer to a single circular linked list, which code places H on the last node(i.e., just before starting H)?

    a. while(H)H=H->next;
    b. P=H; do{H=H->next}while(H->next!=P);
    c. while(H&&H->next)H=H->next;
    d. None

ANSWERS															
1.	(b)	2.	(c)	3.	(d)	4.	(e)	5.	(e)	6.	(b)	7.	(a)	8.	(b)
9.	(b)	10.	(c)	11.	(c)	12.	(c)	13.	(b)	14.	(a)	15.	(a)	16.	(c)
17.	(c)	18.	(a)	19.	(c)	20.	(d)	21.	(a)	22.	(a)	23.	(c)	24.	(c)
25.	(d)	26.	(c)	27.	(a)	28.	(c)	29.	(c)	30.	(c)	31.	(d)	32.	(c)
33.	(d)	34.	(c)	35.	(c)	36.	(b)	37.	(b)	38.	(c)	39.	(c)	40.	(c)

Descriptive Questions

Question 70: See the following linked list of words.

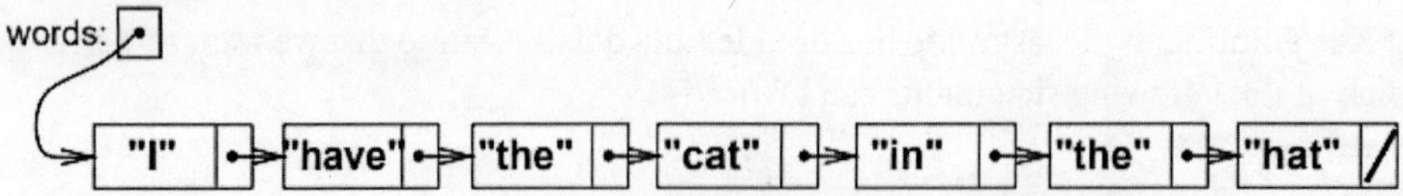

The value of words.value is I. What is the value of words.next.next.value?

Answer: the

Question 71: See the following figure which shows a dummy(sentinel node) with two fields field1, filed2 that are pointing to beginning and ending nodes of a linked list.

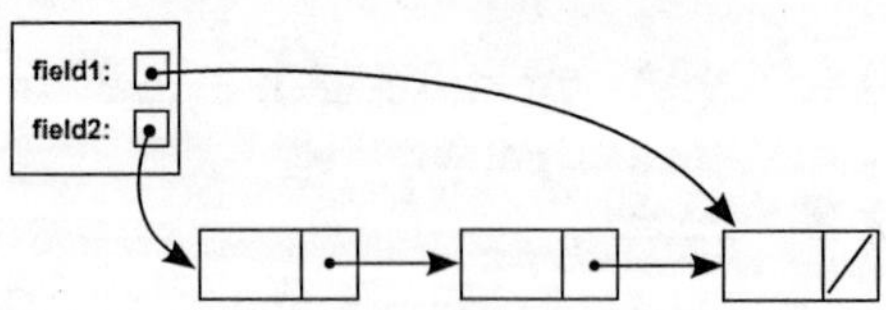

Which field would you use for the back of the queue (where items are enqueued) and which field would you use for the front of the queue (where items are dequeued from)? Briefly explain your choice. What happens if the nodes are of double linked list nodes with pointers to next, previous nodes?

Answer:

Front: field 2

Rear: field 1

It is cheap to add a node after the node that field 1 points at, but it is expensive to delete that node, so this should be where we add nodes.

It is cheap to add or delete nodes at field 2.

If we use double linked list nodes then both insertion removal operations become simple. The following steps are proposed for the operations. Verify whether they are OK or not.

To delete last node:

```
A=field1;
field1=A->prev;
fields1->next=0;
free(A);
```

To delete first node:

```
A=field2;
field2=A->next;
fields2->prev=0;
free(A);
```

To insert after the last node:

```
A=createnode(x);
A->prev=field1;
fields1->next=A;
A->next=0;
```

To insert before the last node:

```
A=createnode(x);
A->next=field2;
fields2=A;
A->prev=0;
```

Implement the above four operations as functions in your program.

Question 72: Suppose the variable myList points to a linked list of three items ("A", "B", and "C"). Draw a diagram of the linked list. How do you represent "null" using only myList and next?

Answer:

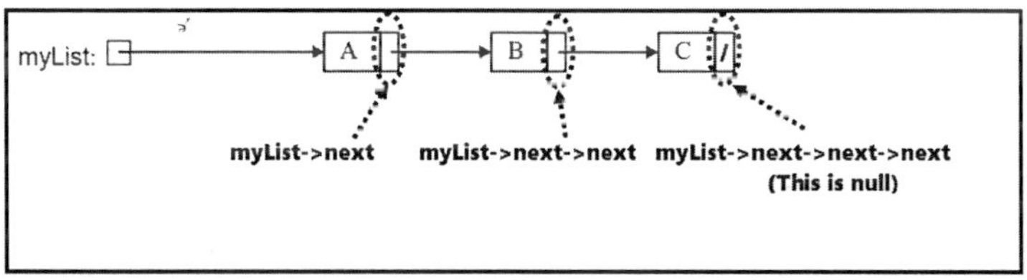

Question 73: Show the changes to the original linked list whose head is pointed by myList after the following statement:

```
myList->next->next = createnode("Y") ;
```

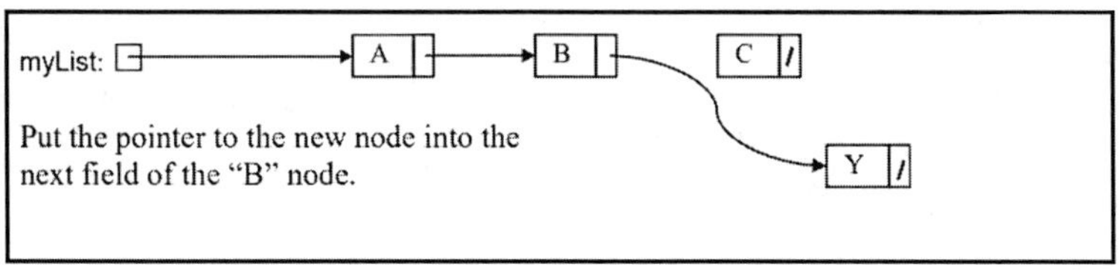

Question 74: Which is the dangling object in the following figure?

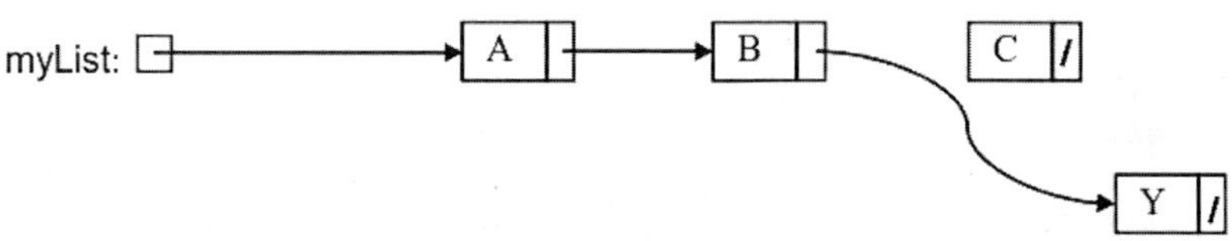

Answer: the node having C.

Question 75: We have a linked list whose head is pointed by myList. What happens if we execute the following instruction?

```
myList->next->next->next=myList->next;
```

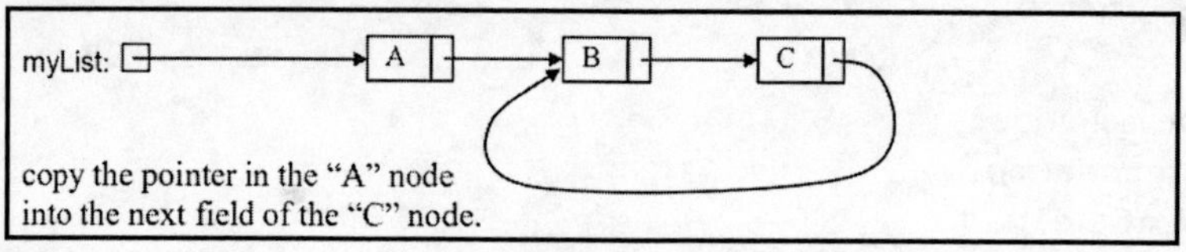

Question 76: Implement the following using linked lists.

Can we work out enough about each element/key in an array to trivialize sorting? Version 1: comparison counting for each element, calculate the number of elements smaller than it, and output the elements in order of fewest "smaller" elements Version 2: distribution counting count the number of elements associated with each value between l and u (l u), and redistribute the array elements according to the number of items associated with each value

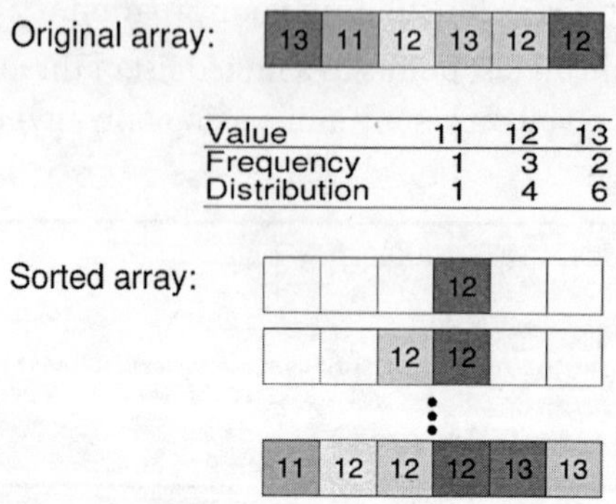

Question 77: Write a function that takes in a pointer to the front(head) of a linked list of integers and returns whether or not the list that's pointed to is in sorted (nondecreasing) order. An empty list is considered to be sorted. You are welcome to explore the following link before answering.

https://tinyurl.com/AICTEDSBOOK37

Also, see the following link also which has a function that takes head of a linked list and returns 1 if its elements are in ascending order; otherwise returns 0.

```
int isSorted(struct lst *H){
int Flag;
Flag=1;
while(H&&H->next){
        if(H->n>H->next->n){
        Flag=0;
        break;
        }
        H=H->next;
}
return Flag;
}
```

You are welcome to explore the following link before answering.

https://tinyurl.com/AICTEDSBOOK63

The following is the recursive version of the above function. Fully working code is also available on the visualization server whose link is given below. Readers are most welcome to verify its working.

```
int isSorted(struct lst *H){
int isOrd;
if(H&&H->next){
        isOrd=(H->n<H->next->n);
        if(isOrd)return(isSorted(H->next));
        else return 0;
        }
else return 1;
}
```

You are welcome to explore the following link before answering.

https://tinyurl.com/AICTEDSBOOK64

Question 78: See the following code fragment. Initially H is the head of the linked list. This code fragment is giving segment violation error(linux). Can you explore why?

```
while(H){
        if(H->n>H->next->n){
        break;
        }
        H=H->next;
}
```

You are welcome to run the following code on a visualization server to find the reason.

https://tinyurl.com/AICTEDSBOOK38

Question 79: The following code fragment is proposed to reverse a linked list. That is, assuming H is the head of the linked list and P, Q are struct lst * type variables, the following code fragment reverses the linked list such that after the execution of this code fragment also yet H points to the head of the linked list, but reversed linked list.

```
Q=0;
while(H){
P=H->next;
H->next=Q;
Q=H;
H=P;
}
H=Q;
```

The following link contains the above code fragment uploaded in a visualization server. You are welcome to run it before answering.

https://tinyurl.com/AICTEDSBOOK39

Question 80: Write a program that takes head of a double linked list and reverses the same. Follow the above solution.

See this https://tinyurl.com/AICTEDSBOOK114

Question 81: Verify whether the following function that takes head of a linked list and returns the number of nodes in the list or not.

```
int Length(struct lst *A){
int c=0;
while(A&&++c)
        A=A->next;
return c;
}
```

The following link contains the above code fragment uploaded in a visualization server.

You are welcome to run this before answering: https://tinyurl.com/AICTEDSBOOK40

Verify whether this function works if we send a null list as an argument to it.

What happens if we modify the above code like the following.

```
int Length(struct lst *A){
int c=0;
while(A&&++c,A=A->next);
return c;
}
```

Verify whether this function works if we send a null list as an argument to it.

The following link contains the above code fragment uploaded in a visualization server. You are welcome to run this before answering.

https://tinyurl.com/AICTEDSBOOK41

The following is the recursive version of the above.

```
int recursiveLength(struct lst *A){
   if(A)return 1+recursiveLength(A->next);
   else return 0;
}
```

The following link contains the above code fragment uploaded in a visualization server. You are welcome to run this before answering.

https://tinyurl.com/AICTEDSBOOK109

Question 82: Using arrays implement adding, subtracting, multiplying two polynomials. You are welcome to visit the following links to get clues.

https://tinyurl.com/polyadditionusingarrays

https://tinyurl.com/polynomialsubtractionarrays

https://tinyurl.com/polymultarrays

Question 83: Discuss how to represent a polynomial in a linked list fashion. Also, write a function that takes a polynomial in the linked list and a float number x and then returns the polynomial value at x. Write functions to implement adding, subtracting, multiplying two polynomials that are in linked list fashion. You are welcome to visit the following links to get clues.

https://tinyurl.com/createPolynomial

https://tinyurl.com/polynomialaslist

https://tinyurl.com/ployEvaluation

https://tinyurl.com/polycreation1

https://tinyurl.com/addingpolynomialsinlists

https://tinyurl.com/polynomialaslist

https://tinyurl.com/AICTEDSBOOKADDMATERIALUNIT3

Question 84: Implement a very large integer in a linked list fashion and discuss how two such numbers can be added.

You are welcome to refer Additional material available at:

https://tinyurl.com/AICTEDSBOOKADDMATERIALUNIT3

Question 85: Implement deque using doubly linked list.

https://tinyurl.com/NBVDoubleQueues1

You are welcome to refer Additional material available at:

Question 86: Write a function getNth() GetNth() function that takes a linked list head and an integer, n, and returns the address of the nth node from the head node if existing; otherwise returns zero. Do assume that the head node is the 1st node, that is if n=1 then the head node address has to be returned from this function.

```
struct lst * getNth(struct lst *A, int n){
  int i;
  for(i=1;A&&i<n;i++)A=A->next;
  return A;
}
```

The following link contains the above code fragment uploaded in a visualization server.

You are welcome to run it before answering.

https://tinyurl.com/AICTEDSBOOK107

Question 87: Write a function that takes heads of two linked lists as arguments and appends the second list to the first one and returns the head of the modified linked list.

```
struct lst * append(struct lst *A, struct lst *B){
  struct lst *C=A;
  if(A==0)return B;
  if(B==0)return A;
  while(A&&A->next)A=A->next;
  A->next=B;
 return C;
}
```

The following link contains the above code fragment uploaded in a visualization server.

You are welcome to run it before answering.

https://tinyurl.com/AICTEDSBOOK108

Question 88: Write a function which takes the head of a linked list having integers in each node then returns the head of the middle node.

Question 89: Assume that we have a single linked list with an even number of elements and at present H is the head of the linked list.

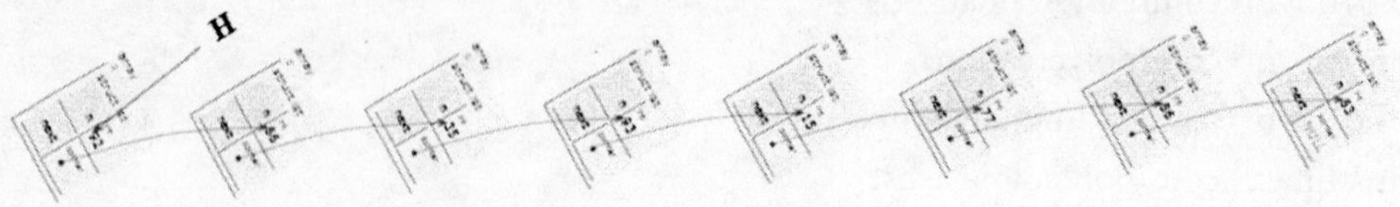

Explore what happens if we apply the following code.

```
H=createlist();
do{
        A=H;
        while(A){
        B=A->next;
        A->n+=B->n;
        A->next=B->next;
        free(B);
        A=A->next;
}
}while(H->next);
```

Is the linked list going to transform like this?

After 1st iteration **After second iteration** **After third iteration**

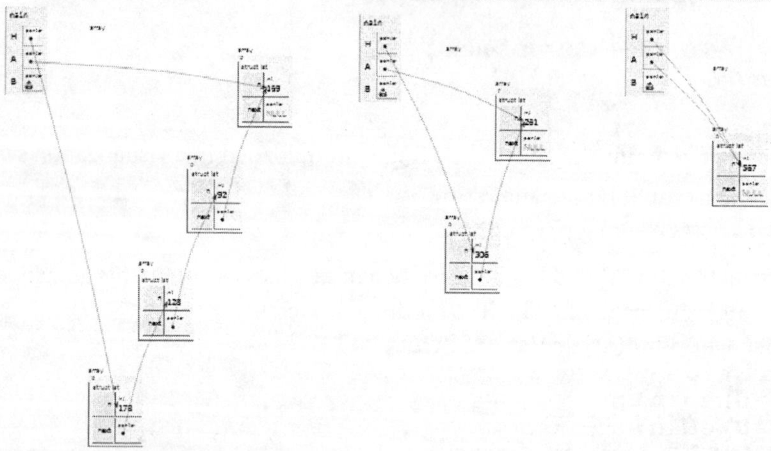

You are welcome to explore the following link before answering https://tinyurl.com/AICTEDSBOOK112

Question 90: Define a structure and write a program such that every node contains a link to the next node and also that next next node. How do you traverse the linked list.

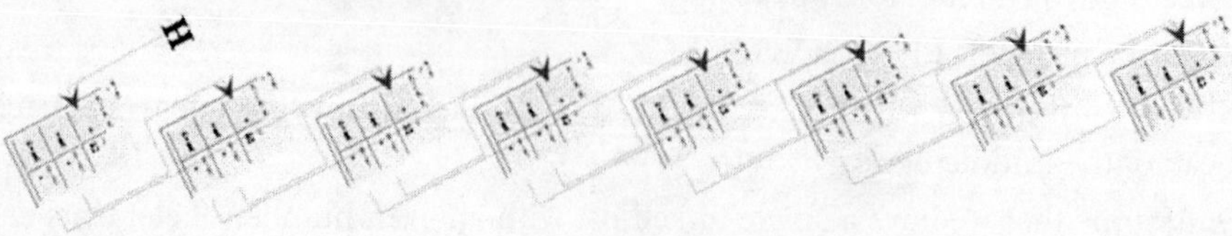

You are welcome to explore the following link before answering. https://tinyurl.com/AICTEDSBOOK113

Question 91: Can you build a linked list such that it contains links to the nodes that are 1, 2, 4, and 8 units from it. Maybe, you can employ the following structure for the node. Probably the previous problem can be your beginning point to start with where links are created for nodes that 1 and 2 units from each node.

```
struct lst{
  int n;
  struct lst *next[4];
};
```

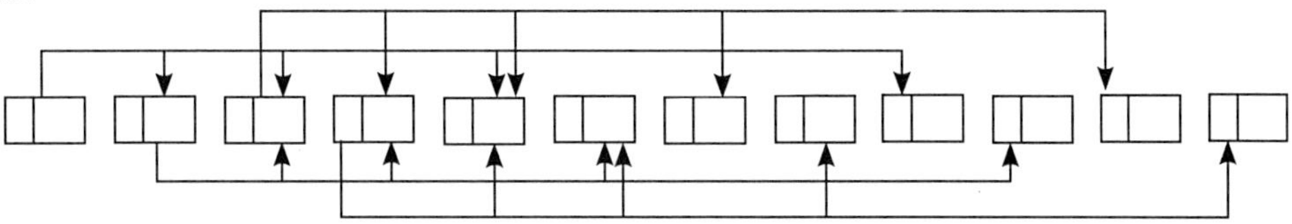

Question 92: See the following figure of a single linked list and some pointers n,x,y and v. At present x is the next to n and y is the previous node to v. We want to exchange x and y (but not their values which is a simple thing to achieve).

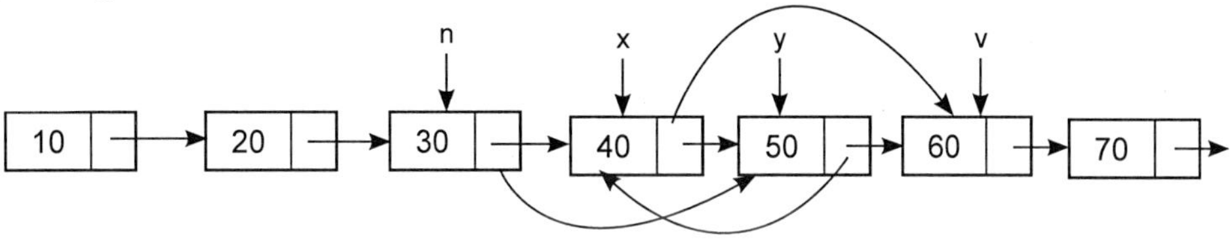

Answer: `n->next=x->next; x->next=v; y->next=x;`

Question 93: See the following figure of a double linked list and some pointers n,x,y and v. At present x is the next to n and y is the previous node to v. We want to exchange x and y (but not their values which is a simple thing to achieve)

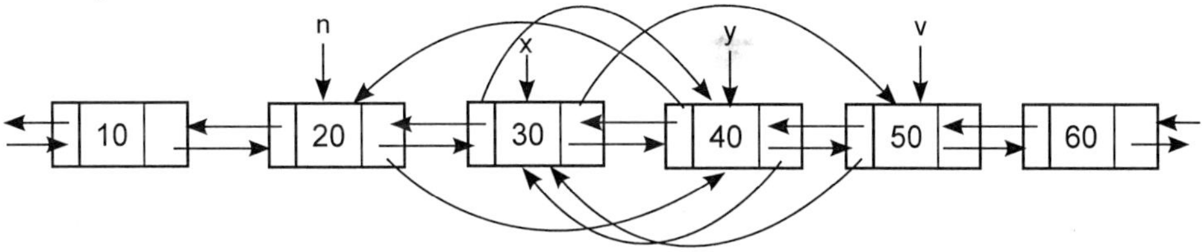

Question 94: See the following program. Here, are the linked lists nodes are sequential in memory or not?

```
int main() {
struct lst A[8];
int i;
for(i=0;i<8;i++){
  A[i].n=rand()%100;
  if(i<7)A[i].next=A+i+1;
  else A[i].next=0;
}
display(A);
  return 0;
}
```

You are welcome to explore the following before answering.
https://tinyurl.com/AICTEDSBOOK116

Laboratory programming tasks

1. Write a program to implement a singly linked list.
2. Write a program to create a sorted linked list.
3. Write a program to implement a doubly linked list.
4. Write a program to implement a circular single linked list.
5. Write a program to implement a circular doubly linked list.
6. Write a program to implement deque using a doubly linked list.
7. Write a program to implement stack operations using a linked list.
8. Write a program to implement queue operations using a linked list.

Welcome to participate in the online competition

We are hosting a competition so as to encourage students to build their competence in coding. This will be very useful for placements also in the coming years. Thus, welcome students to attempt the competition at the following link.

https://www.hackerrank.com/aictedsbook

Programming puzzles

Some programming puzzles along with their solution around linked list concept are made available at the following link.

https://tinyurl.com/AICTEDSBOOKLINKEDLISTQUIZZES

REFERENCES

1. Fundamentals of Data Structure in C, Horowitz, Ellis, Sahni, Sartaj, Anderson-Freed, Susan, University Press, India.
2. Data Structures: A Pseudocode approach with C, Richard F. Gilberg, Behrouz A. Forouzan, CENGAGE Learning, India.
3. My class notes on Algorithmic Complexity, now a refresher for craving teachers and knowledge greedy students: A must primer for GATE(India), Adv. GRE appearing students. https://www.amazon.com/dp/B09DJCW78T
4. C and Data Structures, NB Venkateswarlu & EV Prasad, 2010, S Chand & Co, New Delhi http://cslibrary.stanford.edu/105/LinkedListProblems.pdf

4 Non-Linear Data Structures

UNIT COVERAGE

Non Linear Data Structures-Trees: Basic Terminologies, Definition and Concepts of Binary Trees, Representations of a Binary Tree using Arrays and Linked Lists, Operations on a Binary Tree-Insertion, Deletion, Traversals, Types of Binary Trees.

Graphs: Graph Terminologies, Representation of Graphs-Set, Linked, Matrix, Graph Traversals.

OBJECTIVES OF THE UNIT

By the end of this unit, student will be able to:

- describe and use the Binary Search Tree(BST) abstract data types.
- explain inorder, preorder, postorder traversal of trees and how they are used in development of compilers.
- describe sequential storage of BST.
- describe and use stacks for traversal of trees.
- explain the relevance of graphs in operating systems design, network design, etc.,
- give typical examples of topological sorting in practical applications.

LEARNING OUTCOMES OF THE UNIT

After completing the Unit, the student

- has detailed knowledge of BST **(U4-01).**
- has detailed knowledge of **graphs, minimum distance problems** (U4-02).
- has detailed knowledge of how trees and graphs are used in practical SW systems such as operating systems, networks, etc**(U4-03).**
- is familiar with use of minimum spanning trees in network routing **(U4-04).**
- **is** familiar with recursive implementations of various operations trees.**(U4-05)**
- has knowledge of implementing trees sequentially **(U4-06)**
- has detailed knowledge of implementing various traversing methods of trees, graphs. **(U4-07)**

Unit-4 Outcomes	Expected Mapping with Course Outcomes (1- Weak Correlation; 2- Medium correlation; 3- Strong Correlation)				
	CO-1	CO-2	CO-3	CO-4	CO-5
U4-O1			3	-	
U4-O2			3		
U4-O3			3	2	
U4-O4			2		
U4-O5			1		
U4-06				2	
U4-07			2		3

Non-Linear Data Structures

In the previous chapters, we have discussed linear data structures stack, linked lists, queues. All of them are linear in the sense that elements of them can be accessed one after another. Also some of them like arrays are physically linear in the sense that their elements occupy consecutive memory locations in the physical memory(RAM); whereas some others, especially the ones which are realized through linked lists are logically linear. However, in the non linear data structures their elements will not be having such a linear association; instead they may be having hierarchical (parent-child-grandparent) association like trees. Of course, a tree is considered as a special case of a graph known as an acyclic graph. Also, in the case of linear structures such as arrays, linked lists either next or previous elements of any of their elements are at most one. Whereas in the case of non linear structures such as trees or graphs, this can be any number. **Because of this property, if you change one element, its impact may be on more than one element of them.** For example, since the beginning of the Ukraine war, all of us have been hearing about some statements such as supply chain disruption, etc. Also, we are all facing one or other problems because of this single incident.

4.1 INTRODUCTION TO TREES

In real life, we may be using a variety of trees. A good example for a tree is a directory tree of an operating system such as Windows or Unix. For example, the following figure 4.1 shows a Unix/Linux style directory tree with the top most directory as the root(/)[59].

59 Do you know the three 'root's in Linux/Unix? Answer: 1. Root directory (/) 2. The home directory of super user is /root, 3. super user username is 'root'.

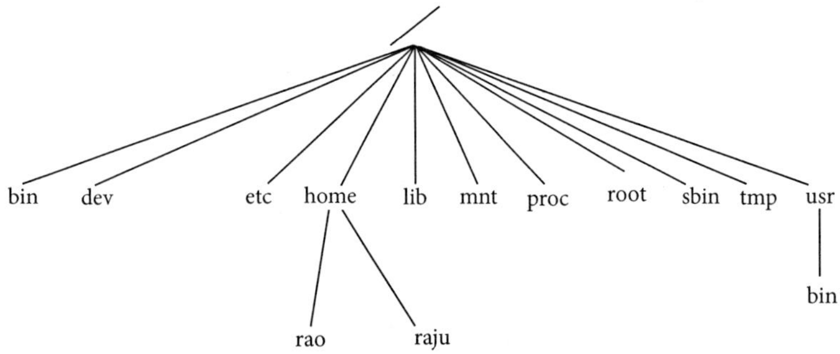

Fig. 4.1: Directory Tree

The above tree is a logical tree. We also have physical trees. We all know that our data is saved onto secondary memory devices such as hard disks. An important concept of operating systems known as file systems deals with this aspect. For example, the NTFS file system of Windows uses B+Tree in storing the data into data blocks on the disk (see Fig 4.2). This can be called a physical tree as it is very much available in the disk.

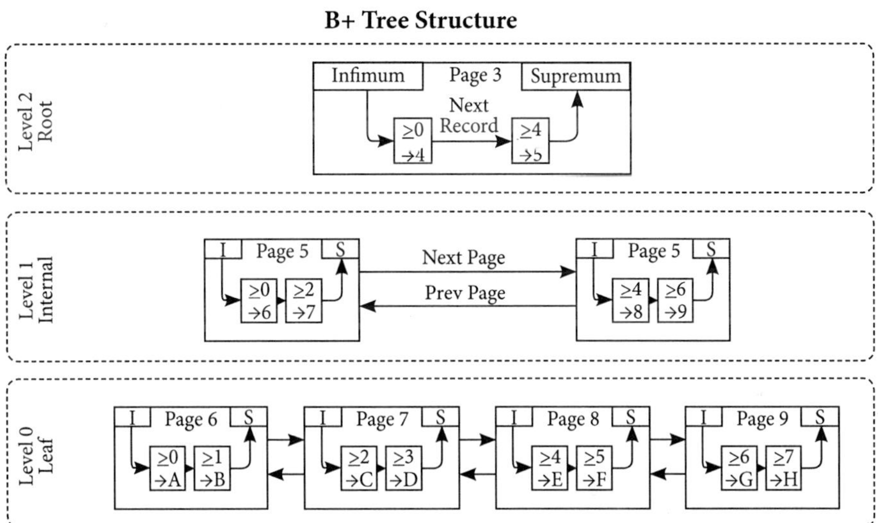

Fig. 4.2: NTFS File system (Courtesy: https://www.ntfs.com/refs-architecture.htm Last accessed, 6th Sep, 2022)

We can create a family tree of ours with the details of our parents, grandparents, etc. You may visit https://geni.com or some other sites as shown in the following figure 4.3.

Fig. 4.3: A family tree template at https://www.FreeFamilyTreeTemplates.com Last accessed: 6th Sep 2022)

Another live example is an administrative structure chart in a University with the Vice Chancellor being at the top most level, Deans/Directors in the next level, and vice versa (see Fig. 4.4).

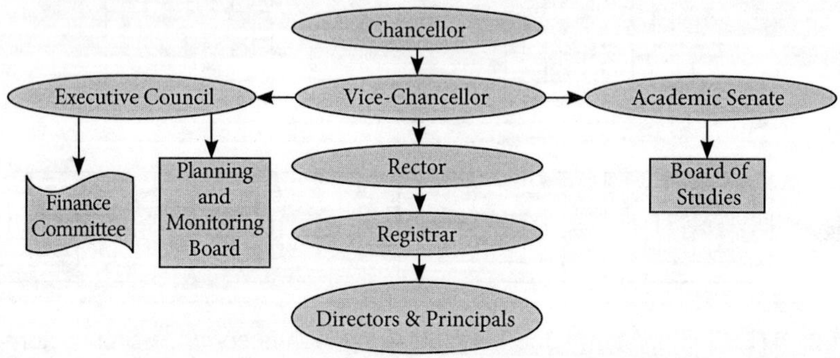

Fig. 4.4: An Administrative Structure at a typical University (source www.jntu.ac.in Last accessed in Apr 2016)

In recent years, many companies such as Amway are following multi-level marketing(MLM[60]) to improve their sales. Here, a person can join as a member under an existing member. Whenever he purchases items from Amway, some percentage of the profit will be given to the person under whom he has joined. Also, a person can introduce new members under him; they can introduce new members under them and vice versa. However, whenever a member purchases some items, the profit of the company on this purchase is given to people (members) above him at some company decided fractions. Thus, here we have a tree of people with some hierarchical relationship.

60 https://www.thebalancesmb.com/the-likelihood-of-mlm-success-1794500

4.1.1 Definition of a Tree

A tree is a collection of vertices/nodes (G) and links/edges (E) connecting the vertices. Of course, the same definition is used for graphs also. However, the main difference is that the tree is also a graph, to be specifically an acyclic graph. **Evidently the tree contains parent, child and grandchild type hierarchical relationships.**

If a tree contains a single node, x, root node then it can be represented as T={x}. This representation is called a set representation. In the following figure we have a tree which can be represented as (see Fig. 4.5):

T={x, {b,{c,{d}},{e},{f,{g,{h},{i},{j}}}}}

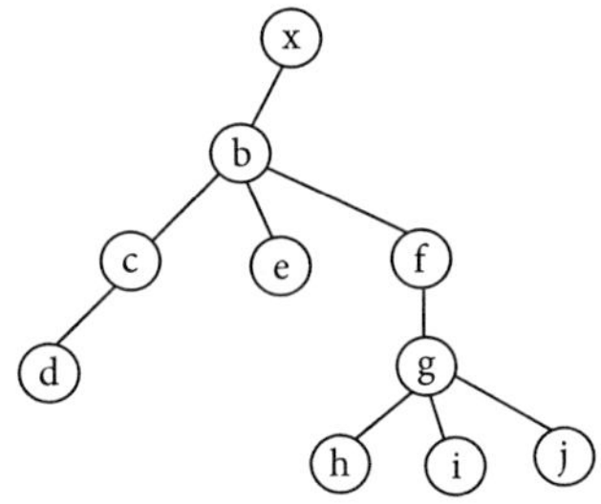

Fig. 4.5: A Sample Tree

Do remember that a null is also considered as a tree. That is, T={} is a valid tree.

In compiler construction, expression or parse trees (see Fig. 4.6) are used for verifying the validity of expressions.

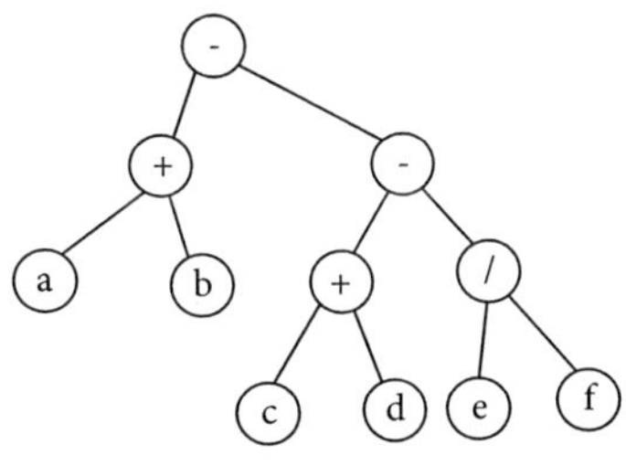

Fig. 4.6: An example parse or expression tree.

Another important tree in Computing or Computer Science is a **call tree** which is used in representing the recursive function execution. The following figure shows the call tree for the function FIB() that is written to compute n^th^ Fibonacci number(see Fig. 4.7). For the reasons of terseness, the function name FIB() is shown as f().

```
int FIB(int n){
        int x,y;
                if(n<=1) return n;
        else{
                x=FIB(n-1);
                y=FIB(n-2);
                return(x+y);
        }
}
```

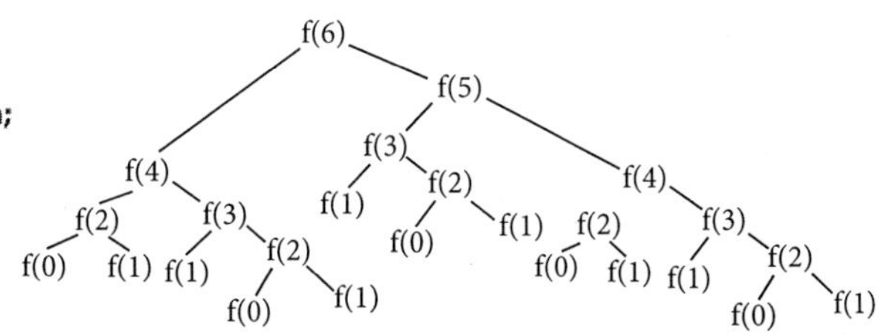

Fig. 4.7: Call tree for function FIB() (source www.wikipedia.com, last accessed: 10 Aug, 2015)

4.1.2 Basic terminology

Root Node: It is the top most node in the tree hierarchy. It is the only one node which does not contain any parent. This is also simply referred to as root.

Degree of the vertex: The degree of a vertex is the number of siblings or subtrees of a vertex/node.

Leaf Node: Leaf node is the one which does not have any children. That is, leaf node's degree value will be zero.

Non-Leaf Node: The nodes that contain child nodes are termed as non-leaf nodes. Thus, the non-Leaf node's degree value will be greater than zero.

Level: Root node is said to be at 0th level. Level numbers increase downwards. The immediate children of the root node are said to be at 1st level. Their immediate children are said to be at 2nd level. Like this, in trees we have hierarchy (see Fig. 4.1).

Height (or depth) of the Tree: Height of a tree is the number of levels in which nodes of the tree are organized. The depth of a tree is the maximum level of the nodes in a tree.

Left subtree or sibling: Left side portion of any non-leaf node is called its left subtree or sibling.

Internal node: An Internal node (or non-leaf node) is the node that is neither root nor a leaf node.

Parent: A node is a parent node if it has child nodes. That is, a parent node's out degree value will be greater than 0.

Child: A node is a child node if it has a parent. That is, a child node's in-degree value will be greater than 0.

Siblings: Two nodes with the same parent are said to be siblings.

Path: A sequence of adjacent nodes is termed as a path.

Right subtree or sibling: Right side portion of any non-leaf node is called its right subtree or sibling.

Ancestor: Any node in the path from the root to the given node is called the ancestor to the given node.

Descendent: Any node in a path from the given node to a leaf node is called the descendent node to the given node.

Subtree: A connected tree structure below any non-leaf node is called a subtree(Fig. 4.8).

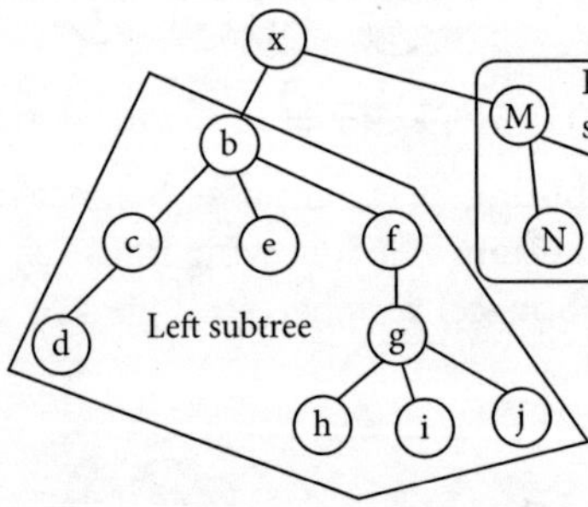

Fig. 4.8: Shows left and right subtrees of a binary tree.

Balance of a node: Balance of a node is the difference of heights of its left and right subtrees. For leaf nodes, the balance value will be 0. For a complete binary tree, every node will have a balance value of zero. If the balance value of a node is positive then its left subtree height is more than its right subtree; If the balance value of a node is negative then its left subtree height is smaller than its right subtree; if the balance value of a node is zero then both of its left and right subtrees are of same height. However, do remember there is nothing wrong in taking the balance value of a node = height of its right tree - height of its left subtree.

Trees and its variants

Binary trees are the ones in which any node contains at most two children. That is the maximum allowed degree of any node in a binary tree is 2. Violation of the above rule is seen in the multi-way trees. That is the nodes may have more than two children. An example binary tree is given in Figure 4.9.

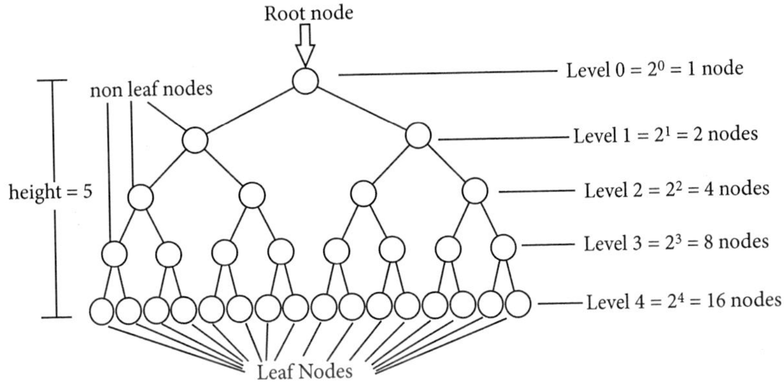

Fig. 4.9: An example binary tree with levels, height, leaf nodes, non leaf nodes.

An example multiway tree known as B-Tree is shown in Fig. 4.2. Of course, the tree that is shown in Fig. 4.1 is also a multiway tree because if you observe you will find that the root directory (/) is having more than two children(sub directories).

Some important points related to binary trees:

- A **binary tree** may contain at most 2n nodes at level n.
- **A strictly binary tree** is the one whose non-leaf or internal nodes contain exactly two children; i.e., all of its non-leaf nodes will have degree value of 2.

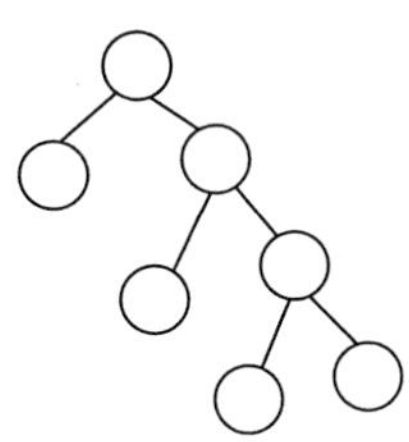

- A **complete binary tree** (see the tree in Fig, 4.10) of depth N will be having exactly 2k nodes for k=0,...,N-1. Complete binary tree is the one in which all leaf nodes will be at the lowest level and every non-leaf node will have exactly two children. Thus, a complete binary tree is evidently a strictly binary tree.
- **Almost complete binary tree** is the one in which all the leaf nodes will be at the lowest level or one level above it. Some authors further divide these trees as "**almost complete strictly binary tree**" and "**almost complete binary tree**", where strictness is not maintained(see Fig. 4.10).

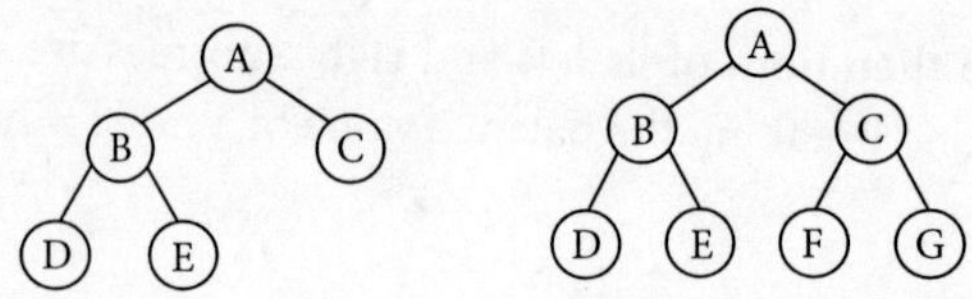

Fig. 4.10: Almost complete binary tree and complete binary tree

- **Balanced Binary tree or AVL tree:** The tree whose node's balance values are between -1 to 1. Here, the balance value of anode is defined as left subtree height minus right subtree height.
- The complete binary tree is called a **full** tree as each of its levels will be a fully possible number of nodes. That is, its nth level contains 2^n nodes for all the possible levels of that tree.
- If all nodes of a tree are having their degree values as 1 then the tree is a degenerate tree (or simply linked list).
- If a node in a binary search tree contains two children (leaf), then its successor has no left child and its predecessor has no right child.
- If N is the number of nodes then the depth of an almost complete strictly binary tree will be less than or equal to $\log_2(N)$.
- For a given height, a complete binary tree will have more nodes than any binary tree organizations.
- For any strictly binary tree, the equality "No. of Leaf Nodes – No. of Non-Leaf Nodes = 1" will be satisfied.
- Given the number of keys, height of the tree becomes minimum if they are organized in complete binary tree fashion compared to any other binary tree configurations.
- If the lowest level in a complete binary tree is K, then the number of leaf nodes with 2^K and number of non-leaf nodes will be 2^{K-1}. Total number of nodes will be 2^{K+1} -1.
- If H is the height of the complete binary tree, the number of leaf nodes are 2^{H-1}, the number of non-leaf nodes are 2^{H-1}-1 and the total number of nodes are 2^{H-1}. This you can verify from the figure where the height of the tree is 5, number of leaf nodes are 16 (2^{5-1}), number of non-leaf nodes are 15(2^{5-1} – 1), total nodes are 31(2^{5-1}).

Question 1: A tree has an odd number of nodes, n, where n>1. What is the worst possible height of a strict binary tree which we can make from these n nodes?

Answer: (n+1)/2

Binary Search Trees

From the name itself we can know that Binary search trees are used for searching applications. Binary search tree is the one in which some order exists among the information of the nodes. For example, if the nodes contain numbers, then all the nodes which are left to a node will be having their node values smaller and right to it will be having their values larger as shown in Figure 11. In fact, not only numerical data, but any other type of elements also can be organized as BST.

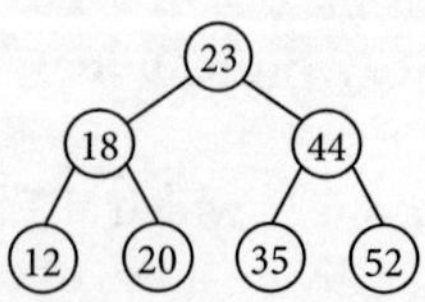

Fig. 4.11: Binary search tree

Of course, one way we can think of a linked list with ascending ordered values also as a binary search tree. To be critical, such trees are called skewed trees or degenerate trees.

Max Heap & Min Heaps

Max heap is a special type of tree in which any non leaf node value will be more than its children. For example, see Figure 4.12.

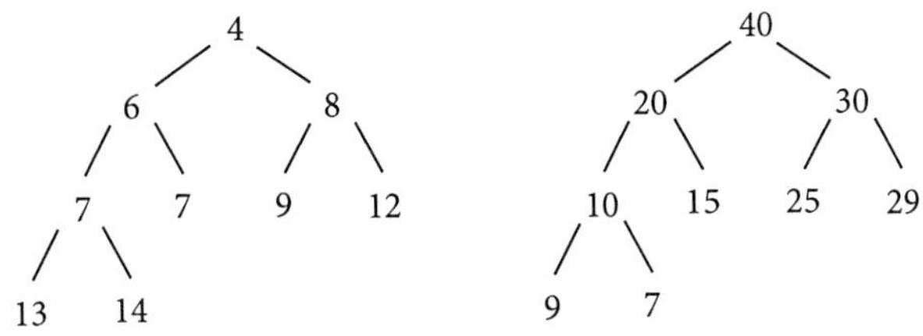

Fig. 4.12: Min Heap

Min Heap is a complimentary to max heap. That is, any node value will be less than its children values. Moreover, heaps are nearly complete binary trees. That is all nodes at the lowest level will be on the left side as shown in Figure 4.13.

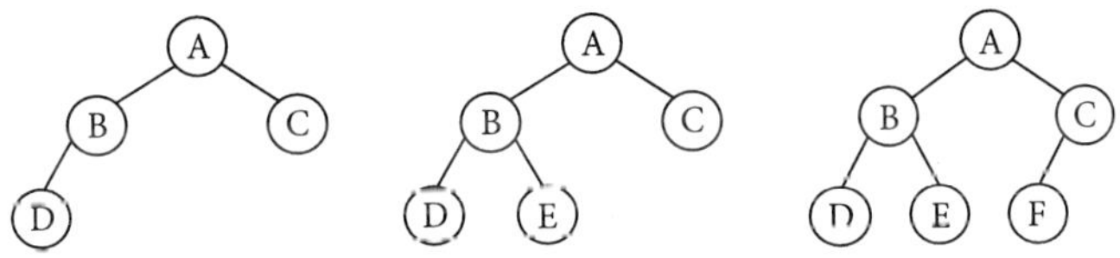

Fig. 4.13: Acceptable heaps.

4.1.3 Tree Traversals

In previous chapters, we have discussed various structures like linked lists, doubly linked lists, circular lists, etc., Always, and we have demonstrated first creation of them followed by traveling them. In the case of a single linked list we have freedom only to traverse from head node to tail node. While with a double linked list, we can also traverse from tail to head node; also from any node to node in any direction, forward or backward. In the case of circular lists we can traverse cyclically. In the same fashion, trees also can be traversed in the following ways.

1. In-Order Traversal
2. Pre-Order Traversal
3. Post-Order Traversal
4. Level-Order or Breadth First Traversal

While traversing the information in the node will be processed. Here, processing can be simply **printing/displaying** or comparing with a search key, etc. **Always, we assume traversal starts from the root node.**

In-Order Traversal (Left-Center-Right)

At each node, A, we have to apply the following sequence of operations recursively:

- First, traverse the **left subtree** of the node A in **In-Order** manner,

- then process the node A (here, we assume process means simply displaying the node A's data or value or label),
- then traverse the **right subtree** of the node A in **In-Order** manner.

For example, if we traverse the tree in Figure 4.14., we get the sequence: **DBEAHFICJGK**

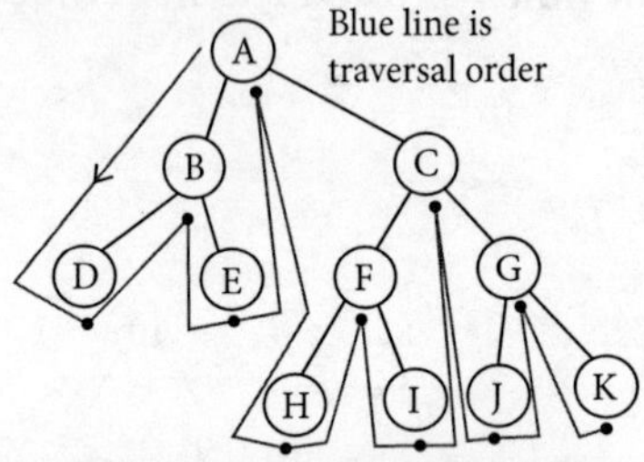

Inorder traversal: **DBEAHFICJGK**

Fig. 4.14: Inorder traversal

Pre-Order Traversal(Center-Left-Right)

At each node, A, we have to apply the following sequence of operations recursively:

- First process node A (here, we assume process means simply displaying the node A's data or value or label),
- then traverse the **left subtree** of the node A in **Pre-Order** manner,
- then traverse the **right subtree** of the node A in **Pre-Order** manner.

For example, if we traverse the tree in Figure 4.15 we get the sequence: **ABDECFHIGJK**

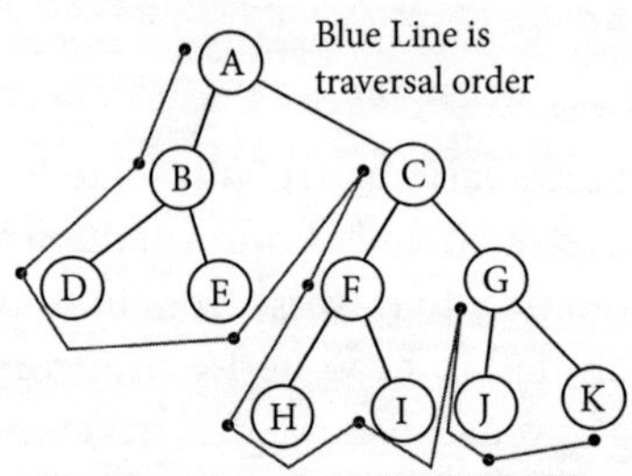

Preorder traversal: **ABDECFHIGJK**

Fig. 4.15: Pre-Order Traversal

Post-Order Traversal(Left-Right-Center)

At each node, A, we have to apply the following sequence of operations recursively:

- Traverse the **left subtree** of node A in **Post-Order** manner,
- then traverse right subtree of node A in **Post-Order** manner,
- then process node A (here, we assume process means simply displaying the node A's data or value or label).

For example, if we traverse the tree in Figure 4.16 we get the sequence: **DEBHIFJKGCA**

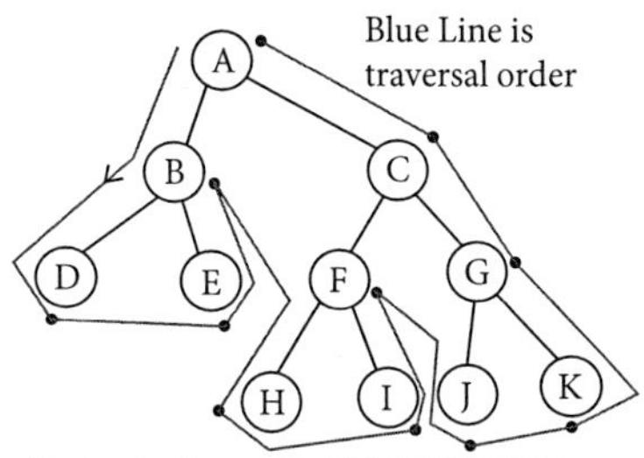

Postorder traversal: **DEBHIFJKGCA**

Fig, 4.16: Post-Order Traversal

If we traverse an expression tree (Fig 4.6) in In-Order fashion, we will get its infix representation; pre-order fashion we will get its prefix representation; post-order traversal gives postfix representation. For example, three traversals on expression tree in Figure 4.6 gives:

inorder traversal: a+b–(c+d)*(e/f)

postorder traversal: ab+cd+ef/*–

preorder traversal: –+ab*+cd/ef

Similarly, if we traverse a binary search such as the one in Figure 4.11 in In-Order fashion, we get an ascending ordered sequence of the node values. For example, the In-Order traversal of the BST in Figure 4.11 gives: 12, 18, 20, 23, 35, 44, 52.

Level-order Traversal

This is somewhat different from previous traversals. Here, all the nodes at each level will be processed from left-to-right starting from 0th level. For example, level order traversal of the Figure 4.17 gives sequence: **ABCDEFGHIJK**

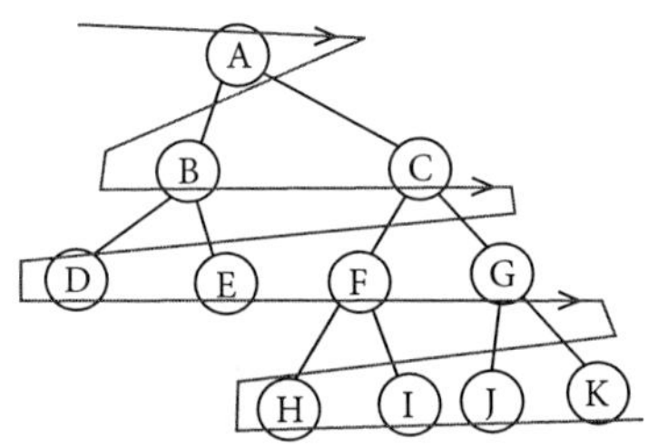

Level order traversal: **ABCDEFGHIJK**

Fig. 4.17: Level Order Traversal

Question 2: See the following figure which contains an ascending ordered array and a BST. Do you get the ascending ordered array if we traverse the BST in in-order fashion? Is the given BST a max-heap?

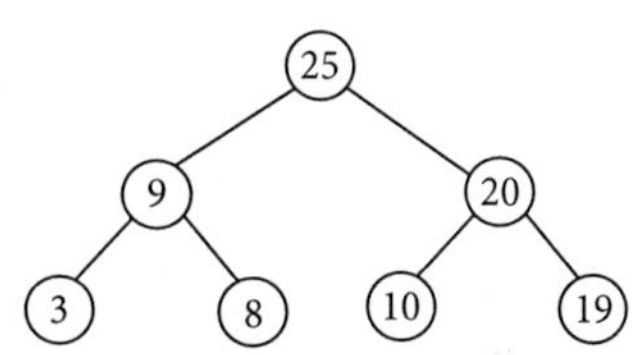

3	8	9	10	19	20	25

If we traverse this tree in level order fashion, we get {25}, {9,20},{3,8,10,19}. If you observe, values of each level are in ascending order. Do you get the same order for any max-heap?

4.1.4 Creating Binary Search Tree

Assume that we want to organize a set of integers as a BST fashion. Thus, the node data becomes an integer. We employ the node structure of a binary search tree with an integer information (or data element) as:

```
struct Node
{
int n;
struct Node *left;
struct Node *right;
};
```

That is, it is made to have an integer member n and two Node type of pointers which may point to left and right subtrees.

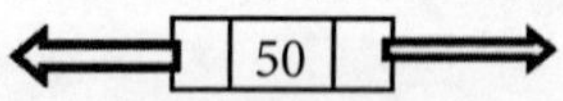

Question 3: Is it OK to take any of the following as the node structure of a binary search tree whose node data is an integer?

struct Node{
int n;
struct Node *left;
struct Node *right;
};
	struct Node{
	struct Node *left;
	int n;
	struct Node *right;
	};
		struct Node{
		struct Node *left;
		struct Node *right;
		int n;
		};

struct Node{
int n;
struct Node *right;
struct Node *left;
};
	struct Node{
	struct Node *right;
	int n;
	struct Node *left;
	};
		struct Node{
		struct Node *right;
		struct Node *left;
		int n;
		};

struct Node{
int n;
struct Node *left, *right;
};
	struct Node{
	int n;
	struct Node *right, *left;
	};
		struct Node{
		struct Node *right, *left;
		int n;
		};

Answer: Yes.

Example 1: The following simple program creates a simple binary search tree with statically created nodes. Please do visualize the same and observe how the links are getting created.

```
struct Node
{
int n;
struct Node *left;
struct Node *right;
};
```

```
int main(){struct Node *tree;
 struct Node A={12,0,0},B={33,0,0},C={25,&A,&B},D={50,0,0};
 tree=&C;
 B.right=&D;
return 0;
}
```

or

```
int main(){
 struct Node *tree;
 struct Node A={12,0,0};
 struct Node B={33,0,0};
 struct Node C={25,&A,&B};
 struct Node D={50,0,0};
 B.right=&D;
 tree=&C;
return 0;
}
```

The following table explains what happens in a step by step fashion.

Node A will be created with data value 12.	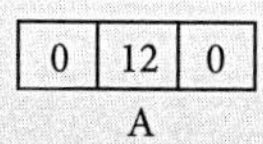
Node B will be created with data value 33.	
Node C will be created with data value 25 and also Node A will be made its left while Node B will be made its right.	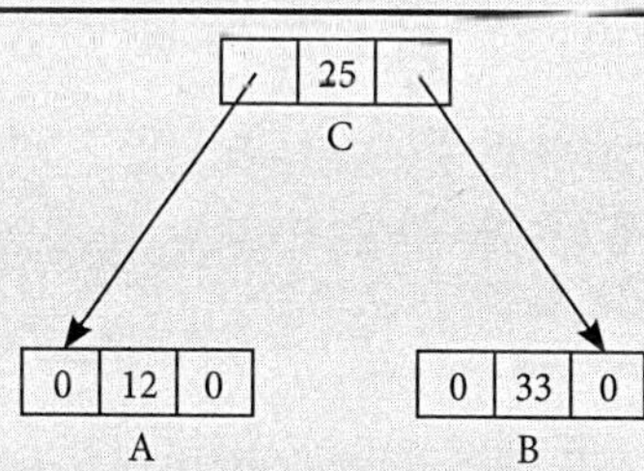
A new Node D will be created with data value 50.	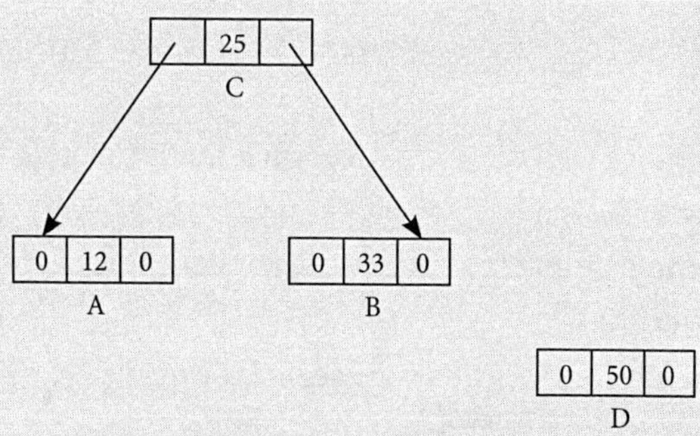

Node D will be made Node B's right by executing B.right=&D.	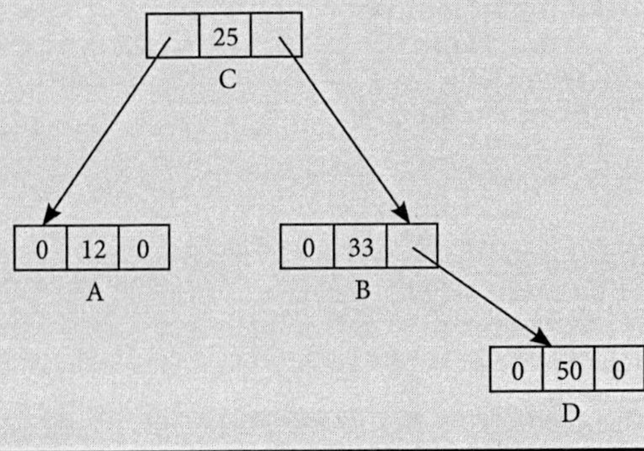

You are welcome to play with the following links which have the above code.

https://tinyurl.com/AICTEDSBOOK121

https://tinyurl.com/AICTEDSBOOK120

Question 4: In the above tree, what does **tree->n** convey?

Answer: 25.

Question 5: In the above tree, what is the **root node** value?

Answer: 25.

Question 6: In the above tree, what does **tree->right->right->n** convey?

Answer: 50.

Question 7: In the above tree, what does **C.right->right->n** convey?

Answer: 50.

Question 8: In the above tree, what does *(**tree->right).right->n** convey?

Answer: 50.

Question 9: In the above tree, what does *(*(**tree->right).right).n** convey?

Answer: 50.

Question 10: In the above tree, what does &(*(*(**tree->right).right))->n** convey?

Answer: 50.

Question 11: In the above tree, what does *(&(*(*(**tree->right).right))).n** convey?

Answer: 50.

Question 12: In the above tree, what does **tree->left->n** convey?

Answer: 12.

Question 13: Does this code segment work?

```
struct Node{
int n;
struct Node *left;
struct Node *right;
}A={12,0,0},B={33,0,0},C={25,&A,&B},D={50,0,0};
int main(){
  B.right=&D;
return 0;
}
```

You are welcome to play with the following link which has the above code. https://tinyurl.com/AICTEDSBOOK122

Question 14: Does this code segment work?

```
struct Node{
int n;
struct Node *left;
struct Node *right;
}A={12,0,0},B={33,0,0},C={25,&A,&B},D={50,0,0},B.right=&D;
int main(){
  return 0;
}
```

You are welcome to play with the following link which has the above code.

https://tinyurl.com/AICTEDSBOOK123

Question 15: Does this code segment work?

```
struct Node{
struct Node *left;
int n;
struct Node *right;
}A={12,0,0},B={33,0,0},C={25,&A,&B},D={50,0,0};
int main(){
  B.right=&D;
return 0;
}
```

Question 16: Does this code segment work?

```
struct Node{
  int n;
struct Node *left;
struct Node *right;
};
int main(){
struct Node *A={12,0,0};
struct Node *B={33,0,0};
struct Node *C={25,A,B};
struct Node *D={50,0,0};
B->right=D;
return 0;
}
```

Question 17: Does the following code segment work? What is the output?

```
struct _{
int ___;
struct _ *_;
struct _ *__;
};
int main(){
  struct _ _={12,0,0};
  struct _ __={33,0,0};
  struct _ ___={25,&_,&__};
  struct _ ____={50,0,0};
  __.__=&____;
```

```
    printf("%d\n", _.___);
    printf("%d\n",__.___);
    printf("%d\n", ___.__->__->___);
    printf("%d\n", (*(___.__)).__->___);
    printf("%d\n", (*((*(___.__)).__)).___);
  return 0;
  }
```

You are welcome to visit the following link to understand its working.
https://tinyurl.com/AICTEDSBOOK134

Question 18: Does the following code segment work? What will be the output?

```
  struct _{
  int ___;
  struct _ *_;
  struct _ *__;
  };
  struct _ * L(struct _ *_){
    return _->_;
  }
  struct _ * R(struct _ *_){
    return _->__;
  }
  int N(struct _ *_){
    return _->___;
  }

  int main(){
    struct _ _={12,0,0};
    struct _ __={33,0,0};
    struct _ ___={25,&_,&__};
    struct _ ____={50,0,0};
    struct _ *_____=&___;
    __.__=&____;
    printf("%d\n", R(_____)->___);
    printf("%d\n",N(&___));
    printf("%d\n",  N(R(_____)));
    printf("%d\n", N(R(R(_____))));|
    printf("%d\n", R(R(_____))->___);
  return 0;
  }
```

You are welcome to visit the following link to understand its working.
https://tinyurl.com/AICTEDSBOOK135

Question 19: In the following program, we have written a function createNode() which takes an integer as an argument. It creates a one tree node dynamically by calling malloc() function. It stores the integer argument as the newly created data (that is, assigns argument of this function to data member 'n' of tree node). It also initializes the new node's left and right members to null or zero. In the main program, some nodes are created by calling the above createNode() function and a simple binary tree is created.

```
struct Node* createNode(int x){
struct Node*A;
A=(struct Node*)malloc(sizeof(struct Node));
A->n=x;
A->left=0;
A->right=0;
return A;
}
int main(){
struct Node *A=createNode(12),
       *B=createNode(33),
       *C=createNode(25),
       *D=createNode(50);
       C->left=A;
       C->right=B;
       B->right=D;
return 0;
}
```

The above code is available in the following link for experimentation and visualization.

https://tinyurl.com/AICTEDSBOOK124

Question 20: In the following code fragment, we have another variant to create a dynamic node of a tree. The function createNode1() takes node's data value(an integer, x) and two node types of addresses which can be made as this new node's left and right subtrees. Also, a main program is included to explain how this function can be used to create a binary search tree manually.

```
struct Node* createNode1(int x, struct Node *X, struct Node *Y){
struct Node*A;
A=(struct Node*)malloc(sizeof(struct Node));
A->n=x;
A->left=X;
A->right=Y;
return A;
}
int main(){
struct Node *A=createNode1(12,0,0),
       *B=createNode1(33,0,0),
       *C=createNode1(25,A,B),
       *D=createNode1(50,0,0);
       B->right=D;
return 0;
}
```

The above code is available in the following link for experimentation and visualization.

https://tinyurl.com/AICTEDSBOOK125

Question 21: Does this code segment work?

```
struct Node;
struct Node * createNode1(int x,struct Node *, struct Node *);
struct Node{
  int n;
struct Node *left;
struct Node *right;
};
```

```
int main(){
 struct Node *A=createNode1(12,0,0),
       *B=createNode1(33,0,0),
       *C=createNode1(25,A,B),
       *D=createNode1(50,0,0);
return 0;
}
struct Node* createNode1(int x, struct Node *X, struct Node *Y){
struct Node*A;
A=(struct Node*)malloc(sizeof(struct Node));
A->n=x;
A->left=X;
A->right=Y;
return A;
}
```

The above code is available in the following link for experimentation and visualization.

https://tinyurl.com/AICTEDSBOOK126

Question 22: Is there any advantage of defining a binary tree's node in the following manner?

```
struct Node;
struct links{
 struct Node *left;
 struct Node *right;
};
typedef struct links childs;
struct Node{
 int n;
 childs sibl;
};
int main(){
 struct Node A;
return 0;
}
```

The above code is available in the following link for experimentation and visualization.

https://tinyurl.com/AICTEDSBOOK127

Question 23: Can you compare the structure used for the trees and double linked lists?

Example 2: The following program creates a simple binary tree. However, it does not guarantee to be good for efficient searching. We use the createNode() function that was explained previously.

For the first integer, a new node is created by calling createNode() function and itself is taken as the root node of the tree.

For each of the subsequent integers, a new node will be created and inserted to the such that binary search property is maintained. For this purpose, search is always carried out from the root node and the node(C) to which this new node will have to be added as a child is found.

This program creates a binary search tree by finding the (leaf) node for which a new node to be added. That is, whenever a new value to be added to the binary search tree, search starts from the root node and continues till we find a leaf node for which this new values to be added as a either left or right node. Table 4.1 shows how the tree grows as numbers are inserted. For example, in the following tree, to add the number 17, first we find the node with 19 by searching from the root node. We start from the root. Root node value is 22. As 17 is less than 22, we move to the left child of 22, which is the node with value 14. Again, we do the same comparison operation. That is, we compare 17 with 14. As 17 is more than 14, we move to the right child of 14. That is, we arrive at the node with value 19. As it is a leaf node we stop our search process. Then, as 17 is smaller than 19, we let 17 be the left child of 19. Similarly, number 21 is added to the tree by traversing the tree from top to bottom checking the binary tree sequence values. Incidentally, this will be also added as the child of node with 19.

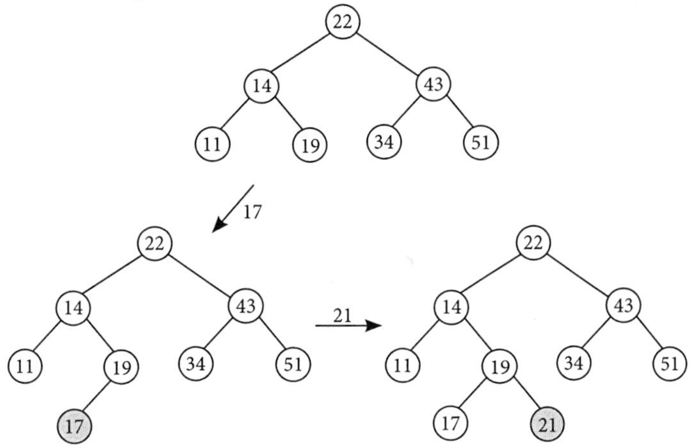

```
int main(){
int m,n=7, a[10]={123,26,44,23,34,22,91};
struct Node*A, *B, *H=0,*C;
srand(time(0));
while(n--){
A=createNode(a[n]);
if(H==0)H=A;
else{
B=H;
while(B){
C=B;
if(B->n<a[n]) B=B->right;
else
B=B->left;
}
if(C->n<a[n]) C->right=A;
else C->left=A;
}
}
return 0;
}
```

The following link contains the above code hosted on a visualization server. You are welcome to use the same. Here, we take unique element values only into the tree.

https://tinyurl.com/AICTEDSBOOK119

The following link contains a little variant of the above in which duplicates will be avoided. You are welcome to observe the necessary changes to take care of duplicates in the input while creating the binary search trees.

https://tinyurl.com/NBVCreatingAbinarytree

Table 4.1: Explains the binary search tree creation

Let us assume that the user has taken 91 the first time. A new node is created with 91 which obviously is the root node.	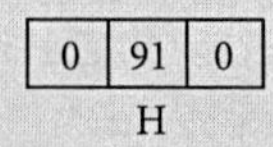
Let us assume that the user has taken 22 now. A new node is created with 22. When the while(B) loop is exited, C will be pointing to the root node. As 22 is less than the root node value, this new node will be made as the left node of the root node.	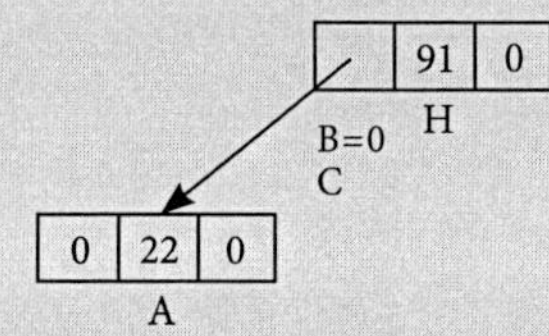
Let us assume that the user has taken 34 now. A new node is created with 34. When while(B) loop is exited C will be pointing to the node with 22. As 34 is larger than 22, the new node will be made as right to C.	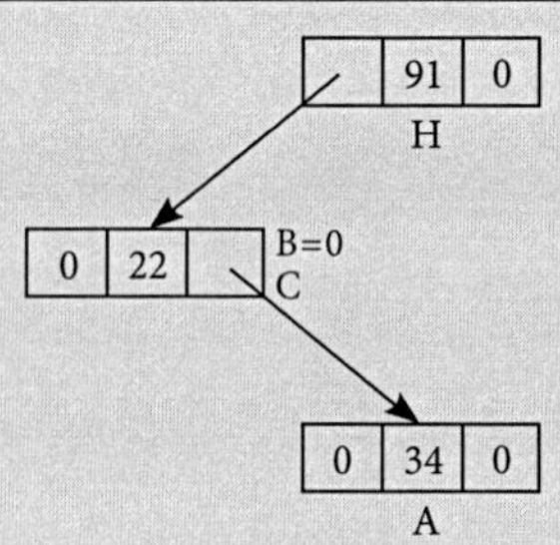
Let us assume that the user has taken 23 now. A new node is created with 23. When while(B) loop is exited C will be pointing to the node with 34. As 23 is smaller than 34, the new node will be made as left to C.	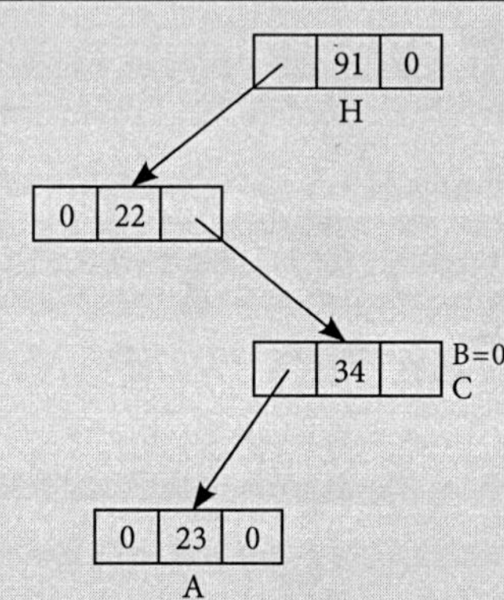
Let us assume that the user has taken 44 now. A new node is created with 44. When while(B) loop is exited C will be pointing to the node with 34. As 44 is larger than 34, the new node will be made as right to C.	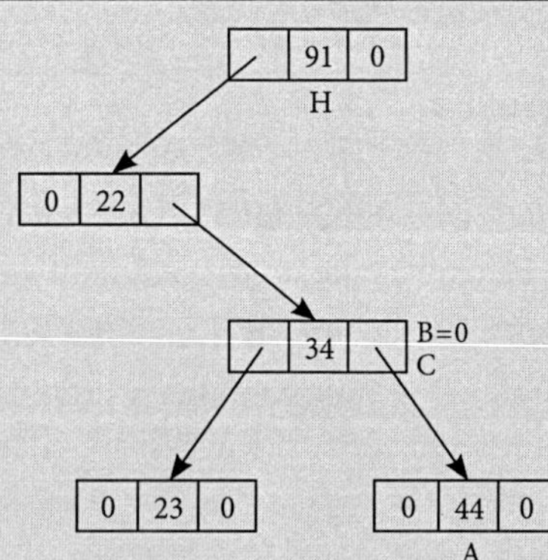

Let us assume that the user has taken 26 now. A new node is created with 26. When while(B) loop is exited C will be pointing to the node with 23. As 23 is smaller than 25, the new node will be made as right to C.	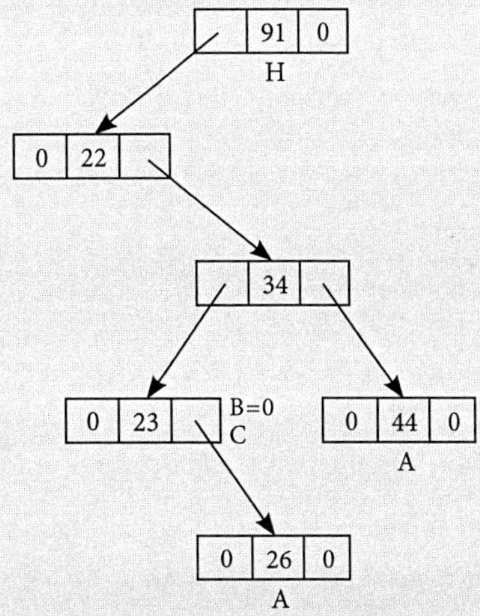
Let us assume that the user has taken 123 now. A new node is created with 123. When while(B) loop is exited C will be pointing to the node with 91(root node). As 123 is more than 91, the new node will be made as right to C.	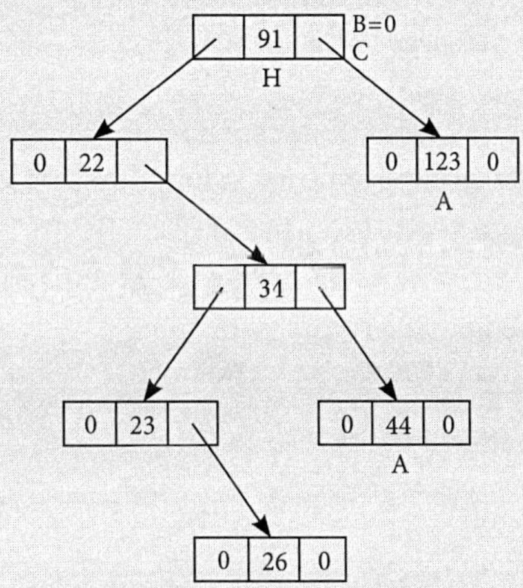

Question 24: Assume that in the above program, what each of the the following lines displays?

```
printf("%d\n", H->n);
printf("%d\n", (*H).n);
printf("%d\n",*&(*H).n);
printf("%d\n", H->left->right->n);
printf("%d\n", (*(H->left->right)).n);
printf("%d\n", H->left->right->left->n);
printf("%d\n", H->left->right->left->right->n);
printf("%d\n", (*(H->left->right->left)).right->n);
printf("%d\n", (&*(H->left->right->left))->right->n);
printf("%d\n", (*(H->left->right->left->right)).n);
printf("%d\n", (&*(H->left->right->left->right))->n);
```

You are welcome to visit the following link to answer the question.

https://tinyurl.com/AICTEDSBOOK128

Question 25: The above main program now we have converted into a function createTree() such that it takes a 1-D integer array, number of elements of the array as arguments and organizes all the elements of the array in a binary search tree fashion and returns the address of the root node. If you observe the following code, you find that it is almost the same as the previous program's main.

```
struct Node * createTree( int a[], int n){
struct Node *A, *B, *H=0,*C;
srand(time(0));
while(n--){
 A=createNode(a[n]);
if(H==0)H=A;
else{
B=H;
while(B){
C=B;
if(B->n<a[n]) B=B->right;
else
B=B->left;
}
if(C->n<a[n]) C->right=A;
else C->left=A;
}
}
return H;
}
```

The following link contains the above createTree() code and a simple main program to test the same. You are welcome to explore the same with the following link.

https://tinyurl.com/AICTEDSBOOK129

Example 3: The following program illustrates how inorder traversal of the binary search tree can be implemented in a recursive manner.

```
void INORD(struct Node *A){
if(A){
INORD(A->left);
printf("%d\n", A->n);
INORD(A->right);
}
}

int main(){
int m;
struct Node*A, *B, *H=0,*C;
while(1){
scanf("%d", &m);
if(m==0)break;
A=createNode(m);
if(H==0)H=A;
else{
B=H;
while(B){
C=B;
if(B->n==m){ free(A);
          printf("Duplicate\n");
          break;
          }

else if(B->n<m) B=B->right;
else
B=B->left;
}
if(B==0){
```

```
if(C->n<m) C->right=A;
else C->left=A;
}
}
}
printf("\nInorder Traversal\n");
INORD(H);
return 0;
}
```

You are welcome to play with the following links which have the above code.

https://tinyurl.com/NBVInorderTraversalofTree

https://tinyurl.com/AICTEDSBOOK131

Example 4: The following program illustrates how preorder traversal of the binary search tree can be implemented in a recursive manner.

```
void PREORD(struct Node *A){
if(A){
printf("%d\n", A->n);
PREORD(A->left);
PREORD(A->right);
}
}

int main(){
int m;
struct Node*A, *B, *H=0,*C;
while(1){
scanf("%d", &m);
if(m==0)break;
A=createNode(m);
if(H==0)H=A;
else{
B=H;
while(B){
C=B;
if(B->n==m){ free(A);
        printf("Duplicate\n");
        break;
        }
else if(B->n<m) B=B->right;
else
B=B->left;
}
if(B==0){
if(C->n<m) C->right=A;
else C->left=A;
}
}
}

printf("\nPreorder Traversal\n");
PREORD(H);
return 0;
}
```

You are welcome to play with the following links which have the above code.

https://tinyurl.com/NBVPreorderTraversalTree

https://tinyurl.com/AICTEDSBOOK132

Example 5: The following program illustrates how postorder traversal of the binary search tree can be implemented in a recursive manner.

```
void POSTORD(struct Node *A){
if(A){
POSTORD(A->left);
POSTORD(A->right);
printf("%d\n", A->n);
}
}

int main(){
int m;
struct Node*A, *B, *H=0,*C;
while(1){
scanf("%d", &m);
if(m==0)break;
A=createNode(m);
if(H==0)H=A;
else{
B=H;
while(B){
C=B;
if(B->n==m){ free(A);
          printf("Duplicate\n");
          break;
          }
else if(B->n<m) B=B->right;
else
B=B->left;
}
if(B==0){
if(C->n<m) C->right=A;
else C->left=A;
}
}
}
printf("\nPostOrder Traversal\n");
POSTORD(H);
return 0;
}
```

You are welcome to play with the following links which have the above code.

https://tinyurl.com/NBVPostorderTraversalofTree

https://tinyurl.com/AICTEDSBOOK133

Question 26: What will be the result of the following function on a binary search tree?.

```
int xyz(struct Node *A){
if(A==0) return 0;
while(A->left)A=A->left;
return A->n;
}
```

You are welcome to play with the following links which have the above code.

https://tinyurl.com/AICTEDSBOOK136

Question 27: What will be the result of the following function on a binary search tree?.

```
int PQR(struct Node *A){
if(A==0) return 0;
while(A->right)A=A->right;
return A->n;
}
```

You are welcome to play with the following links which have the above code.

https://tinyurl.com/AICTEDSBOOK137

Example 6: The following program allows us to create a binary search tree by calling a recursive function. We have not taken care of repeated numbers here.

```
void insertbst(struct Node **H, struct Node *A){
   if(*H==0)*H=A;
   else if((*H)->n <A->n) insertbst(&(*H)->right, A);
   else insertbst( &(*H)->left, A);
}

int main(){
        struct Node *tree=0, *A;
        int m;
        printf("Enter Numbers\n");
        while(1){
                scanf("%d", &m); if(m==0)break;
                insertbst(&tree,createNode(m));
        }
        printf("Inorder Traversal results\n");
        INORD(tree);
        return 0;
}
```

Output: Enter Numbers

50 67 80 25 34 1 0

Inorder Traversal results

1

25

34

50

67

80

You are welcome to play with the following links which have the above code.

https://tinyurl.com/AICTEDSBOOK139

https://tinyurl.com/AICTEDSBOOK138

Example 7: This problem explains the creation of a binary tree with a father node.

This example is exactly the same as Example 1 with a little modification. Here, our nodes are made to have another link field known as father field which may be supposed to point to father's node. Of course, the root node will not be having any father. This node structure is useful for iterative traversal of the trees and also for some backtracking applications.

The program has few extra lines that are shown in red and underlined compared to the code in Example 1. We can happily use the functions INORD(), PREORD(), POSTORD() with the BST tree created with the father field. Why? Because we have used only left, right, n, data members in these functions which are also available in this new structure and also they mean the same.

```
struct Node{
int n;
struct Node *left;
struct Node *right;
struct Node * father;
};
struct Node* createNode(int x){
        struct Node*A;
        A=(struct Node*)malloc(sizeof(struct Node));
        A->n=x;
        A->left=0;
        A->right=0;
        A->father=0;
        return A;
}
int main(){
        int m;
        struct Node*A, *B, *H=0,*C;
        while(1){
        scanf("%d", &m);
        if(m==0)break;
        A=createNode(m);
        if(H==0)H=A;
        else{
        B=H;
        while(B){
        C=B;
        if(B->n==m){
                        free(A);
                        printf("Duplicate\n");
                        break;
           }

        else if(B->n<m) B=B->right;
        else
                B=B->left;
        }
        if(B==0){
                if(C->n<m) C->right=A;
                else C->left=A;
                A->father=C;
        }
        }
        }
        printf("\nInorder Traversal\n");
        INORD(H);
        printf("\nPreOrder Traversal\n");
        PREORD(H);
        printf("\nPostOrder Traversal\n");
        POSTORD(H);
        return 0;
}
```

The above code is available at the following link for your experimentation.
https://ideone.com/gGSXUy

Table 4.2: How BST with father tree is created

Let us assume that the user has taken 91 the first time. Thus, a new node is created such that it contains 91. Its left and right members are made as 0s. It will be taken as the root node of the tree.	| 0 | 91 | 0 | 0 | H

Let us assume that the user has taken 22 now. A new node is created with 22. When the while(B) loop is exited, C will be pointing to the root node. As 22 is less than the root node value, this new node will be made as the left node of the root node. At the same time the new node A's father node becomes C.	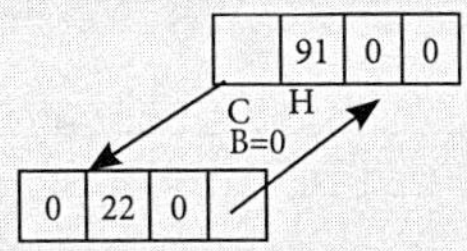
Let us assume that the user has taken 34 now. A new node is created with 34. When while(B) loop is exited C will be pointing to the node with 22. As 34 is larger than 22, the new node will be made as right to C. At the same time the new node A's father node becomes C.	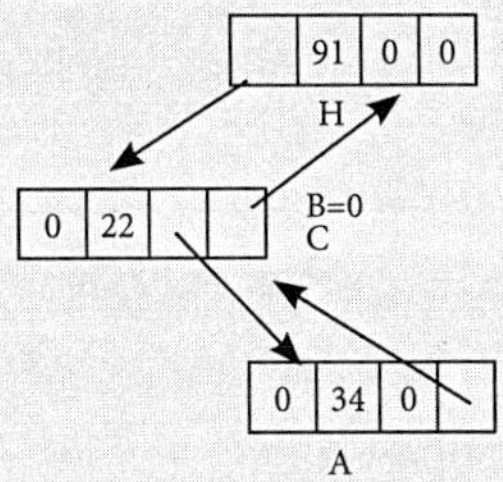
Let us assume that the user has taken 23 now. A new node is created with 23. When while(B) loop is exited C will be pointing to the node with 34. As 23 is smaller than 34, the new node will be made as left to C. At the same time the new node A's father node becomes C.	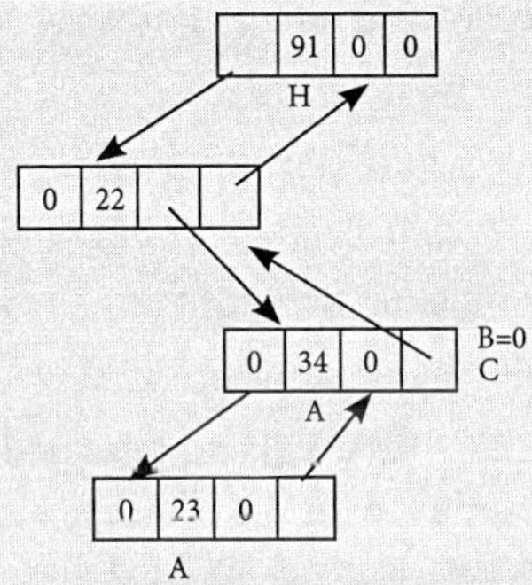
Let us assume that the user has taken 44 now. A new node is created with 44. When while(B) loop is exited C will be pointing to the node with 34. As 44 is larger than 34, the new node will be made as right to C. At the same time the new node A's father node becomes C.	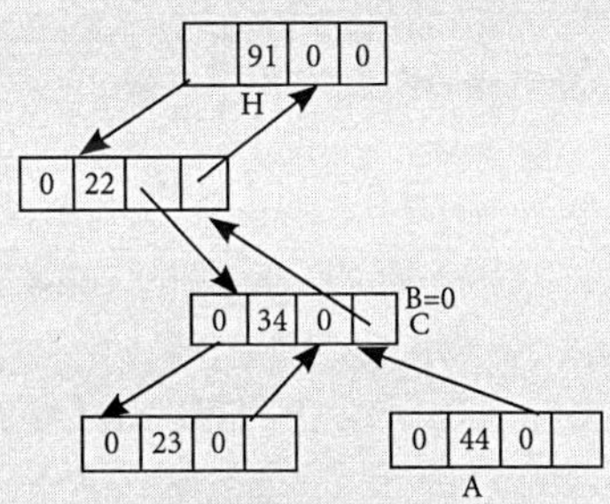
Let us assume that the user has taken 26 now. A new node is created with 26. When while(B) loop is exited C will be pointing to the node with 23. As 23 is smaller than 25, the new node will be made as right to C. At the same time the new node A's father node becomes C.	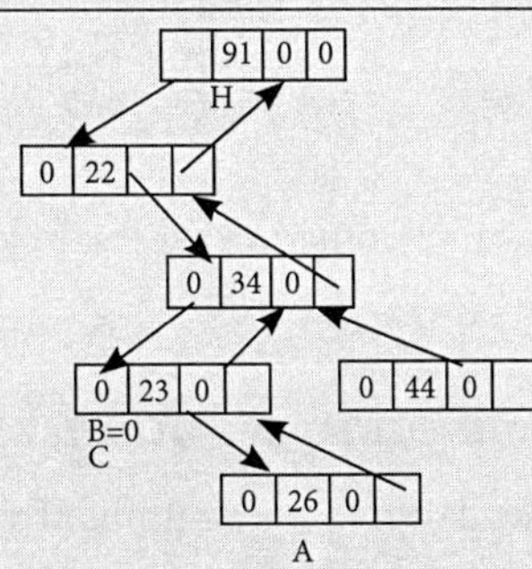

Let us assume that the user has taken 123 now. A new node is created with 123. When while(B) loop is exited C will be pointing to the node with 91(root node). As 123 is more than 91, the new node will be made as right to C. At the same time the new node A's father node becomes C.

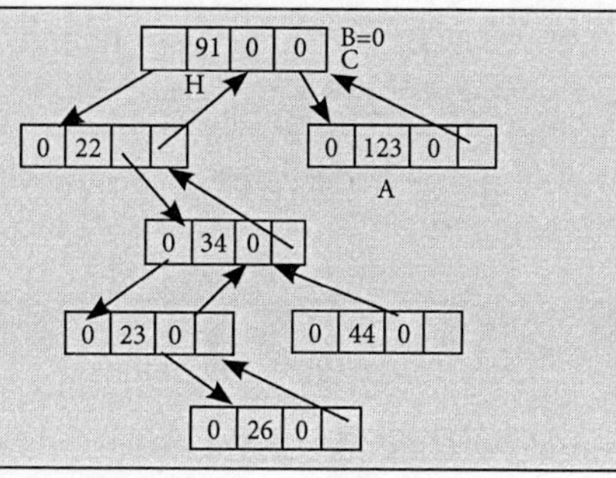

You are also welcome to the following links also where the father field is used in creating a BST.

https://tinyurl.com/AICTEDSBOOK140

https://tinyurl.com/NBVBinTreeCreatwithFather

The following link contains the **inorder** traversal code for the tree with the father node.

https://tinyurl.com/AICTEDSBOOK141

The following link contains the **preorder** traversal code for the tree with the father node.

https://tinyurl.com/AICTEDSBOOK142

The following link contains the **postorder** traversal code for the tree with the father node.

https://tinyurl.com/AICTEDSBOOK143

Question 28: What will be returned value from the following function when we send the root node address of a BST with the father node?

```
struct Node * XYZ (struct Node *root)
 if (! root -> left)
        return (root)
 else return XYZ (root -> left);
}
```

You are welcome to visit the following link before exploring the answer.

https://tinyurl.com/NBVleftmostnode

Question 29: What will be the returned value from the following function when we send the root node address of a BST with the father node?.

```
struct Node * PQR(struct Node *  root ){
  if (! root -> right)
              return (root)
  else return PQR(root -> right)
}
```

You are welcome to visit the following link before exploring the answer.

https://tinyurl.com/NBVrightmost

4.1.5 Deleting a node from BST

We may need to remove a number from the binary search tree. After removal also, the tree should satisfy the BST property. The following situations may occur during the deletion.

- **Leaf node**: If the node required to be deleted is a leaf node(A), then, set its link (A->father->left or A->father->right) in its parent to null and free the node required to be deleted (free(A)).

- **Node having only right subtree**: If the node (A) required to be deleted is having only right subtree, then attach the right subtree A to A's parent.
- **Node having only left subtree**: If the node(A) required to be deleted is having only left subtree, then attach A's left subtree to A's parent.
- **Node having both left and right subtrees**: The node required to be deleted (C) may be having both left and right subtrees. Then, identify the node B having the smallest element in the right subtree of the node to be deleted, and assign C->n as the B->n and remove B. See Figure 4.18 where to remove 18, the smallest node in the right subtree of 18 is identified (i.e node with 19) and 19 is stored as shown in the figure.

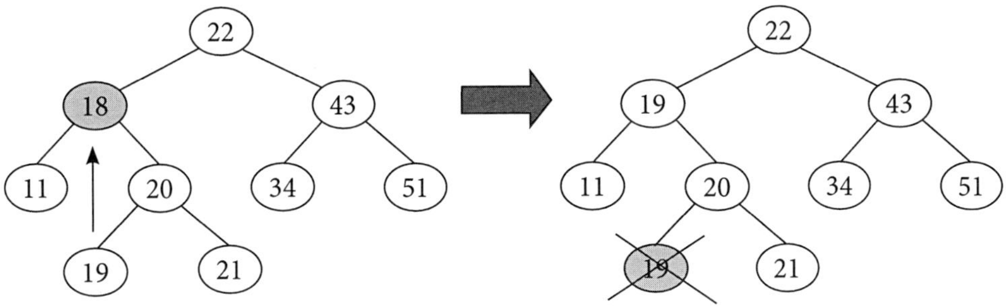

Fig. 4.18: Deleting the node which contains both the children.

Example 8: Deleting a node from binary search tree is implemented below

```
int deletenode(struct Node **H, int x){
    struct Node *A;
    if( *H==0) return 0;
    else if(x< (*H)->n) deletenode( & (*H)->left, x);
    else if( x > (*H)->n)deletenode( & (*H)->right,x);
    else{
      if( (*H)->left == 0){
                  A=*H;
                  *H=(*H)->right;
                  free(A);
                  return 1;
                }
      else if( (*H)->right ==0){
                  A=*H;
                  *H=(*H)->left;
                  free(A);
                  return 1;
                    }
      else{
        A=(*H)->left;
        while(A->right)A=A->right;
        (*H)->n=A->n;
        return deletenode(& (*H)->left, A->n);
        }
    }
}
```

```
int main(){
struct Node *tree=0, *A;
int m;
printf("Enter numbers\n");
while(1){
      scanf("%d", &m); if(m==0)break;
      insertbst(&tree,createNode(m));
}
printf("Inorder Traversal results\n");
INORD(tree);

printf("Inorder Traversal after removing 25\n");
deletenode(&tree,25);
INORD(tree);
system("PAUSE");
return 0;
}
```

Output: Enter numbers

40 50 60 25 35 34 41 10 21 0

Inorder Traversal results

10 21 25 34 35 40 41 50 60

Inorder Traversal after removing 25

10 21 34 35 40 41 50 60

The following link contains a little variant of the above code.

https://ideone.com/ZATY0i

4.1.6 Traversing Tree Using Stacks

We can traverse the trees using stacks such that we can avoid recursive calls which are used in all the three functions INORD(), PREORD(), POSTORD().

The following pseudo code gives us an idea of how traversal can be done using stack. Let p is the pointer to the root node of the tree.

```
do{
while(p !=NULL){
                    push(p);
                    p=p->left;
                  }
if(stack if not empty){
 p=pop();
Print information of node p;

p=p->right;
}
}while(stack is not empty or p is not NULL);
```

A snapshot of the working of the above algorithm along with the sample tree is shown in Figure 4.19.

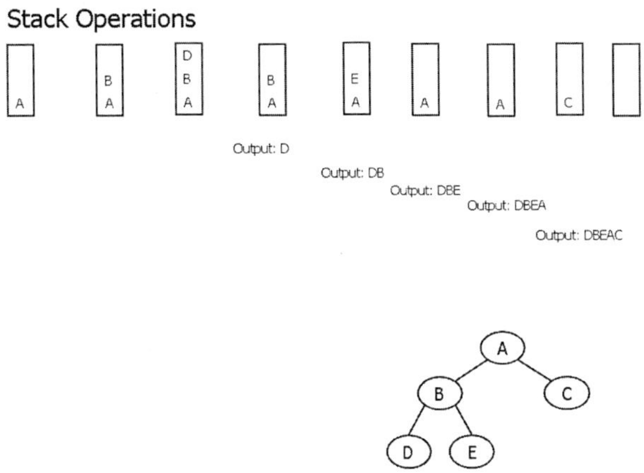

Fig. 4.19: Tree traversal using a stack.

Inorder traversal of a BST using a stack is implemented and is available in the following link. Because of book size limitations, we are unable to give the full listing in the book.

https://ideone.com/Gn3H7H

Question 30: Implement the preorder traversal of a BST using a stack by modifying the code at https://ideone.com/Gn3H7H.

Question 31: Implement the postorder traversal of a BST using a stack by modifying the code at https://ideone.com/Gn3H7H.

Example 9: The in-order and pre-order traversals of a tree are: "BDFAEC", "ABDFCE". Find out the topology of the tree.

Explanation:

1. From the pre-order sequence, we can understand that A is the root node.
2. If we observe the in-order sequence, BDF will be on the left hand side of node A while EC will be on the right hand side of root node A. That is, the root node A's left subtree's in-order traversal is BDF while its right subtree's in-order traversal is EC. We can even say that root node A's left subtree contains three nodes, while the right subtree contains two nodes.
3. Now, if observe pre-order sequence of the left subtree of A, it is BDF("A**BDF**CE"). Which indicates that the root of the left subtree of A is B. That is, A's immediate left child is B.
4. Now if we observe the given in-order sequence, DF will be on the right side of B. Thus, D becomes the right child of B.
5. Now , by observing the given in-order sequence "BDFAEC", we can say that F is right to D.
6. We already understood that EC is on the right of the root A. When we observe the pre-order sequence, we can see that C is the root of A's right subtree. That is, C is the immediate right child of root node A.
7. By observing in-order sequence of A's right tree (i.e. EC), we can conclude that E is left of C. This can be concluded from the given pre-order sequence also..

Thus, the tree topology of the given tree is:

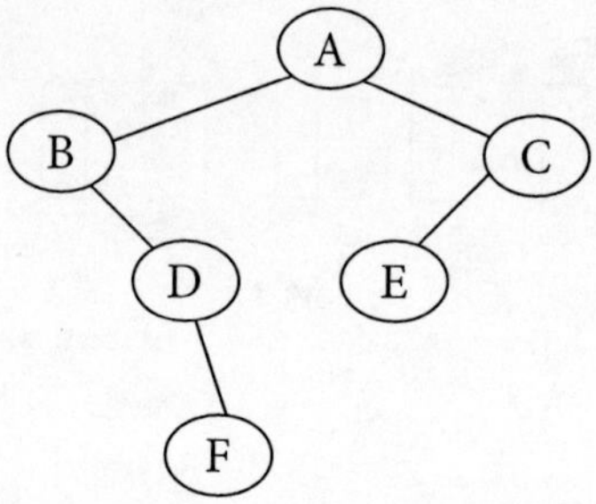

Question 32: The in-order, pre-order traversals of a tree are "ABCDEFGHI", "DBACIEGFH". What is the topology of the tree?.

Example 10: The following program evaluates the various functions with a BST. Detailed discussion on each of the functions follows subsequently.

```
int H(struct Node *A){
if(A==0) return 0;
else if(A->left==0 && A->right==0) return 1;
else
return(1+H(A->left)+ H(A->right) );
}

int NL(struct Node *A){
if(A==0) return 0;
else if(A->left==0 && A->right==0) return 1;
else
return(NL(A->left)+ NL(A->right) );
}

int NONL(struct Node *A){
if(A==0) return 0;
else if(A->left==0 && A->right==0) return 0;
else
return(1+NONL(A->left)+ NONL(A->right) );
}

int HEIGHT(struct Node *A){
int L,R;
if(A==0) return 0;
else if(A->left==0 && A->right==0) return 1;
else{
 L=HEIGHT(A->left);
 R=HEIGHT(A->right);
return(1+ ( L<R? R:L) );
}
}

int COMPLETE(struct Node *A){
int L,R;
if(A==0) return 0;
else if(A->left==0 && A->right==0) return 1;
else{
 L=COMPLETE(A->left);
 R=COMPLETE(A->right);
 if( (L==-1) || (R==-1) || (L!=R)) return -1;
return(1+L);
}
}
```

```
int BAL(struct Node *A){
int L,R;
if(A==0) return 0;
else if(A->left==0 && A->right==0) return 1;
else{
 L=BAL(A->left);
 R=BAL(A->right);
 if( (L==-1) || (R==-1) || (abs(L-R)>1 )) return -1;
return(1+(L<R?R:L));
}
}

int STRICT(struct Node *A){
int L,R;
if(A==0) return 0;
else if(A->left==0 && A->right==0) return 1;
else{
 L=STRICT(A->left);
 R=STRICT(A->right);
return(L*R);
}
}

int main(){
struct Node *tree;
tree=createtree();
printf("\nTotal Number of Nodes=%d\n", H(tree));
printf("\nTotal Number of Leaf Nodes=%d\n", NL(tree));
printf("\nTotal Number of Non Leaf Nodes=%d\n", NONL(tree));
printf("\nHeight of the Tree=%d\n", HEIGHT(tree) );
if(COMPLETE(tree)) printf("Complete Binary Tree\n");

 else printf("Not a Complete Binary Tree\n");

 if(BAL(tree)) printf("Balanced Binary Tree\n");
 else printf("Not a Balanced Binary Tree\n");
  if(STRICT(tree)) printf("Strict Binary Tree\n");
 else printf("Not a Strict Binary Tree\n");
 return 0;
 }
```

You are welcome to play with the following links which have the above code.

https://ideone.com/YCllLL

Also,

https://tinyurl.com/NBVtotalnodesinatree

You are welcome to play with the following links which have the above code.

https://tinyurl.com/NBVisstrict

Analysis of the function STRICT()

This is a recursive function which takes the root node of a binary tree and returns 1 if it is a strictly binary tree, otherwise returns 0. The function is written such that if we send a null node to the function it returns 0; if we send a leaf node to then it returns 1. We know that to call a tree strictly binary, all its non-leaf nodes should contain exactly two children. To call a tree a strictly binary tree, its left and right subtrees should be strict binary trees. Thus, we have written the recursive function as shown above.

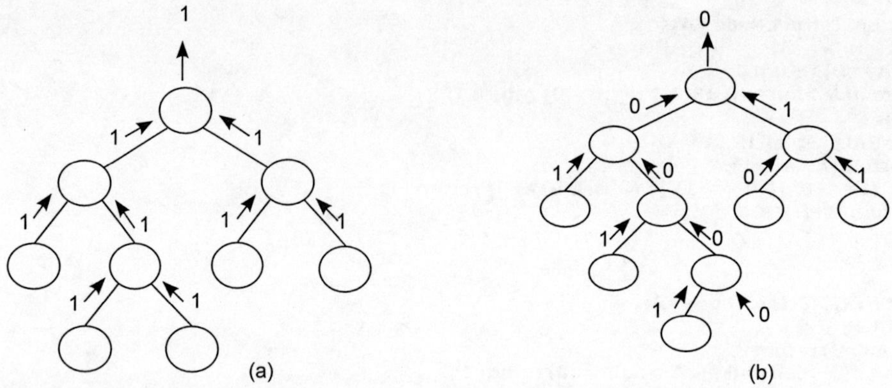

Fig. 4.20: (a) strictly binary Tree (b) Not a strictly binary tree

If we observe Figure 4.20.(a), we see that if a node receives 1 from both of its children, it returns their product, i.e., 1 to indicate strict property is satisfied with it. If any where that condition is not satisfied, it returns 0 (See Figure 4.20.(b)). One of the node in a subtree returns 0, then all of its parent nodes will bound to return 0, indicating that tree is not strict.

Analysis of the function NL() which returns the number of leaf nodes

This is also a recursive function which takes the root node of a binary tree and returns the number of leaf nodes in that tree. We consider the total number of leaf nodes of a tree is the sum of the leaf nodes in its left subtree plus number of leaf nodes in its right subtree. Thus, we apply this function recursively on both left and right subtrees recursively. The function is written such that if we send a null node to the function, it returns 0; if we send a leaf node to a function then it returns 1. See the Figure 4.21 that shows the returned values from each of the recursive calls.

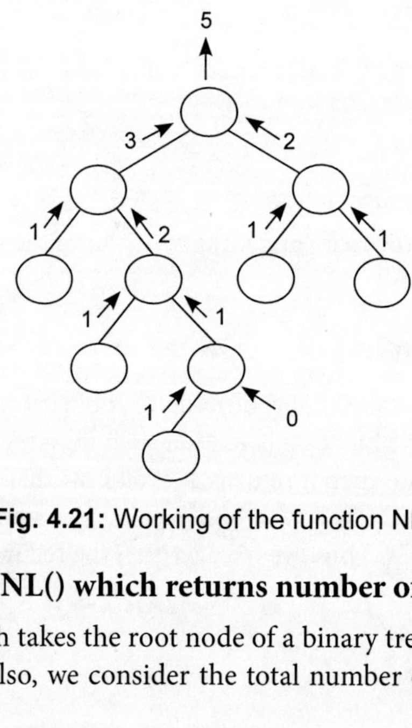

Fig. 4.21: Working of the function NL.

Analysis of the function NONL() which returns number of non-leaf nodes

This is a recursive function which takes the root node of a binary tree and returns the number of non-leaf nodes available in it. Here also, we consider the total number of non-leaf nodes at any non-leaf node is the sum of non-leaf nodes in its left subtree plus the number of non-leaf nodes in its right subtree. We apply the function recursively on both left and right subtrees recursively. The function will return 0 if we send a null or leaf node to it. See Figure 22, which shows the returned values from each of the recursive calls.

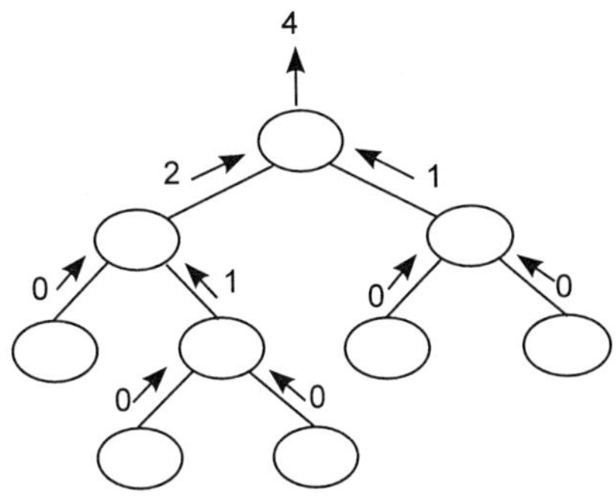

Fig. 4.22: Total Non-Leaf Nodes

Analysis of the function H() which returns Total number of nodes

This is also a recursive function which takes the root node of a binary tree and returns the total number of nodes (sum of leaf and non-leaf nodes) in it. Here too we consider the total number of nodes at any given node as the sum of nodes in its left subtree plus number of nodes in its right subtree. Thus, we apply the function recursively on both left and right subtrees recursively. The function will return 0 if we send a null node to it; if we send a leaf node it returns 1. See the Figure which shows the returned values from each of the recursive calls.

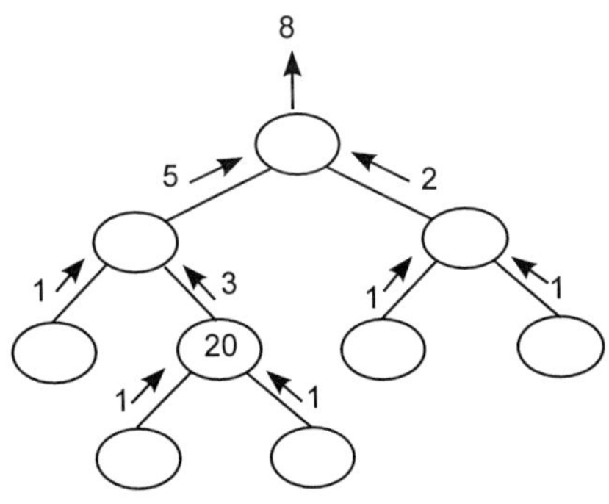

Fig. 4.23: Total Nodes in a tree

Calculating the Height of the tree Recursively

This is also a recursive function which takes the root node of a binary tree and returns the height of the tree. We consider height at any given node is the maximum of the heights of the left subtree and the right subtree plus one (i.e. including the current node). Thus, we apply the function recursively on both left and right subtrees recursively. The function is written such that if we send a null node to the function, it returns 0; if we send a leaf node to the function then it returns 1. See Figure 4.24 which shows the returned values from each of the recursive calls.

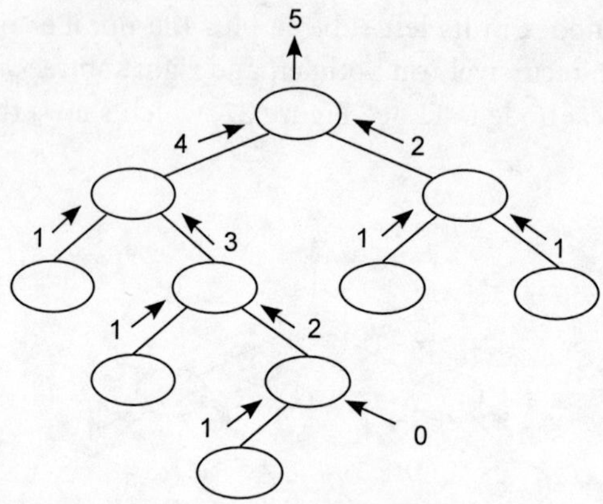

Fig. 4.24: Recursively calculating the height of a tree.

Recursive Function to test whether a tree is a Complete Tree or not.

This is also a recursive function which takes the root node of a binary tree and returns height of the tree if it is complete binary tree else returns -1. We know that in a complete tree, all non-leaf nodes will be having their left and right subtrees are of the same height. Thus, we apply the function recursively on both left and right subtrees recursively and check whether this property is satisfied or not. Anywhere if this property is violated then -1 is returned. At any node, if we receive -1 from any side, we will simply return -1 to the previous function call. The function is written such that if we send a null node to the function, it returns 0; if we send a leaf node to the function then it returns 1. See Figure 4.25 which shows the returned values from each of the recursive calls.

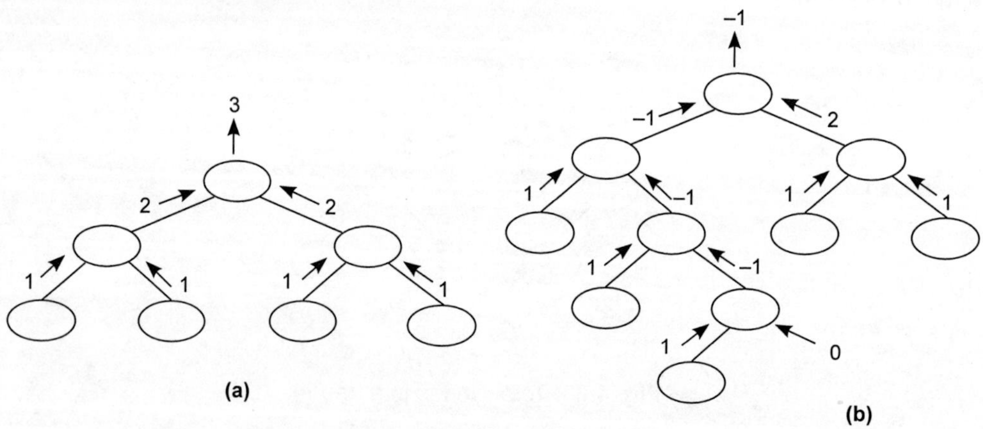

Fig. 4.25: Recursive way of checking whether a tree is complete or not.
a) tree is not complete. b)tree is complete

We can see in Figure 24 (b) that the right most node in level 3 is not having the right child and thus it returns -1. Thus, all along the path from that node to the root node, the returned value becomes -1. Thus, the tree is not a complete binary tree. See Figure 24.(a) where at any non leaf node, left and right subtree heights are the same. Thus, the height of the node is returned to the previous function call.

Recursive way of finding whether a tree is a balanced tree or not.

This is also a recursive function which takes the root node of a binary tree and returns height of the tree if it is a balanced binary tree else returns -1. We know that for all node's if the balance values are in between -1 to 1 then the tree can be called a balanced binary tree. We apply the function recursively on both left and right subtrees recursively and check whether this property is satisfied or not. Anywhere, if this property is violated then -1 is returned. At any node, if we receive -1 from any of its sides, we will simply return -1 to its previous function call. The function is written such that if we send a null node to the function, it returns 0; if we send a leaf node to the function then it returns 1. See Figure 4.26 which shows the returned values from each of the recursive calls.

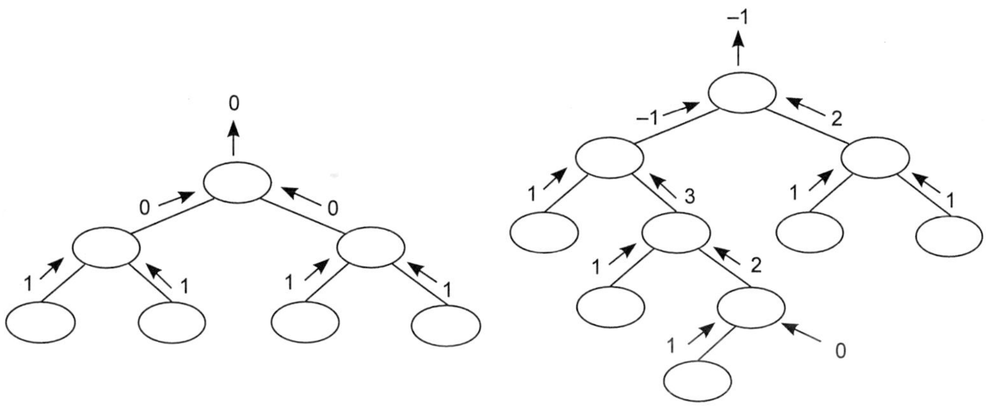

Fig. 4.26: Recursive function trace for finding whether the tree is a balanced tree or not.

We can see from the above figure b, that if one node balance is missing then the recursive function call gets rewinded immediately and returns -1 for all the previous function calls.

Example 11: The following program checks whether two trees are topologically and content-wise the same or not.

```
int identicaltopology(struct Node* a, struct Node* b) {
if (a==NULL && b==NULL){return(1);}
else if (a!=NULL && b!=NULL) {
return(
identicaltopology(a->left, b->left) &&
identicaltopology(a->right, b->right));
}
else return(0);
}

int identical(struct Node* a, struct Node* b) {
if (a==NULL && b==NULL){return(true);}
else if (a!=NULL && b!=NULL) {
return(a->n == b->n &&
identical(a->left, b->left) &&
identical(a->right, b->right));|
}
else return(0);
}

int main(){
int i;
struct Node *A,*B;
printf("Creating first tree\n");
```

```
A=createtree();
printf("\nCreating Second Tree\n");
B=createtree();
if(identicaltopology(A,B))printf("\nTopologically Same\n");
else
printf("\nTopologically Not Same\n");

if(identical(A,B))printf("\nTopologically and Contentwise Same\n");
else
printf("\nTopologically and content wise Not Same\n");
return 0;
}
```

Output:

Test1: Creating first tree 20 30 40 50 60 0 Creating Second Tree 20 30 40 50 60 0 Topologically Same Topologically and Content wise Same	Test2: Creating first tree 20 30 40 50 60 0 Creating Second Tree 50 60 70 80 90 0 Topologically Same Topologically and content wise Not Same	Test 3: Creating first tree 20 30 40 50 60 0 Creating Second Tree 20 30 40 50 60 70 80 0 Topologically Not Same Topologically and content wise Not Same

You are welcome to play with the following links which have the above code.

https://ideone.com/HDvMNd

The above functions identical topologically() is used to test whether two given trees are having topological structure or not. In order to call two trees topologically the same, at each level they have the same topological structure. The same is tested with the above recursive function. Here, we have employed a rule to check in any recursive call if both a&b either true or null then trees are topological; else trees are not identical. That is, in any recursive call, a is pointing to a meaningful node while b is 0; or vice versa. Then, trees are not having same topological structure. Thus, the function returns 0. At one node, if zero is received, then the same is returned to previous function calls. See Figure 4.27 for the analysis.

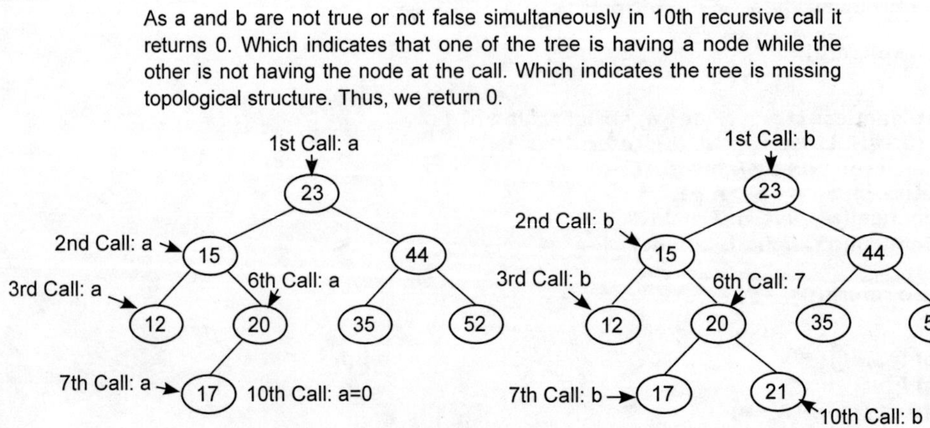

Fig. 4.27: Checking whether two trees are identical or not.

The function identical() used in the above program is same is identicaltopology() with some extra constraint. That is, we will check the information of nodes pointed by both a and b in each recursive call.

Example 12: The following code is to create a copy of a given tree.

```
struct Node *copy(struct Node *root){
struct Node *temp;
if(root==NULL)return(NULL);

temp = (struct Node *) malloc(sizeof(struct Node));
temp->n = root->n;
temp->left = copy(root->right);
temp->right = copy(root->left);
return(temp);
}

int main(){
struct Node *H, *B;
H=createtree();
printf("\nInorder Traversal of Tree\n");
INORD(H);
B=(H);
printf("\nInOrder Traversal of copied tree\n");
INORD(B);
return 0;
}
```

Output: 20 30 21 22 33 0

Inorder Traversal of Tree

20 21 22 30 33

Inorder Traversal of copied tree

20 21 22 30 33

We have our side code made available at https://ideone.com/C4yNTL . Check any problem here.

Example 13: The following program calculates the mirror of a tree.

```
void mirror(struct Node* node) {
struct Node *temp;
if (node==NULL) {
return;
}
else {
mirror(node->left);
mirror(node->right);

// Swap the pointers of this node
temp = node->left;
node->left = node->right;
node->right = temp;
}
}

int main(){
  struct Node *H;
H=createtree();
printf("\nInorder Traversal of Tree\n");
INORD(H);
mirror(H);
```

```
mirror(H);
printf("\nInOrder Traversal After Mirroring\n");
INORD(H);
return 0;
}
```

Output: 20 30 40 50 70 0

Inorder Traversal of Tree

20 30 40 50 70

Inorder Traversal After Mirroring

70 50 40 30 20

You are welcome to play with the following links which have the above code.

https://tinyurl.com/AICTEDSBOOK151

Question 33: Check whether the following function will allow us to check whether a tree having its left and right subtrees are mirrors to each other not.

```
int mirror(struct Node* a, struct Node* b) {
if (a==NULL && b==NULL)return(1);
else if (a!=NULL && b!=NULL) {
return(
mirror(a->left, b->right) &&
mirror(a->right, b->left));
}
else return(0);
}
```

Example 14: The following function checks the existence of a node with value x in a BST whose root node is A.

```
struct Node * Find(struct Node *A, int x){
if(A==0) return 0;
while(A){
if(A->n==x)return A;
else if(A->n<x) A=A->right;
else A=A->left;
}
return A;
}
int main(){
struct Node *tree;
tree=createtree();
printf("%d\n", Find(tree,23)->n);
return 0;
}
```

You are welcome to play with the following links which have the above code.

https://tinyurl.com/AICTEDSBOOK147

Recursive Version for Find

This is the recursive version of Find(). If A is null, we return null. If A contains x then it returns A. Otherwise, we will search for x in its left and right subtrees **recursively** with the same function.

Example 15: The following function checks the existence of a node with value x in a BST whose root node is A in a recursive manner.

```
struct Node * RFind(struct Node *A, int x){
if(A==0) return 0;
else if(A->n ==x) return A;
else if( A->n<x) return(RFind(A->right,x));
else  return (RFind(A->left,x));
}
```

You are welcome to play with the following links which have the above code.

https://tinyurl.com/AICTEDSBOOK148

Question 34: Assume that our binary tree node contains one extra data member, link count, which indicates the number of nodes left of it.

```
struct Node{
int n;
int linkcount;
struct Node *left;
struct Node *right;
};
```

You are welcome to play with the following links which have the above code.

https://tinyurl.com/AICTEDSBOOK149

Find out whether the following function returns the address of kth element of the ordered list or not.

```
struct Node * kthelement(struct Node *H, int k){
if( H==0) return 0;
while( H && ( H->left || H->right ) ){
if(H->linkcount >= k) H=H->left;
else{
k -=H->linkcount;
H=H->right;
}
return H;
}
```

You are welcome to play with the following links which have the above code.

https://tinyurl.com/AICTEDSBOOK150

Question 35: Write a program to find out the in-order successor of a node with a given value.

In-Order successor of Node, A, can be calculated by employing the following rules.

- If A is left child to its parent and A does not have any right subtree then its parent itself becomes an in-order successor of A.
- If A is left child to its parent and A has right subtree, then the leftmost child of A's right subtree becomes the A's in-order successor.
- If A is the right child of its parent and A has the right subtree, the leftmost child of A's right subtree becomes the A's in-order successor.
- If A is the right child of its parent and A does not have any right subtree, then backtrack using the father field till we will find a node B which is left to its parent and then return B's father as A's in-order successor.

- If A is the rightmost node of a tree then its in-order successor is NULL.
- If A is the root node then the leftmost child of its right subtree is its in-order successor.

In Figure 4.28 for nodes marked as A,B, the in-order successors are their parents as A, B do not have right subtrees.

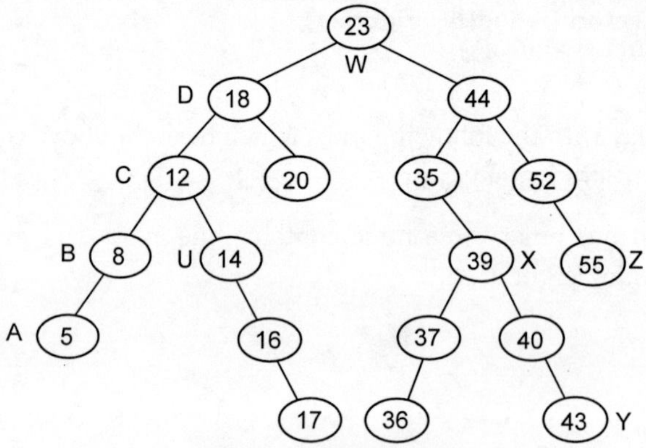

Fig. 4.28: In-Order Successors

For nodes C,D, in-order successors are the left most nodes of its right subtrees. In this case, they are 14 and 20 respectively.

For nodes Y, Z (which are right children for their parents and do not have any right subtrees), in-order successors are 35 and NULL.

For nodes, U, X in-order successors are left most children of their right subtrees. That is, 16 and 40 respectively.

For root node, W, in-order successor is 35.

Note: In-Order predecessors of a node can be easily calculated by replacing left with right and right with left in the above statements.

Threaded Binary Trees are the ones which may contain nodes with their links pointing to in-order successors or predecessors. A binary tree can be made as a right *threaded* tree by making all right pointers point to the inorder successor of the node. If we make left child pointers to point to in-order predecessors, the resulting tree is called as left-threaded tree (see Figure 4.29)

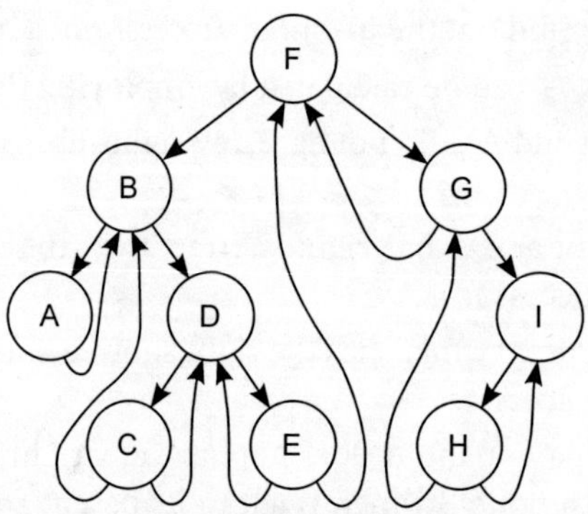

Fig. 4.29: Threaded tree

Height Balanced Trees or AVL(Adelson-Velsky and Landis) Trees

We have mentioned that binary search trees are primarily meant for searching applications. In example 1, we have created a binary search tree by reading a set of numbers. If we give the following input for the above program, the resulting tree will be a skewed tree which is also called a degenerate tree as shown in figure 4.30.

10 23 44 52 55 90 100

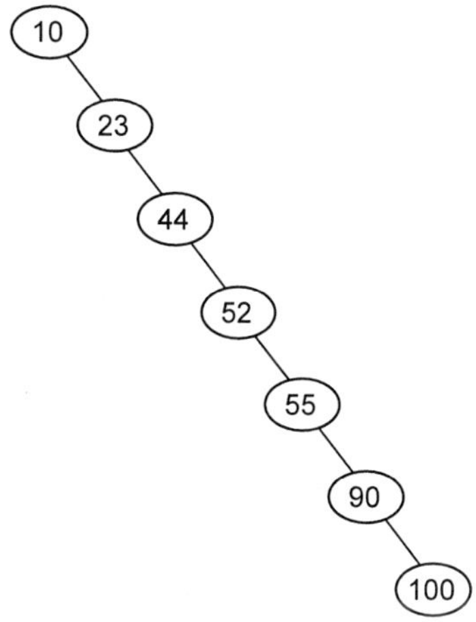

Fig. 4.30: Skewed Tree

Is it not looking like a single linked list?. Indeed it is. What is the cost of finding an element in this tree, a.k.a. singled linked list?. If the number we wanted is 10, then we will succeed with one search only (O(1)). If the number we are looking for is 100, then we have to visit all the nodes, in the worst case with order O(n). Thus, its behavior is more like linear search. Of course, if the given number is not in the tree also, worst case complexity of O(n).

Now consider what if the same set of numbers are organized as a binary search tree as shown in Figure 4.31:

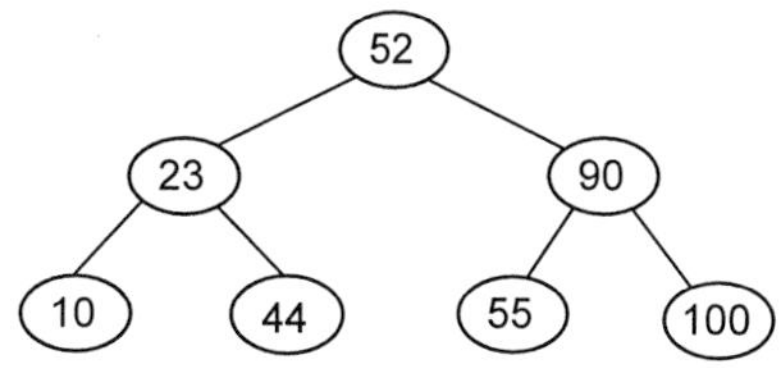

Fig. 4.31: Balanced Binary Search Tree

Is there any advantage of this tree over the previous degenerate tree?. Here, if the search number is 52, we will succeed with only one comparison, i.e., it is O(1) order. If we observe the tree, at most we have to visit three nodes only while searching for a number . Thus, this organization is better. What have we done here?. We have organized the numbers such that the tree is balanced in some sense such that we don't face worst case situations such as the skewed tree. Thus, in practice, while building binary search trees, we apply some rotations on the tree nodes such that the tree becomes height balanced or optimal binary tree. Of course, we have to remember that the inorder sequence has to be preserved (or maintained) during these rotations. If you verify inorder traversal results of both the above trees, you will find that both will be giving the same inorder sequences. This idea of rotation is proposed by G.M. Adelson-Velskii and E.M. Landis, in 1962. Thus, these trees are called AVL trees. **What are rotations, how they are carried is beyond the scope of this book because of the book size limitations.**

We find the following site has marvelous BST visualization tools and AVL tree visualization tools. It illustrates the rotations of the node while AVL tree is created.

https://www.cs.usfca.edu/~galles/visualization/BST.html

4.1.7 Sequential Representation of the Tree

Sequential representation of a tree means, tree nodes information is stored in an 1-D array fashion such that ith node's left, right children values are stored in 2*i+1 and 2*i+2 elements of the array (see Figure 4.32). Index of the root node is considered as 0. Sequential representation is employed to reduce time required to read/write tree information from disk to RAM and vice versa where the tree contains trillions of numbers. That is, if nodes are located sequentially in memory, then time required to save tree information onto the disk becomes very less. However, after reading the tree information into RAM, we may need some computations to have new links depending on to which memory tree is loaded.

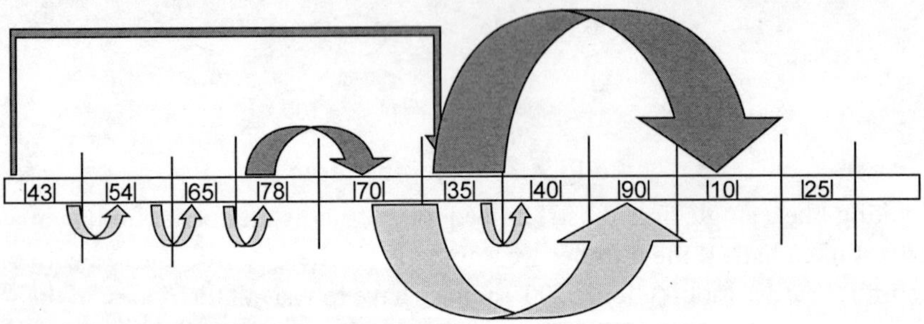

Fig. 4.32: Sequential storage of a binary tree.

Example 16: The following example explains about creating a sequential tree.

We will be asking the user to enter the number of nodes to be maintained in the tree. Then, we allocate a 1-Dimensional array of Node type of objects by calling malloc. Whenever a new node is required to be added, one element of this array is assigned. If one observes, we have changed importantly one statement; A=D+i. In previous examples, whenever a node is required to be added, it will be created at that time and assigned to A. Here, we are simply assigning the address of one the node which is already created. This is the major change. Of course, loop control is changed to run for n times.

```
int main(){
int i,m,n;
struct Node*A, *B, *H=0,*C,*D;
printf("Enter number of integers we wanted to maintain in binary search
tree\n");
scanf("%d", &n);
D=(struct Node *)malloc(n*sizeof(struct Node));
for(i=0;i<n;i++) {
        D[i].left=0;
        D[i].right=0;
        }
```

```
for(i=0;i<n;i++){
printf("Enter Number to be inserted in the tree\n");
scanf("%d", &m);
A=D+i;
        /* Assigning the one of address of already allocated nodes */
A->n=m;
if(H==0)H=A;
else{
B=H;

while(B){
C=B;
if(B->n==m){ i--;
        printf("Duplicate\n");
        break;
        }
else if(B->n<m) B=B->right;
else
B=B->left;
}
if(B==0){
if(C->n<m) C->right=A;
else C->left=A;
}
}
}
printf("\nInorder Traversal\n");
INORD(H);
return 0;
}
```

Output: Enter number of integers we wanted to maintain in binary search

10

Enter number to be inserted in the tree

29

Enter number to be inserted in the tree

34

Enter number to be inserted in the tree

29

Duplicate

Enter number to be inserted in the tree

35

Enter number to be inserted in the tree

9

Enter number to be inserted in the tree

10

Enter number to be inserted in the tree

22

Enter number to be inserted in the tree

33

Enter number to be inserted in the tree

45

Enter number to be inserted in the tree

78

Enter number to be inserted in the tree

89

Inorder Traversal

9 10 22 29 33 34 35 45 78 89

The above code is available for experimentation at:

https://tinyurl.com/AICTEDSBOOK145

The following picture illustrates how a tree is stored in sequential memory.

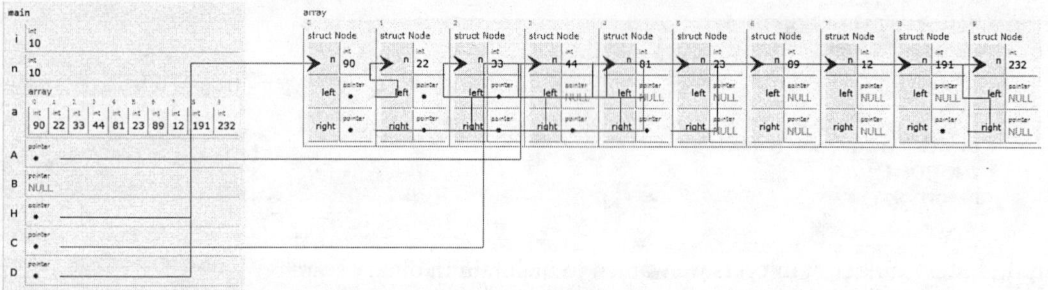

Question 36: If we have N keys (numbers) and organized as a binary tree fashion such that every node contains exactly two children. What is the worst possible height of the tree?. Assume, N value is more than or equal to 3. What is the nature if N is even or odd?. In this type of tree, what are the number of leaf and non-leaf nodes available?

Example 17: The following example demonstrates the tree creation using a structured array. We do not use any pointers. It is more like a sequential tree itself.

```
struct {
char data[16];
int left;
int right;
} list[100];

int length=0; // assume root is 0

void print_tree(int root) {
  if(root !=-1) {
    print_tree(list[root].left);
    puts(list[root].data);
    print_tree(list[root].right);
  }
}

int search(int i,char s[]) {
if(i==-1) return 0; // This is recursive version
```

```
if(strcmp(s,list[i].data)<0) return search(list[i].left,s);
if(strcmp(s,list[i].data)>0) return search(list[i].right,s);
return 1; // found
}
void newnode(int n, char s[], int side) {
     if(side==0) list[n].left=length;
     if(side==1) list[n].right=length;
     strcpy(list[length].data,s);
     list[length].right=-1;
     list[length].left=-1;
     length++;
}
void insert(int i,char name[]) {
 if (strcmp(name,list[i].data) < 0) {
     if(list[i].left==-1) newnode(i,name,0);
     else
     insert(list[i].left,name);
 }
 else if (strcmp(name,list[i].data) > 0){
     if(list[i].right==-1) newnode(i,name,1);
     else
     insert(list[i].right,name);
 }
}
void insert_node(char name[]) {
 if(length == 0) {
  newnode(0,name,-1);
 } else
 insert(0,name);
}
void main(){
int t1;

 insert_node("Ramesh");
 insert_node("Anuj");
 insert_node("Sarada");
 insert_node("Appu");
 insert_node("Venkat");

 insert_node("VVN Rao");
 insert_node("Gandhiji");

 print_tree(0);

 t1=search(0,"Rao");
 if (!t1)
  puts("Rao Not Found");

 t1=search(0,"Gandhiji");
 if (!t1)
  puts("Gandhiji Not Found");

  system("PAUSE");

}
```

You are welcome to play with the following links which have the above code.

https://tinyurl.com/AICTEDSBOOK146

4.2 INTRODUCTION TO GRAPH THEORY

A marvelous tool for graph analysis is available at:

https://snapapps.github.io/edgy/app/edgy.html

We strongly recommend teachers to use this tool without missing much before starting their lectures on Graphs. Teachers really can design tasks to raise the interest of students.

Graph theory is the one area which is used in almost all areas including biology, sociology, engineering, chemistry, etc., Most of the renowned Universities are offering a minimum 2 to 3 courses on this theme for their Computer Science and allied students. The development of graph theory is very much inspired by the study of games and recreational mathematics.

Generally speaking, we use graphs in many situations of daily life also. A graph is a very convenient and natural way of representing the relationships between objects (such as cities, people, molecules). Objects are represented with vertices while the relationships between them by lines or arcs. Thus, a graph can be said as a collection of vertices (**V**) and edges (**E**). Do remember that we have used the same definition for a tree also.

Undoubtedly in many situations (including intricate problems), a pictorial representation may help a lot in illustrating the things easily. In crystallography, the three dimensional structure of atoms (topoly) structures is explored using graph theoretic approaches. For example, a chemical molecule and its graph representation is shown in Figure 4.33.

Fig. 4.33: A sample chemical molecule and its graph representation.

Also, there are some problems which are referred to as matching problems. Consider we have the following set of applicants and the jobs they can do. No applicant is accepted for two jobs, and no job is assigned to two applicants. The problem is to find a worker for each job.

Applicants:	**p**	**q**	**r**	**s**	**t**
Suitable jobs:	**a b c**	**b d**	**a e**	**e**	**c d e**

The possible solution can be given as (Figure 4.34) a graph:

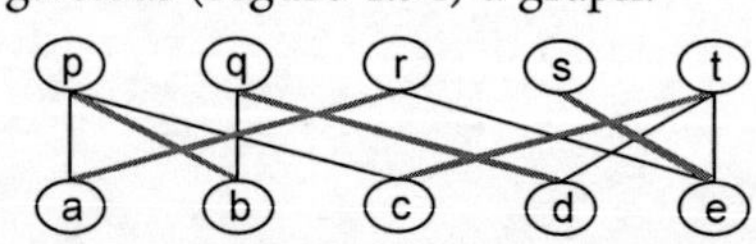

Fig. 4.34: A job assignment problem.

We often look for a route map (such as the one in Figure 4.35) of a place which we may plan to visit during your next vacation. Such a map may contain details about roads and rail routes in the area of interest.

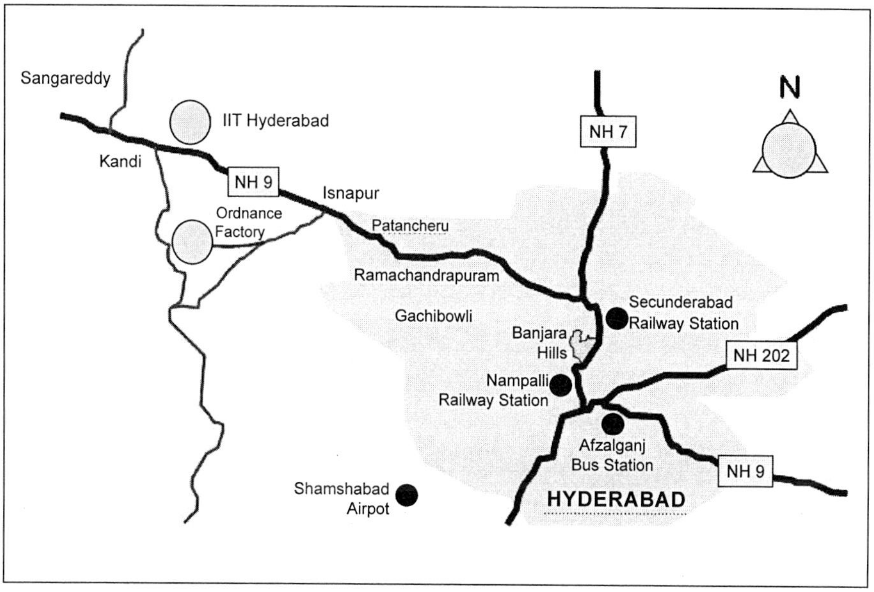

Fig. 4.35: A sample route map (source www.iith.ac.in Last accessed: Aug 2016)

Similarly, we may encounter applications of graph theory in the design of water supply systems, gas supply systems, etc. Of course, their applications may differ from problem to problem. For example, in the case of water supply systems design supply water at maximum possible rate with expected minimum pressure. Here, we can consider the pipes are the edges and intermediate valves etc., can be considered as nodes. Same is applicable to gas supply systems such as the one shown in Figure 4.36.

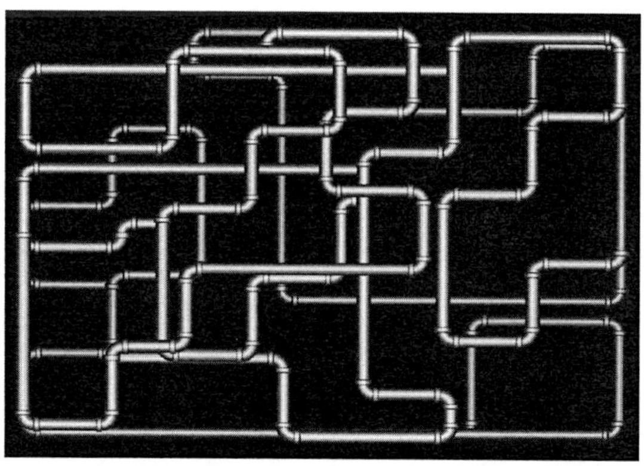

Fig. 4.36: An example Pipe distribution system

Some graph structures(see Figure 4.37) employ some weights to each edge of the graph like distance between two places in the road network, or delay between two routers on the Internet, etc. They are called weighted graphs.

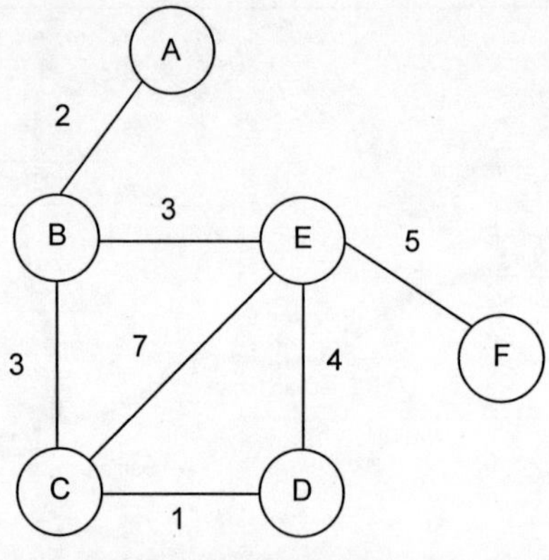

Fig. 4.37: A sample weighted graph.

A website is also represented by a directed graph with web pages as the vertices, urls being the edges. A directed edge from page *A* to page *B* is assumed if page *A* contains a hyperlink to *B*.

A **graph** *G* consists of *vertices* and *edges*. Every edge connects (joins)two vertices. An edge is represented with two vertices which it is connecting. Here, the vertex order is important to disambiguate the direction of the connection. For example, two places A, B in a city have a connecting road which is a one way road for all the time, then we say A —> B, indicating we can reach B from A, but not the other way wrong. These types of edges are called directed edges; otherwise undirected edges. The following is a graph (see Figure 4.38) with all of its edges as undirected. This type of graph is referred to as an undirected graph; otherwise the graphs are called directed graphs. Even the existence of a single directed edge makes us refer to that graph as a directed graph.

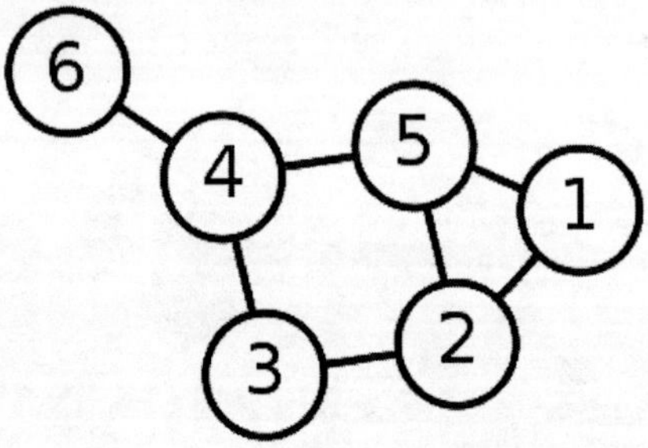

Fig. 4.38: A sample graph

The collection of vertices of a graph G is represented as V(G) and is also referred to as the vertex **set** of G. The total number of elements of vertex set is known as the order of the graph and the same is represented as $|V(G)|$.

The set of edges of a graph G is referred to as the **edge set** of *G or E(G).* The collection of edges of a graph is known as its size, i.e. $|E(G)|$.

A **self loop** is a special single edge that starts at a vertex and ends at the same vertex. Anything is getting into your mind? Yes. Marvelous examples can be ring roads that are typically constructed to control the traffic of cities.

A **link** or **edge** connects two distinct vertices. It is very much possible for two vertices to have more than one edge. In which case that edge is referred to as multiple **edge**; otherwise it is **simple.**

The number of multiple edges between two given vertices is called that edge's **multiplicity** while the maximum multiplicity of a graph's edges is called **multiplicity of that graph**. Based on this multiplicity concept, graphs are classified as:

- a **simple graph** if it has no multiple edges or loops
- a **multigraph** if it has multiple edges, but no loops,
- a **multigraph** or **pseudograph** if it contains both multiple edges and loops.

A graph *G's* **complement** $\overline{G}$ is a graph with the same V(G) but with an E(G) which is the set of edges that are not there in G.

A graph with zero or more vertices without any edges is referred to as an edgeless **graph** or an **empty graph.**

A **null graph** is a graph with no vertices and no edges. However, a graph with no edges and any number *n* of vertices is called the **null graph on *n* vertices**.

A graph with infinitely many vertices or edges or both is referred to as an infinite graph; otherwise **finite** graph. Do remember in this course, we shall deal with finite graphs only.

An alternating sequence of vertices and edges that starts and ends with a vertex is called a **walk/path.** If a path starts and ends at the same vertex it is a closed path or **cycle**; otherwise it is an open path. The number of edges of a path is called the length of the path. A path without any repeated vertices is called a simple path. A path with distinct edges and vertices is referred to as a **chain.**

In the example graph in Figure, (1, 2, 5, 1, 2, 3) is an open path of length 5 while (4, 5, 2, 1, 5, 4) is a closed path of length 5.

The path with distinct edges is referred to as a **trail;** while a closed trail is called a **tour** or **circuit.**

Do you remember that we have mentioned that a tree is also a graph and is without any cycles; rather it is **acyclic** (cycle less graph). If a graph contains a single cycle then the graph is **unicyclic** otherwise **pancyclic**. A cycle that uses all vertices exactly only once is known as spanning or **hamiltonian** and that graph is **hamiltonian graph**. If a cycle uses all of its edges exactly once then it is **Eulerian.**

A graph's shortest possible cycle length is its **girth** while the longest possible simple cycle is its **circumference.**

A graph node's **indegree** is the number of edges ending there while **outdegree** is the number of edges leaving from that node; total of these two is the **degree** of that node. Can you guess what is the degree of an isolated vertex? Zero.

The **distance** of a pair of vertices is the length of the shortest path between them.

If every node can be reached[61] from every other node in a graph then that graph is a connected graph. The worst possible path length in a connected graph with n vertices is *n-1*.

The largest possible subgraph of a graph in which all nodes are reachable from every other node is its **connected component.**

If the removal of any vertex of a graph leads to more connected components then that any vertex is called a cut point. The set of such a vertex is known as the cutset of that graph.

If the removal of any edge of a graph leads to more connected components then that any edge is called a bridge. The set of such edges is known as the edge cutset of that graph.

61 A node is reachable from another node if there exists a path of any length from one to the other.

4.2.1 Graph Representations

Pictorially, graphs are drawn with filled or empty circles for their vertices and lines (or arrows) for their edges. However, we are very much interested in doing some manipulations using a computer program. There are many approaches that are widely used. We shall discuss each of them in the following pages.

4.2.1.1 Adjacency Matrix Representation of the Graph

An NxN matrix that is known as an adjacency matrix stores the edge details of a graph with N number of vertices. If we assume vertices are represented as numbers 0 to N-1 (or 1 to N), then in the given graph if there exists an edge between i[th] vertex and j[th] vertex then i[th] row j[th] column element of the adjacency matrix will be set to 1; otherwise it is set to zero. Of course, if the stations are having more than one edge, the respective element of the adjacency matrix will be initialized with that count. From this adjacency matrix, we can draw the graph at any time.

Figure **4.39** contains a sample graph and its adjacency matrix. Observe the principal diagonal element's values. All are zeros. This indicates that the stations are not having self cycles or self loops.

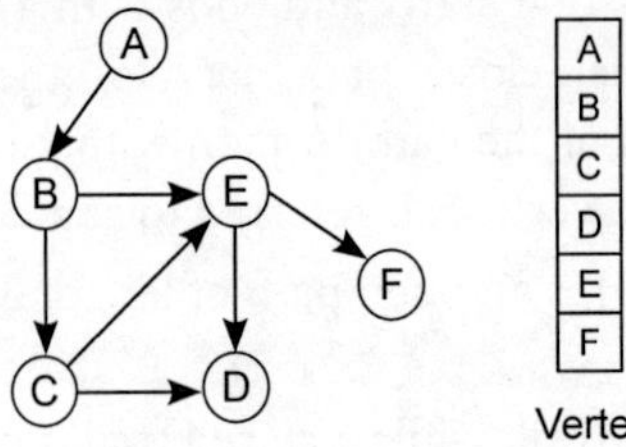

Vertex Vector

	A	B	C	D	E	F
A	0	1	0	0	0	0
B	0	0	1	0	1	0
C	0	0	0	1	1	0
D	0	0	0	0	0	0
E	0	0	0	1	0	1
F	0	0	0	0	0	0

Adjacency matrix

Fig. 4.39: A sample graph with its adjacency matrix.

If we observe the last row of the above adjacency matrix, we may find all 0's indicating that the station is sink. Which means, there are no edges emanating from that station.

If the above graph is an undirected graph, the adjacency matrix will be created by considering each undirected edge as two directed edges, one forward and one backward. The resultant adjacency matrix will be given in Figure 8. However, for a weighted graph (such as the one shown in Figure 4.40), the adjacency matrix will be having weight values of the edges.

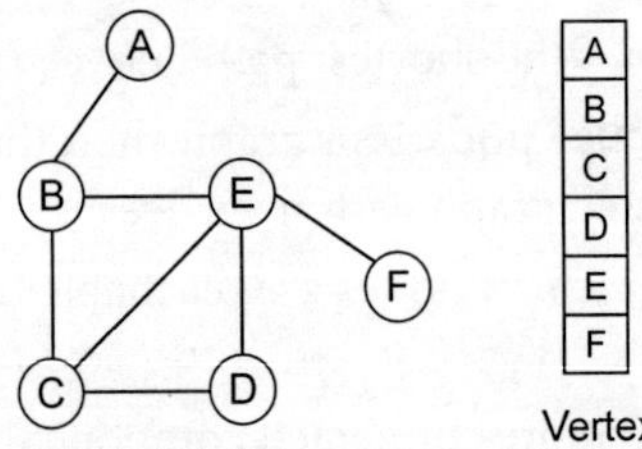

Vertex Vector

	A	B	C	D	E	F
A	0	1	0	0	0	0
B	0	0	1	0	1	0
C	0	1	0	1	1	0
D	0	0	1	0	1	0
E	0	1	1	1	0	1
F	0	0	0	0	1	0

Adjacency matrix

Fig. 4.40: Adjacency matrix for an undirected graph

If we observe the adjacency matrix of an undirected graph, we may find it as a symmetric matrix. Of course, one has to remember that a graph is called a directed graph (or di-graph) even if a single edge is directed. On the contrary, to call it an undirected graph, all the edges should be un-directed. Of course, there are some algorithms which work only on directed graphs. In order to apply those algorithms on undirected graphs, we can replace each un-directed edge with two directed edges, one forward and one backward as shown in Figure 4.41.

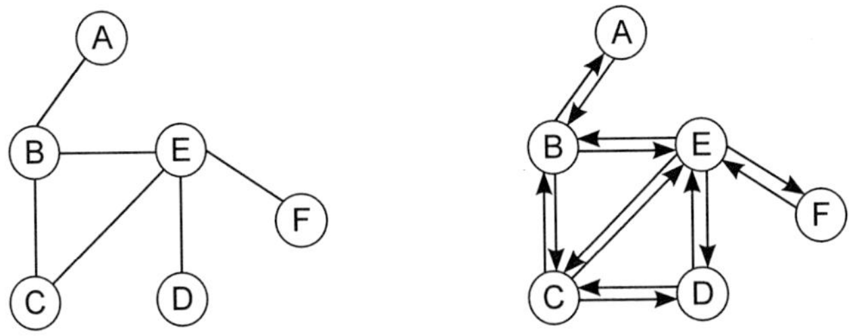

Fig. 4.41: Converting an undirected graph to directed graph.

As mentioned in the above paragraph that the adjacency matrix of a un-directed graph is symmetric about its principal (or main) diagonal. In un-directed graphs, self loops are not allowed. Thus, the adjacency matrix contains its main diagonal elements as zeros.

Sum of the elements of an adjacency matrix of an un-directed graph will be even. That is, the sum of the degrees of all the vertices of an un-directed graph G is equal to twice the number of edges in G.

If an adjacency matrix of a graph (with N vertices) contains only 1's in main diagonal and all remaining elements are 0s, then we can say that the graph containing N connected components are N isolated points with self cycles (see Figure 4.42).

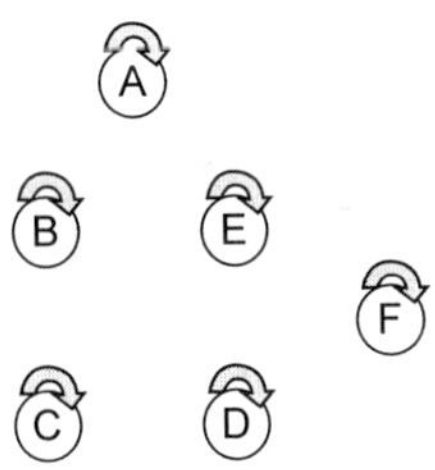

Graph

	A	B	C	D	E	F
A	1	0	0	0	0	0
B	0	1	0	0	0	0
C	0	0	1	0	0	0
D	0	0	0	1	0	0
E	0	0	0	0	1	0
F	0	0	0	0	0	1

Adjacency matrix

Fig. 4.42: Graph with isolated points with self cycles and their adjacency matrix.

If an adjacency matrix of a graph (with N vertices) contains all 0s, then we can say that the graph containing N connected components are N isolated points as shown in Figure 4.43.

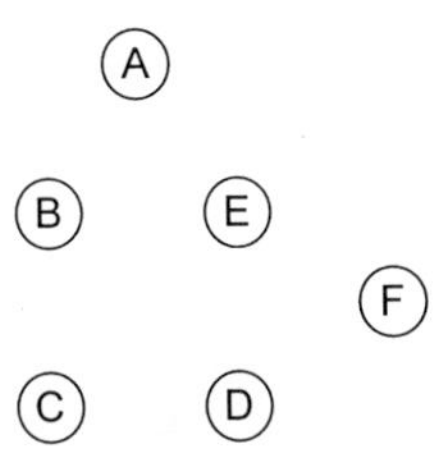

Graph

	A	B	C	D	E	F
A	0	0	0	0	0	0
B	0	0	0	0	0	0
C	0	0	0	0	0	0
D	0	0	0	0	0	0
E	0	0	0	0	0	0
F	0	0	0	0	0	0

Adjacency matrix

Fig. 4.43: Graph with isolated points and their adjacency matrix.

An Adjacency matrix of a graph with N nodes contains all 1's in i^{th} row (except i^{th} element) and all

0's in the ith column, then i^{th} station can be said as source. Similarly, An Adjacency matrix of a graph with N nodes contains all 0's in i^{th} row (except i^{th} element) and all 1's in the ith column, then i^{th} station can be said as sink.

An Adjacency matrix of a graph with N nodes contains all 1's in i^{th} row (except i^{th} element) and all 0's in the remaining portion of the matrix, then the graph can be said as star shaped with i^{th} station as center and directed edges for all other stations as shown below.

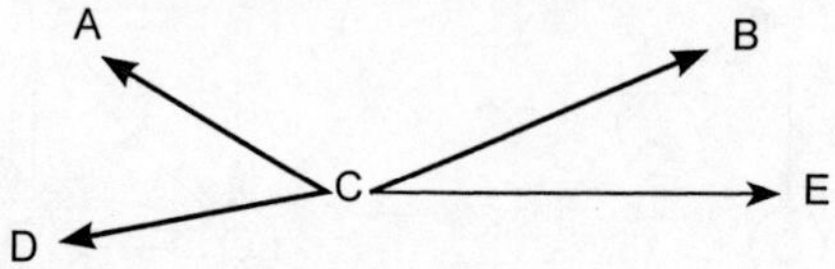

An Adjacency matrix of a graph with N nodes contains all 1's in i^{th} row (except i^{th} element), all 1's in i^{th} column (except i^{th} element), and all 0's in the remaining portion of the matrix, then the graph can be said as star shaped with i^{th} station as center and un-directed edges for all other stations as shown below.

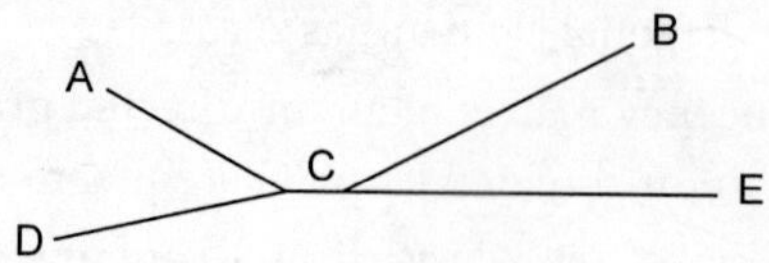

If all the stations are connected with exactly one directed edge and all are in a cycle as shown in Figure 4.44 then the related adjacency matrix looks as shown in Figure 4.44.

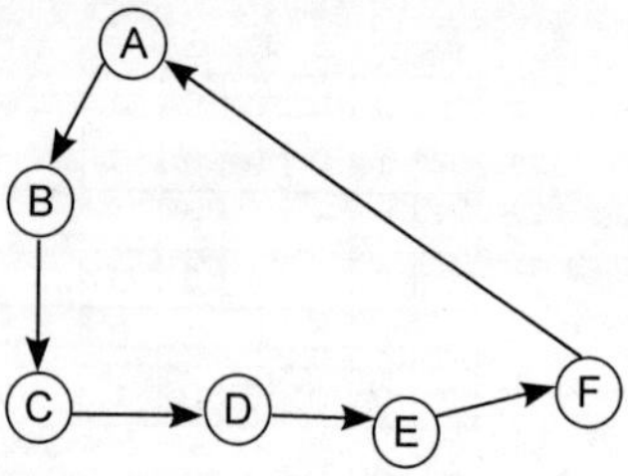

Graph

	A	B	C	D	E	F
A	0	1	0	0	0	0
B	0	0	1	0	0	0
C	0	0	0	1	0	0
D	0	0	0	0	1	0
E	0	0	0	0	0	1
F	1	0	0	0	0	0

Adjacency matrix

Fig. 4.44: Adjacency matrix of directed graph with a cycle.

If the directed edges of the above graph are replaced with undirected edges, then the adjacency matrix looks like (Figure 4.45)

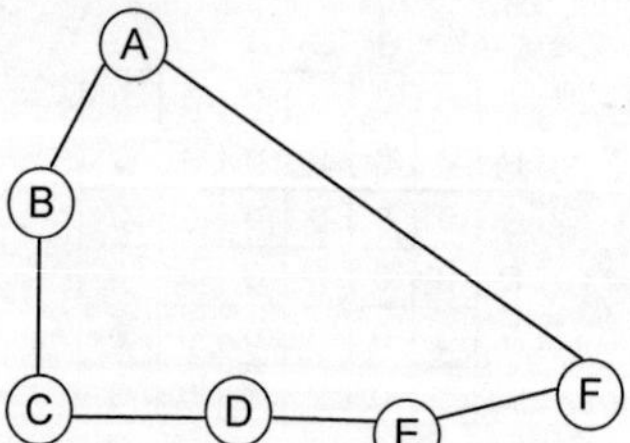

Graph

	A	B	C	D	E	F
A	0	1	0	0	0	1
B	1	0	1	0	0	0
C	0	1	0	1	0	0
D	0	0	1	0	1	0
E	0	0	0	1	0	1
F	1	0	0	0	1	0

Adjacency matrix

Fig. 4.45: Adjacency matrix of a graph with single cycle and undirected edges.

What will be the nature of stations if the adjacency matrix looks like a band matrix of width 3 as shown is Figure ?. All the stations will be having self loops and all are connected through un-directed edges except last two stations (see Figure 4.46)

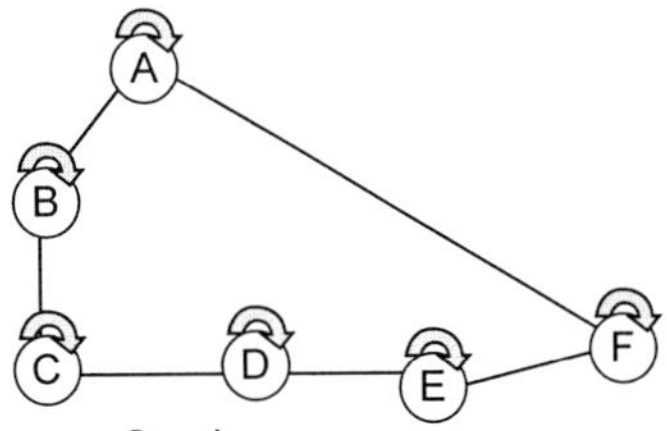

Graph

	A	B	C	D	E	F
A	1	1	0	0	0	0
B	1	1	1	0	0	0
C	0	1	1	1	0	0
D	0	0	1	1	1	0
E	0	0	0	1	1	1
F	0	0	0	0	1	1

Adjacency matrix

Fig. 4.46: Adjacency matrix of a graph in which all the nodes in a circular chain with self cycles.

Adjacency matrix of a weighted graph is shown in Figure 4.47.

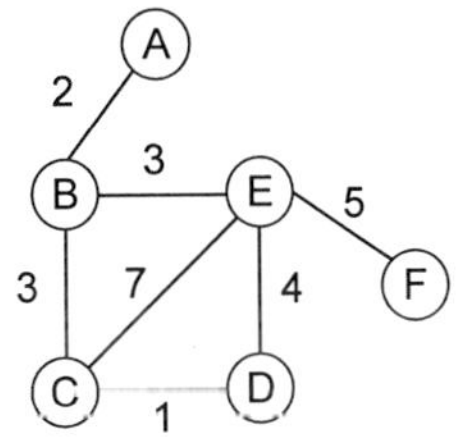

Vertex Vector
A
B
C
D
E
F

	A	B	C	D	E	F
A	0	2	0	0	0	0
B	2	0	3	0	3	0
C	0	3	0	1	7	0
D	0	0	1	0	4	0
E	0	3	7	4	0	5
F	0	0	0	0	5	0

Adjacency matrix

Fig. 4.47: Adjacency matrix of a weighted graph.

4.2.1.2 Adjacency List Representation

Graph information is maintained in another format known as adjacency list representation. Here, for each node, its neighbor's information is maintained in a linked list fashion as shown in Figure 4.48.

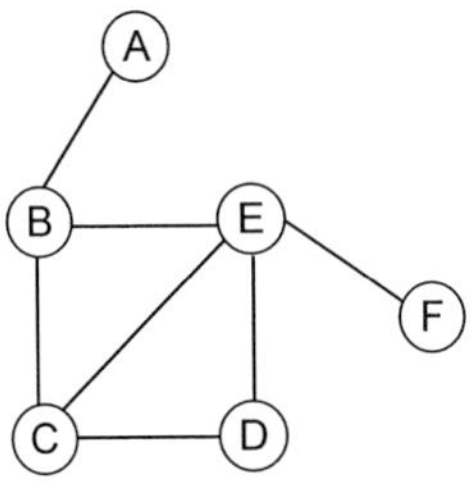

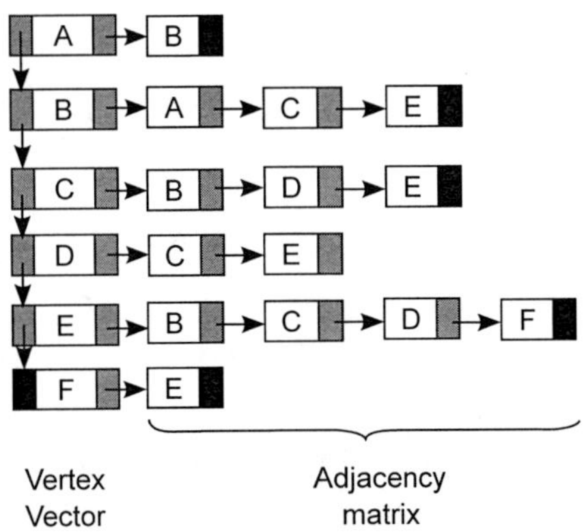

Fig. 4.48: Adjacency List representation of the graph

Question 37: From the above adjacency list representation, can you arrive at a suitable C language structure to represent nodes in the adjacency list and nodes in the vertex vector list?

Answer: If you observe the above figure, in each node of the adjacency list a vertex label and address of the next node. Thus, it can be defined as:

```
struct alst{
char label;
struct alst *next; };
```

Also, from the above figure that the node for vertex vector list has to have, vertex label, pointer or reference to its list of neighbors and a reference to the next node in vertex vector list. Thus, the following type is an apt one.

```
struct vlst{
char label;
struct alst *neighbors;
struct vlst *next; };
```

Obviously, people may be getting doubts about which representation is better. The answer is, in practical applications, a combination of both is used. Thus, we really do not want to enter into the debate of which is better. However, for the sake of comparison, we shall discuss their relative merits and demerits in Table 4.3.

Table. 4.3: Comparison of adjacency matrix and lists

Theme	Adjacency list	Adjacency Matrix
Memory requirement	O(|V|+|E|)	O(|V|2)
Insertions/deletions	Easy	Difficult
Is the memory requirement vertices are fixed?	No. Varies if extra edges are added.	Yes.
When is it preferred?	If the graph is sparse.	If the graph is dense.
Ease of Programmability	Difficult.	Ease as matrix operations can be used.

Figure 4.49 displays the adjacency matrix and adjacency list of a sample weighted graph.

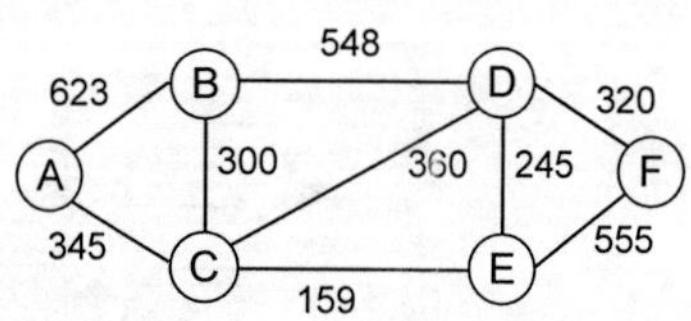

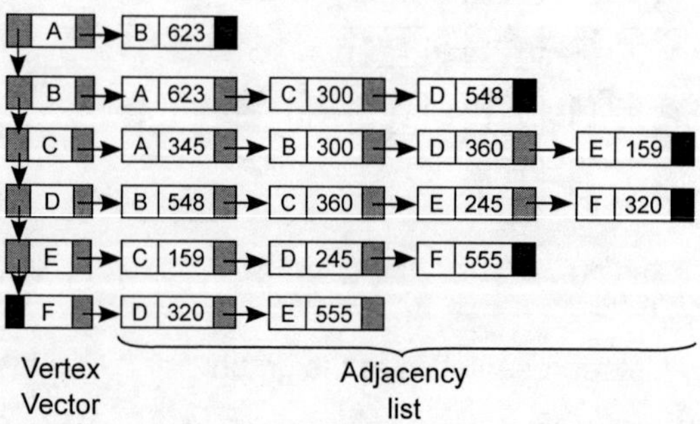

	A	B	C	D	E	F
A	0	623	345	0	0	1
B	623	0	300	548	0	0
C	345	300	0	360	159	0
D	0	548	360	0	245	320
E	0	0	159	245	0	555
F	0	0	0	320	555	0

Adjacency matrix

Fig. 4.49: Adjacency Matrix and Adjacency List of a weighted graph

Question 38: From the above adjacency list representation, can you arrive at a suitable C language structure to represent nodes in the adjacency list and nodes in the vertex vector list?

Answer: If you observe the above figure, in each node of the adjacency list a vertex label, weight value, and address of the next node. Thus, it can be defined as:

```
struct alst{
char label;
int weight;
struct alst *next; };
```

Also, from the above figure that the node for vertex vector list has to have, vertex label, pointer or reference to its list of neighbors and a reference to the next node in vertex vector list. Thus, the following type is an apt one.

```
struct vlst{
char label;
struct alst *neighbors;
struct vlst *next; };
```

4.2.1.3 Set representation

In this representation, edges details are maintained as shown below:

(6, 4)
(4, 5)
(5, 1)
(1, 2)
(2, 3)
(3, 4)
(2, 5)

The following picture 4.50 shows the set representation of a directed graph and its set representation. That is, edges and their weights are maintained in a table.

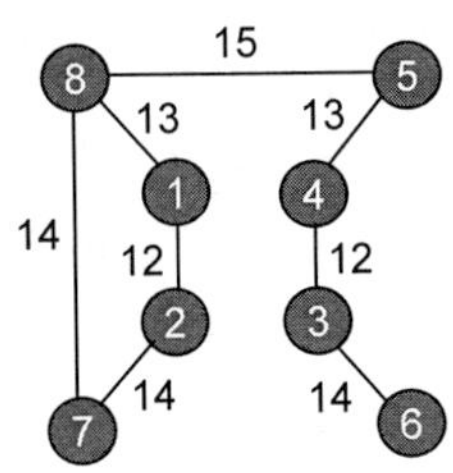

{1.2}	12
{3,4}	12
{1,8}	13
{4,5}	13
{2,7}	14
{3,6}	14
{7,8}	14
{5,6}	14
{5,8}	15
{6,7}	15
{1,4}	16
{2,3}	16

Fig. 4.50: Set representation of a weighted graph

4.2.1.4 Array List representation

Here a 1-dimensional array is used to store the edges details of a graph. In the graph of Figure, edges details are stored in the following array. We have one edge (1,2). Thus, 2 stored. We have two edges from vertex 2. They are (2,3), (2,5). Thus, 3, 5 are stored in the array. Like this, edge details are stored. However, we do need some extra information about each vertex like their degree (number of edges) has to be stored. However, compared to adjacency list, adjacency matrix this representation found to be little complex to implement to manipulate the graphs.

2	3	5	4	5	1	4
1	2		3	4	5	6

4.2.2 Transitive Closure and Path Matrix or reachability matrix

The transitive closure of a graph G conveys the existence of a nontrivial directed path from one station to another station. Here, a nontrivial directed path indicates the path of any length. The transitive closure of a graph is usually represented with an binary valued (0 or 1) NxN matrix (here N is the number of nodes of the given graph), with the value 1 at an element of ith row j^{th} column conveying the existence of the route (or path or walk) from i^{th} vertex to j^{th} vertex; otherwise non-existence of the path.

Consider the following sample undirected graph(see Figure 4.51).

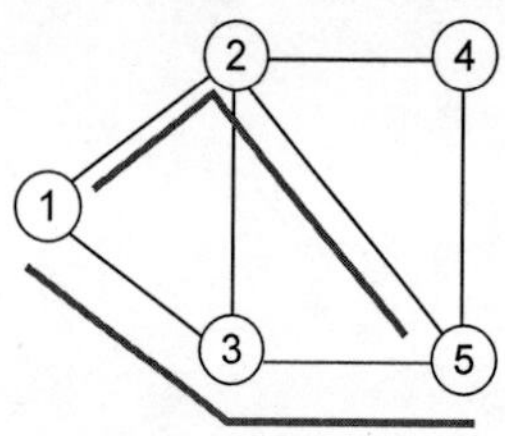

Graph

0	1	1	0	0
1	0	1	1	1
1	1	0	0	1
0	1	0	0	1
0	1	1	1	0

Adjacency matrix A

2	1	1	1	2
1	4	2	1	2
1	2	3	2	1
1	1	2	2	1
2	2	1	1	3

A^2

Fig. 4.51: Paths of square of an adjacency matrix

What is the physical significance of the above matrix A^2?. For example, station 1-5, the value is given as 2. This indicates the existence of two routes between 1 to 5 with 2 hops or jumps. We can verify the same as: 1-2-5 and 1-3-5. Similarly, we have 2-2 as 4. The possible routes are: 2-1-2, 2-3-2, 2-4-2, and 2-5-2 with two jumps. Like this, this matrix A^2 indicates the number of paths with two jumps. Similarly, A^3 will indicate the possible routes from one station to another station with 3 jumps or hops. If we add A, A^2 and A^3 then the resultant matrix indicates the existence of routes between stations with at most 3 jumps.

We know that any path length can not be more than N edges in a graph with N nodes. Thus, we can calculate the path matrix or transitive closure by binarising the summation matrix of $A+ A^2 +A^3+..+A^N$. That is,

$$X = A + A^2 + A^3 \ldots + A^N$$

$$P[i][j] = \begin{cases} 1 & \text{if } X[i][j]>0 \\ 0 & \text{otherwise} \end{cases}$$

This approach of calculating, A, A^2, A^3,.., A^N is computationally demanding. We know that the matrix multiplication algorithm for two NxN matrices has a time complexity of $O(N^3)$. Thus, this method of finding transitive closure will be of order of complexity as $O(N^4)$.

Question 39: Assuming A as an adjacency matrix of a star shaped directed graph with N vertices (with one center vertex), what will be the matrices A^2, A^3,..,A^N ?.

Question 40: Assuming A as an adjacency matrix of a star shaped un-directed graph with N vertices (with one center vertex), what will be the path matrix?.

4.2.2.1 Warshall's Algorithm

The basis of this algorithm is a very simple theme. Let's assume that we have three stations x,y and z. There exists a path between x to y and y to z. Which means, we have the path for x to z also, but of course via y. Thus, in this algorithm, we try to explore the existence path between stations by exploring existing paths of the stations. If we do not have a path currently from station I to J. Then, we search whether there is a path between I to K and K to J. If path exists, we consider now that there is a path between I to J. We will vary K such that all the stations are verified by assuming them as intermediate stations between I and J. However, in order to alleviate unnecessary computations, if there already exists a path between I and J, we don't explore further with intermediate stations.

Pseudo-Code of Warshall's Algorithm

```
Input:      A – the N-by-N adjacency matrix of the graph.
Output:     P – the N-by-N path matrix of the graph.

Step1: Binarising the adjacency matrix
For I = 1 to N Do
        For J = 1 to N Do
                if A[I, J]>0 Then
                   P[I, J]=1
                Else
                   P[I,J]=0
        End Do
End Do

Step 2: Exploring the intermediate stations or vertices
For K = 1 to N Do
        For I = 1 to N Do
                For J = 1 to N Do
                        P[I,J]=P[I,J] ∨ (P[I,K] ∨ P[K,J])
                End Do
        End Do
End Do

Return P
```

This is an algorithm that is computationally less intensive. Its order of complexity is $O(N^3)$. Moreover, the operations involved here are simple AND, OR operators.

4.2.3 Graph Traversals

Like tree traversals, linked lists traversals discussed in the previous chapters, we do have some methods to traverse graphs also. They are:

- Depth First Traversal (DFT) or Depth First Search(DFS)
- Breadth First Traversal(BFT) or Breadth First Search(BFS)

The basic object of the graph traversal is to visit each node at least once. However, the algorithms will actually give us much more than that. For instance, DFS can be used to find the path from one vertex to another vertex.

The DFT algorithm is quite famous and can be used to solve a variety of graph problems. We employ stacks to traverse the graph in DF manner. As the algorithm proceeds, node status will be changed. Initially, we assume all the nodes will be in an un-processed state. When they are in the stack, we assume they are in the ready state. When they leave the stack, we consider that they are processed.

Phase	Condition of Node	Status
1	Undiscovered	Un-Processed
2	Discovered and being processed	Ready
3	Finished	Processed

4.2.3.1 DFT Algorithm

1. Select any node of the graph and push into the stack while making its status as Ready.
2. Repeat step 3 till the stack becomes empty.
3. Pop a node (A) from the stack and make its status as processed. Push all the un-processed nodes of A into the stack while making their status values as ready.

We try to apply the above algorithm for the graph shown in Figure 4.52 and show how the stack changes.

1. We assume here that we will be traversing from the node A. We will push the same into the stack.
2. When we pop, we will get A as output. The same will be displayed in the output string. Its unprocessed neighbor, X, is pushed into the stack.

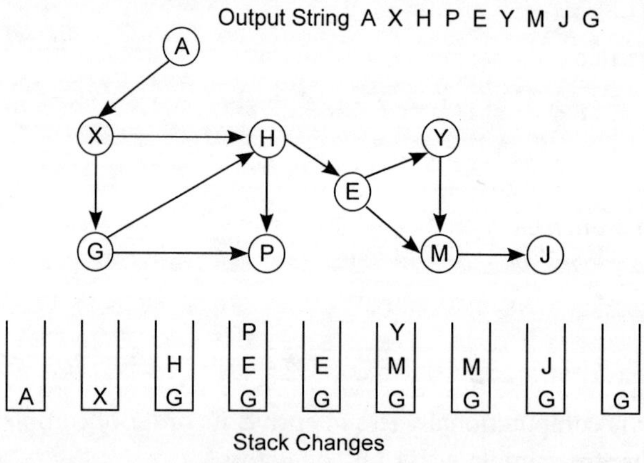

Fig. 4.52: Depth First Traversal snap shot on a selected graph.

3. Now, when we pop, we will get X. The same will be printed and its unprocessed neighbors, G and H are pushed into the stack.
4. Now, when we pop, we will get H. The same will be printed and its unprocessed neighbor, E,P are pushed into the stack.
5. When we pop, we will get P as output. The same will be printed. As it does not have any unprocessed neighbors, nothing is pushed into the stack.
6. This time, when we pop, we will get E. The same will be printed and its unprocessed neighbors, M,Y are pushed into the stack.

7. Now, when we pop, we will get Y. The same will be printed. Though it has a neighbor M, as M is already in the stack (i.e. its status is ready), nothing will be pushed into the stack.
8. Next when we pop, we will get M as output. The same will be printed. Its unprocessed neighbor is pushed into the stack.
9. Next, when we pop, we will get J as output. The same will be printed. As it does not have any neighbors, nothing will be pushed into the stack.
10. Next when we pop, we will get G as output and the same will be printed. As G does not have unprocessed neighbors, nothing will be pushed into the stack. Remember, though G as neighbors, all of them are in processed state (i.e. they went to stack and came out. That is, they are processed).
11. Now, stack empty. Thus, it terminates.

The following figure (4.53) explains how the edges get discovered. If you observe the figure, you will find it visits the deepest vertex first.

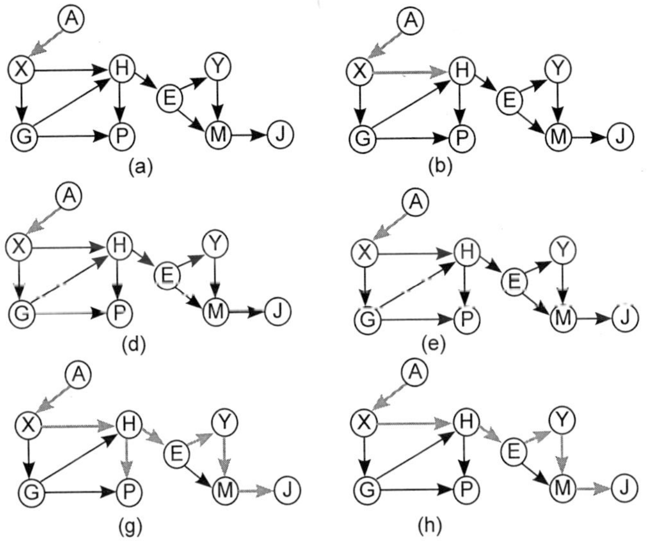

Fig. 4.53: DFS traversal of a graph

Backtracking to find the path

Assume that we want to find a path for vertex A(source) to vertex G(destination). See the following diagram which shows by processing which node, its neighbors are becoming pushed into the stack or changing their status as Ready.

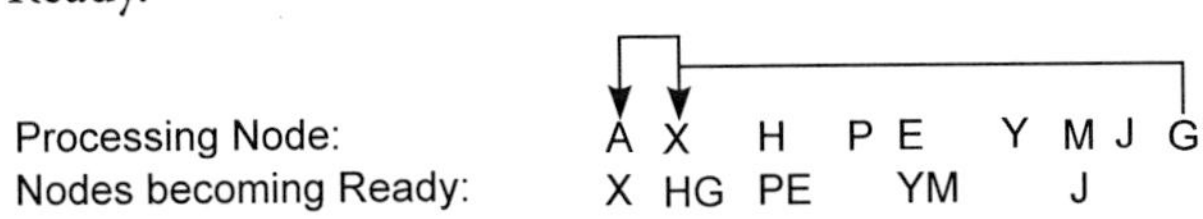

We start from the destination node in the top row. We check how it has entered into the stack. We know when we have processed vertex X, G has entered into the stack. Now, we select X in the top row and find how it has entered into the stack. That is, X has entered into the stack when we have processed vertex X. Thus, the route becomes G-H-A, a.k.a A to G route is via H, A-H-G.

Let us take one more example of finding the path for A to J. By applying the above backtracking approach, we can find the path as: A-X-H-E-M-J. See the following workout diagram.

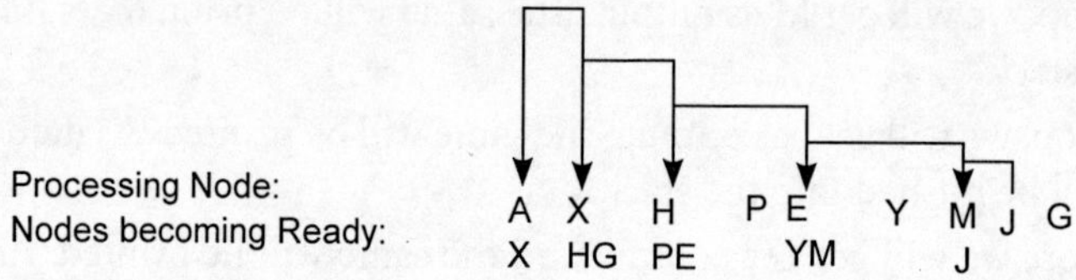

One useful aspect of the DFS algorithm is that it traverses connected components one at a time, and thus it can be used to identify the connected components in a given graph.

We welcome readers to visit the following visualization resource for experiencing real time BFS on a graph. You may set animation speed to a small value such that you can feel the working of BFS algorithm in an easy manner.

https://www.cs.usfca.edu/~galles/visualization/DFS.html

4.2.3.2 BFT Algorithm

In the case of the BFT algorithm, we employ the queue. Other notations are the same as above.

1. Select any node of the graph and insert into the queue while making its status as Ready.
2. Repeat step 3 till the queue becomes empty.
3. Remove a node (A) from the queue and make its status as processed. Insert all un-processed nodes of A into the queue while making their status value as Ready.

Let us apply the BFT traversal algorithm on the graph given in Figure 4.54.

1. We assume that traversal starts from node A. Thus, we insert the same into the queue while making its status as Ready.
2. We will remove a node from the queue. Obviously, it is A itself. We will mark the same as processed and insert its unprocessed neighbors into the queue while making their status as Ready. The following figure illustrates the snapshot of the above algorithm.

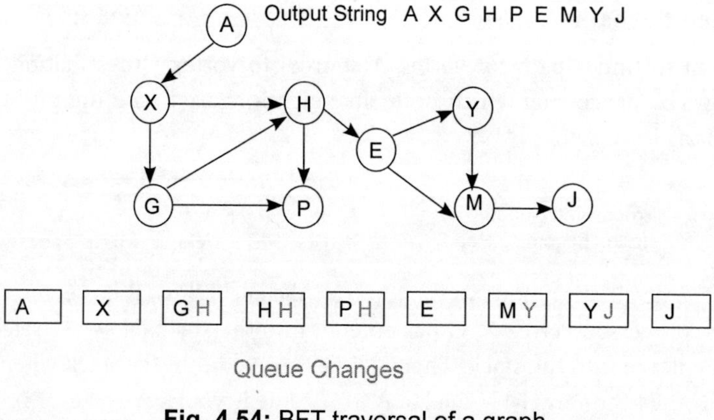

Fig. 4.54: BFT traversal of a graph

3. Next, when we remove a node from the queue, we will get node X. The same will be printed. Its unprocessed neighbors G, H are inserted into the queue.
4. Next, when we remove a node, we will get node G. The same will be printed. Its unprocessed neighbor is inserted into the queue while making its status as ready (Of course, though H is also G's neighbor it is not inserted as it is already in the queue).
5. Next, when we remove a node from the queue, we will get node H. The same will be printed. Its unprocessed neighbor, E, is inserted into the queue.
6. When we remove a node from the queue, we will get node P. It does not have any neighbors to be inserted into the queue.
7. Next, we remove a node, we will get node E. The same will be printed. Its unprocessed neighbors, M.Y are inserted into the queue while making their status as ready.
8. Next, when we remove, we will get M as output. Its unprocessed neighbor is inserted into the queue.
9. Next, when we remove, we will get Y as output. As it does not have any unprocessed neighbors. Nothing will be inserted into the queue.
10. Next, when we remove a node from the queue, we will get node J. The same will be printed. As it does not have any neighbors, nothing will be inserted into the queue.
11. Now, the queue is empty. Thus, the algorithm terminates.

The following figure (4.55) explains how the nodes get discovered. If you observe the figure, you will find it traverses all the possible edges of a vertex before going further downwards. For instance, for vertex (X), two edges are available. Both the edges get discovered one after another before going further downwards. Similarly, consider another vertex, E. For this node also two edges are available. They will be traversed one after another.

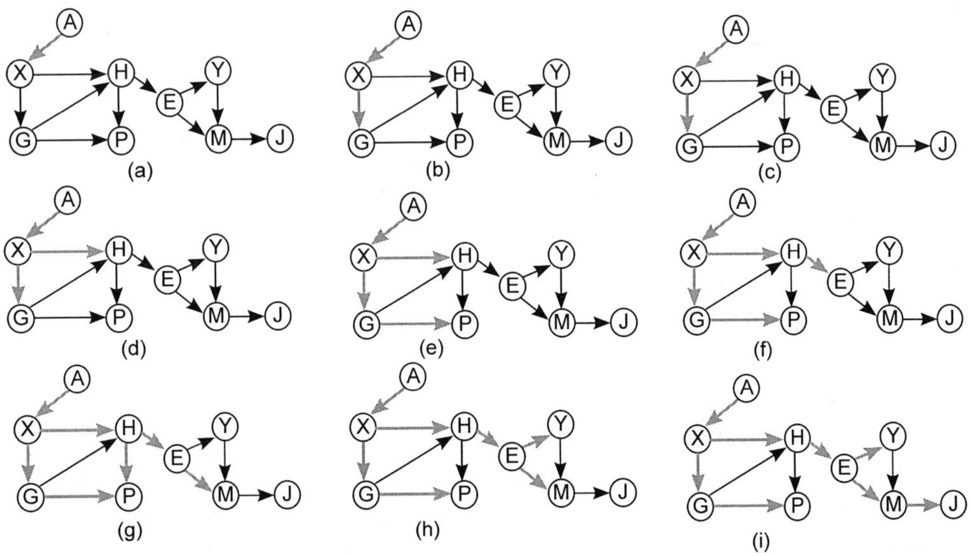

Fig. 4.55: Breadth first traversal of a graph

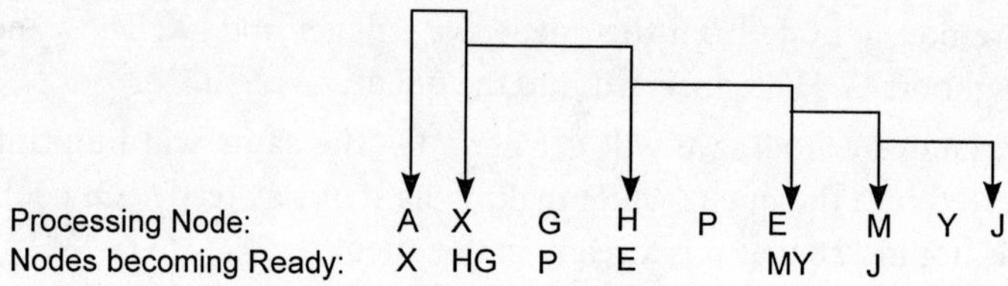

We welcome readers to visit the following visualization resource for experiencing real time BFS on a graph. You may set animation speed to a small value such that you can feel the working of BFS algorithm in an easy manner.

https://www.cs.usfca.edu/~galles/visualization/BFS.html

The following link can be used to understand about the connected component analysis.

https://www.cs.usfca.edu/~galles/visualization/ConnectedComponent.html

4.2.4 Minimum Distance Problems

There are a plethora of problems in which we need to find out the minimum distance between two nodes of a graph. For example, while planning our holiday trip, we need to find minimum distances between the places which we have identified to visit. Similarly, in computer networks (i.e., in Internet), we need to find our best route to rout the packet. Here, we may consider many parameters such as minimum delay or minimum cost, minimum jitter, etc. In some other applications also we may have to find minimum cost routes.

In all the above problems, we will be given a weighted graph and we need to find out the minimum distance route between any given two stations. In the literature, we may find many solutions to solve this problem. However, Dijkstra's algorithm is the most popular out of all.

4.2.4.1. Dijkstra's Algorithm

Here also, we assume the same notations as in the graph traversals algorithm. Initially, all the stations are at infinite distance from the source station. That is their state is considered as unprocessed. When we find a route (may not be the best route) for a station from source, those stations are said to be in ready state. If we have found the best possible route to a station, we mark its status as processed. The algorithm is given as follows.

1. Select the source node and mark it as processed.
2. Select all the neighbors of the source station and mark them as ready and update their minimum distances as the distances from source.
3. Repeat step 4 till destination station status becomes processed.
4. Select the station (B) which is having minimum distance out of the stations which are in the ready status. Make status of B as processed and update all of its unprocessed, ready state nodes minimum distance (by adding distance from B to this station to distance of B from source) while making their status as ready (see Figure 4.56)

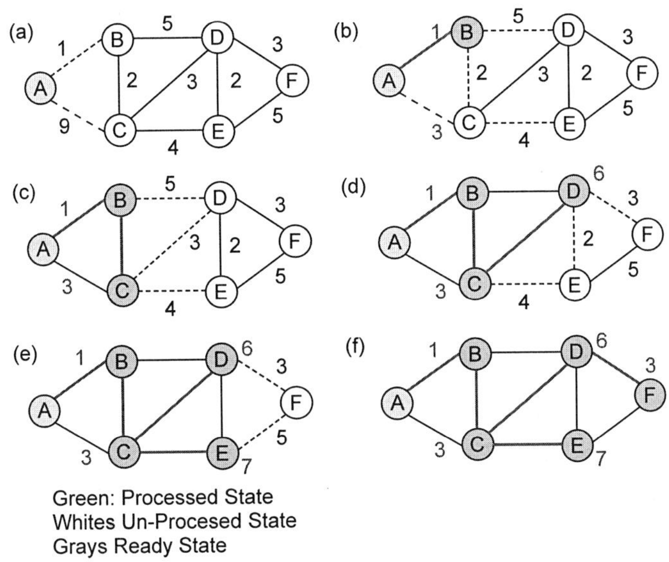

Fig. 4.56: Dijkstra's Algorithm's working

Let us apply Dijkstra's algorithm to the above graph shown in Figure 19 .

1. We have assumed the source station is A and destination station is F.
2. We have marked A's status as Processed. Its neighbors, B, C are kept in ready state and their minimum distances from A is marked as their actual distances themselves. That is, 1 and 9 respectively.
3. As of now, we have B and C in ready state. We select B as it has minimum distance. We will make B's status as Processed. Also, we make B's neighbors C, D as ready and their distances are updated.
4. As of now, C and D are in ready state and their distances from A are 3 and 6 respectively (via B). Thus, we select C as it has the smallest distance. Make its status as processed. Make its neighbors, D,E as ready while adjusting their distances.
5. As of now, we have D, E in the ready state with minimum distances of 6 and 7. Of course, for D, we have two routes with minimum distance. That is A-B-D or A-B-C-D. We can select any one of them. We have selected A-B-C-D. Now, we select D and make its status as processed. Make its unprocessed neighbors as Ready and update their minimum distances.
6. Now, E and F are in ready state with distance 7 and 9. We select E and make its status as processed. Its neighbor F minimum distance will not change.
7. Now, we have only F in the ready state. Make it processed. We will come out of the algorithm.

The figure contains red edges which form the minimum route from A to F. Observe all the red edges which connect all the nodes. These edges make the minimum spanning tree for node A. This tree contains shortest routes from A to all other nodes. In computer networks, if A is a router and wants to broadcast (broadcast means sending to all) a message, it can select these routes to send messages.

Example 18: The following is our C implementation of Dijkstra's Algorithm. This code deals with graphs having utmost 10 vertices. One can modify this code while dealing with large graphs.

```
int main(){
   int DIST[10][10], STA[10], MIN[10], VIA[10];
   int  i,j,k,source,dest,AMIN,n,dd,t;

   printf("Enter Number of Nodes\n");
   scanf("%d", &n);

   printf("Enter Weights\n");
   for(i=0;i<n;i++)
   for(j=0;j<n;j++)
   scanf("%d", &DIST[i][j]);

   for(i=0;i<n;i++){
            STA[i]=0;
            MIN[i]=32767;  /*largest possible 2 byte integers*/
            }

   printf("Enter Source and Destination Station Indexes\n");
   scanf("%d%d", &source,&dest);

  k=source;
  AMIN=0;
  while(STA[dest]!=2){
   STA[k]=2;
   for(i=0;i<n;i++){
    if(DIST[k][i]&&STA[i]!=2){
      dd=AMIN+DIST[k][i];
      if(dd<MIN[i]){ MIN[i]=dd; VIA[i]=k; }
      STA[i]=1;
    }
   }
    AMIN=32767;
   for(i=0;i<n;i++)
   if(STA[i]==1&&MIN[i]<AMIN){AMIN=MIN[i]; k=i;}
    }
   printf("Backtracking\n");
  printf("%c->", 'A'+dest);
  for(k=VIA[dest]; k!=source; k=VIA[k])printf("%c->", 'A'+k);
  printf("%c",'A'+source);

    return 0;

  }
```

Output: Enter Number of Nodes

6

Enter Weights

0 1 9 0 0 0

1 0 2 5 0 0

9 2 0 3 4 0

0 5 3 0 2 3

0 0 4 2 0 5

0 0 0 3 5 0

Enter Source and Destination Station Indexes

0 5

Backtracking

F->D->B->A

Note: Please note the difference in the path solved in the figures. We have mentioned B is having two routes with the same minimum distance. While solving, we have taken one route. The program has taken the other. The following link contains the above code, graph data loaded into a server for experimentation.

https://ideone.com/kFXF8C

The following link contains the visualization tool for this algorithm.

https://www.cs.usfca.edu/~galles/visualization/Dijkstra.html

Example: Run the above program for the weighted graph given in Figure 15.

Output: Enter Number of Nodes

```
6
Enter Weights
0 623 345 0 0 0
623 0 200 548 0 0
345 200 0 360 467 0
0 548 360 0 245 320
0 0 467 245 0 555
0 0 0 320 555 0
Enter Source and Destination Station Indexes
0 5
Backtracking
F->D->C->A
```

The following link contains the above code, graph data loaded into a server for experimentation.

https://ideone.com/wigttc

Note: In our discussion, we have assumed that the graph is having positive edges. If anyone wants to know more about what happens when there are negative edges and negative cycles, we advise to refer to a simple discussion at http://www.cs.berkeley.edu/~jordan/courses/170-fall05/notes/lecture7.pdf .

4.2.4.2 Minimum Spanning Tree

In network design, we often need to find the need to send a packet from one router to all the routers of a network in the optimal manner. For this purpose, we need to find a minimal spanning tree that connects all the n nodes with n-1 best edges such that total delay will be minimal (see Figure 4.57).

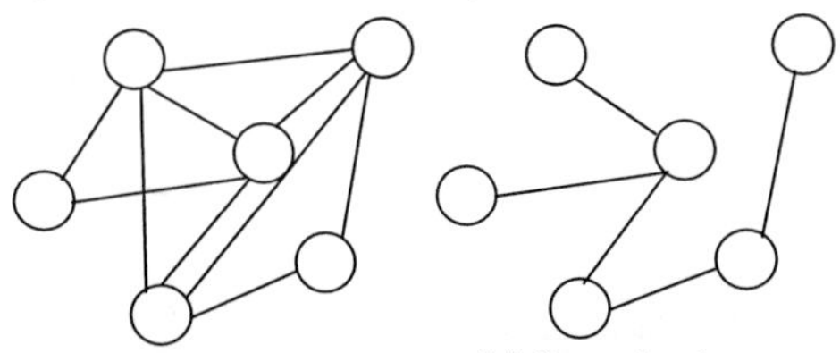

(a) A graph (b) Spanning tree

Fig. 4.57: Spanning tree

We know that a tree is the one that does not have any cycles. In some algorithms in computer networks such as flooding, a packet is required to be broadcasted, that is it has to be sent to all the nodes or routers of a network. To achieve this a spanning tree is used. The spanning tree is the one that connects n nodes (or routers) with n-1 edges as shown in the above figure. For a graph, there can be more than one spanning tree possible based on its topological structure. However, if the graph is weighted, which is often true in the case of computer networks, we need to find the minimum (cost) spanning tree, where a spanning tree cost is the sum total of weights of its edges.

4.2.4.2.1 Kruskal's Algorithm

1. Arrange all edges in a list (L) in non-decreasing order
2. Select edges from L, and include that in set T, if its inclusion does not induce a cycle.
3. Repeat 2 until T all vertices of the graph without any cycles.

Let us apply this algorithm. The given figure 4.58 a-j below illustrates its application.

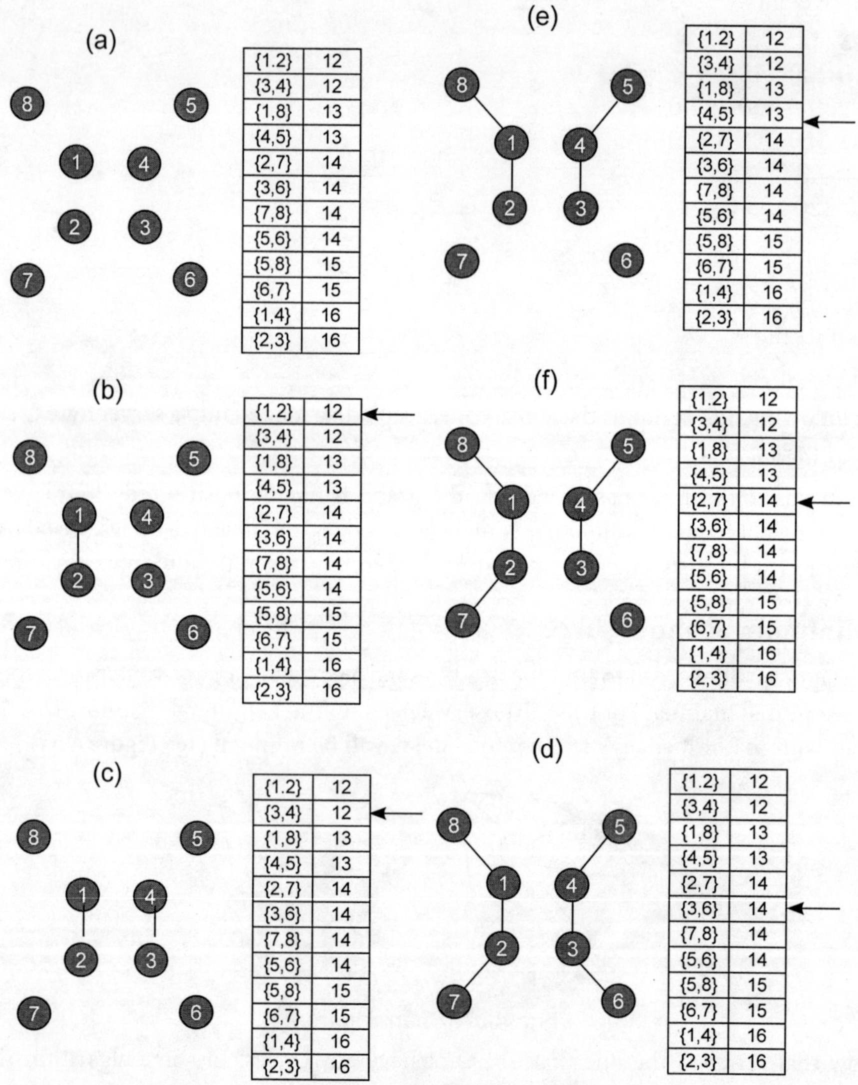

(d)

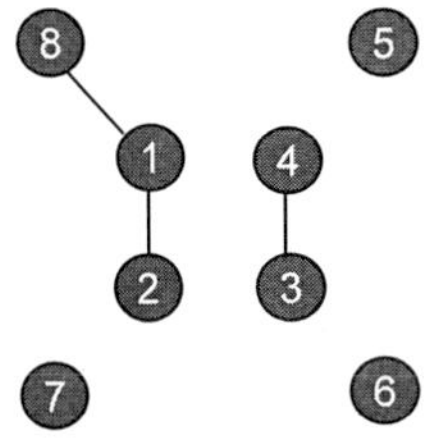

{1.2}	12
{3,4}	12
{1,8}	13
{4,5}	13
{2,7}	14
{3,6}	14
{7,8}	14
{5,6}	14
{5,8}	15
{6,7}	15
{1,4}	16
{2,3}	16

(h)

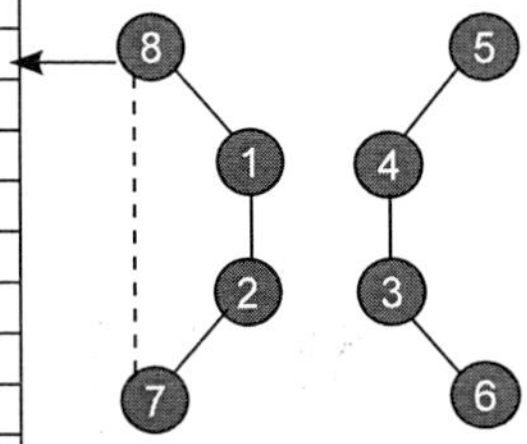

{1.2}	12
{3,4}	12
{1,8}	13
{4,5}	13
{2,7}	14
{3,6}	14
{7,8}	14
{5,6}	14
{5,8}	15
{6,7}	15
{1,4}	16
{2,3}	16

Cycle. So don't select

(i)

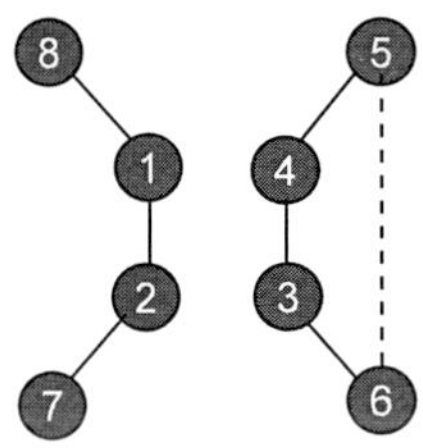

{1.2}	12
{3,4}	12
{1,8}	13
{4,5}	13
{2,7}	14
{3,6}	14
{7,8}	14
{5,6}	14
{5,8}	15
{6,7}	15
{1,4}	16
{2,3}	16

Cycle. So don't select

(j)

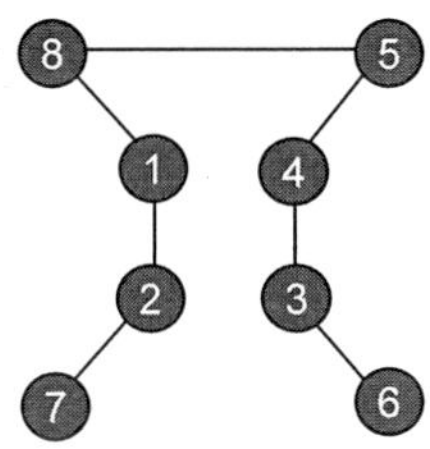

{1.2}	12
{3,4}	12
{1,8}	13
{4,5}	13
{2,7}	14
{3,6}	14
{7,8}	14
{5,6}	14
{5,8}	15
{6,7}	15
{1,4}	16
{2,3}	16

Fig. 4.58: Kruskal's algorithm in working

1. First edge {1,2} is selected (see Figure b). Its inclusion did not give any cycle in the graph.
2. Edge {3,4} is selected (see Figure c). Its inclusion did not give any cycle in the graph.
3. Edge {1,8} is selected (see Figure d). Its inclusion did not give any cycle in the graph.
4. Edge {4,5} is selected (see Figure e). Its inclusion did not give any cycle in the graph.
5. Edge {2,7} is selected (see Figure f). Its inclusion did not give any cycle in the graph.
6. Edge {3,6} is selected (see Figure g). Its inclusion did not give any cycle in the graph.
7. Edges {7,8}, {5,6} are not selected as their inclusion may lead to a cycle in the graph.
8. Edge {5,8} is selected (see Figure h). Its inclusion did not give any cycle in the graph.
9. By now, we have selected all the necessary edges (8-1, where 8 is the number of nodes in the graph). Thus, the algorithm terminates.

We welcome readers to visit this link for playing with Kruskal's algorithm.

https://www.cs.usfca.edu/~galles/visualization/Kruskal.html

4.2.4.2.2 Prim's Algorithm

This is a complementary approach to Kruskal's algorithm.

1. Maintain all the edges in the descending order.

2. Select an edge and identify whether its removal leads to breaking the connectivity of the graph. If the graph breaks then retain that edge else remove.
3. Repeat step 2 till all n-1 edges are selected.

Application of the above algorithm of the same graph of the previous example.

1. Edge {2,3} is not important as its removal is not disturbing the connectivity. So, remove it from the list.
2. Edge {1,4} is not important as its removal is not disturbing the connectivity. So, remove it from the list.
3. Edge {6,7} is not important as its removal is not disturbing the connectivity. So, remove it from the list.
4. Edge {5,8} is important as its removal is disturbing the connectivity. So, retain.
5. Edge {5,6} is not important as its removal is not disturbing the connectivity. So, remove it from the list.
6. Edge {7,8} is not important as its removal is not disturbing the connectivity. So, remove it from the list.
7. By now, N-1 edges (8-1) are left in the list. They form the MST of the graph.

Let us apply this algorithm. The given figure 4.59 a-f below illustrates its application

(a)

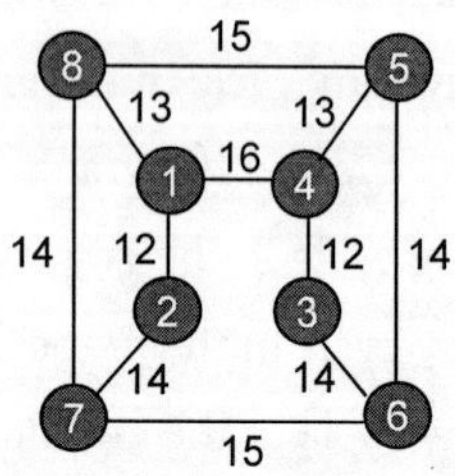

{1.2}	12	
{3,4}	12	
{1,8}	13	
{4,5}	13	
{2,7}	14	
{3,6}	14	
{7,8}	14	
{5,6}	14	
{5,8}	15	
{6,7}	15	
{1,4}	16	
{2,3}	16	←

(c)

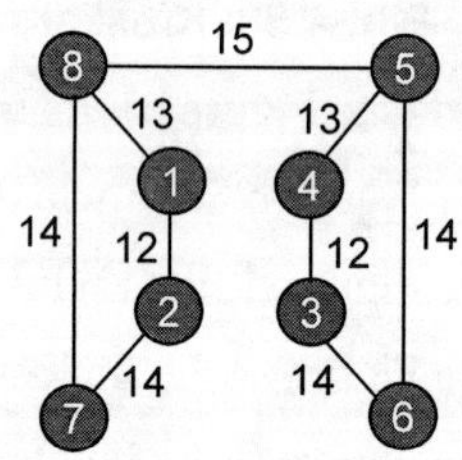

{1.2}	12	
{3,4}	12	
{1,8}	13	
{4,5}	13	
{2,7}	14	
{3,6}	14	
{7,8}	14	
{5,6}	14	
{5,8}	15	
{6,7}	15	←
{1,4}	16	
{2,3}	16	

(b)

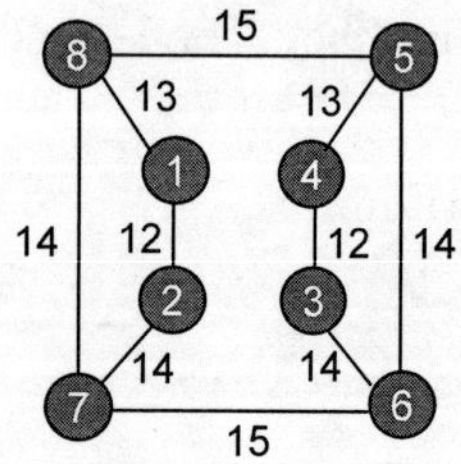

{1.2}	12	
{3,4}	12	
{1,8}	13	
{4,5}	13	
{2,7}	14	
{3,6}	14	
{7,8}	14	
{5,6}	14	
{5,8}	15	
{6,7}	15	
{1,4}	16	←
{2,3}	16	

(d)

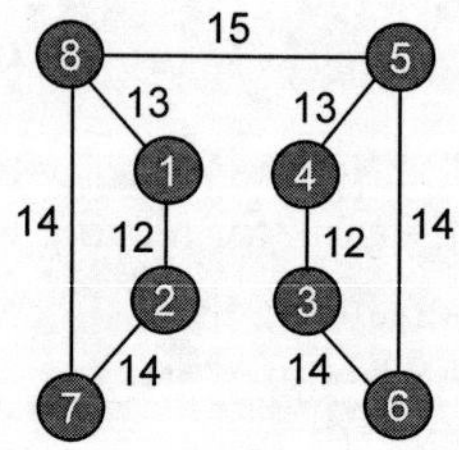

{1.2}	12	
{3,4}	12	
{1,8}	13	
{4,5}	13	
{2,7}	14	
{3,6}	14	
{7,8}	14	
{5,6}	14	
{5,8}	15	←
{6,7}	15	
{1,4}	16	
{2,3}	16	

Retain as connectivity breaks

(c)

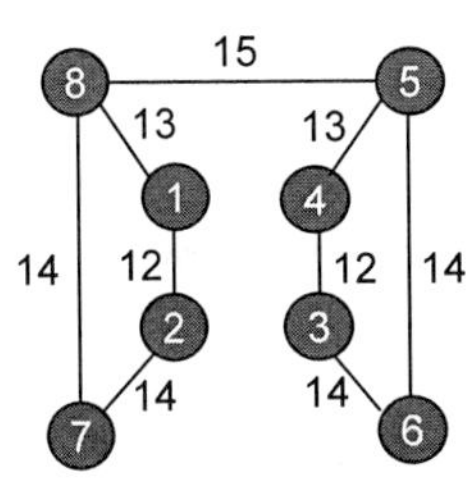

{1.2}	12
{3,4}	12
{1,8}	13
{4,5}	13
{2,7}	14
{3,6}	14
{7,8}	14
{5,6}	14
{5,8}	15
{6,7}	15
{1,4}	16 ←
{2,3}	16

(f)

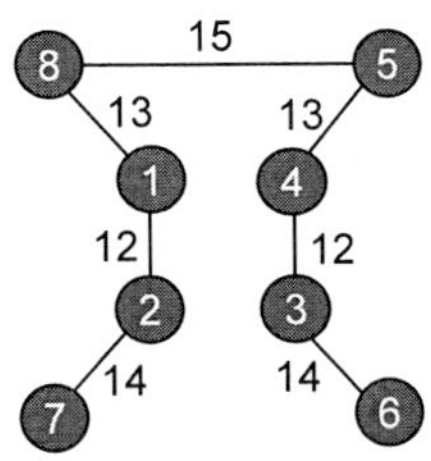

{1.2}	12
{3,4}	12
{1,8}	13
{4,5}	13
{2,7}	14
{3,6}	14
{7,8}	14 ←
{5,6}	14
{5,8}	15
{6,7}	15
{1,4}	16
{2,3}	16

Fig. 4.59: Prim's algorithm in working

We welcome readers to visit the following link to experiment with Prims algorithm.

https://www.cs.usfca.edu/~galles/visualzation/Prim.html

4.2.5 Topological Sorting

In some applications, we need ordering of the nodes while maintaining some ordering information. For example, consider an example of course registration rules in an academic system as shown in Figure 4.60. That is, to register in CS234, students have to complete CS232. Of course, to register in CS232, students have to complete CS231, and vice versa.

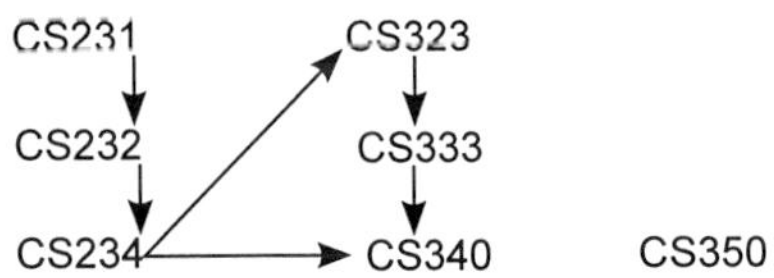

Fig. 4.60: A sample course registration in a University

We can know from the above graph that one can register in the course CS350 without any constraint. That is, there is no prerequisite for CS350. However, in order to register in CS340 they have to complete CS231, CS232 and CS234 or they can do extra CS323, CS333 and join.In this type of problem if we want to order the course names, we have some acceptable ordering and some or not acceptable. Topological sorting is used to find out the acceptable orderings.

For the above problem, the legal ordering can be : CS231, CS350, CS232,CS234, CS323, CS333, and CS340.

Consider another example, related to construction of a house. Here, we have shown activities as the nodes. The possible sequence is also shown in Figure 4.61.

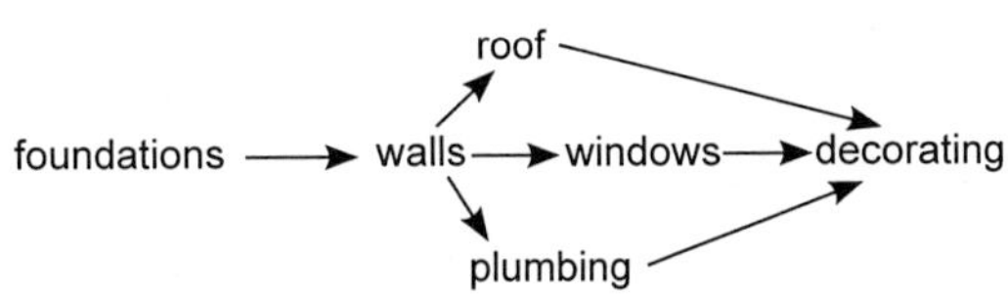

Possible sequence:
Foundations-Walls-Roof-Windows-Plumbing-Decorating

Fig. 4.61: Sample graph for possible topological sorting.

Topological sorting is applicable only to DAGs. Here, if there is a path from vertex v to vertex w in the given graph, vertex v is assumed to be coming before vertex w in the final ordering. That is, we want to generate vertex ordering satisfying this constraint.

In a graph with no cycles, there must always be at least one vertex with 0 indegree, so we will start at one of these vertices.What do you mean by zero indegree means?. If you take our course registration example, the course which does not have any prerequisites. We print it and remove all of its outgoing edges. We repeat this till all the nodes are printed on the output sequence.

The Steps in a topological ordering can be mentioned as:

1. For each vertex calculate in-degree values.
2. Repeat step 3 till there are no more vertices in the graph.
3. Select a vertex whose indegree value is zero and print the same in the output list while reducing the indegree values of all other nodes which are having an outgoing edge from this node.
4. The graph has 7 vertices as shown in Figure a.
5. We found that both A and F are the nodes with zero indegree value. We have selected vertex A and printed the same in the output list. Also, edges coming out from A are removed.
6. Now, vertex F is printed as output as its indegree value is zero.
7. Now, vertex B is identified to be having zero indegree. Thus, the same is printed. Its outgoing edges are removed.
8. Now, C is selected as its in-degree is zero and printed. Outgoing edges from it are removed.
9. Now, D is selected as its in-degree is zero and printed. Outgoing edges from it are removed.
10. Finally, E is printed as its in-degree is zero.

To find a node with an in-degree value of zero, we need to scan the array of vertices. Thus, we need N comparisons. The same operation we need to do with each of the outputting vertices, thus the complexity of this algorithm will be $O(N^2)$. The following figure 4.62 illustrates the working of topological sorting algorithm.

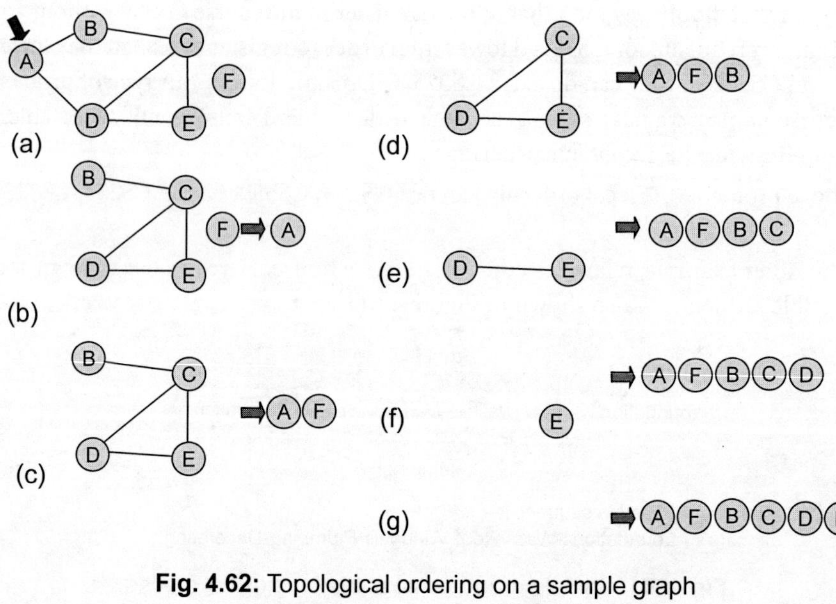

Fig. 4.62: Topological ordering on a sample graph

Example 19: The following is our implementation of topological sorting given the adjacency matrix details of a graph.

```
int main(){
        int i,j,k,n,a[10][10],indeg[10],flag[10],count=0;
        printf("Enter the no of vertices:\n");
        scanf("%d",&n);
        printf("Enter the adjacency matrix:\n");
        for(i=0;i<n;i++)

        for(j=0;j<n;j++) scanf("%d",&a[i][j]);
                for(i=0;i<n;i++){
                        indeg[i]=0;
                        flag[i]=0; }

                for(i=0;i<n;i++)
                for(j=0;j<n;j++)indeg[i]=indeg[i]+a[j][i];

                        printf("The topological order is:");
                        while(count<n){
                                for(k=0;k<n;k++){
                                        if((indeg[k]==0) && (flag[k]==0))
                                        {
                                                printf("%d",(k+1));
                                            flag [k]=1;
                                        }

                                        for(i=0;i<n;i++){
                                                if(a[i][k]==1) indeg[k]--;
                                                        }
                                }
                                count++;
                        }

                        return 0;
}
```

Output: Enter the no of vertices:

7

Enter the adjacency matrix:

0 1 0 0 0 0 0

0 0 1 0 0 0 0

0 0 0 1 0 0 0

0 0 1 0 1 0 0

0 0 0 0 0 1 0

0 0 0 0 0 0 0

0 0 0 0 0 0 0

The topological order is:1723456

You are welcome to play with the following links which have the above code.

https://ideone.com/a8hkHF

The following site contains a visualization tool to animate the working of the above topological sorting algorithm. We welcome readers to use the same.

https://www.cs.usfca.edu/~galles/visualization/TopoSortIndegree.html

EXERCISES

Multiple Choice Questions

1. The maximum number of leaves for a BST with 15 nodes are ________.
   (a) < 8 (b) 8
   (c) 7 (d) 11
2. Sixteen integers are maintained in almost complete BST then the number of leaf nodes in the resulting tree are ________.
   (a) < 8 (b) 8
   (c) 7 (d) 11
3. If a complete BST with 500 nodes is sequentially stored in an array b[0]..b[499], where will be the parent and the left child of the node b[100]?
   (a) at 49,200 (b) at 49, 201
   (c) at 50, 200 (d) at 50, 201
4. If total number of nodes in an almost complete binary tree are 2**q**, where q is a positive integer then the number of leaf nodes at the lowest level are
   (a) 1 (b) q
   (c) 2q (d) None
5. If total number of nodes in an almost complete binary tree are 2q, where q is a positive integer then the number of levels with full nodes are
   (a) 1 (b) q
   (c) 2q (d) None
6. In the following graph, ________ cut point(s).

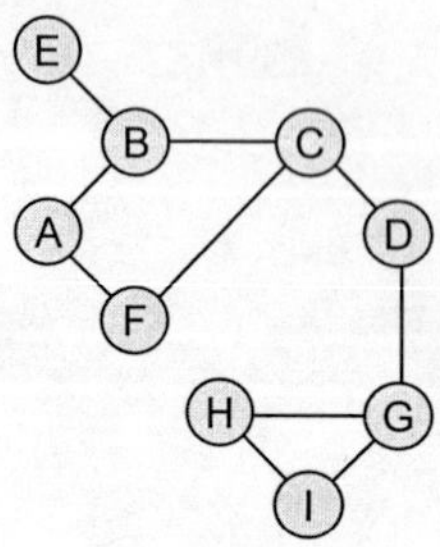

   (a) D (b) C
   (c) D & C (c) None

7. In the graph given in question 6, bridges are
   (a) DG edge (b) CD edge
   (c) EB edge (d) a, b and c
8. Row sums of an adjacency matrix represents
   (a) Rank of the graph (b) Order of the graph
   (c) Out degree of the vertices (d) None
9. A vertex is seen in adjacency lists of all the vertices and also that vertex'es adjacency list is empty then that vertex is
   (a) Given string itself (b) Reverse of the given string
   (c) A series of characters (d) None
10. Assume that we have a series of n (n is divisible with 3) numbers of character stacks and queues (that is stack, queue, queue, stack, queue, queue, and vice versa). We take a string and push all the characters of the string from beginning to till null ('\0', excluding null) are pushed into the first stack of the chain of stacks. Then, we go on pop() from the first stack and insert to the next available queue. This, we repeat for each of the stacks/queues except the last stack/queue. Whatever we get from the last stack/queue when we apply pop()/remove operations, we simply display the popped/removed characters from it. Assume none gives any overflow errors. What do we get on the screen?
   (a) Given string itself (b) Reverse of the given string
   (c) A series of characters (d) None
11. Queue is also called as
   (a) MEMO (b) FIFO
   (c) LIFO (d) None
12. The ADT which can be used both as a stack and queue is
   (a) Circular queue (b) Double stack in a array
   (c) Deque (d) None
13. The ADT which can allows insertion and removal at both the ends is
   (a) Circular queue (b) Double stack in a array
   (c) Deque (d) Dequeue
14. In our RPN expression evaluation code, we are using 48, why?
   (a) Every author uses this, so
   (b) 48 is ASCII code of symbol 0
   (c) We are using char stack and RPN expression is processed character by character while the operands are considered as single digit operands. To get digit value, we are subtracting 48.
   (d) None
15. Assume that we have an ADT stack of character stacks. Assume A is such a type of variable. Assume both stack of stacks and character stacks are realized using an array. Do we need to take the same size (sz) for both types of stacks?
   (a) Yes (b) No
   (c) Not necessary (d) I don't kno

ANSWERS															
1.	(b)	2.	(b)	3.	(b)	4.	(a)	5.	(b)	6.	(c)	7.	(d)	8.	(c)
9.	(c)	10.	(a)	11.	(b)	12.	(a)	13.	(b)	14.	(c)	15.	(a)		

Descriptive Questions

Question 41: See the following graph.

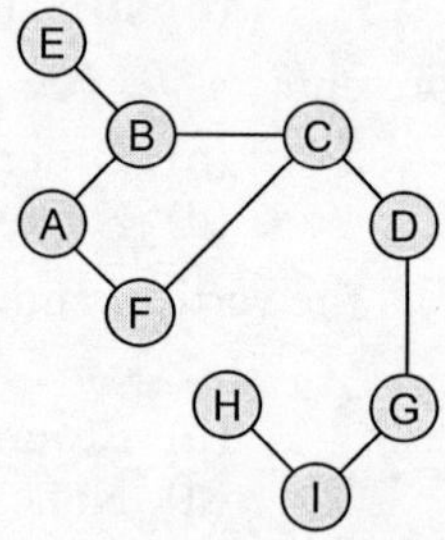

Is the graph a tree?
What is its DFS sequence starting from A?
What is its BFS sequence starting from A?

Question 42: Assume that two BS trees are created using the following two sets of integers.

(a) 5, 7, 9, 11, 13, 15, 17
(b) 11, 7, 5, 9, 15, 13, 17

Which of them are better from a search point of view?

Answer: Tree (b) is preferred because of the smaller tree height. That is, the search cost is smaller than tree (a).

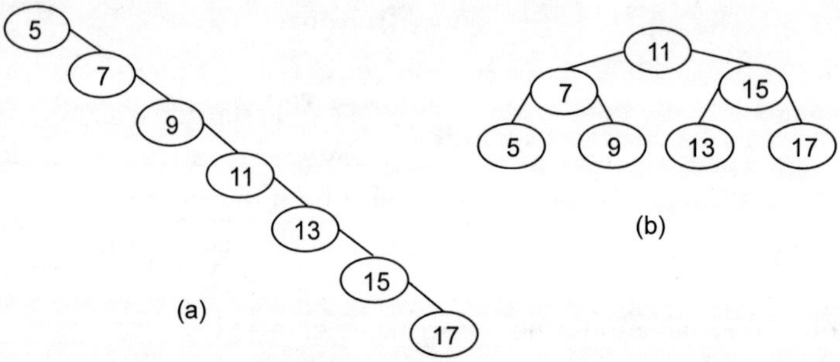

Question 43: Write a function called maximumDegree that takes the adjacency matrix and number of nodes of the undirected graph as arguments then returns the vertex index that has the maximum number of neighbors of the undirected graph.

Question 44: What is the maximum and minimum number of nodes that could be in a binary tree of depth 2 (three levels of nodes)

Answer: 7 & 3: Maximum number of nodes will be seen if the tree is a complete binary tree with depth 2; while minimum number of nodes will be seen if the tree is a degenerate tree (left or right degenerate tree).

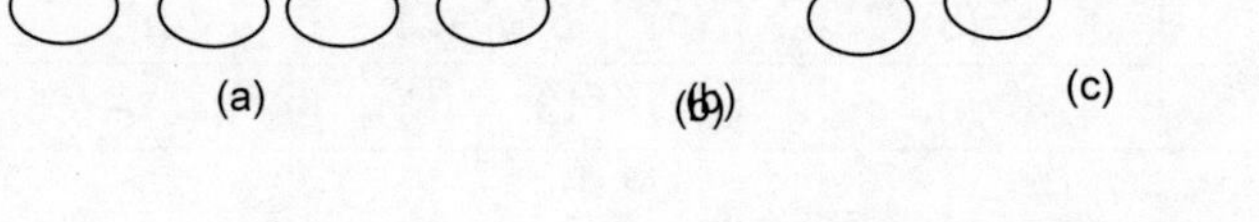

(a) (b) (c)

Question 45: The following code is proposed to find the maximum value out of the leaf nodes of a given tree whose root is H? Is it going to suffice our requirement?

```
int max=-32767;
void traverse(struct Node *H){
if(H==0) return;
else if((H->left==0)&&(H->right==0)){
if(H->n>max)max=H->n;
}
else{
traverse(H->left);
traverse(H->right);
}
}
```

After you return from the function, the global variable max contains the maximum value among the leaf nodes values.

Question 46: Write a program that takes the root of a binary tree having integers in each of its nodes as the data and returns 1 if the data of its nodes satisfies binary search property; otherwise returns 0.

Question 47: The ring, the star, and the fully connected mesh are three possible network topologies.

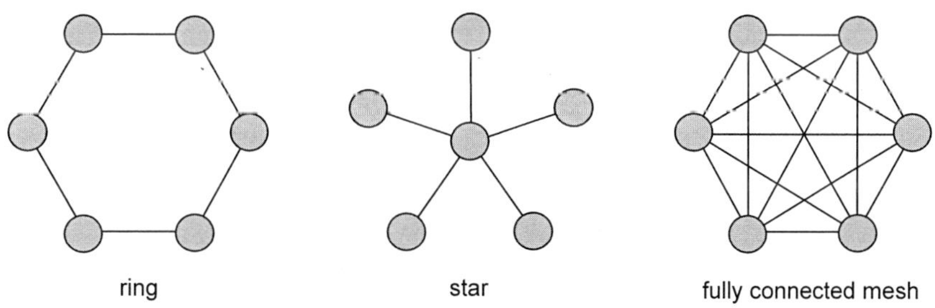

You were given the adjacency matrix of a graph and you need to explain how to distinguish them.

Answer: For fully connected mesh, the adjacency matrix looks like the following. That is, except diagonal, all elements are 1's.

011111
101111
110111
111011
111101
111110

If we assume A is nxn adjacency matrix, if we check all diagonal elements are zeroes and all off diagonal elements are 1s then we can decide whether the graph is fully connected or not.

```
int isFullyConnected(int A[][n],int n){
int i,j;
for(i=0;i<n;i++)
for(j=0;j<n;j++){
```

```
if(i==j){
if (A[i][j]!=0) return False;
}
else{
if(A[i][j]!=1)return False;
}
}
return True
}
```

Best case occurs when A[0][0] is not zero. That is, the 0th node has a self cycle. Thus, the best case complexity is O(1). Worst case situation arises when the matrix is indeed a fully connected matrix. That is, when we reach the last return statement. Thus, the worst case complexity can be said as $O(n^2)$.

Let us explore a star shaped graph. If we assume the middle most node as 1st node of the graph, then the adjacency matrix looks like:

```
011111
100000
100000
100000
100000
100000
```

If we assume the middle most node as last node of the graph, then the adjacency matrix looks like:

```
000001
000001
000001
000001
000001
111110
```

If we assume the middle most node as the fourth node of the graph, then the adjacency matrix looks like:

```
000100
000100
000100
111011
000100
000100
```

What is your observation from the above adjacency matrices? Total number of 0's are exactly n^2-2*(n-1). Also, all the 1s will be either in the kth row or kth column. We need to traverse the adjacency matrix once to verify the total number of zeros as n^2-2*(n-1). For this, we need an $O(n^2)$ algorithm.

After that we need to check other patterns such as 1s in a row and 1s in a column for which we may need at most O(n) efforts. Thus, the worst case complexity of this algorithm can be said as $O(n^2)$.

Let us take the ring network. If we take left, top most as the 1st node and then prepare the adjacency matrix, it looks like the following.

```
010001
101000
010100
001010
000101
100010
```

How many 0s and 1's do you find? Every row and every column has two 1s. This is acceptable, in the ring network every one will be having its in-degree and out degree as 2. Total number of 1s=2n. Total number of 0s=n^2-2n. It looks to me that we need to traverse the adjacency matrix once. Thus, its worst case order is $O(n^2)$.

Question 48: You were given an acyclic directed graph G with n vertices v1, v2, ..., vn. All the edges of the graph are forward; that is, if (vi, vj) is an edge then i < j.

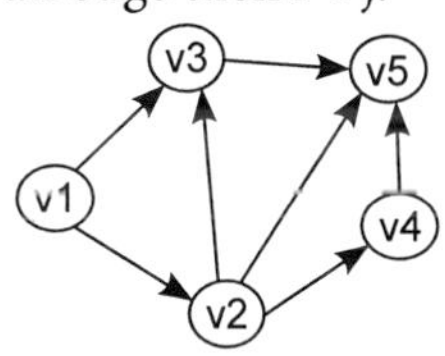

Suggest an efficient algorithm to compute the number of paths from vertex v1 to vertex vn of the given graph. What is the running time of the same?

Answer: See the following code segment.

```
numOfPaths[1]=1
for( j=2;j<n;j++){
numOfPaths[j] =0
for all edges (vi, vj) ∈ E do
numOfPaths[j] =numOfPaths[j] + numOfPaths[i]
end for
}
return numOfPaths[n]
```

Answer: Running Time: Let m = |E|. Assume G is represented by an adjacency list. The external loop has O(n) iterations, while the internal loop considers each edge only once, so the running time is O(m + n).

Question 49: Assuming that you were given a valid tree that is represented in set notation as:

T={a,{b,{c,{d}},{e},{f,{g,{h},{i}}}}

Write a program to find each node's level in the given tree. Hint: Refer chapter on Stacks and example of matching parenthesis.

Question 50: We have N numbers (where N = 2^q-1, for some positive integer value of q) are to be organized in a binary search tree fashion such that there exists N/2 non-leaf nodes, N/2+1 leaf nodes and at any level (other than 0th level) exactly two nodes are seen, one leaf and the other is non-leaf. Physically they are proposed to be stored in an array. Root node will be stored in the 0th location in the array. Its two children are stored in locations 1 and 2. That is, ith node's left and right childrens will be at 2i+1 and 2i+2 locations in the array. Calculate the number of empty elements in the array as a function of N.

Question 51: See the following function to calculate the sum of the node's values of a BST with integers as its data. Is it going to work?

```
int sum(struct Node *A){
if(A==0) return 0;
else if(A->left==0 && A->right==0) return A->n;
else return(A->n+sum(A->left)+ sum(A->right) );
}
```

You may experiment with the above code at the following link before answering.

https://tinyurl.com/AICTEDSBOOK153

Laboratory programming tasks

1. Write a program to create a binary tree of integers.
2. Write a program to traverse a binary tree of integers in inorder fashion.
3. Write a program to traverse a binary tree of integers in preorder fashion.
4. Write a program to traverse a binary tree of integers in postorder fashion.
5. Write a program to traverse a binary tree of integers in inorder fashion using a stack.
6. Write a program to traverse a binary tree of integers in preorder fashion using a stack.
7. Write a program to traverse a binary tree of integers in postorder fashion using a stack.
8. Write a program to traverse a binary search tree that is sequentially stored in an array in inorder fashion.
9. Write a program to find the minimum depth of a binary tree.
10. Write a program to implement Warshall's algorithm.
11. Write a program to implement Breadth First Search (BFS).
12. Write a program to implement Depth First Search (DFS)

Welcome to participate in the online competition

We are hosting a competition so as to encourage students to build their competence in coding. This will be very useful for placements also in the coming years. Thus, welcome students to attempt the competition at the following link.

https://www.hackerrank.com/aictedsbook

Programming puzzles

Some programming puzzles along with their solution around trees and graph concepts are made available at the following link. We request teachers to use them in their teaching and encourage students to attempt such a type of puzzles to win placements.

https://docs.google.com/document/d/1xhNJU8jq2Xi5bL2a_StUK0G6diu-0oTQahJ3f9Fp8hc/edit?usp=sharing

REFERENCES

1. Fundamentals of Data Structure in C, Horowitz, Ellis, Sahni, Sartaj, Anderson-Freed, Susan, University Press, India.
2. Data Structures: A Pseudocode approach with C, Richard F. Gilberg, Behrouz A. Forouzan, CENGAGE Learning, India.
3. My class notes on Algorithmic Complexity, now a refresher for craving teachers and knowledge greedy students: A must primer for GATE(India), Adv. GRE appearing students. https://www.amazon.com/dp/B09DJCW78T
4. C and Data Structures, NB Venkateswarlu & EV Prasad, 2010, S Chand & Co, New Delhi
5. http://cslibrary.stanford.edu/105/LinkedListProblems.pdf

LIST OF APPENDICES

1. The following link contains discussion on logarithms with computation point of view. https://tinyurl.com/AICTEDSBOOKAPPENDIX-A
2. The following link contains row and column major order storage concepts and their impact on designing algorithms. https://tinyurl.com/AICTEDSBOOKAPPENDIX-B
3. The following link contains a brief explanation of various searching and sorting algorithms along with their implementations. Because of the book size limitations, we have made this content available as an appendix. https://tinyurl.com/AICTEDSBOOKAPPENDIX-C

CO AND PO ATTAINMENT TABLE

Course outcomes (COs) for this course can be mapped with the programme outcomes (POs) after the completion of the course and a correlation can be made for the attainment of POs to analyze the gap. After proper analysis of the gap in the attainment of POs necessary measures can be taken to overcome the gaps.

Table for CO and PO attainment

Course Outcomes	Attainment of Programme Outcomes *(1- Weak Correlation; 2- Medium correlation; 3- Strong Correlation)*											
	PO-1	PO-2	PO-3	PO-4	PO-5	PO-6	PO-7	PO-8	PO-9	PO-10	PO-11	PO-12
CO-1												
CO-2												
CO-3												
CO-4												
CO-5												
CO-6												

The data filled in the above table can be used for gap analysis.